Race,
Ethnicity,
and
Urbanization

Other Books by
Howard N. Rabinowitz

Race Relations in the Urban South, 1865–1890

Southern Black Leaders of the Reconstruction Era (editor)

The First New South, 1865–1920

Howard N. Rabinowitz

Race, Ethnicity, and Urbanization

Selected Essays

University of Missouri Press

Columbia and London

Copyright © 1994 by

The Curators of the University of Missouri

University of Missouri Press, Columbia, Missouri 65201

Printed and bound in the United States of America

5 4 3 2 1   98 97 96 95 94

Library of Congress Cataloging-in-Publication Data

Rabinowitz, Howard N., 1942–

    Race, ethnicity, and urbanization : selected essays /
Howard N. Rabinowitz.

      p. cm.

    Includes index.

    ISBN 0-8262-0930-0 (alk. paper)

    1. Afro-Americans—Southern   States—History—19th
century. 2. Urbanization—Southern States—History—
19th century. 3. Southern States—Race relations.
4. Southern States—History—1865–1950. I. Title.

E185.6.R17 1993   93-32413

975'.00496073—dc20   CIP

⊗™ This paper meets the requirements of the
American National Standard for Permanence of Paper
for Printed Library Materials, Z39.48, 1984.

Designer: Kristie Lee

Typesetter: Connell-Zeko Type & Graphics

Printer and Binder: Thomson-Shore, Inc.

Typeface: Optima

In Memory of Arthur Mann

Uncle, Mentor, Colleague

Contents

Part Three: Reconstruction and Its Legacy

Part Four: Jews and Other Ethnics

Part Five: Continuity and Change

Acknowledgments

Although most of the essays reprinted in this collection include their own acknowledgments of assistance, I need to take this opportunity to thank various institutions and individuals for helping to make this volume possible.

I want to thank the following publishers and journals for permission to use the articles reprinted here: "More than the Woodward Thesis: Assessing *The Strange Career of Jim Crow,*" *Journal of American History* 75 (December 1988): 842–56; "Segregation and Reconstruction," in *The Facts of Reconstruction: Essays in Honor of John Hope Franklin,* ed. Eric Anderson and Alfred Moss, Jr. (Baton Rouge: Louisiana State University Press, 1991), 79–98; "From Exclusion to Segregation: Health and Welfare Services for Southern Blacks, 1865–1890," *Social Service Review* 48 (September 1974): 327–54, copyright © 1974 by The University of Chicago. All rights reserved; "Half a Loaf: The Shift from White to Black Teachers in the Negro Schools of the Urban South, 1865–1890," *Journal of Southern History* 40 (November 1974): 565–94; "From Reconstruction to Redemption in the Urban South," *Journal of Urban History* 2 (February 1976): 169–94; "From Exclusion to Segregation: Southern Race Relations, 1865–1890," *Journal of American History* 63 (September 1976): 325–50; "The Conflict between Blacks and the Police in the Urban South, 1865–1900," *The Historian* 39 (November 1976): 62–76; "Three Reconstruction Leaders: Blanche K. Bruce, Robert Brown Elliott, and Holland Thompson," in *Black Leaders of the Nineteenth Century,* ed. August Meier and Leon Litwack (Urbana: University of Illinois Press, 1988), 191–217; "A Comparative Perspective on Race Relations in Southern and Northern Cities, 1860–1900, with Special Emphasis on Raleigh, N.C.," in *Black Americans in North Carolina and the South,* ed. Jeffrey J. Crow and Flora J. Hatley (Chapel Hill: University of North Carolina Press, 1984), 137–59, copyright © 1984 by The University of North Carolina Press. Used by permission of the publisher; "Race, Ethnicity, and Cultural Pluralism in American History," in *Ordinary People and Everyday Life: Perspectives on the New Social History,* ed. James D. Gardner and George R. Adams (Nashville: The American Association for State and Local History, 1983), 23–49; "Writing Jewish Community History," a review of *Richmond's Jewry: Shabbat in Shockoe, 1769–1976,* by Myron Berman, and *Jews and Judaism in a Midwestern Community: Columbus, Ohio, 1840–1975,* by Marc Lee Raphael, *American Jewish History* 70 (September 1980): 119–27; "Nativism, Bigotry, and Anti-Semitism in the South," *American Jewish History* 77 (March 1988): 437–51; "Continuity and Change: Southern Urban Development, 1860–1900," in *The City in Southern History,* ed. Blaine A. Brownell and David R. Goldfield (Port Washington, N.Y.: Kennikat Press, 1977), 92–122, 204–9; "The Weight of the Past vs. The Promise of the Future: Southern Race Relations in Historical Perspective," in *The Future South: An Historical Perspective for the Twenty-first Century,* ed. Joe P. Dunn and Howard L. Preston (Urbana: University of Illinois Press, 1991), 100–22.

I began thinking about the possibility of putting together a collection of my essays while I was a fellow at the Center for Advanced Study in the Behavioral Sciences during 1989–1990. That year marked my first exposure to elements of poststructuralism and other approaches to knowledge that were beginning to alter the discipline and profession of history. I was also given the opportunity to assess the meaning of my own work when I introduced several of the essays that appear in this volume to my interdisciplinary race and ethnicity group. The Center provides an unrivaled intellectual environment, and I am thankful to have been able to be a part of it. All that is missing is tenure.

Nothing more would have been done with these essays, however, had not University of Missouri Press Director and Editor-in-Chief Beverly Jarrett invited me to prepare this collection for publication. I want to thank her for her persistence, encouragement, and help with the Introduction. She also deserves credit for assembling such a professional staff at Missouri, including Jane Lago, Tim Fox, and Karen Caplinger, who ably followed up on Bev's pledge to "do right by the book." Thanks to Linda Webster as well for a fine index.

Anne Boylan, Daniel Feller, Peter Kolchin, Charles McClelland, Virginia Scharf, and Melvin Yazawa provided careful critiques of the Introduction. They didn't always agree—indeed, they often strongly disagreed—with what I said or the way I said it, but they gave me constructive criticism that forced some rethinking and buoyed my flagging enthusiasm by saying they had fun reading the piece. Once again I am indebted to my wife, Diane Wood, for her unique nonacademic perspective.

As in the past, however, my greatest intellectual debt is to Arthur Mann. Arthur had read all of the previously published essays, most of them before they were published. He did not, however, live to read the Introduction. I like to think it would have pleased him, but I know it would have been better had he been able to apply his unsurpassed editorial skills, which inevitably brought him (and you) to the core of things that really mattered.

Author's Note

These essays are reprinted essentially as they originally appeared. Typos have been corrected, some occasional infelicitous phrasing has been altered, and punctuation, capitalization, citation, and similar matters were made to conform to University of Missouri Press practices. Although I have eliminated some unnecessary repetition, in certain places I have intentionally left in factual material, themes, and sentences that appear in more than one essay. Such duplication was unavoidable, given the interrelationship among many of the topics that interest me, and to have eliminated it entirely would have seriously weakened the internal integrity of individual essays, a particularly serious matter for those readers who will be dipping selectively into this collection. I hope that those of you who are reading the volume in its entirety will excuse this repetition and greet its examples more with a welcomed sense of familiarity at meeting old friends than with anger at having to relive unpleasant past experiences. In addition to these changes, I have inserted brief introductory remarks when additional background information was needed. Acknowledgments have also been added to many of the essays.

No attempt was made to update usage of the words *Negro* or *black.* It is now common among many high-profile black leaders, white liberals, and elements of the media to "privilege" the term *African American.* One prominent black leader even erroneously claims that all previous referential terms were assigned by whites, and then compounds his error by failing to recognize the degree to which whites have helped spread the new terminology. Polls indicate that the overwhelming majority of group members reject *African American.* That might change by next year, but it is just as likely that there might be a new trendy favorite. (The terms *Latino* and *Native American,* pushed by a similar politically correct coalition of activists, white liberals, and the media, have likewise been rejected by their intended beneficiaries.)

But we don't need polls to reveal the kind of force-feeding that is going on.

Watch TV or talk to friends of both races. Even those who start off carefully using *African American* less self-consciously end up with more than a sprinkling of *black*. Besides, what does one call a white South African who becomes an American citizen? For that matter, what about a black South African? I hope that we eventually get to the point where terminology is worth this kind of attention. It will mean that the problems that really matter have been finally overcome. For now, I hope that the use of *Negro* and *black* will not detract from what I have to say.

Race,
Ethnicity,
and
Urbanization

Introduction

Selected Reflections on Thirty Years of History as a Discipline and a Profession

This book is a collection of essays selected from the three major fields in which I do most of my writing: race relations, ethnicity, and urban history. I think these essays are particularly noteworthy for what they have to say about the nature of black leadership, the origins of segregation, the writing of ethnic history, and the urban dimension of southern history.[1] Despite some overlap, they generally reinforce rather than duplicate one another. Although most of them were initially prepared for an academic audience, they were written in jargon-free English, and I hoped that they might somehow reach the informed general reader. Publication of this volume will now make that possible, while bringing to the attention of other academics those essays that were buried in anthologies, or in journals that were outside their areas of specialization. At the time they were written, most challenged the accepted wisdom in their fields. A number have already contributed to the reevaluation of that wisdom. Others, however, might now have a

1. I have also been part of the effort to incorporate urban history into Western history. In order to provide a better focus for this volume, however, I have omitted this body of work. For those interested in the growing subfield of Western urban history and its relationship to the broader fields of urban and Western history, see my essays "Albuquerque: City at a Crossroads," in *Sunbelt Cities: Politics and Growth since World War II,* ed. Richard M. Bernard and Bradley R. Rice (Austin: University of Texas Press, 1983), 255–67; "Reps on the Range: An Anti-Turnerian Framework for the Urban West," *Journal of Urban History* 8 (November 1981): 91–98; "The New Western History Goes to Town; or, Don't Forget that Your Urban Hamburger Was Once a Rural Cow," *Montana: The Magazine of Western History* 43 (Spring 1993): 73–77; and (with David R. Goldfield) "The Vanishing Sunbelt," in *Searching for the Sunbelt,* ed. Raymond A. Mohl (University of Tennessee Press, 1990), 224–33.

greater impact than they originally had, given a book's greater visibility and ac-
cessibility.

There is no need to sum up the contents of the essays; their titles make clear
what they are about, and most provide sufficient historiographical guidance. Nor
is it necessary to show how my thought "evolved." Indeed, although my work,
especially on segregation, has matured over time, I still accept the major points
made in all the essays—otherwise I wouldn't have chosen to reprint them. In any
case, the essays should be able to stand on their own. This reflects my more
general opinion that it's the stories that count, not the storyteller.

It might help, however, to provide some context for the essays you are about to
read.

In the beginning, that is, when I entered the University of Chicago for graduate
study in history in September 1964, there was the story, or as E. M. Forster might
put it, the plot.[2]

We were taught, and most of us believed, that there was a "truth," if not "the
truth," out there in the past. It was our job to find it and relate and explain it in
clear, precise prose. Few of us were naive enough to believe that we could be
entirely "objective" either in terms of the questions we asked or the answers we
found. After all, we carried our own "cultural baggage," reflecting, among other
things, our racial, regional, religious, gender, and class origins. And we certainly
knew, or came to know, that history's sources were often unavailable, contradictory, or unreliable. Yet our job was to get straight with the past. In the process we
did our best to identify and put aside our biases, without, of course, expecting to
be entirely successful. We had read Carl Becker and knew that "everyman [is]
his own historian." But we felt quite comfortable with what Peter Novick subsequently termed our "practical objectivity."[3] Unlike Gertrude Stein's Oakland,
when it came to the past, there was a there there.

Our primary tool in seeking to unlock the secrets of the past was the historical
method. It involved an inductive approach, often, however, informed by tenta-

---

2. Forster defined a story as "a narrative of events arranged in their time-sequence,"
such as "the king died and then the queen died." A plot is "also a narrative of events, the
emphasis falling on causality," as in "the king died and then the queen died of grief." In
this sense, according to historian Lee Benson, the historian becomes a "plot-teller" rather
than a "chronicler." See Forster, *Aspects of the Novel* (New York: Harcourt Brace and
World, 1927), 86; Benson, "Causation and the American Civil War," in his *Toward the
Scientific Study of History: Selected Essays* (Philadelphia: J. B. Lippincott, 1972), 81–82.
See also Allan Megill, "Recounting the Past: 'Description,' Explanation, and Narrative in
Historiography," *American Historical Review* 94 (June 1989): 627–53.

3. Becker, "Everyman His Own Historian," *American Historical Review* 37 (January
1932): 221–36; Novick, *That Noble Dream: The "Objectivity Question" and the American Historical Profession* (Cambridge: Cambridge University Press, 1988), 628.

tive hypotheses to be tested by close immersion in the sources. In the history department's historical methods course, for example, our major assignment was to ask an extremely narrow question and then try to answer it. (I pursued "Who Were the Chicago Populists?") We were also reminded, however, that we, as the French historian Louis Gottschalk, echoing Newton, put it, "stood on the shoulders of giants." Those giants were historians who had come before us and had contributed to an understanding of the past that we would build on. We were free, indeed encouraged, to correct their errors, but to do so with civility and with the higher goal, always in mind, of doing justice to the past. Many of us failed the civility test, though in doing so we were violating the explicit tenets of our public culture. But however we chose to pursue our task, historical understanding was thus viewed as unilinear and progressive. Most of all, the past was "knowable."

In that search for a knowable and, for many, "usable" past, we had the assistance of what we referred to as our sister disciplines, all the while assuming the superiority, or at least parity, of our own discipline. In those days and most certainly for a budding urban historian like myself, *interdisciplinary* tended to mean reliance on sociology, political science, geography, and, to a lesser extent— except for Marxists and (Milton) Freedmanites—economics. We read Robert Merton on functionalism, Robert Dahl on political elites, and Allen Pred on information networks. Too often, we blindly assumed that their ideas were unchallenged by other sociologists, political scientists, or geographers, but we never turned such major figures into demigods. It was their ideas that interested us, and only to the degree they helped us lay bare the past and tell our stories. Rarely did we invoke their names in the texts of our writings or even cite their work in our notes.

But in whatever we did we were encouraged to think broadly. The narrow specialization so dominant in the study of history today was already beginning to take its toll on the profession, even as it often produced startling new windows to the past,[4] but I thankfully was braced against the temptation to indulge myself. As a fellow of Chicago's Center for Urban Studies, I mixed with students from throughout the social sciences and heard lectures by leading scholars in those disciplines. Within the Department of History, we were required to select five different M.A. and Ph.D examination fields. I chose U.S. history before and after 1860, American urban history from colonial times to the present, British history since 1800, and Russian history to 1917. Further impeding any lust to specialize

4. Thomas Bender, "Wholes and Parts: The Need for Synthesis in American History," *Journal of American History* 73 (June 1986): 120–36. See also "A Round Table: Synthesis in American History," ibid. 74 (June 1987): 107–22, which contains responses to Bender's article by David Thelen, Nell Irvin Painter, Richard Wightman Fox, and Roy Rosenzweig, and Bender's rejoinder.

was the requirement that we take twenty-seven quarter-length courses spread over our five fields. As a result, I remember saying after my orals that I didn't feel like an "urban historian," "social historian," or "southern historian." Instead, I felt like an "American historian." Today, I continue to describe myself as an American historian, with a particular interest in things ethnic, urban, and southern.

Thus when it came time to choose a dissertation topic, I was drawn to a broadly defined, comparative study. I chose to examine, despite a somewhat misleading title ("The Search for Social Control: Race Relations in the Urban South, 1865–1890"), both the system of race relations and the nature of black urban life in five post–Civil War southern cities—Atlanta, Montgomery, Richmond, Nashville, and Raleigh.[5] This work grew out of a unique seminar on Reconstruction in North Carolina taught by John Hope Franklin. Franklin arranged to have the seven students and himself spend two weeks in Raleigh, where we were free to roam through the North Carolina Archives and the State Library, and the libraries at Duke and the University of North Carolina.[6] My seminar topic, "Raleigh Negroes, 1865–1885," reflected both the research and personal interests of Franklin and another of my teachers, urban historian Richard Wade, and my own desire to write about something "relevant." Little did I realize that when it became the nucleus for the dissertation, the conjunction of southern, black, and urban history would basically set the research agenda for much of my academic career.[7]

The mid-to-late 1960s were by no means an academic golden age, in terms of either how the history profession was run or what we knew about the chaos of the past.[8] Although Jews, Catholics, and a variety of white ethnics had begun to make their mark, the WASP Old Guard was not totally reconciled to the changing shape of the profession. In his presidential address to the American Historical Association in 1962, to take one now commonly cited example, Carl Bridenbaugh observed:

5. Approved in 1973, it was subsequently published as *Race Relations in the Urban South, 1865–1890* (New York: Oxford University Press, 1978; paperback, with a foreword by C. Vann Woodward, Urbana: University of Illinois Press, 1980).

6. John Hope Franklin, *Race and History: Selected Essays, 1938–1988* (Baton Rouge: Louisiana State University Press, 1989), 3–9.

7. For more details concerning my decision to study black history, see August Meier and Elliott Rudwick, *Black History and the Historical Profession, 1915–1980* (Urbana: University of Illinois Press, 1986), 217–18.

8. It is all to easy to romanticize one's academic roots. For an otherwise perceptive and telling critique of the profession circa the early 1970s that is marred by the creation of an earlier academic golden age (ca. 1930s–1950s), see Oscar Handlin, *Truth in History* (Cambridge: Harvard University Press, 1979). Despite its seemingly naive title, this often unfairly maligned book was really less about "truth" than the importance of evidence in the writing of history.

> Today we must face the discouraging prospect that we all . . . have lost much of what . . . earlier generation[s] possessed, the priceless asset of a shared culture. . . . Furthermore, many of the younger practitioners of our craft, and those who are still apprentices, are products of lower middle-class or foreign origins, and their emotions not infrequently get in the way of historical reconstructions.[9]

And partly due to subtle or even overt discrimination, the recruitment and advancement of other minorities, and especially well-qualified women, still lagged. As in all eras, there was also too much uninteresting, poorly written, and easily forgotten history being published; indeed, that is one of the reasons some of us now tend to elevate the best work to such great heights. But the profession and the writing of history were, in my view, on the correct trajectory.

The historical profession seems very different today. Much of that difference is to the good, as the positive trends already underway in the 1960s have borne fruit. Women and an ever more representative range of ethnic minorities now make up a significant portion of the profession and produce some of its most valuable work. And the new fields of the 1960s provided the foundation for a continuing broadening of our understanding of what was worth studying. Indeed, the best of this work often goes beyond the pioneering efforts in both methodology and substance. Social and cultural history have illuminated the lives of ordinary Americans and particularly enriched our understanding of colonial, black, women's, and twentieth-century history, to cite only the most obvious examples; American Indian and Asian-American history have now been integrated into the study of ethnic history; and exciting new work has reinvigorated the traditional fields of southern and Western history. But matters of tone, style, and approach to knowledge now have begun to overwhelm and undermine the considerable progress in more substantive matters. The level of contempt for what came before also threatens to homogenize the academic writing of history to an extent not seen since the early days of the profession, if then. This problem is most evident in lectures and conference presentations, but it is increasingly revealed in print as well.

The historian's focus is now too often on the storyteller rather than the story. Books and articles are filled with proselytizing for new methods, approaches, or "perspectives," and not simply in prefaces or notes (or when otherwise unavoidable, as in this Introduction), but in the text. There, too, are found "confessions" about past mistakes or other examples of self-criticism. This tendency was al-

---

9. "The Great Mutation," *American Historical Review* 68 (January 1963): 322–23. For examples of discrimination against Jews and others of "foreign origins," see Novick, *That Noble Dream,* 172–74, 339–40, 364–66.

ready emerging in the late 1960s, but it is now fueled by a self-absorption and self-indulgence that is relatively new. Few today would agree with Lord Acton that "there is virtue in the saying that a historian is seen at his best when he does not appear."[10] Such a role would be dismissed as either naive or dishonest. In short, there is little concern for the audience, as we learn more about the storyteller than we need or want to know. The author informs us, "This is what I'm going to do, and in my own way, because this is what I need, or want, to do. Come along if you like, this should interest you because it interests me, and because everyone before me has gotten it wrong. Whether you need to know it or not, I do." Books have become voyages of personal discovery.[11]

Historians, of course, have always pursued subjects because they interested them, but that was a given and there was a sense their stories needed to connect with an audience outside themselves. But now there is also the compulsion to spell out their own approach to the subject. And despite occasional protestations of merely seeking "parity," what many authors are claiming is the superiority of their approach and the worthlessness of others. Clinching their argument, of course, is one of the few devices they borrow from earlier generations of historians—the straw man. Even one otherwise gracious and perceptive article on new directions in the study of "ethnicization" could not resist contemptuously dismissing the once prevalent "hackneyed concern with individual assimilation to a host society." And the author of a prize-winning book that treats the encounter between Franciscans and Pueblo Indians in colonial New Mexico proudly announced that he had refused to read any of the earlier work on that subject because of its racial and sexual biases.[12] No standing on giants, here;

10. John Emerich Edward Dalberg-Acton, *Lectures on Modern History,* ed. J. N. Figgs and R. V. Laurence (London: Macmillan, 1926), 12.

11. This tendency is most common in women's and minority history, but it has spread to other fields as well. Examples are practically limitless. Two that I am particularly familiar with are Eric H. Monkkonen, *America Becomes Urban: The Development of U.S. Cities and Towns, 1780–1980* (Berkeley: University of California Press, 1988) and William Cronon, *Nature's Metropolis: Chicago and the Great West* (New York: W. W. Norton and Co., 1991). For a fuller discussion of the problems with this approach, see my two review essays "The (Urban) World According to Monkkonen," *Reviews in American History* 20 (June 1992), 194–99, and "The New Western History Goes to Town."

12. Kathleen Neils Conzen, David A. Gerber, Ewa Morawska, George E. Pozzetta, and Rudolph J. Vecoli, "The Invention of Ethnicity: A Perspective from the U.S.A.," *Journal of American Ethnic History* 12 (Fall 1992): 31. For a thoughtful response that emphasizes the need to continue to study the Americanization process, see Herbert J. Gans, "Comment: Ethnic Invention and Acculturation, A Bumpy-Line Approach," ibid., 42–52. Response of Ramon A. Gutierrez, "A Symposium on Ramon A. Gutierrez's *When Jesus Came, the Corn Mothers Went Away: Marriage, Sexuality, and Power in New Mexico, 1500–1846,*" Organization of American Historians Convention, Anaheim, California, April 16, 1993.

indeed, given the frequent absence of citations to seemingly relevant earlier work, not even pygmies are acknowledged.

Those who prefer other approaches, including some traditional Marxists, are, thanks to a mixture of tactical reasons and sloppy thinking, dismissed as "conservatives."[13] The less fortunate get branded "racist," "sexist," or "elitist." It is no longer sufficient to simply call someone wrong. C. Vann Woodward's sensible proposal in 1982 to unite the new and old history in order to produce narrative syntheses for the general reader was labeled "anti-intellectual Luddism" and equated with "Reaganism and the New Right" because it allegedly demanded "a return to simpler times and simpler tales, for a world no longer mired in complexity and opacity."[14]

The penchant for self-identification means that authors expressly write from a "black," "Marxist," or "feminist" perspective. What Joan Wallach Scott says is needed—and she will pursue it by using gender as a category of analysis—is "a more radical feminist politics (and a more radical feminist history)."[15] This suggests that there is one "black," "Marxist," "feminist," or "Babylonian" perspective, which is, of course, nonsense.[16] But even if there were only one per defined group, why should that perspective be any more legitimate, or as the new lingo puts it, "privileged," than a patriarchal, "white," or "liberal" perspective? There is, after all, no inherent worth here comparable to, say, claims of being God or even Nature ordained.

If historical work is well-written and consistent, an author's perspective should be easily discernible to a careful reader, and therefore such admissions should be superfluous. Most of all, they are overly self-conscious and self-important. "Hi, I'm Jim, I'll be your waiter tonight." Who cares? Just deliver the food. And I don't need to know about the chef either—the menu will tell me all I need to know.

But the concern for the storyteller goes beyond the author. It has become central to poststructural "readings" of the past. Since meaning and language are

13. For a typical example, see Joan Wallach Scott, "History in Crisis? The Others' Side of the Story," *American Historical Review* 94 (June 1989): 682 and passim.

14. Woodward, "A Short History of American History," *New York Times Book Review,* August 8, 1982, 3, 14; Eric H. Monkkonen, letter to the editor, ibid., September 5, 1982, 21. In his introduction to the reprinted version of "A Short History," Woodward quoted some of Monkkonen's attack "in the hope it might help explain my concern for restoring mental balance in the profession" (Woodward, *The Future of the Past* [New York and Oxford: Oxford University Press, 1989], 315).

15. *Gender and the Politics of History* (New York: Columbia University Press, 1988), 4. See also Scott, "Gender: A Useful Category of Historical Analysis," *American Historical Review* 91 (December 1986), 1053–75.

16. For more on the forgotten impact of Babylonian Americans, see Philip Roth, *The Great American Novel* (New York, Chicago, and San Francisco: Holt Rinehart Winston, 1973), especially 266–68.

no longer seen as a transparent reflection of experience, history's sources become storytellers. In this case the storyteller might be an individual witness—
diarist, observer, orator, etc.—whose objectivity is automatically suspect and
whose observations therefore fair (or unfair) game, or rituals—parades, picnics,
banquets, etc.—whose structure and placards are subjected to close readings as
text, without making any attempt to ascertain their correspondence to an unknowable or multiple "reality."[17]

Thankfully, only a minority of academic historians embrace this view of history (plus a handful of what academics with a combination of envy and contempt label "popularizers"). But this is a centrally placed minority, which is
extremely influential if not dominant in the American Historical Association and
especially the Organization of American Historians and its journal, the *Journal of
American History.* For much of this minority, the rest of the profession might as
well consist of "popularizers" whose work shouldn't be taken seriously. These
historians also influence, or even control, the graduate training in many history
departments, especially in the most prestigious institutions. Formidable among
their ranks are what have been termed with some justification "tenured radicals"
or "academic capitalists."[18] Both are loaded terms, of course, and, for that and
other reasons, I prefer not to use them. Besides, there are too many exceptions—
the tenured radicals are not monolithic; many of the trendy young radicals,
though powerful, lack tenure; and there are too many liberal-to-conservative
academic capitalists.

Whatever we call this new elite—I prefer Historians with Attitude—its students are often more familiar with the intricacies of theory than with the skills
of solid archival research. The first products of this graduate generation are
beginning to enter the profession, and they and the remainder of their cohort can
be expected to spread the new learning to their own students. Just as the genera-

17. Again examples are too numerous to list, but see the interesting but ultimately
frustrating Leon Fink, "The New Labor History and the Powers of Historical Pessimism:
Consensus, Hegemony, and the Case of the Knights of Labor," *Journal of American
History* 75 (June 1988): 115–36. See also the reactions to this article by Jackson Lears,
George Lipsitz, Mari Jo Buhle and Paul Buhle, and, especially, John P. Diggins, and Fink's
response, ibid., 137–61. For a broader debate over such techniques and the "invented"
history it can produce, see "AHR Forum: *The Return of Martin Guerre,*" *American Histori-
cal Review* 93 (June 1988) consisting of Robert Finlay, "The Refashioning of Martin
Guerre," 553–71, and Natalie Zemon Davis, "'On the Lame,'" 572–603.

18. Roger Kimball, *Tenured Radicals: How Politics Has Corrupted Our Higher Education* (New York: Harper and Row, 1990); Harold Fromm, *Academic Capitalism and
Literary Value* (Athens: University of Georgia Press, 1991). John Patrick Diggins makes a
good case for the use of the term *academic left* in his perceptive and nuanced *The Rise
and Fall of the American Left* (New York: W. W. Norton and Co., 1992), especially
chapters 7–9.

tion of the 1960s now controls academia, the present version's strength will not peak until twenty years from now. Unfortunately, the current generation seems particularly impressionable, and while far more varied in demographic terms, it is intellectually less diverse than its 1960s counterpart.

The newest "New History" is also spreading from its initial base in intellectual history.[19] It is now well established in social history and popular culture, particularly in work dealing with "raceclassandgender." It is also at the core of the so-called "cultural studies" movement, which early on got a foothold in law schools and is moving through the social sciences. But like any imperialistic, truth-bearing movement it shows no inclination to stop at the boundaries of more "traditional" areas. A variant that is less theory-driven has spread through the once conceptually dormant field of Western history. And of only three sessions at the 1993 convention of the Organization of American Historians even pretending to be about foreign relations, one was entitled "Gendered Discourses in Twentieth-Century United States Foreign Policy."[20]

The transformation in the writing of American history is in part due to the recent course of American history itself. Today's historians have unavoidably been affected by the end of the civil rights movement, urban riots, the Vietnam War, the assassination of two Kennedys and Martin Luther King, Jr., Watergate, and the Reagan Revolution. Most can be fairly described as being to the left of the general public, and that includes not only the profession's self-described "radicals" but also an amorphous group ranging from "liberals" to "moderates" to "conservatives." The style of Historians with attitude was often influenced by the highly personalized and self-important "new journalism" of Norman Mailer, Jimmy Breslin, and Tom Wolfe, or the "gonzo journalism" of Hunter Thompson. Current events also made them more susceptible than they otherwise might have been to a variety of guru-scholars whose approaches and ideas, even when quite different from one another, emphasized the exploitiveness, brutality, arrogance, and insensitivity of Western civilization in general, and American society in particular.

Introductions, texts, and especially lengthy discursive footnotes proclaim an intellectual and analytical indebtedness to a series of theorists who have gotten more than their allotted share of Andy Warhol minutes. All of these theorists were employed to varying degrees to raise our historical "consciousness." Many were Marxists who sought to work out some of the kinks in the master's argument, including sociologist Immanuel Wallerstein and his world-system approach

19. John E. Toews, "Intellectual History after the Linguistic Turn: The Autonomy of Meaning and the Irreducibility of Experience," *American Historical Review* 92 (October 1987): 879–907.

20. Organization of American Historians, *Program of the Eighty-sixth Annual Meeting, April 15–18, 1993,* (Bloomington, Ind.: Organization of American Historians, 1993), 86.

and dependency theory; theoretician Antonio Gramsci and his belief in cultural hegemony as a substitute for overt class rule; and historian E. P. Thompson and his self-actuating working class. There are also social historians of the Annales School, like Fernand Braudel, with their "long duree," "deep structures," and "total history"; "interpretative" anthropologist Clifford Geertz with his "deep play" and "thick description"; and historian Thomas Kuhn with his "paradigms" of scientific revolutions that challenged the foundations of scientific "objectivity." Most recently, there has been the invasion of the French poststructuralists, bringing with it a new vocabulary ("privileging," "discourse," "contested terrain" and "decoding") and the, hopefully temporary, triumph of "theory." Most ubiquitous are philosopher Michel Foucault and his power/knowledge nexus, which sees all knowledge as the result of the will to power and domination, and deconstructionist literary critics Jacques Derrida and Roland Barthes and psychoanalyst Jacques Lacan, who proclaim the indeterminate meaning of the text, the death of the author, and the subjective construction of sexual identity.[21]

Despite their many differences, collectively these theorists, especially the literary critics (a group not consulted by my 1960s more materially-oriented generation), reject the traditional Western-centered—"ethnocentric" or "logocentric"—approach to history, culture, and knowledge itself. There are, after all, as guru linguist Mikhail Bakhtin reminds us, "many voices" in the world and in each society.[22] And if Michel Foucault is correct, the only reason we choose to "privilege" some of those voices is because of power relationships. There is no right, no wrong, no "correct" or "superior" interpretation of the past, only

21. For a guru sampler, see Wallerstein, *The Modern World-System* (New York: Academic Press, 1974); Gramsci, *Selections from the Prison Notebooks,* ed. Quintin Hoare and Geoffrey Nowell-Smith (New York: International Publishers, 1971); Thompson, *The Making of the English Working Class* (New York: Vintage, 1963); Braudel, *The Mediterranean and the Mediterranean World in the Age of Philip II,* 2 vols., trans. Sian Reynolds (New York: Harper and Row, 1966); Geertz, *The Interpretation of Cultures: Selected Essays* (New York: Basic Books, 1973) and *Local Knowledge: Further Essays in Interpretive Anthropology* (New York: Basic Books, 1983); Kuhn, *The Structure of Scientific Revolutions,* enlarged ed. (Chicago: University of Chicago Press, 1970); Foucault, *Power/Knowledge: Selected Interviews and Other Writings, 1972–1977,* ed. Colin Gordon (New York: Pantheon, 1980); Derrida, *Of Grammatology,* trans. G. C. Spivak (Baltimore: Johns Hopkins University Press, 1974) (but see also Jonathan Culler, *On Deconstruction* [Ithaca: Cornell University Press, 1982]); Barthes, *The Pleasure of the Text,* trans. Richard Miller (New York: Hill and Wang, 1975); Juliet Mitchell and Jacqueline Rose, eds., *Feminine Sexuality: Jacques Lacan and the Ecole Freudienne* (New York: W. W. Norton and Co., 1982). For a useful introduction to this body of literature, see Lynn Hunt, ed., *The New Cultural History* (Berkeley and Los Angeles: University of California Press, 1989).
22. *The Dialogic Imagination: Four Essays,* trans. Michael Holquist (Austin: University of Texas Press, 1981).

power. The "real" past remains "unknowable." To search for it or to rely on other traditional categories of ascription, including good and evil, man and woman, black and white, is to suffer from "essentialism."

Race, gender, and ethnicity are "inventions." Everything then is "a construct" or "constructed," and it is the act of "invention" or "construction" that is supposed to interest us. Such insights can be useful, as in the case of more closely examining historical definitions of *black*, but once you have made this point, then what? Similar comments about the power of gender or ethnicity can lead to dead ends rather than open new vistas. Besides, such points are not all that new. We have long known, for example, about the difference between America's tendency to define race according to the "one drop of black blood rule" and Latin America's use of *mulatto* as an intermediate category between black and white. But identifying constructions is exactly the kind of thing that scores points among academics while turning off our potential popular audience. Rightly or wrongly, most people consider Martin Luther King, Jr., "black" and don't worry too much about how he became so designated. They take his race as a given and want to know more about what he did.

Even when interesting and perceptive, the new historical writing has become sadly predictable. In practically every article in a given issue of the *American Historical Review* or *Journal of American History* one encounters values, memories, symbols, language, and the like that are "contested," with the outcome of those conflicts determined by "power" or "power relationships." Citations will include reference to, with apologies to Claude Rains, "the usual suspects." Not only will the words and sources be the same, but in most cases so, too, will be the author's feelings toward the prospective winners and losers. The values and attitudes of the oppressed are explicitly preferred to those of the oppressor, local cultures to national culture, traditional to market economies, and the common folk to elites. Yet history is simply too complex to allow for such easy pickings.

Derrida, Foucault, and their disciples miss the irony that not only do they seem to have come up with the one proper reading of texts, whether taken to mean "works" of literature or the "facts" and "events" of historical experience, but also that the rest of us are able to grasp correctly the "essence" of their arguments. When we don't, we are taken to task for "careless reading."[23] Imagine— refusing to accept the "truth" that there is no "Truth." Welcome to the land of the closed system and the nonfalsifiable hypothesis.

Such gurus have, despite often impenetrable prose,[24] helped us gain greater

23. For Derrida's complaints about being "misread," see Fromm, *Academic Capitalism,* 212–14.

24. As Thomas Haskell has put it, "Only people of angelic patience and much time on

insight into the past—some, of course (in my view, Thompson, Geertz, and Kuhn), have contributed more positively than others. And unlike assorted knee-jerk critics, I welcome their contributions. The problem is that their theories have too often been blindly embraced and treated as gospel, to the point of being used in footnotes for purposes of proof. As Derrida might put it, a case of signifiers being used to signify other signifiers.

Early in my career, historians commonly debated the "causes" or "essence" of events and movements. Often we did so rather simplistically: "The American Revolution: Was It Over Home Rule or Who Shall Rule at Home?" or "Industrial Revolution: Was It or Wasn't It?"[25] But now rather than debate "The Causes of the Civil War," we debate why we once debated about the causes of the Civil War. In short, there has been a shift from "cause" to "meaning." And there is always a "subtext" to the effect that we should have been looking at something else and would have been except for. . . . We waste endless words on "To Foucault or Not," "Gender vs. Class as a Mode of Analysis," or "Geertzian Model vs. Deconstruction Model." History itself—that is, what happened and why—gets lost, indeed becomes unknowable, except in the most limited sense and perhaps not even then. Intellectual word games and reflecting on the reflections of others is now in; doing history is out.

The best thing about gurus is not that they come, but that they go. Unfortunately, American historians seem to take longer than necessary to appreciate this fact. And when we finally wise up, we have to expose the limitations of a theory that most of the rest of us never bought in the first place.[26] Although I disagree with many elements of her jeremiad against what she calls the "New History" (really the "Newest History"), and especially her blanket disdain for social history, Gertrude Himmelfarb is right on the mark when she writes, "It has been said that when ideas die in France, they are reborn in America; one might add that when they are past their prime in other disciplines, they are belatedly adopted by historians."[27]

Exposure to such academic ideas has encouraged many historians to embrace

---

their hands read Jacques Derrida" ("The Curious Persistence of Rights Talk in the 'Age of Interpretation,'" *Journal of American History* 74 [December 1987]: 992).

25. David Hackett Fischer, *Historians' Fallacies: Toward a Logic of Historical Thought* (New York: Harper and Row, 1970), especially chapter 1.

26. For how this works in the study of a single subject—popular culture and its relationship to "hegemony" and "power"—see the articles by Lawrence W. Levine, Robin D. Kelley, Natalie Zemon Davis, and T. Jackson Lears in "AHR Forum," *American Historical Review* 97 (December 1992): 1369–1430.

27. "Some Reflections on the New History," *American Historical Review* 94 (June 1989): 662.

the politically correct frenzy in the real world over "multiculturalism" and "diversity." Despite the claims of opponents that the assorted "new historicism" is politicizing history, history has always been "politicized." With the possible exception of the American Civil War, the winners have always written the history. And in America, as elsewhere, that has normally meant the white, the male, and the well off. Yet the new true believers seem relatively unconcerned that there should have been so much disagreement among "dead [whether living or not] white males" over the years. What united the earlier generations, of course, was a belief that American, and for that matter Western, society, with all their faults, were no worse than and maybe even superior to all others. Often that view was a "given," that is, taken for granted and expressed more implicitly than explicitly.

Now the poststructurally and the politically correct have explicitly challenged this earlier mindset. To begin with, they say, all cultures are equal; but many are willing to go further and argue that Western civilization in general, and American history in particular, are less worthy because of their long history of racial, class, and gender oppression. No matter that other cultures have at the very least comparable histories; they evidently were not powerful enough to do the kind of damage we inflicted. Blacks, as the argument goes, can't be guilty of racism, or women guilty of sexism, because they lack the power. (In the 1970s it was common to refer to "white racism," so common in fact that I thought that all typewriters should have a key labeled "white racism." Today "white" is a given and we could get by with a computer macro for "racism.") Few seem to notice that the originators, if not necessarily the implementers, of such insights are all Western white males.[28]

In its most extreme form, this approach has led to the assertion that traditional history writing is, in Michel Foucault's sense, political, and also imperialistic. Emerging as some sort of revealed truth is the startling fact that "history is not purely referential but is rather structured by historians."[29] So what else is new? In

---

28. The Columbus Quincentennial seemed to encourage the profession's worst tendencies. Many of them, including white-male bashing and celebration of the "Other," poststructural overtheorizing and underresearching, extreme self-importance and impenetrable trendy prose, are on display in the *Journal of American History* 79 (December 1992), a special issue devoted to "Discovering America." Thankfully it contains some exceptions, but see especially the articles by Carroll Smith-Rosenberg, Ronald Takaki, Patricia Nelson Limerick, and Michael Rogin.

29. On Foucault, power, politics, and inclusion, see Scott, "History in Crisis?" passim, quote 681. For the issue and implications of historical imperialism or "colonialism," as it applies to one field, see Antonia I. Castaneda, "Women of Color and the Rewriting of Western History: The Discourse, Politics, and Decolonization of History," *Pacific Historical Review* 61 (November 1992): 501–33, and the more sensible Virginia Scharff, "Else Surely We Shall All Hang Separately: The Politics of Western Women's History," ibid., 535–55.

fact, the writing of history is by its nature imperialistic. It must seek dominance, that is, order; it must expropriate other people's experiences and culture, though hopefully with sensitivity, understanding and, above all, humility, in an effort to be as "true" as possible to the past. And it cannot be totally inclusive. There will always be voices or "Others" omitted, no matter our best intentions. And if we accept the power/knowledge nexus, then we can expect to be privileging some group or other. No matter that some of those groups might actually have "earned" that privileging.

In order to make amends we are now called upon to celebrate the diversity of people and study the oppressed. Preferably, the oppressed should be studied by members of their own groups. Only they, it is argued, will be sensitive and worthy enough to undertake such investigations and report the results whether through scholarship or teaching. Few seem aware that the two most impressive accounts of nineteenth-century American society and the seminal treatment of twentieth-century race relations were written respectively by a Frenchman, Englishman, and Swede.[30] No one tries to explain the extensive list of superior books about American ethnic groups written by nonmembers. But then again, what often seems to matter more is the need to have role models. Getting "your" history from "your own kind" is most likely to bring about increased "self-esteem."[31] Alas, if it were that easy to attain self-esteem, Woody Allen wouldn't have needed all those years in analysis.

One expects such ignorance or selective amnesia from neophytes and activists, but academics, especially at "elite" institutions, often defend such positions. In the case of black history, there are now many fewer explicit calls for blacks—and only blacks—to teach black history than during the late 1960s and 1970s, but, despite some notable hirings and tenurings of whites, that clearly remains the unstated goal of many departments. Prominent white historians of black history are regularly asked to assess the qualifications of blacks for senior positions in black history for which they themselves are not considered. The same pattern is even more evident and explicit in the fields of women's and "Latino" history. In those two instances, however, there are fewer nonmembers of those groups with a scholarly interest in those subjects, so reverse discrimination, while present, is not as great a problem. In all three cases, the opportunity to increase the number of female and "minority" members of a department is at

30. Alexis de Tocqueville, *Democracy in America* (New York: Alfred A. Knopf, 1945); James Bryce, *The American Commonwealth,* 2 vols. (New York: Macmillan, 1893); Gunnar Myrdal, *An American Dilemma: The Negro Problem and Modern Democracy* (New York: Harper and Brothers, 1944).

31. Arthur M. Schlesinger, Jr., *The Disuniting of America* (New York: W. W. Norton and Co., 1992), especially chapters 2–4.

least as important as having courses taught in these fields. But things could be worse. For a while I feared my department might authorize a position in children's history.

Viewed within this context much of my work seems a throwback to an earlier time. A few comments about major themes and my approach to the subjects under discussion might therefore be in order. The current crop of literary theorists, of course, would argue that my "reading" of my own work is no more valid than that of other "readers." "Every text at the very moment of its inception," claims intellectual historian David Harlan, "has already been cast onto the waters. . . . No text can ever hope to rejoin its father. . . . It is the fate of every text to take up the wanderings of a prodigal son that does not return."[32] But I'm not ready to surrender my words so easily.

First, I'm a nuts and bolts kind of guy. As my earlier comments suggest I'm suspicious of big, all-encompassing theories, especially when associated with trendy gurus who rail against "universal truths" that I never subscribed to for the same reason I make only limited use of their work. My generation has been damned, after all, for embracing "situational ethics" and "secular humanism." You will find no "webs of significance," "layered meanings," or "hegemonic relationships," although there is an awareness of what we used to call causal links, complex meanings, and subtle uses of power. Some of these essays might have benefited from more attention to theory, but on balance I think they are better off without it. I'm an empiricist at heart, and the highest compliment I can pay an author is that he or she displays common sense based on a thorough reading of the sources. Too often, overattention to theory results in obfuscation in language and simplistic generalizations. Many of my findings might seem "obvious," but they were not at the time. Some of them still are not.

These essays were written to be read. They sought to illuminate specific aspects of the American past. Above all, they sought to ask what, how, and why, and to find answers without too much self-consciousness about the inherent biases of the historical method. And I certainly felt no need to try to provide a substitute for the way others look at history and then have the chutzpah to preach inclusion.

Not surprisingly then, these essays reflect a belief in the need to immerse oneself in the documents that I learned in graduate school. They were, of course, to varying degrees affected by what was going on in society at the time and perhaps in my own life as well. Try as we might, there are limits to our filters. But it is worth noting that when I discovered in 1967 that nineteenth-century south-

32. "Intellectual History and the Return of Literature," *American Historical Review* 94 (June 1989): 600.

ern urban blacks often called for separate but equal treatment in the post–Civil War South, it was at a time when both I and most of my graduate colleagues, to say nothing of the great mass of blacks and black leaders, were pushing an integrationist agenda.

Let there be no mistake, this early work and its conclusions were not, as one favorable reviewer argued in 1978, simply the product of "the late 1970s, when legal segregation is ended and there is less *de facto* segregation in southern than in northern schools, [and thus] the 'relatively fluid' race relations and the exceptional 'degree of integration' a century ago seem of limited significance."[33] The new true believers will find this difficult to accept, but I simply reported what the research turned up. Indeed, if I had been looking for anything in particular it was signs of white oppression that would have forced segregation on blacks well before the time commonly claimed. Prodded by the evidence, my teachers, my own curiosity, and a deepening, if at times grudging, respect for the work of my predecessors, I insisted on asking why blacks were taking the position they were, and thankfully was able to avoid the twin traps of presentism and parasitic history.

My work can also be described as "nontribal." I believe strongly in a comparative approach, be it explicit, or implicit. I'm concerned about the current tendency to isolate the study of one group (or region). As I've already noted, I find this particularly troubling when the study of that group or region becomes the sole property of privileged constituencies. In part, I believe this for philosophic reasons. Although there is no denying the special insight that insiders bring to the study of a given group's or region's culture or history, we too often discount the value of what an outsider brings to such a study.

I also have more narrow, self-serving reasons. For I am a truly marginal man when it comes to the subjects I study. I'm a white studying black history, a suburban product studying cities, a northerner studying the South and the West, and a Jew studying the two most heavily Protestant regions of the country. Even my work on other Jews has concentrated not on my native North, but on the South. And, as should be clear in my essays "Writing Jewish Community History" and "Nativism, Bigotry, and Anti-Semitism in the South," unlike those who champion the redemptive power of filiopietistic history, I undertook the latter work for the same reasons that drew me to black history. The study of history can, of course, provide grounds for groups to feel good about themselves, but history that stops there or is undertaken only for that reason is propaganda and no history at all. Perhaps, this explains not only my antipathy toward those who

---

33. C. Vann Woodward, review of *Race Relations in the Urban South, 1865–1890,* by Howard N. Rabinowitz, *Journal of Southern History* 44 (August 1978): 477.

loudly proclaim their "perspective" to the world, but also my own attempt to view the people and events I study, to the greatest extent possible, on their own terms. To those who nevertheless insist on seeing these essays on blacks as the product of a "white" perspective, I can only say—let's get it right: what you'll find is a white, middle class, liberal, college educated, Jewish, heterosexual male from Albuquerque, New Mexico, by way of South Brooklyn perspective.

And most obviously, as I've said in "Race, Ethnicity, and Cultural Pluralism in American History"—initially prepared for oral delivery and thus more confessional than the other essays—I think of myself in ethnic terms as a partial identifier and am a firm believer in maximizing personal choice and equal opportunity. Members of minority groups and women should be able to write the kind of history they want, with the kind of perspective that suits them. If they want to write about black history, or women's history, fine; if not, that's fine too, indeed, in my view perhaps even better since other fields might be enriched. The point is, they should be and feel free to choose. And they certainly can do what I did; that is, specialize in certain nontribal fields, but then return to their "roots" if the spirit moves them.

While teaching at Grinnell College in 1970–1971, I saw for the first time the kind of group pressure put on black students who wanted associations and a life beyond the confines of the campus's black student "community." Such internally enforced segregation continues to be a problem at universities throughout the country. More recently, I have encountered various forms of indirect and direct pressure used to influence the field selections of female and nonwhite male graduate students. Thirty years ago you would have lost a lot of money betting that every Jewish, Irish, or female graduate student you met was primarily interested in the history of his or her own kind; indeed, the best bet to make in the case of Jews was that they were interested in black history. Predictable, yes; but not parochial. Today a similar wager on, for example, female and Chicano students would turn a tidy profit.

C. Vann Woodward termed such tendencies toward the match of individuals and fields, induced by both personal choice and job-market pressures, "ghettoization." He was labeled racist by some, paternalistic by others, and simply dismissed as past his prime by still others. But he was right. He would have been "racist" or "patronizing" had he not spoken up. One of his black students, Barbara J. Fields, was so conscious of such pressures and tendencies within the profession that she refused to be interviewed for a broad-ranging study of the writing of black history in America between 1915 and 1980 on the grounds that she was a southern or social historian and didn't want to be typed as a "black historian." She went a bit overboard, I think, but I, for one, can't blame her. History, both as a profession and a discipline, would be better served if there were more men doing women's history, Protestants, Catholics, and Muslims doing Jewish history, and more blacks and Hispanics doing Russian history.[34]

If much of the above can be considered "old-fashioned," one final aspect of my work is certainly not. I try to treat the various ethnic groups and indeed, the individual members of those groups, as subjects rather than mere objects of history, actors and not merely passive victims. As indicated in several of the essays, particularly those involving *The Strange Career of Jim Crow,* when I began graduate school blacks and "Others" in general were rarely treated as actors. Instead they were "the oppressed," and the focus was on their "oppressors." My work was thus part of a basic shift in the writing of American history that is too often simply summed up as "writing history from the bottom up."

I think this shift has important implications for the study of what the lives of so-called "ordinary people" are like and *why* they are that way. It certainly speaks to our current preoccupation with "power." This approach to blacks has been most rewarding in my writing about the origins of segregation and the shift from exclusion to segregation that occurred in the late– nineteenth-century South as a result of the demands of both whites and blacks, and in my functional approach to black leadership. The trendy term for this approach is now *historical agency,* as in the need to focus on the "oppressed" as agents of their own destiny. As is true of so much else in contemporary scholarship, the historians who use the term seem to have picked it up from literary theory or other disciplines, ignoring the extent to which they are simply reinventing the wheel, an item already to be found in history's garage. Yet in too much of the current work authors ignore the extent to which whites still set the basic ground rules. In the end, the limits of black power—or agency—and the interaction of whites and blacks rather than some ill-defined black "autonomy" is most significant in charting relations between the races.[35] And this remains true for other ethnic groups as well.

Viewing people and cultures on their own terms, or with regard to a comparative dimension, means that these essays try not to be judgmental. It is easy to damn the dead—they are, after all, poorly equipped to defend themselves. It is much tougher to try to understand the dead. Although it is fashionable today for historians to condemn explicitly the instances of racism, sexism, classism, or

34. A second black historian, Armstead Robinson, also declined to be interviewed for the same reason. Meier and Rudwick, *Black History and the Historical Profession,* 299–300.

35. For a perceptive discussion of the limits of slave autonomy, especially with regard to the existence of an allegedly cohesive and powerful slave "community," see Peter Kolchin, "American Historians and Antebellum Southern Slavery, 1959–1984," in *A Master's Due: Essays in Honor of David Herbert Donald,* ed. William J. Cooper, Jr., Michael F. Holt, and John McCardell (Baton Rouge: Louisiana State University Press, 1985), 87–111.

environmental destruction they write about (another of their ironic concessions to "universalism"), the following essays lack such expressions of committed passion. I did not feel the need to point out that reprehensible behavior was "bad." I simply assumed that readers would realize, for example, that I oppose all forms of racial discrimination and think that our society would be better off without them. As a product of the mid-1960s graduate cohort, it never occurred to me that I needed to say so or that anyone would care. But it's the 1990s, so I've now come clean.

Part One

Historians
and
Segregation

More than the Woodward Thesis

Assessing *The Strange Career of Jim Crow*

Since Its publication in 1955, C. Vann Woodward's *Strange Career of Jim Crow* has had a fundamental impact on the study of American race relations. Although best known for its so-called "Woodward thesis," that is only part of the book as it emerged through four editions over twenty years, and no one has assessed the work in its entirety since the final edition appeared in 1974.

What I want to do, then, is to consider three of the contributions of *Strange Career*. The first, of course, is the Woodward thesis concerning the origins, timing, and nature of segregation or, as Woodward sometimes calls it, Jim Crow. The second is the concept of the Second Reconstruction as a way of gaining perspective on Reconstruction or, in Woodward's term, the "First Reconstruction." The third is the masterful but neglected concluding chapter to the 1974 edition, whose strengths ironically point up some of the limitations of the earlier sections and editions of *Strange Career*.

I suspect that I have read *Strange Career* in its various forms more often than I have read any other book, except perhaps Woodward's *Origins of the New South*. Nevertheless, as I began to prepare this essay, I was surprised to discover not only that the book was even more subtle and substantive than I had remembered, but also that there was a need to get the different editions straight. In fact, the *Strange Career* has had several careers, and I think it important to review briefly the structure of the four editions before we consider the contributions.

Earlier versions of this essay were presented at the annual meeting of the American Historical Association, Chicago, December 1986, and to the University of Chicago Social History Workshop, October 1987. I would like to thank all participants for their helpful comments, and also David Thelen for his perceptive prodding during preparation of the published version for *Journal of American History*.

What we really need is something comparable to Woodward's edition of the Mary Chesnut diaries.[1]

Everything began with the James W. Richard Lectures, which Woodward wrote during the summer months immediately following the *Brown v. The Board of Education* decision and presented before a biracial audience of about one hundred at the University of Virginia in October 1954. The manuscript for the lectures became the copy for the first edition of *Strange Career,* published in 1955. A brief preface and an introduction entitled "Of Reconstructions and the South" argued for the use of history to help understand the present and asserted the essential discontinuity of southern history. Woodward then turned in chapter 1 to the "Forgotten Alternatives" of fluid race relations in the post-Reconstruction South; in chapter 2 to the "Capitulation to Racism" at the turn of the century; and in chapter 3, "The Man on the Cliff," to the course of race relations from World War I to the *Brown* decision.[2]

Two years later in a paperback edition, Woodward added a chapter 4, "'Deliberate Speed' vs. 'Majestic Instancy,'" which brought events up to 1957. He sought not only to explain the worsening of race relations in the South since 1954 but also to provide renewed grounds for optimism by noting that the prospects for change were more promising than during the First Reconstruction. The 1957 edition remains a strangely forgotten one. It was the only one in which the subtitle, *A Brief Account of Segregation,* appeared on the cover; its foreword, which modified some of Woodward's original argument, was not reprinted with the other prefaces in successive editions; and much of its final chapter was later eliminated, including an extended comparison of the two reconstructions.[3]

The 1966 revision proved longer lasting. The preface said the new version sought to take advantage of the new perspective provided by the additional years since 1955, as well as to bring the account up to date and to consider new scholarly contributions to the field. The original introduction remains intact, though without a title; the original three chapters appear as chapters 2 to 4 with sections slightly altered, especially to include more information on northern race relations. A new chapter 1, "Of Old Regimes and Reconstructions," incorporates

1. *Mary Chesnut's Civil War,* ed. C. Vann Woodward (New Haven: Yale University Press, 1981). Woodward's biographer devotes a thoughtful chapter to the *Strange Career,* but concentrates on the origins of the segregation issue. There are merely scattered references to other parts of the book, and he misses the significant differences among the various editions. See John Herbert Roper, *C. Vann Woodward: Southerner* (Athens: University of Georgia Press, 1987), 171–200, 247, 338.

2. Woodward, *Thinking Back: The Perils of Writing History* (Baton Rouge: Louisiana State University Press, 1986), 82–83; Roper, *C. Vann Woodward,* 194; Woodward, *The Strange Career of Jim Crow* (New York: Oxford University Press, 1955).

3. *The Strange Career of Jim Crow* (New York: Oxford University Press, 1957).

some of the modifications expressed in the 1957 foreword, adds some new ones, and considers the most serious challenges to Woodward's view of segregation as a product of the turn-of-the-century South. There is also a new concluding chapter (chapter 5), "The Declining Years of Jim Crow," which incorporates part of the final chapter of the 1957 edition and carries the story to the climactic week in August 1965 that witnessed both the signing of the Voting Rights Act and the outbreak of the Watts riot. The 1966 edition also marks the coming-of-age of *Strange Career* as a textbook with the addition of an index and an updated list of suggested reading.[4]

The process of "textbookization" was completed in the 1974 edition. Following a brief but important preface, this version is identical to the previous one until page 181; except for the deletion of some material on northern race relations, the rest of the book differs significantly from the 1966 version only in the addition of a sixth chapter, "The Career Becomes Stranger." The new chapter begins with Watts and closes with a typically ironic assessment of the seeming high tide (in the early 1970s) of black separatist rejection of Jim Crow's end.[5]

During the process of revision, *Strange Career* evolved from a lecture series meant for a local, predominantly southern audience, which aimed to provide a historical foundation for hopes that desegregation would be peaceful and successful, into the most widely used survey text on the nature of American race relations since the Civil War. Along the way, Woodward drew attention to his initial qualifiers and provided further modifications. After all, as he put it in the original edition, "Since I am . . . dealing with a period of the past that has not been adequately investigated, and also with events of the present that have come too rapidly and recently to have been properly digested and understood, it is rather inevitable that I shall make some mistakes. I shall expect and hope to be corrected."[6] In that spirit and with the benefit of additional years of scholarship and perspective, it is time to turn to three of the contributions of the *Strange Career*.

The heart of the book remains the Woodward thesis. In his recent memoirs, Woodward confirms the definition of the thesis he gave in a 1971 essay, "The Strange Career of a Historical Controversy." It was, he wrote, "First, that racial segregation in the South in the rigid and universal form it had taken by 1954 did not appear with the end of slavery, but toward the end of the century and later; and second, that before it appeared in this form there occurred an era of experi-

---

4. *The Strange Career of Jim Crow*, 2d rev. ed. (New York: Oxford University Press, 1966). For the addition of material on postbellum northern race relations, see especially 71–72.

5. *The Strange Career of Jim Crow*, 3d rev. ed. (New York: Oxford University Press, 1974).

6. Ibid. (1955), ix.

ment and variety in race relations of the South in which segregation was not the invariable rule."[7] As Woodward put it in the original and subsequent editions of *Strange Career,* it was not until the post-1890 period that a rigid segregation code "lent the sanction of law to a racial ostracism that extended to churches and schools, to housing and jobs, to eating and drinking. Whether by law or by custom, that ostracism eventually extended to virtually all forms of public transportation, to sports and recreations, to hospitals, orphanages, prisons, and asylums, and ultimately to funeral homes, morgues, and cemeteries."[8] The reference to custom is misleading, however, since for Woodward, despite his partial disclaimers, the existence of a law enforcing segregation has always been the key variable in evaluating the nature of race relations. And in all editions of the book, most of the examples of flexibility before the 1890s have come from the moderate South Atlantic states.

Woodward easily weathered and even incorporated the first wave of criticism that appeared. In the new first chapter of the 1966 edition, he accepted Richard C. Wade's depiction of segregation in antebellum southern cities but discounted its importance because an all-pervasive, legally enforced system was absent and the region's urbanization limited. Leon F. Litwack's revelations about the extent of segregation in the pre–Civil War North impressed Woodward more, and he broadened his treatment of the North as a result, but he reminded readers that his concern had been primarily with the roots of segregation in the South. Joel Williamson's argument for the existence of a "duo-chromatic order" by the end of Reconstruction in South Carolina, like Wade's, was found lacking because South Carolina "may have been exceptional in some respects," but more importantly because there, as elsewhere in the South, race relations had not yet crystallized. Having dealt firmly but graciously with his critics and even included some additional examples of early segregation, Woodward then added a new section to the beginning of chapter 2 ("Forgotten Alternatives") that spotlighted Charles E. Wynes's support for the Woodward thesis in Virginia.[9]

Woodward did not consider further historiographical developments in his 1974 edition, instead referring readers to "The Strange Career of a Historical

7. *Thinking Back,* 82–83. For the original quote in the earlier essay, see Woodward, *American Counterpoint: Slavery and Racism in the North-South Dialogue* (Boston: Little, Brown and Company, 1971), 237.

8. *Strange Career* (1955), 8; ibid. (1957), 8; ibid. (1966), 7; ibid. (1974), 7.

9. Ibid. (1966), 13–29, 33–34. For the criticisms brought against the book, see Wade, *Slavery in the Cities: The South, 1820–1860* (New York: Oxford University Press, 1964); Litwack, *North of Slavery: The Negro in the Free States, 1790–1860* (Chicago: University of Chicago Press, 1961); Williamson, *After Slavery: The Negro in South Carolina during Reconstruction, 1861–1877* (Chapel Hill: University of North Carolina Press, 1965); Wynes, *Race Relations in Virginia, 1870–1902* (Charlottesville: University Press of Virginia, 1961).

Controversy." Other studies had appeared since Woodward's 1971 essay that aimed to document the prevalence and early appearance of segregation or to argue for its later crystallization, and more would follow after 1974. Woodward was correct to think that those subsequent works did not significantly alter the debate, and they do not merit detailed consideration here.[10]

Increasingly, however, some historians sought to go beyond the narrow question of what segregation did the South have, and when did the South have it, a debate that often seemed to come down to whether the bourbon glass was half full or half empty. For example, although I had entered the fray in 1967 geared to write parasitic history and was therefore delighted to discover widespread legally enforced cemetery segregation by 1865 and the presence of Jim Crow Bibles in 1868, I soon sought to move the debate in a new direction. Instead of simply chronicling the considerable segregation that existed prior to 1890, I asked what it had replaced. I discovered that it was normally exclusion of blacks, rather than integration; ironically, segregation often therefore marked an improvement in the status of blacks, rather than a setback. That view has been widely accepted, most notably and generously by Woodward himself.[11] John

10. *Strange Career* (1974), viii. In addition to Wynes, *Race Relations in Virginia,* and George Brown Tindall, *South Carolina Negroes, 1877–1900* (Columbia: University of South Carolina Press, 1952; reprint ed., Baton Rouge: Louisiana State University Press, 1966), which anticipated the basic thrust of *Strange Career,* the following works explicitly or implicitly support the Woodward thesis: Frenise A. Logan, *The Negro in North Carolina, 1876–1894* (Chapel Hill: University of North Carolina Press, 1964); Henry C. Dethloff and Robert P. Jones, "Race Relations in Louisiana, 1877–1898," *Louisiana History* 9 (Fall 1968): 301–23; John W. Blassingame, *Black New Orleans, 1860–1880* (Chicago: University of Chicago Press, 1973); Dale A. Somers, "Black and White in New Orleans: A Study in Urban Race Relations, 1865–1900," *Journal of Southern History* 40 (February 1974): 19–42; John William Graves, "Town and Country: Race Relations and Urban Development in Arkansas, 1865–1905" (Ph.D. diss., University of Virginia, 1978). In addition to Williamson, *After Slavery,* Wade, *Slavery in the Cities,* and Vernon Lane Wharton, *The Negro in Mississippi, 1865–1890* (Chapel Hill: University of North Carolina Press, 1947), which can be used to challenge the thesis, the following works provide contrary evidence for the South: Roger A. Fischer, "Racial Segregation in Ante Bellum New Orleans," *American Historical Review* 74 (February 1969): 926–37, and *The Segregation Struggle in Louisiana, 1862–1877* (Urbana: University of Illinois Press, 1974); Ira Berlin, *Slaves without Masters: The Free Negro in the Antebellum South* (New York: Pantheon, 1974); Joseph H. Cartwright, *The Triumph of Jim Crow: Tennessee Race Relations in the 1880s* (Knoxville: University of Tennessee Press, 1976). For a discussion of additional titles, see Woodward, *American Counterpoint,* 234–60. For a convenient summary of the initial stages of the debate, see Joel Williamson, ed., *The Origins of Segregation* (Lexington, Mass.: D. C. Heath and Co., 1968). I have dealt more thoroughly with the debate, including its most recent developments, in my essay "Segregation and Reconstruction," reprinted below.

11. See my essay "From Exclusion to Segregation: Southern Race Relations, 1865–1890," reprinted below, and my book *Race Relations in the Urban South, 1865–1890*

Cell embraced my view and then shed further light on the issue by comparing the origins of segregation in the American South and South Africa in a book that Woodward considers more supportive of the Woodward thesis than I do. It is worth noting, however, that Cell's experiment in comparative history and George Fredrickson's before it owed much to the pioneering comparisons with South Africa found in *Strange Career,* whose title for the "Man on a Cliff" chapter is taken from an essay by Alan Paton.[12]

The debate over the Woodward thesis has been fruitful. Yet it has often been frustrating for Woodward's critics, since the master continues to absorb what they see as knockout blows and even to incorporate adversaries' weapons into his own arsenal. A careful reading of *Strange Career* helps explain why this could happen. For despite all that has been written about it, the contours of the Woodward thesis are not at all clear. Rather than being a firmly etched thesis, Woodward's argument is hedged, as he recalled in his memoirs, by "the carefully noted exception, the guarded qualification, the unstated assumption, the

---

(New York: Oxford University Press, 1978). For Woodward's reaction, see his foreword to the paperback edition of *Race Relations in the Urban South* (Urbana: University of Illinois Press, 1980), ix–x, his review of *Race Relations in the Urban South* in *Journal of Southern History* 44 (August 1978): 476–78, and *Thinking Back,* 96–97. For the response of others, see, for example, Eric Anderson, *Race and Politics in North Carolina, 1872–1901: The Black Second* (Baton Rouge: Louisiana State University Press, 1981), ix; Lawrence O. Christensen, "Race Relations in St. Louis, 1865–1916," *Missouri Historical Review* 78 (January 1984): 123–36; John Cell, *The Highest Stage of White Supremacy: The Origins of Segregation in South Africa and the American South* (New York: Cambridge University Press, 1982), 133–34, 175–76, 180; George Fredrickson, *White Supremacy: A Comparative Study in American and South African History* (New York: Oxford University Press, 1981), 262–63.

12. Cell, *Highest Stage of White Supremacy,* 133–34, 175–76, 180; Fredrickson, *White Supremacy.* For Woodward's assessment of Cell's book, see his "The Edifice of Domination," *New Republic,* December 27, 1982, 33–35, and *Thinking Back,* 97. In addition, Joel Williamson, who had been largely responsible for opening the original debate, sought to "move to one side, and begin again," though in fact he is still using Woodward's work as a jumping-off point. See Williamson, *The Crucible of Race: Black-White Relations in the American South since Emancipation* (New York: Oxford University Press, 1984), viii–ix, 491–93. Woodward himself sought to go beyond the debate by applying "competitive" and "paternalistic" models of race relations to the late nineteenth-century southern experience; see Woodward, *American Counterpoint,* 243–60. For two other efforts to save the Woodward thesis by approaching it from a different perspective than had Woodward, see the cyclical explanation in August Meier and Elliott Rudwick, "A Strange Chapter in the Career of 'Jim Crow,'" in *The Black Community in Modern America,* 14–19, vol. 2 of *The Making of Black America: Essays in Negro Life and History,* 2 vols., ed. Meier and Rudwick (New York: Atheneum, 1969), and J. Morgan Kousser and James M. McPherson, eds., *Region, Race, and Reconstruction: Essays in Honor of C. Vann Woodward* (New York: Oxford University Press, 1982), xxv–xxvii.

cautionary warning [which] was often overlooked or brushed aside." Indeed, Woodward went to great lengths in the various editions to avoid misinterpretation. Despite his emphasis on the importance of laws, he wrote in the first edition, "Laws are not an adequate index to the extent and prevalence of segregation and discriminatory practices in the South." The same phrase appears in all subsequent editions, but beginning in 1966, Woodward italicized it to make sure no one missed the point.[13] He also sought to be even more precise in his use of evidence. In all editions, Woodward uses Negro journalist T. McCants Stewart's recollections of his 1885 trip along the South Atlantic seaboard to illustrate the absence of rigid segregation. The treatments are identical, except that the 1955/1957 account is introduced by the sentence, "More pertinent and persuasive is the testimony of the Negro himself"; the 1966/1974 account begins, "More pertinent, whether typical or not, is the experience of a Negro."[14]

Yet the fault for missing Woodward's point does not always rest with the careless reader, for in matters besides the importance of law, *Strange Career* is often contradictory. Often that is to the good, making the book more comprehensive. Woodward regularly claims that he is looking simply at segregation, defined as the physical distance between the races, but there is a wealth of valuable information about political participation, jury service, and other matters that go well beyond mere segregation. At other times the contradictions are less fortunate. Despite Woodward's reference to the progressive extension of segregation, the original edition makes clear that the claims about the fluidity of race relations did not include churches, militia companies, schools, state and private welfare institutions, and a wide range of activities. In the 1966 and 1974 versions of the book, an addition to the original paragraph on state and private welfare institutions, for example, makes Woodward's point more explicitly by noting, "Both types had usually made it [segregation] a practice all along."[15] Not only was segregation the norm in many areas from at least 1865 on, but it was often, as in the case of schools, admittedly enforced by law. The Woodward thesis is therefore much

13. *Thinking Back,* 93; *Strange Career* (1955), 87; ibid. (1966), 102; ibid. (1974), 102. Woodward struggles with the relative importance of laws in many places. The best examples, in addition to the pages already cited, are the prefaces to the last three editions: ibid. (1957), xi–xvii; ibid. (1966), v–ix; ibid. (1974), v–viii. See also ibid. (1966), 24–25, 29, 31, and ibid. (1974), 24–25, 29, 31.

14. Ibid. (1955), 19; ibid. (1957), 19; ibid. (1966), 38; ibid. (1974), 38. Although Woodward does not mention T. McCants Stewart's color, he was a very light-skinned Negro, and that may help explain the ease with which he traveled through the South.

15. See ibid. (1955), 15–16, 83–84; ibid. (1957), 15–16, 83–84; ibid. (1966), 99; ibid. (1974), 99. Exclusion from welfare institutions had been the initial policy. See my essay "From Exclusion to Segregation: Health and Welfare Services for Southern Blacks, 1865–1890," reprinted below.

narrower than commonly believed and ironically had little relevance for the cause that most concerned Woodward at the time he conceived the book, that is, school desegregation. In essence, the thesis covered the situation in public conveyances and in hotels, theaters, restaurants, and other places of public accommodation. Woodward wrote out whole aspects of southern life from the bounds of his argument, thus at the very beginning, depending on your point of view, either loading the dice or conceding much of the game to his critics.

Woodward has obviously fared best within the strict ground rules he had established. The thesis is particularly true of public conveyances, where segregation laws were generally of post-1890 origin and where a degree of integration certainly existed, though rarely on first-class railroad cars. Yet the evidence about various forms of public accommodation, most notably the limited impact of the 1875 Civil Rights Act, suggests that segregation by custom was almost certainly more common than integration.[16] On Woodward's terms, that conclusion might be a victory for the thesis, but a somewhat hollow one.

The weight of the evidence seems to be on the side of those who find segregation deeply ingrained in southern life in the immediate postwar years, if not before. More importantly, it is not clear that the system of segregation became so rigid after the turn of the century as Woodward suggests, or that it did so when he averred. Recent studies of early twentieth-century Georgia and Tennessee blacks, for example, note that while segregation was pervasive, integrated activities continued to exist. I suspect further probing will reveal many instances of inter-racial mixing through at least the 1930s and even later, particularly among the lower classes.[17] Similarly, despite Woodward's surprising assertion that after 1900 "blacks ceased to vote," only indirectly corrected in a later chapter, scattered blacks continued to vote throughout the South and sometimes, in cities such as Atlanta and Memphis, even played a pivotal role in local politics.[18] By

16. John Hope Franklin, "The Enforcement of the Civil Rights Act of 1875," *Prologue* 6 (Winter 1974): 225–35; Charles A. Lofgren, *The Plessy Case: A Legal-Historical Interpretation* (New York: Oxford University Press, 1987), 132–37; Rabinowitz, *Race Relations in the Urban South,* 186–89, 195–96.

17. John Dittmer, *Black Georgia in the Progressive Era, 1900–1920* (Urbana: University of Illinois Press, 1977); Lester C. Lamon, *Black Tennesseans, 1900–1930* (Knoxville: University of Tennessee Press, 1977). Woodward notes that a 1940 park segregation ordinance in Atlanta provided an exception for the Grant Park Zoo; see *Strange Career* (1955), 104; ibid. (1957), 104; ibid. (1966), 117; ibid. (1974), 117. Yet there might be some confusion here between exclusion and segregation since the zoo had been segregated at its opening in 1890. See Rabinowitz, *Race Relations in the Urban South,* 190. For the passage of new laws during the 1930s and even 1940s, see Woodward, *Strange Career* (1955), 102–4; ibid. (1957), 102–4; ibid. (1966), 116–18; ibid. (1974), 116–18.

18. *Strange Career* (1955), 91; ibid. (1957), 91; ibid. (1966), 106; ibid. (1974), 106. For reference to the "virtual exclusion for nearly half a century" of Negro voters, see ibid.

juxtaposing the American South and South Africa, Cell and Fredrickson remind us that the twentieth-century social, political, and especially economic barriers between the races in the South were never as great or rigid as Woodward posits. Indeed, I think we have probably been spending too much time on the wrong end of the Woodward thesis. We need to know as much about the fluidity during the allegedly rigid period of segregation as we know about the rigidity during the allegedly fluid years.[19] It would also help to know if supposedly new forms of segregation such as those involving phone booths, elevators, and water fountains merely coincided with the appearance of new inventions.

What then has been the significance of the Woodward thesis? Woodward seems to have been wrong about the extent of nonsegregated behavior and the prospects for forgotten alternatives in that realm during the Reconstruction and post-Reconstruction periods, but he did inject the issue of segregation into the study of nineteenth-century southern history. Woodward stated that previous observers had assumed the prevalence of segregation in the postwar period, but he does not give any names. In fact, segregation, while certainly taken for granted, was not a major issue in the study of the postbellum South prior to *Strange Career.* Even George Tindall's penetrating, though more limited, anticipation of the Woodward thesis for South Carolina had aroused little attention.

It can be as difficult to explain "great leaps" in the writing of history as in the unfolding of history itself. Perhaps even Woodward cannot fully account for the timing and shape of his argument. He certainly was able to draw on the work of Tindall and of social scientists, especially social psychologists interested in the uses of scapegoats and the nature of prejudice, such as Konrad Lorenz and Gordon Allport. Nor should we forget Woodward's own primary research for *Origins of the New South* and a supporting brief in the *Brown v. The Board of Education* case. But more was involved than the "facts" of history or the theories

---

(1955), 124; ibid. (1957), 124. For reference to the exclusion of "all but a tiny percentage of the Negroes from the polls in the Southern states for nearly half a century," see ibid. (1966), 141; ibid. (1974), 141. On the political role of blacks in Atlanta, see Dittmer, *Black Georgia,* 147–48; on Memphis, see Lamon, *Black Tennesseans,* 42–47, 55–58, 222–23. For a broader discussion of black voting before the 1950s, see V. O. Key, Jr., *Southern Politics in State and Nation* (New York: Alfred A. Knopf, 1949).

19. Cell, *Highest Stage of White Supremacy,* 192–275; Fredrickson, *White Supremacy,* 199–282. For a largely unsuccessful attempt to minimize the differences between the South African and southern experiences, see Robert J. Norell, "Caste in Steel: Jim Crow Careers in Birmingham, Alabama," *Journal of American History* 73 (December 1986): 669–94, especially 671, 694. Although in *Strange Career* Woodward frequently admitted exceptions even at the peak of legalized Jim Crow, in *Thinking Back* he argued that "the new laws were of profound significance. They rigidified practice, eliminated exceptions, and applied to all on the basis of race alone" (96).

of others. Critical to opening a whole new field for study and infusing it with a startling perspective was Woodward's desire to provide southerners with a more hopeful, diverse, and discontinuous "usable past" with which to confront the challenges of desegregation.[20] And in the controversy that followed in its wake, the Woodward thesis led to new findings that transcended the narrower issue of the origin and extent of segregation.

Even more important than the injection of the segregation issue into southern historiography has been Woodward's profound insight into the importance of discontinuity in the study of southern race relations and especially the watershed nature of the 1890s. It is now clear that something highly significant happened in southern race relations during the 1890s. Though many segregation laws were already on the books, Woodward is right about the importance of post-1890 legislation. Those later laws, however, even when coming in new areas, did not create a new system of segregation. Rather, they added the force of additional laws to a system already widespread in practice. Cell reached a similar conclusion, noting that the shift during the 1890s came, not in the reality of racial contact, but in political rhetoric and law. In his recent tour de force, *The Crucible of Race,* Joel Williamson agrees but adds to the equation the sharp increase in racial violence.[21]

The question remains: Why did things change in the 1890s? Woodward attributed the altered racial climate to the erosion of northern liberalism and the weakened commitment of southern conservatives and agrarian radicals to defending black political rights. Yet recent scholarship has demonstrated that most Populists were, at best, always ambivalent about having a biracial coalition and that Conservatives, rather than following, actually led in the fight for disfranchisement legislation.[22] Besides, both those groups had already long ex-

20. Tindall, *South Carolina Negroes.* In the original edition, Woodward cited several books concerned with the legal status of blacks but did not single out the most important, Gilbert Thomas Stephenson, *Race Distinctions in American Law* (London: D. Appleton and Company, 1910), which he may have had in mind since Stephenson had argued that Jim Crow laws often simply gave the force of law to customary practices. For influences on Woodward's new approach to the subject, including work on a brief for *Brown v. The Board of Education,* 347 U.S. 483 (1954), see Roper, *C. Vann Woodward,* 171–200, and Woodward, *Thinking Back,* 81–90.

21. Rabinowitz, *Race Relations in the Urban South,* 330–33; Cell, *Highest Stage of White Supremacy,* 82–102; Williamson, *Crucible of Race,* 180–223.

22. For Woodward's explanation, see *Strange Career* (1955), 51–64, which is reproduced in ibid. (1957), 51–65; ibid. (1966), 69–82; ibid. (1974), 69–82. For challenges to Woodward's interpretation of Populist racial attitudes and behavior, see Gerald H. Gaither, *Blacks and the Populist Revolt: Ballots and Bigotry in the "New South"* (University: University of Alabama Press, 1977) and Barton C. Shaw, *The Wool-Hat Boys* (Baton Rouge: Louisiana State University Press, 1984). For conservative responsibility for dis-

pected to be segregated from blacks in schools, churches, and places of public accommodation.

The withdrawal of northern support for blacks alone remains a convincing reason for the changes of the 1890s. But there were other forces, treated only indirectly by Woodward. As Williamson notes, the economic hard times of the late 1880s and early 1890s and the threat of renewed northern Republican interference in southern affairs encouraged a shift in racial attitudes. Cell, drawing inspiration from Woodward's *Origins of the New South,* also emphasizes the altered economic situation in the South during the 1890s.[23] Although I would agree with Cell and Williamson, I think they both ignore a possible source encouraging the creation of a more de jure pattern of racial segregation. As I have argued elsewhere, segregation emerged during Reconstruction in part due to the efforts of white Republicans and their black allies, two groups Woodward largely ignores. Because segregation replaced exclusion, they could see it as an improvement in the status of blacks, especially when it was presented as providing separate but equal treatment. By the 1890s white Republicans were, except in a few parts of the South, no longer a major factor in the racial equation. Blacks were, however, and their resistance to de facto segregation may have helped move white southerners in the direction of additional laws. No one, to my knowledge, has sought to follow up that line of inquiry systematically since I presented it in the mid-1970s, but I think it worth pursuing, particularly given Cell's conclusion about the role of South African blacks' "growing uppityness" in forcing whites to resort to apartheid in an effort to control them.[24] And strange as it might seem, during the entire debate over the Woodward thesis, there has been remarkably little interest in the Jim Crow statutes themselves, and no one

---

franchisement, see J. Morgan Kousser, *The Shaping of Southern Politics: Suffrage Restriction and the Establishment of the One-Party South, 1880–1910* (New Haven: Yale University Press, 1974). Woodward has only partly accepted the views of his critics on Populism but finds Kousser's argument more compelling. See Woodward, *Thinking Back,* 39–40, 69, 97.

23. Williamson, *Crucible of Race,* 112–14; Cell, *Highest Stage of White Supremacy,* 82–170. Although he acknowledged the role of political and economic forces, Williamson emphasized, misguidedly in my view, psychosexual reasons for the rise of "Radicalism" after 1889. See Williamson, *Crucible of Race,* 111–79. See also my essay "Psychological Disorders, Socio-Economic Forces, and American Race Relations," *Slavery and Abolition* 7 (September 1986): 188–94.

24. Rabinowitz, *Race Relations in the Urban South,* 333–39, and "From Exclusion to Segregation: Southern Race Relations," reprinted below; Cell, *Highest Stage of White Supremacy,* 192–229, especially 212. For an endorsement of my position, but without new evidence, see Lofgren, *Plessy Case,* 25–26. For a mention of white fears of the "new Negro" that does not give enough credence to the justification for such fears, see Linda M. Matthews, "Keeping Down Jim Crow: The Railroads and the Separate Coach Bills in South Carolina," *South Atlantic Quarterly* 73 (Winter 1974): 117–29.

has satisfactorily followed the life of a statute from its origins through passage and the effects of implementation.[25] I might add that in the process of sorting out the reasons for change in the 1890s it would help to be more precise in the use of "Jim Crow" and to avoid the linkage of segregation, proscription, and disfranchisement that clouds the thinking of both the supporters and critics of the Woodward thesis. For long before the de jure disfranchisement of blacks or the frightening increase in lynching, segregation had become the norm in much of southern society.[26]

A second contribution of *Strange Career* has been less controversial. Just as Woodward felt that the recent origins of segregation might make it easier to overcome, he believed that the forces of reform were better positioned in the 1950s than they had been during Reconstruction. In his view, the nation in 1955 was in the midst of a "New Reconstruction," a term later used interchangeably with "Second Reconstruction," until the latter unaccountably completely replaced "New Reconstruction" in the 1966 edition.[27] For Woodward, the New or Second Reconstruction had far better prospects for success than the First Reconstruction. In the 1955, 1966, and 1974 editions, he kept comparisons to a minimum, stressing the impact of World War II and the cold war, the greater power of

---

25. Two attempts would have benefitted from greater attention to roll-call analysis and to the effects of the laws: Matthews, "Keeping Down Jim Crow," and John William Graves, "The Arkansas Separate Coach Law of 1891," *Journal of the West* 7 (October 1968): 531–41. On white Republican commitment to separate but equal train accommodations in Tennessee in 1881, see Stanley J. Folmsbee, "The Origin of the First 'Jim Crow' Law," *Journal of Southern History* 15 (May 1949): 243–47. For a suggestive, but only partially convincing, economic interpretation, see Walter E. Campbell, "Profit, Prejudice, and Protest: Utility Competition and the Generation of Jim Crow Streetcars in Savannah, 1905–1907," *Georgia Historical Quarterly* 70 (Summer 1986): 197–231. For an economic interpretation marred by misleading claims of originality and an inadequate grasp of the secondary literature, see Jennifer Roback, "The Political Economy of Segregation: The Case of Segregated Streetcars," *Journal of Economic History* 46 (December 1986): 893–917.

26. Woodward expressed this view in its classic form in a passage retained in subsequent editions: "The policies of proscription, segregation, and disfranchisement that are often described as the immutable 'folkways' of the South, impervious alike to legislative reform and armed intervention, are of more recent origin [than the immediate post-Reconstruction period]" (*Strange Career* [1955], 47). John Cell's definition of segregation is comparable to Woodward's "Jim Crow" (which Woodward often used interchangeably with "segregation" but sometimes more broadly): "An interlocking system of economic institutions, social practices and customs, political power, law, and ideology, all of which function both as means and ends in one group's efforts to keep another (or others) in their place" (*Highest Stage of White Supremacy,* 14). On Cell's approach, see my essay "The Not So Strange Career of Jim Crow," *Reviews in American History* 12 (March 1984): 58–64.

27. *Strange Career* (1955), 9–10, 124; ibid. (1957), 9–10, 124, 155, 175, 179; ibid. (1966), 9–10, 135, 139; ibid. (1974), 9–10, 135, 139, 209.

the federal government, and the commitment of both political parties to desegregation in the twentieth century. In the 1957 edition, however, during a time of
renewed southern resistance to desegregation, Woodward devoted five pages of
his concluding chapter to reasons why conditions favoring change were more
encouraging in the mid-1950s than in the 1860s and 1870s. Unlike the earlier
Reconstruction, the new one was not so strongly tied to the fortunes of a single
party, blacks were in a stronger position, there was more support in the South,
churches were unified in their support, the border states and mid-South were on
the right side, and there were already tangible results, as in the desegregation of
higher education. This time Reconstruction was national, rather than sectional,
in scope and support.[28]

By 1966, Woodward evidently no longer felt the need to be so defensive about
the prospects for change, and he eliminated the extended comparison while
incorporating most of the chapter's remaining material in the new edition. The
rest of his treatment was essentially the same except for the expanded account of
the new period of reconstruction and the name change. Unfortunately, the
persistence of language from the earlier editions resulted in some confusion as to
periodization. Woodward continued to date the origins of the Second Reconstruction from the late 1930s; he argued that it reached full momentum in the first
decade after the war and was divided into two eras by the *Brown* decision. But
although he retained in the 1974 edition the earlier statement, "The Second
Reconstruction shows no signs of having yet run its course or even of having
slackened its pace," in his new concluding chapter be observed, "The foundations of the Second Reconstruction had, in fact, begun to crumble during the
Johnson Administration."[29]

Most other scholars and politicians still use the term to describe the situation
today, though, given the policies of the Reagan administration, the number is
understandably shrinking. Disregarding the questions about duration for the
moment, the concept of the Second Reconstruction seems to have great value
as a means of enlarging our understanding of the limitations of the First Reconstruction. For Woodward, of course, the contrast was especially useful because
it suggested that the new effort had a better chance for success than the first.
Yet as Woodward realized, it is best to use the term as a shorthand way of
noting that after World War II federal policy once again became vitally concerned with the status of blacks in America. Obviously there were the differences between the two reconstructions with regard to prospects for success, as
already noted, but in a passage found in all editions, which has been over-

28. Ibid. (1957), 174–78.
29. Ibid. (1974), 8, 209.

looked by those who glibly use the term, Woodward observed that the Second Reconstruction "addressed itself to all the aspects of racial relations that the first attacked and even some that the First Reconstruction avoided or neglected." He then mentions as examples the attacks on segregation in the armed services and in the public schools.[30]

And here, I think, is the key point. Unless extreme caution is employed when using the term *Second Reconstruction,* the effect will be to distort the meaning of the First Reconstruction. It seems to me that the First and Second Reconstructions not only differed in their chances for success; they were about very different things. For that reason Woodward might have been better advised to stick to the term *New Reconstruction,* which has a stronger connotation of difference. The only policy aim that really links together the two reconstructions is the desire to increase the political power of blacks, though in its enforcement provisions the Voting Rights Act is much stronger than anything earlier. For if I am correct about the First Reconstruction's emphasis on equal access and acceptance of segregation, even for those areas in which Woodward does not acknowledge its existence, then there is no comparison with the integrationist thrust of the Second Reconstruction. Similarly, it is clear that the emphasis on jobs, housing, and other economic conditions had no counterpart in the First Reconstruction, other than perhaps the largely abortive efforts at land redistribution and tax reform. And certainly there is a world of difference between the call for equal opportunity that dominated the First Reconstruction and the demand for equality of condition that, at least after 1965, threatened to control the Second Reconstruction. But I don't think we should be surprised by those differences. Nor should we succumb, as some have, to the temptation to damn the proponents of the First Reconstruction for not going far enough in their reform efforts, a temptation Woodward staunchly resists.[31] After all, it would be ahistorical and unjust to expect mid-nineteenth-century Americans to believe and act like their late twentieth-century descendants or to create comparable institutions to promote change.

Woodward's treatment of the Second Reconstruction led him naturally into the penetrating concluding chapter of the 1974 edition. Its contribution does not

30. Ibid. (1955), 10–11; ibid. (1957), 10–11; ibid. (1966), 9–10; ibid. (1974), 9–10.
31. See, for example, Lawrence J. Friedman, *The White Savage: Racial Fantasies in the Postbellum South* (Englewood Cliffs, N.J.: Prentice Hall, 1970); Forrest G. Wood, *Black Scare: The Racist Response to Emancipation and Reconstruction* (Berkeley and Los Angeles: University of California Press, 1970), and Wood, *The Era of Reconstruction, 1863–1877* (New York: AHM Press, 1975). Woodward was even more sympathetic to the aims, legacy, and problems of the First Reconstruction in an article that also marked his full commitment to the term *Second Reconstruction.* See Woodward, "The Political Legacy of the First Reconstruction," *Journal of Negro Education* 26 (Summer 1957): 231–40.

stand out like the Woodward thesis or the concept of the Second Reconstruction. Many of the ideas are derivative, and the events have been increasingly covered in more detail by others. Its greatness lies in the way Woodward has brought together an impressive amount of material in a brief space, presented it in the elegant and eloquent style that characterizes the rest of the book, and made sound judgments that continue to fly in the face of much liberal and radical cant now, as they did when written fourteen years ago.

Woodward began with the obvious question: Why, after the great success in desegregation and voting rights, did black urban America explode? His answer was that the issues being settled did not affect poor blacks and that the emphasis on integration ignored the growing nationalist thrust of many black leaders. The fight for the end of legal Jim Crow that seemed so critical in 1954 now paled next to a rash of socioeconomic problems that neither integration nor the ballot could solve. Woodward wrote with compassion of the frustration and deprivation that produced the northern riots and the shift to new leaders who espoused "liberation and separation," rather than "integration and assimilation."[32] Yet in the midst of both black and white liberal support for such a shift, Woodward remained committed to the hopes of 1954, that is, to an integrated America.

John Roper, Woodward's biographer, interprets the 1974 concluding chapter as a product of Woodward's allegedly conservative drift during the years between the mid-1960s and 1974, a period characterized by William McFeely as Woodward's "Tory Period," and by Woodward as his "times of trouble." Another scholar, who is probably not alone, has discerned a "hostile tone" in that chapter.[33] That period was a depressing one for Woodward, both in his personal life and in the life of the country, but it would be wrong to see the chapter as part of some psychologically induced move to the right or an example of hostility toward or deviation from the struggle for equal rights. If anything had changed, it was the times, not the man. There was, however, some overreaction on his part and even some patronizing. Though he attempted to be fair minded, his language often gave him away—"the separatist impulse infected" civil rights organizations; Stokely Carmichael moved more and more "toward a license to hate, to violence and to rage." Yet at times Woodward seemed disturbed by his own pessimism—the 1974 chapter reminds us that despite all the attention they re-

32. *Strange Career* (1974), 195.
33. Roper, *C. Vann Woodward,* 198, 232–67, especially 246–47; remarks of an anonymous reader of a previous version of this essay (in my possession). Roper tends to treat Woodward's views of society and history that he agrees with as "liberal" or "radical"; when he disagrees with the assessments, Woodward is wrong and "conservative." Much of Roper's evidence, including Woodward's vote for George McGovern in 1972, undercuts claims for a Tory Woodward.

ceived (and in the face of his own overemphasis), the separatists captured only a small segment of black America. His heroes remained the National Association for the Advancement of Colored People (NAACP), Bayard Rustin, and others committed to integration, and he was equally harsh toward black separatists and toward the guilt-ridden white liberals who gave in to their demands. About the latter, he said "at times it was a question whether it was guilt or cowardice that prevailed." Nevertheless, he provided thoughtful, if largely negative, portraits of the new black leaders like Malcolm X (his favorite), Carmichael, Huey Newton, Eldridge Cleaver, and the rest and the groups they led. Throughout the chapter, Woodward kept in mind the difference between race and class interests, as when noting that the benefits of "black power" accrued to the black bourgeoisie, a process hidden by the "myth of black unity." He presents an equally compelling analysis of the white backlash.[34]

In short, this is perceptive and strong stuff. No one is spared. In addition to the divisions among blacks, there were many reasons for the end of the Second Reconstruction, including sheer exhaustion, the political and judicial undercutting of federal agencies' integration efforts, and the defection of white allies, especially Jews who became concerned about rising black anti-Semitism and liberals and students who became preoccupied with the Vietnam War. Woodward concludes with an essentially positive assessment of the Second Reconstruction, but he raises a number of penetrating questions about the prospects for integration in a society where "the brute facts of demography," among other forces, were moving in the opposite direction. One could therefore expect, he concluded sadly rather than bitterly, both "demand for integration and a demand for separation. Both demands would likely be heard for a long time, for the means of satisfying neither seemed yet at hand."[35]

It has been fourteen years since the appearance of that chapter. Like many Americans who had hoped that the end of legalized Jim Crow would lead to even greater progress, Woodward had been sobered by the experience of the previous twenty years. It is not surprising that there has been no fifth edition of *Strange Career*. Fortunately, Woodward has left us with a chapter that is the best single place to go in order to understand what happened to Martin Luther King, Jr.'s, dream. Yet it is also a chapter ironically out of place in the book as it was conceived in 1954 and nominally existed in 1974. Although Woodward had continued to add material on the North to the earlier editions, because of developments at the time the new 1974 chapter devoted unprecedented space to northern race relations. Similarly, for a book devoted to the origins and demise

34. *Strange Career* (1974), 196, 197–98, 205, 206–7.
35. Ibid., 219, 220.

of legal segregation, the chapter gave a surprising degree of attention to matters unrelated to segregation and to the effects of de facto, rather than de jure, discrimination. The most important reason for those changes was a new emphasis in a book that had admittedly been concerned with white attitudes and behavior toward blacks. Now blacks moved to center stage, and the focus was on black attitudes and behavior.

Woodward's shift to viewing blacks as subjects, rather than objects, of history was part of a general trend in black and ethnic history then underway, but he was among the pacesetters, as had been indicated by his 1969 presidential address to the Organization of American Historians.[36] In more subtle ways he had moved in that direction in the previous edition of *Strange Career*. In the 1955 and 1957 editions, for example, in discussing the origins of the Second Reconstruction, he had said, "The chief agent for the advance against southern peculiarities of racial discrimination and segregation has been the federal government in its several branches and departments, both civil and military." In 1966, in a change kept in 1974, he substituted, "Among the chief agents," thus implicitly at least increasing the importance of other elements, including blacks, who were subsequently discussed.[37] There is nothing, however, to compare with the emphasis in 1974's new chapter.

It is worth noting the greater attention to blacks in 1974, not only because it would be impossible to understand the preceding years and Woodward's reaction to them without doing so, but also because by largely ignoring black attitudes and behavior for the earlier years, Woodward missed an opportunity to provide a more compelling treatment of the origins and development of segregation. Early generations of blacks are viewed as "not aggressive in pressing their

36. Rabinowitz, "Race, Ethnicity, and Cultural Pluralism in American History," reprinted below; Woodward, "Clio with Soul," *Journal of American History* 46 (June 1969): 5–20.
37. *Strange Career* (1955), 123; ibid. (1957), 123; ibid. (1966), 134; ibid. (1974), 134. At times the new emphasis produced puzzling results. In his discussion of the 1965 disturbances in Selma in the 1966 edition, Woodward mentioned the murders of "Jimmie Lee Jackson, a Negro," "one of the clergymen, James Reeb," and "a woman on the highway to Selma" (187). In the 1974 edition, he repeats the reference to Jackson, but now notes "one of the clergymen died" and "a woman demonstrator" was murdered on the highway. Neither the race nor name of the two whites is given. The woman was, of course, Viola Liuzzo, whose death received more national attention than Jackson's (184–85). The new approach also gave less emphasis to the contributions of white southerners. For the omission of Judge J. Waites Waring of South Carolina, who presides over a key white primary case, see ibid. (1955), 125–27; ibid. (1957), 125–27; ibid. (1966), 140–42; ibid. (1974), 140–42. Note especially the deletion of "As so frequently happens in this New Reconstruction, a Southern man played one of the key roles," indicating that by 1966 Woodward was less concerned about providing the South with white role models. Compare ibid. (1955), 125; ibid. (1957), 125; ibid. (1966), 141; and ibid. (1974), 141.

rights," "confused and politically apathetic"; Booker T. Washington is described as favoring a "submissive philosophy."[38] Only in the preface to the final edition did Woodward seek "to recall a certain ambivalence that black people have felt all along toward integration in white America," but he still incorrectly asserted that it had "been buried and put aside during the long struggle against segregation and discrimination." Unfortunately, it was too late to rewrite the early sections of the book to incorporate the new approach found in the final chapter. Had he written, for example, about the call of Atlanta blacks in 1875 for the hiring of black teachers in their segregated schools, readers would have appreciated even more the irony of the Atlanta NAACP chapter doing the same thing a hundred years later. And, in general, Woodward would not be so surprised or think it quite as "strange" to find that "black champions of separatism joined hands with white champions of segregation."[39] The 1960s and 1970s were not, after all, the first time that some blacks had opted for "separate but equal treatment."

By 1974, then, and certainly by 1988, *The Strange Career of Jim Crow* no longer held together as well as it had in 1955. New research and further reflection had reinforced the qualifications and modifications already present in the initial edition, thus further lessening the purity of the Woodward thesis. Segregation itself no longer seemed so important an issue, whether in its de facto or de jure form. The guarded optimism of 1955 had given way to a guarded pessimism. The inattention to the actions and attitudes of blacks in the initiation of segregation after the Civil War had been revealed as a crippling shortcoming, not only by the work of others, but by a powerful new concluding chapter. An unquestioning commitment to integration and blindness to the voluntary aspects of ethnic cohesion had obscured the realities of the nation's cultural pluralism. As Woodward himself had feared, but expected, the passage of time and fruits of new research had exposed the risks of writing presentist and "committed history."

But does this mean that *The Strange Career of Jim Crow* must simply be consigned to the ranks of misguided classics that include *The Age of Jackson, An Economic Interpretation of the Constitution,* and *The Frontier in American History,* to be read as a period piece or the progenitor of a historiographical controversy? Woodward himself seems to take this view in his memoirs, as does his

---

38. Ibid. (1966), 28, 59, 82; ibid. (1974), 28, 59, 82. For the latter two quotations, see ibid. (1955), 41, 65; ibid. (1957), 41, 65; ibid. (1966), 59, 82; ibid. (1974), 59, 82. Despite the claim that blacks were "confused," in the same paragraph Woodward shows they were not, by saying that they were beginning to think in economic terms and had seen through Democratic appeals for their votes.

39. Ibid. (1974), vi, 218; Rabinowitz, "Half a Loaf: The Shift from White to Black Teachers in the Negro Schools of the Urban South, 1865–1890," reprinted below.

biographer.[40] Had *The Strange Career of Jim Crow* remained the series of lectures it was intended to be, that probably would have been the case. But in the process of turning the lectures into a textbook, Woodward so broadened and modified his initial effort as to make it the best available brief account of American race relations. Historians will continue to explore the well-trod ground of nineteenth-century segregation, but Woodward has already anticipated and undercut much of what they will find, and no one has yet found fault with the essence of Woodward's twentieth-century account of the subject. As typified by its new concluding chapter, *The Strange Career of Jim Crow* remains a pathbreaking, perceptive, highly readable, judicious, and surprisingly fact-filled effort to understand far more than the roots and nature of segregation, more even than the strange career of Jim Crow.

40. Woodward, *Thinking Back*, 98–99; Roper, *C. Vann Woodward*, 198–200.

Segregation and Reconstruction

The following essay appeared in a collection of essays in honor of my teacher, John Hope Franklin, one of the nation's leading southern and black historians. Contributors were asked to assess some aspect of Reconstruction historiography since the publication in 1961 of Franklin's landmark study, *Reconstruction after the Civil War,* and, when appropriate, to discuss Franklin's contribution to the subject being considered. The editors chose the topic of segregation and Reconstruction for me. Although I initially thought I had nothing new to say on the subject and, indeed, would have turned down the assignment had it not involved Franklin, I was pleased to discover that my fears were unwarranted. The invitation allowed me to document for the first time just how little focus there had been on the subject of segregation during Reconstruction. I was also able to deal more systematically with some of the implications of my "More than the Woodward Thesis" piece, integrate new literature, more thoroughly discuss the old, and provide extended suggestions for further research.

John Hope Franklin's *Reconstruction after the Civil War* devoted little attention to segregation. Indeed, the word does not appear in the index, although there is an entry for separate schools and reference to separate Negro churches. Such neglect was common at the time. In 1961 the origins of segregation in the South had not yet emerged as a controversial issue. Although Franklin had written on the subject in his essays "History of Racial Segregation in the United States" and "Jim Crow Goes to School," he had been concerned primarily with the post-

This essay was completed while I was a fellow at the Center for Advanced Study in the Behavioral Sciences. I am grateful for financial support provided by the National Endowment for the Humanities and the Andrew W. Mellon Foundation. I also thank Peter Kolchin for reading an early version of the essay.

Reconstruction years except in the area of education.[1] In addition, his book was intended mainly as a rebuttal to the Dunning school, which had concentrated on political and economic matters and slighted social relations between the races. Franklin's references to segregation were thus only incidental to the discussion of related issues, such as Reconstruction's considerable achievements in education.

Yet the foundation for the future controversy over the timing and extent of segregation already had been laid six years before the appearance of *Reconstruction* with the publication in 1955 of C. Vann Woodward's *Strange Career of Jim Crow,* a work well known to Franklin, who had read it in manuscript and been influenced by it, although he did not cite it in his bibliography.[2] Woodward's primary aim was to demonstrate that segregation was not a long-standing southern "folkway," but a relatively recent development—more post-1890 than post-1865—and therefore more vulnerable to change than commonly believed.[3]

Woodward stated that previous observers had assumed the prevalence of segregation in the immediate postwar period, but he failed to mention specific names in the text. Among the few possibilities listed in *Strange Career's* brief bibliography, the most likely candidate was Gilbert Thomas Stephenson, who in *Race Distinctions in American Law* had argued that in train travel, "the 'Jim Crow' laws. . . coming later, did scarcely more than to legalize an existing and widespread custom." In fact, segregation was not a major issue in the study of the postbellum South prior to the appearance of *Strange Career.* Woodward thus opened an entire new field for study. In doing so, however, he focused on the

1. *Reconstruction after the Civil War* (Chicago: University of Chicago Press, 1961); "History of Racial Segregation in the United States," *Annals* 304 (March 1956): 1–9; "Jim Crow Goes to School: The Genesis of Legal Segregation in Southern Schools," *South Atlantic Quarterly* 58 (Spring 1959): 225–35. The last was a product of Franklin's "association with Counsel for the plaintiffs" in *Brown v. The Board of Education,* service that indicated Franklin's personal as well as professional interest in the subject (Franklin, "Mirror for Americans: A Century of Reconstruction History," *American Historical Review* 85 [February 1980]: 11).

2. *The Strange Career of Jim Crow* (New York: Oxford University Press, 1955). In the preface, Woodward thanks Franklin for reading the manuscript. Franklin did cite Woodward's *Origins of the New South, 1877–1913* (Baton Rouge: Louisiana State University Press, 1951), which contained the seeds of the *Strange Career* argument.

3. *Strange Career,* 8. Cf. ibid. (New York: Oxford University Press, 1957), 8; ibid. (New York: Oxford University Press, 1966), 7; and ibid. (New York: Oxford University Press, 1974), 7. All subsequent references are to the 1966 and 1974 editions. For Woodward's subsequent reflections on the nature and origins of the "Woodward thesis," see his "The Strange Career of a Historical Controversy," in Woodward, *American Counterpoint: Slavery and Racism in the North-South Dialogue* (Boston: Little, Brown and Company, 1971), 237, and *Thinking Back: The Perils of Writing History* (Baton Rouge: Louisiana State University Press, 1986), 82–83.

period between the end of Reconstruction and the proliferation of Jim Crow legislation around the turn of the century. Like others, he devoted scant space to Reconstruction itself. Although in subsequent editions he acknowledged the greater presence of segregation in certain areas of southern life during Reconstruction, it was assumed that integration or at least fluidity was the more common experience during those years.[4]

Woodward's interpretation was quickly accepted by historians, especially those sympathetic to the aims of the civil rights movement then gathering momentum. In his 1956 article on the history of segregation, Franklin was probably the first scholar to employ the Woodwardian framework. Although careful to acknowledge the existence of earlier de facto and even de jure segregation, he argued, "It was not until the final quarter of the nineteenth century that states began to evolve a systematic program of legally separating whites and Negroes in every possible area of activity. And it was not until the twentieth century that these laws became a major apparatus for keeping the Negro in 'his place.'" Some conservatives, such as E. Merton Coulter, were restrained in their reactions to *Strange Career,* and most southern state historical journals chose not to review it, but southern white liberals and blacks were laudatory in initial reviews.[5]

This pattern reappeared in the first wave of articles and monographs aimed at testing the Woodward thesis. The southern white liberal Charles E. Wynes, in *Race Relations in Virginia,* and the black historian Frenise A. Logan, in *The Negro in North Carolina,* gave the thesis its earliest and most important support. Both scholars emphasized the flexibility of Reconstruction-era race relations and the presence of at least occasional integration. According to John W. Graves, Woodward's view also held true for Arkansas. Graves's 1968 study of the 1891 separate coach law concluded, "For many years a degree of racial intermingling prevailed that would be unthinkable in later times." His subsequent dissertation on the broader aspects of race relations in Arkansas between 1865 and 1905 was

---

4. *Race Distinctions in American Law* (London: D. Appleton and Company, 1910), 214. For the modifications and the restrictions of the Woodward thesis over the course of its various editions, see my essay "More than the Woodward Thesis: Assessing *The Strange Career of Jim Crow,*" reprinted above.

5. Franklin, "History of Racial Segregation," 1 and passim. Most academic journals used black reviewers. See, for example, Rufus E. Clement, *Journal of Southern History* 21 (December 1955): 557–59; James Bonner McRae, *Phylon* 16 (December 1955): 472–73; W. M. Brewer, *Journal of Negro History* 40 (July 1955): 379–82; Rayford W. Logan, *American Historical Review* 61 (October 1955): 212–13. For the views of a white liberal, see George B. Tindall, review of *The Strange Career of Jim Crow,* in *Louisiana Historical Quarterly* 38 (October 1955): 100–102. See also the unsigned review—almost certainly Coulter's, in a journal edited by him— in *Georgia Historical Quarterly* 39 (December 1955): 417–18.

justifiably more restrained, but concluded that although considerable discrimination existed, "ambiguity and confusion characterized the Reconstruction legacy in the sphere of civil rights."[6]

In "Race Relations in Louisiana," Henry C. Dethloff and Robert P. Jones used evidence similar to Graves's to present an even stronger endorsement of the Woodward thesis for the Bayou State. Implicit support also could be found in John Blassingame's *Black New Orleans,* Dale A. Somers's "Black and White in New Orleans," and Louis Harlan's narrower study of school desegregation in New Orleans during Reconstruction. Although Joseph H. Cartwright's *Triumph of Jim Crow* depicted a profound shift toward Jim Crow in Tennessee as early as the beginning of the 1880s, Cartwright believed, like the others, that a significant degree of integration existed during Reconstruction.[7] Advocates of such a view also could enlist George Tindall's *South Carolina Negroes.* Writing before the appearance of *Strange Career,* Tindall had anticipated many of its findings, albeit for only one state. He subsequently endorsed Woodward's general assessment for the rest of the South, doing so in a review that called for further studies but asserted, "It is not likely that they will alter substantially the conclusions of Professor Woodward."[8]

By the mid-1970s, then, a consensus on segregation had emerged, substantiated in several state studies and enshrined in college survey texts. According to this consensus, segregation as a rigid, legalized system was a product of the 1890s along with increased lynching and disfranchisement, and at least by impli-

6. Wynes, *Race Relations in Virginia, 1870–1902* (Charlottesville: University Press of Virginia, 1961), passim, especially 149; Logan, *The Negro in North Carolina, 1876–1894* (Chapel Hill: University of North Carolina Press, 1964); Graves, "The Arkansas Separate Coach Law of 1891," *Journal of the West* 7 (October 1968): 531–41, and "Town and Country: Race Relations and Urban Development in Arkansas, 1865–1905" (Ph.D. diss., University of Virginia, 1978), 61. Although it is often misleading, see also Graves, "Jim Crow in Arkansas: A Reconsideration of Urban Race Relations in the Post-Reconstruction South," *Journal of Southern History* 55 (August 1989): 421–48.

7. Dethloff and Jones, "Race Relations in Louisiana, 1877–1898," *Louisiana History* 9 (Fall 1968): 301–23; Blassingame, *Black New Orleans, 1860–1880* (Chicago: University of Chicago Press, 1973); Somers, "Black and White in New Orleans: A Study in Urban Race Relations, 1865–1900," *Journal of Southern History* 40 (February 1974): 19–42; Harlan, "Desegregation in New Orleans Public Schools during Reconstruction," *American Historical Review* 68 (April 1962): 663–75; Cartwright, *The Triumph of Jim Crow: Tennessee Race Relations in the 1880s* (Knoxville: University of Tennessee Press, 1976).

8. Tindall, *South Carolina Negroes, 1877–1900* (Columbia: University of South Carolina Press, 1952; reprint ed., Baton Rouge: Louisiana State University Press, 1966); Tindall, review of *Strange Career,* 102. For an explicit endorsement of the Woodward thesis, albeit one based on limited evidence for a border state that did not undergo Reconstruction, see Margaret Law Callcott, *The Negro in Maryland Politics, 1870–1912* (Baltimore: The Johns Hopkins University Press, 1969), especially ix, 134–38.

cation was less common than integration during Reconstruction. Most significantly, segregation was a relatively recent phenomenon.[9]

This opinion did not go unchallenged, however. Leon Litwack, in *North of
Slavery,* had pointed to the widespread existence of segregation in the antebellum North. Richard C. Wade's *Slavery in the Cities* depicted an entrenched
system of segregation in antebellum southern cities, raising doubts about the fate
of this system during Reconstruction. Ten years later Ira Berlin's study of antebellum southern free Negroes, *Slaves without Masters,* extended Wade's conclusion to include the nonurban areas of the South, although Berlin demonstrated
some ambivalence toward the Woodward thesis itself.[10]

More direct attacks on the thesis were already under way, drawing inspiration
in part from Vernon L. Wharton's earlier documentation of extensive segregation
in *The Negro in Mississippi.* The pivotal work was Joel Williamson's *After Slavery: The Negro in South Carolina during Reconstruction,* the first work in the
debate to focus on Reconstruction per se. Rather than assuming that integration
was the norm during Reconstruction and then tracing its alleged demise in
subsequent years, as his predecessors had done, Williamson sought to establish
its initial extent. In doing so, he gave equal status to customs and laws, unlike
earlier historians. His findings for South Carolina—the state in which blacks had
the most power—directly challenged those of Woodward and his defenders.
Although Williamson acknowledged examples of integration, he found de facto
segregation to be so prevalent that by the end of Reconstruction there existed a
crystallized "duo-chromatic order" in South Carolina.[11] Soon after, Roger A.
Fischer began a series of frontal attacks on the Woodward thesis over ground
that had proved fertile for Woodward's supporters. In "Racial Segregation in
Ante Bellum New Orleans" and "The Post–Civil War Segregation Struggle,"
Fischer argued for the early appearance and persistence of segregation in the
Crescent City. In *The Segregation Struggle in Louisiana,* he expanded his argu-

9. See, for example, Rebecca Brooks Gruver, *An American History,* 2d ed. (Reading, Mass.:
Addison-Wesley, 1976), 547; John Garraty, *A Short History of the American Nation,* 2d ed.
(New York: Harper and Row, 1977), 274–75; John D. Hicks, George E. Mowry, and Robert
Burke, *A History of American Democracy,* 4th ed. (New York: Houghton Mifflin, 1970), 367.

10. Litwack, *North of Slavery: The Negro in the Free States, 1790–1860* (Chicago:
University of Chicago Press, 1961); Wade, *Slavery in the Cities: The South, 1820–1860*
(New York: Oxford University Press, 1964); Berlin, *Slaves without Masters: The Free
Negro in the Antebellum South* (New York: Pantheon, 1974), especially 326–27, 383–84.

11. Wharton, *The Negro in Mississippi, 1865–1890* (Chapel Hill: University of North
Carolina Press, 1947); Williamson, *After Slavery: The Negro in South Carolina during
Reconstruction, 1861–1877* (Chapel Hill: University of North Carolina Press, 1965), espe-
cially 198–99. For an amplification of his views and a convenient summary of the initial
stages of the debate, see Joel Williamson, ed., *The Origins of Segregation* (Lexington,
Mass.: D. C. Heath and Co., 1968), especially the introduction.

ment to include the entire state; in the process, he removed some of his previous ambivalence about the value of the Woodward thesis in order to stress even more the relative importance of segregation during Reconstruction.[12] Although less systematic in their investigations of segregation in Florida, Joe M. Richardson, in *The Negro in the Reconstruction of Florida,* and Jerrell H. Shofner, in *Nor Is It Over Yet,* found evidence similar to Fischer's. As Shofner concluded, "The Jim Crow legislation [of the 1890s] reinforced existing social customs which had remained unchanged by post–Civil War developments."[13]

By the mid-1970s, there seemed to be a stalemate. Various studies had appeared that supported the Woodward thesis, but the works most directly concerned with the extent of segregation during Reconstruction had argued for the practice's prevalence and for an essential continuity in social relations between 1865 and 1900. In "A Strange Chapter in the Career of 'Jim Crow,'" August Meier and Elliott Rudwick had sought to reconcile the opposing views by pointing to an alleged cyclical pattern in the segregation of streetcars. Segregation appeared initially soon after the Civil War and persisted in some places during Reconstruction before being eliminated until its reappearance around the turn of the century.[14] The article was suggestive and demonstrated further the complexity of the issue, but no one followed its lead and it did not resolve the conflict. Not surprisingly, a number of state studies of southern blacks published during these years ignored the controversy and simply made passing reference to the mixture of segregation and integration.[15] Yet textbooks continued at least implicitly to

12. "Racial Segregation in Ante Bellum New Orleans," *American Historical Review* 74 (February 1969): 926–37, "The Post–Civil War Segregation Struggle," in *The Past as Prelude: New Orleans, 1718–1968,* ed. Hodding Carter et al. (New Orleans: Pelican Publishing House, 1968), 288–304; *The Segregation Struggle in Louisiana, 1862–1877* (Urbana: University of Illinois Press, 1974). For a similar emphasis on the essential continuity in Louisiana's pattern of segregation, but without reference to Woodward, see Joe Gray Taylor, *Louisiana Reconstructed, 1863–1877* (Baton Rouge: Louisiana State University Press, 1974), especially 434, 438–39.

13. Richardson, *The Negro in the Reconstruction of Florida, 1865–1877* (Tallahassee: Florida State University Press, 1965); Shofner, *Nor Is It Over Yet: Florida in the Era of Reconstruction, 1863–1877* (Gainesville: University Presses of Florida, 1974), 344 and passim. For a study of the state's post-Reconstruction experience that focuses on de jure segregation but sees a general tightening of de facto practices by 1880, see Wali R. Kharif, "Black Reaction to Segregation and Discrimination in Post-Reconstruction Florida," *Florida Historical Quarterly* 64 (October 1985): 161–73.

14. "A Strange Chapter in the Career of 'Jim Crow,'" in *The Black Community in Modern America,* 14–19, vol. 2 of *The Making of Black America: Essays in Negro Life and History,* 2 vols, ed. Meier and Rudwick (New York: Atheneum, 1969). See also Meier and Rudwick, "The Boycott Movement against Jim Crow Streetcars in the South, 1900–1906," *Journal of American History* 60 (March 1969): 756–75.

15. Peter Kolchin, *First Freedom: The Responses of Alabama's Blacks to Emancipation*

endorse Woodward's position, and in the 1966 and 1974 revisions of *Strange Career,* while modifying some of his earlier remarks, Woodward gently but authoritatively dismissed the criticisms by Litwack, Williamson, and Wade.[16]

In large measure the state of the debate over the extent and role of segregation during Reconstruction reflected the fact that Woodward had been allowed to dictate the ground rules, which both disciples and critics seemed to accept. The most basic agreement involved the relative importance of law and custom. Although Woodward had briefly acknowledged the relevance of custom, his argument centered on the absence of laws requiring segregation prior to the 1890s. Supporters agreed with this emphasis; detractors, although admitting the later appearance of laws, argued that de facto segregation was present much earlier and was firmly in place even during Reconstruction.

Woodward also was permitted to decide which laws would count. After all, during Reconstruction several states had antimiscegenation statutes, and most had laws permitting or requiring separate schools, cemeteries, militia units, and welfare services. Moreover, de jure segregation did not depend only on the passage of laws explicitly requiring segregation. As Charles A. Lofgren argued in *The Plessy Case,* prior to the 1890s courts commonly held that existing legislation permitted racially separate public accommodations, provided they were equal.[17]

Woodward governed the terms of the debate in yet another way in that only certain areas of southern life were included in the argument over segregation. Although Woodward at times had cast a wide net, the Woodward thesis covered much less ground than either its proponents or opponents seemed to appreciate. Whole areas of southern life were written out of the debate. For example, Woodward granted the early and rigid appearance during Reconstruction of segregation in militia service, public education, religion, and a broad range of social welfare provisions. One might also add fraternal organizations, clubs, and other voluntary associations. What was at issue, therefore, was the relative degree of segregation in public accommodations, especially public conveyances. Even such a staunch defender of the thesis as Charles Wynes admitted its weakness when it came to places like restaurants, hotels, and theaters.[18]

---

and Reconstruction (Westport, Conn.: Greenwood Press, 1972); Lawrence D. Rice, *The Negro in Texas, 1874–1900* (Baton Rouge: Louisiana State University Press, 1971). For a later study that takes a similar approach, but seems to emphasize the greater importance of segregation and continuity, see James M. Smallwood, *Time of Hope, Time of Despair: Black Texans during Reconstruction* (Port Washington, N.Y.: Kennikat Press, 1981), especially 122, 127.

16. *Strange Career,* 12–29.

17. Ibid.; Lofgren, *The Plessy Case: A Legal-Historical Interpretation* (New York: Oxford University Press, 1987), especially 9, 147, and chapter 6.

18. See Woodward, *Strange Career,* 24–25; Wynes, *Race Relations in Virginia,* 149–50.

The debate was narrowed further owing to the organization of the books that appeared. Typically, there would be one chapter called "The Color Line" or "Race Relations" that focused on segregation in public accommodations. Other chapters might consider education, justice, and religion. Segregation in those areas would be mentioned, certainly, but basically would be taken for granted and not included in the broader debate. In this process, the extent and meaning of racial separation in southern society became distorted.

In addition, the segregation debate placed too much emphasis on the white majority. Because *Strange Career* was so much a product of the civil rights era, and because segregation was seen as a "bad thing," Woodward concentrated on white attitudes and behavior. Segregation was something done to blacks by hostile and vindictive southern whites. Most scholars embraced this view, even when their own evidence suggested a more complex reality. Neither white Republicans nor blacks were seen as playing critical roles in the emergence of Jim Crow, except perhaps as its tragically overmatched opponents.

Most limiting of all, however, was the confinement of the debate to the alternatives of integration or segregation, with the concomitant unthinking linkage of the various forms of oppression that increasingly plagued blacks by the turn of the century. In the first instance, scholarship sometimes degenerated into a "Can you top this?" contest between examples of segregation and integration, with competing assertions about whether the glass of discrimination was half full or half empty. Each side acknowledged the existence of both alternatives prior to the 1890s but differed as to their relative importance, a judgment often dependent on one's political orientation. The advantage, of course, was with the proponents of the Woodward thesis. No one could deny that integration was at least occasionally a fact of life for some southern blacks under some circumstances. And for those who linked Jim Crow laws with disfranchisement and the increase in lynching, there was no question about there being a decline in status for blacks during the 1890s.

In any case, by the mid-1970s there was growing interest in going beyond the initial terms of the segregation debate. This change resulted partly from an overdue awareness that blacks were not simply objects of history but subjects as well. Inspired both by the role of blacks in current events and by changes in scholarly inquiry, scholars began to carve out a place for blacks as actors, rather than passive victims, in accounting for the development of segregation. James McPherson, for example, in "White Liberals and Black Power in Negro Education," noted that by the end of Reconstruction, blacks had accepted segregated

---

For a fuller discussion of the limits of the Woodward thesis, see my essay "More than the Woodward Thesis: Assessing *The Strange Career of Jim Crow*," reprinted above.

higher education but were pressing for their own black instructors to replace whites. In "Half a Loaf: The Shift from White to Black Teachers in the Negro Schools of the Urban South," I pointed to a similar and even more pronounced pattern below the college level. Sociologists such as E. Franklin Frazier earlier had noted the vested interest that some blacks had in segregated institutions, and historians now began, especially in light of the black power and black nationalist movements, to question the commitment of blacks to integration.[19]

While examining the nature of race relations in five southern cities, I noticed that blacks and their white Republican allies often accepted or actually requested segregated facilities. In a series of articles and in *Race Relations in the Urban South,* I argued that they did so either because provisions were expected to be equal or because even inferior provisions often represented an advance over a previous policy of exclusion. Not only was this frequently the case with theaters, public conveyances, hotels, and other staples of the segregation controversy, but also—and even more significantly—in such previously neglected areas as public education, welfare policy, and militia service. Viewed in this light, segregation might actually have worked as an advance for blacks—especially when couched in terms of equal treatment—because it replaced exclusion. As such, it could be presented and endorsed by both black leaders and their white allies without completely alienating the mass of hostile southern whites. Segregation therefore could be seen as an achievement of Reconstruction rather than as an example of Redeemer or post-Redeemer oppression. Thus, although providing ample evidence of the extent of de facto and even de jure segregation well before the 1890s across a wide spectrum of southern life, I sought to redirect attention not only to new alternatives, but also to the question of *why* segregation emerged, and not simply how much there was or when it appeared.[20]

The concept of a shift from exclusion to segregation has been received favorably by southern historians, including proponents and opponents of the Woodward thesis.[21] However, in an effort to go beyond the narrow terms of the initial debate,

19. McPherson, "White Liberals and Black Power in Negro Education, 1865–1915," *American Historical Review* 75 (June 1970): 1357–86; Rabinowitz, "Half a Loaf: The Shift from White to Black Teachers in the Negro Schools of the Urban South, 1865–1890," reprinted below; Frazier, *Black Bourgeoisie: The Rise of a New Middle Class in the United States* (New York: Free Press, 1957).

20. *Race Relations in the Urban South, 1865–1890* (New York: Oxford University Press, 1978). See also my essays "From Exclusion to Segregation: Health and Welfare Services for Southern Blacks, 1865–1890," "More than the Woodward Thesis," and "Half a Loaf," all reprinted in this volume.

21. See especially the following reviews of my *Race Relations in the Urban South:* Joel Williamson in *American Historical Review* 84 (June 1979): 857–58; George B. Tindall in *Civil War History* 25 (June 1979): 179–81; and even the more critical one by Charles E.

some historians have turned to comparative history. Again, it was Woodward who led the way, this time in his 1971 essay about the debate over his thesis. After a thorough review, he concluded that on the whole, the existing literature had supported his essential interpretation concerning the relatively late appearance of a rigid system of segregation and proscription. He then sought to transcend the old debate in an effort to explain the post-1890 transformation in southern race relations. Rejecting evolutionary, cyclical, and industrialization models, he embraced Pierre L. van den Berghe's race-relations typology, which posited "paternalistic" and "competitive" models based on a comparison of the racial histories of Mexico, Brazil, the United States, and South Africa. To define status, paternalistic systems relied on social distance; competitive systems sought physical distance. Still taking for granted widespread integration during Reconstruction and a transitional post-Reconstruction period, Woodward ascribed the shift during the 1890s to a regionwide change from paternalism to competitiveness.[22] Given disagreements over the actual extent of segregation prior to the 1890s, this analysis was interesting but nonetheless unsatisfying. It has received little support. It did, however, help to direct attention to the comparative dimensions of Jim Crow.

South Africa proved to be an especially productive laboratory for racial comparisons. In *White Supremacy,* George M. Fredrickson emphasized the differences in the origins and institutionalization of segregation in the two countries "in terms both of underlying structures and patterns of historical development." Fredrickson sought to stake out a middle position on the pervasiveness of segregation in the South during Reconstruction, but he fully sided with Woodward on the importance of legal actions during the 1890s, especially with regard to disfranchisement. John Cell, however, in *The Highest Stage of White Supremacy,* found greater similarity between the two countries. Like Fredrickson, Cell employed the exclusion-to-segregation framework and granted the significance of post-1890 developments, but he was more impressed by the extent of de facto segregation during Reconstruction. What was important, he argued, was not a shift

---

Wynes in *Florida Historical Quarterly* 57 (October 1978): 236–38. For C. Vann Woodward's positive reaction—with certain reservations concerning public conveyances—see his forward to the paperback edition of *Race Relations in the Urban South* (Urbana: University of Illinois Press, 1980); his review in the *Journal of Southern History* 44 (August 1978): 476–78; and his *Thinking Back,* 96–97. Although the exclusion-to-segregation framework has not been tested systematically for additional southern cities or states, surprising corroboration of it came in Lawrence O. Christensen, "Race Relations in St. Louis, 1865–1916," *Missouri Historical Review* 78 (January 1984): 123–36. Less surprisingly, examination of another community outside the South produced mixed results in Joanne Wheeler, "Together in Egypt: A Pattern of Race Relations in Cairo, Illinois, 1865–1915," in *Toward a New South? Studies in Post–Civil War Southern Communities,* ed. Orville Vernon Burton and Robert C. McMath, Jr. (Westport, Conn.: Greenwood Press, 1982), 103–35.

22. "Strange Career of a Historical Controversy," 234–60.

in behavior, but changes in rhetoric and the law—changes that served to institutionalize existing social arrangements. And unlike Fredrickson, Cell found South African moderates, who favored intermediate steps, to be similar to the South's advocates of segregation over exclusion, or separate but equal treatment.[23]

The basic points remained at issue. Comparative history revealed a good deal about the formal institutionalization of racial segregation but was less useful in illuminating the impact and extent of the less formal de facto practices of the Reconstruction years. At this point, a leader in the original debate, Joel Williamson, announced that it was time "to move to one side, and begin again." Now less concerned than previously about the amount of segregation during Reconstruction, Williamson pointed to the "Great Changeover" after 1889, with the rise of white extremists advocating lynching, disfranchisement, and legalized segregation, as much for psychological as political or economic reasons. Nevertheless, in *The Crucible of Race,* Williamson argued that whether through law or custom, "during Reconstruction and for some years thereafter, the essential pattern of life of the great mass of black people precluded any significant mixing of the races."[24] This assessment was, of course, the same as the one he had made for South Carolina twenty years earlier. What had changed was his appreciation of the importance of the post-1890 developments.

Published almost thirty years after *Strange Career,* Williamson's *Crucible of Race* provides an excellent opportunity for taking stock. What remains most constant is the need to review Reconstruction within a broader context. Yet surprisingly little of the segregation controversy has focused on the Reconstruction era itself. Far more is known about the pattern of racial relations before and after Reconstruction, especially if the period is defined narrowly as that of Radical Reconstruction, or even as the years between 1865 (or 1862) and 1877. More emphasis has been placed on conditions after Reconstruction than during it. The questions are what we now know and where we go from here.

The key point is that unlike 1961 when *Reconstruction after the Civil War* appeared, today the degree of segregation in southern society has become a major subject for historical inquiry. Rare indeed is an index without the topic's

23. Fredrickson, *White Supremacy: A Comparative Study in American and South African History* (New York: Oxford University Press, 1981), 250 and passim; Cell, *The Highest Stage of White Supremacy: The Origins of Segregation in South Africa and the American South* (New York: Cambridge University Press, 1982), chapters 4–7 and passim. For an earlier appeal for a compromise between the Woodward and anti-Woodward positions based solely on the American context, see Fredrickson, *The Black Image in the White Mind: The Debate on Afro-American Character and Destiny, 1817–1914* (New York: Harper and Row, 1971), especially 202.

24. *The Crucible of Race: Black-White Relations in the American South since Emancipation* (New York: Oxford University Press, 1984), viii, 252, and passim.

presence. For this, of course, we can thank *Strange Career* and the civil rights movement. Yet segregation has become such an accepted subject that scholars are beginning to take it for granted as trendier topics, such as the transformation of the white yeomanry or other class-related matters, take center stage. This is unfortunate, for there is still much to do in the study of segregation, although the Woodward thesis itself is no longer the issue: scholars are now in a position to ask what actually happened rather than which historian was right.

To begin with, a consensus of sorts (although often unacknowledged) has been reached as to the facts about segregation.[25] It is clear that during Reconstruction segregation was a widespread factor in southern life; as even two of Woodward's defenders recently put it, segregation was the "dominant tendency" of the period.[26] Much of this segregation, moreover, was the result of voluntary action on the part of blacks, as found in churches and an impressive array of associations. Other instances, as in public schools, welfare institutions, cemeteries, and militia units often were agreed upon mutually by whites and blacks, although such separation frequently was enforced by law. Still other examples of separation, as in public conveyances, restaurants, hotels, theaters, and the like, were the result of de facto arrangements that had a greater degree of flexibility in some cases—although by no means in very many, especially given the tendency of courts to uphold separate, ostensibly equal arrangements. Whatever its source, segregation often constituted an improvement over a previous policy of excluding blacks from the area in question. Within this environment, the several state civil rights acts and the 1875 federal Civil Rights Act (already stripped of proposed coverage of schools and cemeteries) were, as John Hope Franklin notes in *Reconstruction* and elsewhere, essentially dead letters; at best, they served to assure blacks separate but equal access to facilities.[27]

Furthermore, there is general agreement that something very important happened at the end of the 1880s. Although de jure segregation was more of a factor

25. See especially, in a series edited by John Hope Franklin, a survey of the Reconstruction period by a student of his, Michael Perman, *Emancipation and Reconstruction, 1862–1879* (Arlington Heights, Ill.: Harlan Davidson, Inc., 1987), 81–82, and a penetrating survey of the literature in the field in LaWanda Cox, "From Emancipation to Segregation: National Policy and Southern Blacks," in *Interpreting Southern History: Historiographical Essays in Honor of Sanford W. Higginbotham*, ed. John B. Boles and Evelyn Thomas Nolen (Baton Rouge: Louisiana State University Press, 1987), 250–52. See also Eric Foner, *Reconstruction: America's Unfinished Revolution, 1863–1877* (New York: Harper and Row, 1988), which appeared too late to be included in the body of this essay.

26. J. Morgan Kousser and James M. McPherson, eds., *Region, Race, and Reconstruction: Essays in Honor of C. Vann Woodward* (New York: Oxford University Press, 1982), xxvi.

27. See Franklin, *Reconstruction after the Civil War*, 141, 201–2, 223, and "The Enforcement of the Civil Rights Act of 1875," *Prologue* 6 (Winter 1974): 225–35. See also Lofgren, *Plessy Case*, 132–37, and Rabinowitz, *Race Relations in the Urban South*, 186–89, 195–96.

before the 1890s than Woodward and others have recognized, there is no denying its significant increase at the end of the century. The segregation laws were
important, however, for different reasons from those Woodward argued. The
laws did not represent a shift in the actual degree of segregation between the
races, but rather, as Cell and Williamson argued, a shift in rhetoric and white
attitudes. The essential question should not be why the South went from a fluid
to a rigid system of race relations in the 1890s, but why it became necessary to
legalize customary practices.

Historians must consider the possibility, which I have suggested elsewhere,
that the altered attitudes and especially the behavior of some blacks themselves
might have helped force such changes.[28] Woodward, of course, has argued that
the transformation in the 1890s was caused entirely by the actions of whites—for
example, by the withdrawal of northern support for blacks, the disillusionment
of white insurgents after the failure of the Populist movement, and a capitulation
to racism by Conservatives. Other scholars have followed Woodward's lead in
focusing on whites but have identified different groups and factors. Cell, for
example, pointed to the economic developments of the 1890s and the role of the
white upper classes (although, ironically, he did this in a chapter noting the
important role black actions played in the white push for apartheid in South
Africa). Williamson considered the key to be the extreme white racialists he called
"Radicals," who used a threatening economic and political environment to fulfill
their psychological need to subdue the black population. With less documentation, David Donald has taken a generational approach: having arrived at "middle
adulthood," Civil War veterans in their fifties allegedly sought to safeguard their
legacy of white supremacy through legalized segregation and disfranchisement.
Clearly, the last word has not been written about white Democratic motives for
supporting segregation in either its de facto or de jure forms.[29]

28. Rabinowitz, *Race Relations in the Urban South,* epilogue and passim. See also my
essay "From Exclusion to Segregation: Southern Race Relations, 1865–1890" reprinted
below. For a relatively strong endorsement of this view, see Lofgren, *Plessy Case,* 25–26;
for a more tentative one, see Cox, "From Emancipation to Segregation," 251–52. On the
role of white fears of the "new Negro," for a brief mention that does not give enough
credence to the justification for such fears, see Linda M. Matthews, "Keeping Down Jim
Crow: The Railroads and the Separate Coach Bills in South Carolina," *South Atlantic
Quarterly* 73 (Winter 1974): 117–29.

29. Woodward, *Strange Career* (1974), 51–64; Cell, *Highest Stage of White Sumpremacy,*
chapters 6 and 8; Williamson, *Crucible of Race,* chapter 4 and passim; Donald, "A
Generation of Defeat," in *From the Old South to the New: Essays on the Transitional
South,* ed. Walter J. Fraser, Jr., and Winfred B. Moore, Jr. (Westport, Conn.: Greenwood
Press, 1981), 3–20. See also Fredrickson, *Black Image in the White Mind,* 203, 266–67, for
an earlier version of Cell's argument, which stresses upper-class manipulation of the
concept of "*Herrenvolk* democracy." For the limitations of Williamson's psychological

Whatever the motivating factors, any discussion of segregation during Reconstruction and its aftermath must assess not only the relative importance of de facto and de jure segregation, but also the mixture of voluntary and involuntary segregation. De jure segregation was unquestionably the work of whites, but too often historians have assumed implicitly that de facto segregation also must have been entirely the responsibility of whites. In fact, much of the segregation during and after Reconstruction was initiated or supported by blacks. Most obvious—and often quite troubling to whites—was the black withdrawal from white churches, a movement that began even before Reconstruction. Together with new churches, blacks often established their own schools, welfare institutions, political organizations, and benevolent and fraternal societies, all within increasingly segregated black neighborhoods.[30] Sometimes this self-segregation was in response to white neglect or hostility, but often it was simply a statement of black communal identity. Any discussion of segregation, therefore, must go beyond the narrow limits of white-enforced segregation in public accommodations if it is to illuminate the reality of the cultural urges that southern blacks shared with other American ethnic groups.

Scholars also need to keep in mind the distinction between segregation and other forms of discrimination. A major source for the initial appeal of the Woodward thesis was its linkage of segregation, disfranchisement, and proscription as phenomena of the 1890s. There was, after all, no disputing the increase in lynching and the almost complete denial of the vote to southern blacks after 1890. Joel Williamson and John Cell, among others, also linked these different forms of discrimination even though disagreeing with Woodward over the reasons for, or the degree of, the transformation in race relations.[31] It must be remembered, however, that segregation has a history of its own and that racial separation was widespread during Reconstruction even though blacks voted in large numbers. Segregation also thrived in the supposedly transitional 1880s

approach, see my essay "Psychological Disorders, Socio-Economic Forces, and American Race Relations," *Slavery and Abolition* 7 (September 1986): 188–94. For a fuller discussion of what has been done and needs to be done to account for the post-1890 Jim Crow statutes, see my essay "More than the Woodward Thesis," reprinted above.

30. Clusters of black settlements, formed around the basic institutions of black life, were fixtures of the urban landscape in the years immediately following the war. Indeed, many of these settlements had originated in the antebellum period as areas for free Negroes and hired-out slaves. See Rabinowitz, *Race Relations in the Urban South,* chapter 5. Some historians view residential segregation as having been less pronounced. See, for example, Harold D. Woodman, "Economic Reconstruction and the Rise of the New South," in *Interpreting Southern History,* ed. Boles and Nolen, 298–99.

31. See especially Cell, *Highest Stage of White Supremacy,* 14. For a fuller discussion of Cell's approach, see Rabinowitz, "The Not So Strange Career of Jim Crow," *Reviews in American History* 12 (March 1984): 58–64.

and, for that matter, in much of the twentieth-century North. What was important about the 1890s for southern segregation was not the newness of Jim Crow laws and customs, but the relentless confirmation of them.

Finally, in approaching the issue of segregation during Reconstruction scholars need to do more than examine the attitudes, motivations, and behavior of blacks and southern white Democrats. A great deal remains to be learned about the white Republicans who were, it needs to be emphasized, the critical policy-makers and implementers on the local, state, and national levels during Reconstruction. In *Reconstruction after the Civil War,* Franklin noted the division of opinion on racial matters within this group. As he put it, "Many of the native whites who held office were as opposed to the equality of Negroes as were many of the disfranchised former Confederates." He added, "It was the native whites who insisted on segregated schools and laws against intermarriage."[32] In the years since 1961 most historians have rejected the traditional depiction of congressional Radicals, "carpetbaggers," and "scalawags" as all being unremitting miscegenationists and undifferentiated advocates of "social equality." A substitute view of these men is only beginning to emerge, however, and so far it has focused mainly on a handful of leaders or the most radical faction.[33]

Reflecting the frustrations of the 1960s, historians such as Forest Wood and Lawrence J. Friedman found little difference between Republicans and Democrats with respect to racial discrimination. In Wood's opinion, "One of the most obvious facts about race relations in the 1860s and 1870s was that the vast majority of Americans, white and black, took racial separation for granted." Friedman, arguing that "segregation and integration are not vital issues," saw no need to distinguish among whites as he focused on their drive for Negro "servility."[34] Those who have singled out white Republicans for special treatment usually have been more concerned with other issues and seemingly have taken acceptance of segregation for granted. One partial exception is Ted Tunnell, whose *Crucible of Reconstruction* provides a thoughtful analysis of the range of racial ideas among Louisiana's Unionists, emphasizing their desire to avoid offending potential white

32. *Reconstruction,* 196.
33. See, for example, Kenneth M. Stampp, *The Era of Reconstruction, 1865–1877* (New York: Alfred A. Knopf, 1965), 101–5.
34. Wood, *Black Scare: The Racist Response to Emancipation and Reconstruction* (Berkeley and Los Angeles: University of California Press, 1970), 134; Friedman, *The White Savage: Racial Fantasies in the Postbellum South* (Englewood Cliffs, N.J.: Prentice Hall, 1970), vii and passim. See also Forrest G. Wood, *The Era of Reconstruction, 1863–1877* (New York: AHM Press, 1975). For a criticism of this new tendency to blur distinctions among whites and denigrate the contributions of reconstructionists, see Herman Belz, "The New Orthodoxy in Reconstruction Historiography," *Reviews in American History* 1 (March 1973): 106–13.

voters and their lack of commitment to racial equality.[35] More typical is Sarah Woolfolk Wiggins's study *The Scalawag in Alabama Politics,* which showed that this much-maligned group of white southerners was better off, more honorable, and more respected than the stereotype allowed, but which noted their belief in white supremacy only in passing and without providing a detailed explanation.[36] Still others, such as Michael Les Benedict in *A Compromise of Principle* and Herman Belz in *Emancipation and Equal Rights,* concentrated on suffrage and broader civil rights issues and on the Republicans' constitutionally inspired conservatism (or moderation), which limited the degree to which they would use the federal government to support black rights.[37]

What clearly is needed is a study of white Republicans that examines their attitudes not only toward civil and political rights in general, but also toward the relative desirability in social relations of exclusion, segregation, and—the period's least favored option—integration.[38] Further examination of white Republicans and segregation will help to place in focus the meaning of Reconstruction in general and the ways in which racial policy compared with preceding and subsequent periods. I would argue that Reconstruction was primarily about securing black suffrage and civil rights such as the right to contract, to perform jury service, and the like. With respect to social rights, there was no integrationist thrust, either as a goal or as a reality. The basic aim, as in the rest of Reconstruction policy—indeed, as in American reformist ideology throughout the nation's history—was equal access or opportunity, not equality of condition.

A growing body of work, for example, suggests an essential continuity between the Civil Rights Act of 1875 and the *Plessy v. Ferguson* Supreme Court decision in 1896, legal entities once seen as antithetical. As early as 1967, in

35. *Crucible of Reconstruction: War, Radicalism, and Race in Louisiana, 1862–1877* (Baton Rouge: Louisiana State University Press, 1984), especially 53–65, 117–20, 123–28, 167–69. Tunnell divides the Unionists into conservatives, radicals, and reactionaries but argues that even most radicals did not always favor integration. As a result, Tunnell concludes, even after passage of the state's 1869 civil rights law "segregation in Louisiana remained virtually unchanged."

36. *The Scalawag in Alabama Politics, 1865–1881* (University: University of Alabama Press, 1977). For a study concerned primarily with the economic attitudes and behavior of one type of carpetbagger and arguing that these northern Republicans accepted a generalized racism comparable to that of white southerners despite an avowed dedication to an ideology of free labor, see Lawrence N. Powell, *New Masters: Northern Planters during the Civil War and Reconstruction* (New Haven: Yale University Press, 1980), especially 31, 121, 142–43.

37. Benedict, *A Compromise of Principle: Congressional Republicans and Reconstruction, 1863–1869* (New York: W. W. Norton and Company, 1974); Belz, *Emancipation and Equal Rights: Politics and Constitutionalism in the Civil War Era* (New York: W. W. Norton and Company, 1978).

38. For a modest beginning, see Rabinowitz, *Race Relations in the Urban South,* especially 185–86.

"Racial Segregation in Public Accommodations," Alfred Avins argued that with the exception of a few Radicals, congressional Republicans sought to end unequal treatment of blacks rather than segregation per se, an assessment that I subsequently endorsed and expanded upon. More recently, Charles Lofgren's *Plessy Case* and Stephen J. Riegel's "Persistent Career of Jim Crow" have argued that as designed by the framers of the era's civil rights legislation and as interpreted by the courts, *equality* of accommodation did not necessarily mean *identity* of accommodation, and that *distinction* was not the same as *discrimination*.[39]

Thus, segregation can be seen as an improvement over exclusion or absence of equal access. White southerners reluctantly accepted this shift and continued it into the post-Reconstruction years. The real issue was not segregation as such, but equal treatment within a segregated society. There were times during Reconstruction when this goal was achieved, especially with regard to school appropriations, but by the 1890s such treatment was clearly unequal. When joined to disfranchisement, to the failure of courts to demand truly equal separate accommodations, to increased violence and inflammatory racial rhetoric, and to the expansion of laws into spheres not previously covered, segregation became part of a significant shift in the nature of southern racial relations. Simple physical separation of the races, never *complete* in the South even after 1900, had been the norm at least since Reconstruction, particularly outside the limited sphere of train and streetcar travel.[40] Ironically, in a South committed to Negro inferiority and submission, the idea (and occasionally the reality) of separate but equal treatment was actually one of the few achievements of Reconstruction.

39. Avins, "Racial Segregation in Public Accommodations: Some Reflected Light on the Fourteenth Amendment from the Civil Rights Act of 1875," *Western Reserve Law Review* 18 (May 1967): 125–83; Rabinowitz, *Race Relations in the Urban South;* Lofgren, *Plessy Case,* 70–76, 132–37, and passim; Riegel, "The Persistent Career of Jim Crow: Lower Federal Courts and the 'Separate but Equal Doctrine,' 1865–1896," *American Journal of Legal History* 28 (January 1984): 17–40. See also Jonathan Lurie, "The Fourteenth Amendment: Use and Application in Selected State Court Civil Liberties Cases, 1870–1890—A Preliminary Assessment," *American Journal of Legal History* 28 (October 1984): 295–313. For an interpretation of the Civil Rights Act of 1875 that stresses the act's equalitarian intent despite its minimal impact, see James M. McPherson, "Abolitionists and the Civil Rights Act of 1875," *Journal of American History* 52 (December 1965): 493–510.

40. For a discussion of the incompleteness of the shift after 1890, see my essay "More than the Woodward Thesis," reprinted above. By accepting Woodward's depiction of a rigidly discriminatory twentieth-century South, his critics provided still another example of how they allowed him to determine the terms of the debate over segregation.

Part Two

From
Exclusion
to
Segregation

From Exclusion to Segregation

Health and Welfare Services for Southern Blacks, 1865–1890

Before the Civil War, public officials in the South had been spared the burden of supporting ill and indigent blacks. Slave welfare had been the responsibility of the master, while free Negroes had been left to fend for themselves. The growing number of antebellum local institutions such as orphanages, hospitals, and alms-houses, or state facilities such as insane asylums and institutions for the blind, deaf, and dumb, were limited, with few exceptions, to whites.

The major questions after the war were, Who would assume the responsibility for the freedmen's welfare and on what basis? In other words, Would the antebellum policy of exclusion be retained and, if not, what would replace it? Conflict arose between those who favored public responsibility and those who denied the necessity of such action. At various times from 1865 to 1890 the burden was shouldered by missionary societies, the Freedmen's Bureau, the United States Army, southern whites, and, of course, the Negroes themselves. What finally emerged was a shift from a policy of exclusion to one of segregation. Integrated access to services was rarely considered and even less often permitted. By 1890 the announced goal of southern welfare policy was the acceptance of blacks in institutions on the basis of separate but equal treatment.

This shift from the policy of exclusion has not been systematically studied, since historians of postbellum race relations have concentrated on public accommodations and have framed their arguments in terms of integration versus

I wish to thank John Hope Franklin and Arthur Mann for reading an earlier version of this essay, and the University of Chicago Center for Urban Studies for financial assistance.

segregation. Following the lead of C. Vann Woodward, some scholars have argued that a rigid pattern of segregation did not emerge in the South until the last decade of the nineteenth century and the first decade of the twentieth century; others, led by Joel Williamson, counter that segregation, in practice if not in law, had become firmly established by the end of Reconstruction.[1] The little attention given to welfare services is usually not incorporated into the broader discussion. When they mention the subject, the defenders of the "Woodward thesis" see the area of social services as being among the last to be segregated; their critics see segregated facilities as already present by the mid-1870s. But neither group makes an effort to trace the development of segregation through the three main phases of the postwar era. The first, Presidential Reconstruction, lasted from April 1865 to March 1867, while the Conservatives, most of them former Confederates, controlled local and state government in the South under the benevolent policies of President Andrew Johnson. The second, beginning in March 1867, saw Congress seize control of Reconstruction policy and force the southern states to enfranchise blacks, write new constitutions, and accept governments run by white and black Republicans, or Radicals, as they were known by their enemies. The length of so-called Radical Reconstruction varied from city to city and state to state, but by the mid-1870s the Radicals had generally been driven from power. They were replaced by southern white Democrats, known as Redeemers because they redeemed the South from Radical rule. This third and final phase of the Reconstruction period is therefore referred to as Redemption.

Had historians sought to trace the changes in welfare policy through these three periods, they would have found that the shift from exclusion to segregation was due to three groups: northern Radicals and their southern white allies who initiated it; southern Negroes who supported and at times demanded it; and the Redeemers, the individuals usually considered responsible for segregation, who simply continued and expanded the policy inherited when they took power.

1. Woodward, *The Strange Career of Jim Crow,* 2d rev. ed. (New York: Oxford University Press, 1966); Williamson, *After Slavery: The Negro in South Carolina during Reconstruction, 1861–1877* (Chapel Hill: University of North Carolina Press, 1965). For support of Woodward, see Charles E. Wynes, *Race Relations in Virginia, 1870–1902* (Charlottesville: University Press of Virginia, 1961) and Frenise A. Logan, *The Negro in North Carolina, 1876–1894* (Chapel Hill: University of North Carolina Press, 1964); evidence supporting Williamson can be found in Vernon Lane Wharton, *The Negro in Mississippi, 1865–1890* (Chapel Hill: University of North Carolina Press, 1947) and Roger A. Fischer, "The Post–Civil War Segregation Struggle," in *The Past as Prelude: New Orleans, 1718–1968,* ed. Hodding Carter et al. (New Orleans: Pelican Publishing House, 1968). For a convenient guide to the controversy, see Joel Williamson, ed., *The Origins of Segregation* (Lexington, Mass.: D. C. Heath and Co., 1968).

Public affirmations aside, however, the system rarely functioned on a basis other than separate but unequal treatment.[2]

The Response of Local and State Governments during Presidential Reconstruction, 1865–67

One of the most significant results of emancipation was the migration of large numbers of rural blacks to southern cities. The new urban dwellers left more than their homes and masters when they fled the countryside; they also left their jobs. The high visibility of blacks congregating on street corners or disturbing the peace with loud language and fights emphasized their idleness and confronted whites with the reality of emancipation. At the same time it caused whites to ponder how things might have been if there had been no change. "Hundreds and thousands of lazy negroes who droned off the summer and fall months are now so many pestiferous paupers upon the city," wrote the *Nashville Union and Dispatch* in 1868. It continued: "Some three hundred persons daily eat at the [public] souphouse, and full two hundred of these are negroes of every size, age, color and sex. What a rebuke is this to those who deprived these poor creatures of good homes, and good masters and mistresses, who fed and clothed them, and did it well." The beleaguered cities, short of funds sufficient to perform even their normal services and in any case determined to perpetuate antebellum welfare policy, sought to evade the responsibility of providing food and shelter to this group of blacks. A Montgomery newspaper during the summer of 1865 urged citizens to aid the suffering poor in their midst, but emphasized, "Our remarks are in behalf of the destitute *white* population; the Freedmen's Bureau will doubtless look after the destitute freedmen." Within two years a county poorhouse had been built solely for the use of white paupers.[3]

The bureau, with the aid of the army and northern benevolent societies, at first did care for these Negroes and, by so doing, ironically paved the way for the adoption of segregated facilities by municipal administrations. During the very

2. The discussion that follows is based on a study of five southern states—North Carolina, Georgia, Virginia, Alabama, and Tennessee—and their capitals—Raleigh, Atlanta, Richmond, Montgomery, and Nashville. Together they provide a cross section of the South in terms of geography, length of Radical Reconstruction, and attitudes toward and provisions made for the care of blacks. A perusal of secondary and primary sources concerning other cities and states suggests that the findings for the sample apply to the entire region.

3. *Nashville Union and Dispatch,* January 17, 1868; *Montgomery Daily Ledger,* August 15, 1865 (italics in original); *Montgomery Weekly Advertiser,* April 9, 1867.

cold Richmond winter of 1866–1867, the American Missionary Association daily processed an average of one hundred applicants for relief. These individuals were given sticks of wood and a small amount of meal immediately. If they required further assistance, they were referred to the bureau. Beginning in 1868, the same procedure was used by the bureau in the soup kitchens it had established in the Alabama towns of Montgomery, Mobile, Huntsville, and Selma. The bureau and the societies also cooperated in the founding of orphanages for blacks in Richmond, Atlanta, and Nashville; and in all the cities, the combined northern forces temporarily assumed the role of dispenser of clothing to needy blacks.[4]

It proved difficult to transfer the responsibility for poor Negroes from federal to local officials. This shift, for the most part, is obscured from the historian; but in Richmond the interplay between the two loci of power can be clearly traced in the city council minutes. In November 1865 the council received a letter from the assistant commissioner of the Freedmen's Bureau in Virginia directing it to make provisions for 260 Richmond black paupers then being cared for by the bureau. A month later whites were forbidden from turning out their infirm former slaves until local authorities made arrangements for their support. Yet as of May 1866, the Richmond City Council had not moved in this direction. It instead notified the bureau that supervision of the freedmen would be undertaken only after a corresponding transfer of authority in judicial matters. Besides, added the council, "the colored population [had] . . . been increased by a vast influx from the surrounding country" and the city was "having trouble providing for the white poor." In August 1867, General John Schofield, the state military commander, ordered the overseers of the poor and the superintendents of the almshouse "to receive and provide for all indigent colored people now in the charge of the Freedmen's Bureau." This time the council objected on the ground that it was being forced to assume responsibility for nonresidents, and in any case, the strain on the treasury meant that only inadequate facilities were available. After further foot-dragging, money for the task was appropriated in the fall. In January 1868 the first blacks finally entered the almshouse.[5]

4. Letter of the Reverend W. D. Harris, February 1, 1867, *American Missionary* 11 (March 1867): 50–51; Montgomery City Council Minutes, February 24, 1868, Alabama Department of Archives and History, Montgomery; *Richmond Dispatch,* October 23, 1866; *American Missionary* 11 (February 1867): 29; J. W. Alvord, *First Semi-annual Report on Schools and Finances of Freedmen* (Washington, D.C.: Government Printing Office, 1866), 7; for examples of northern forces dispensing clothing to blacks, see letter of L. E. Williams, April 14, 1866, *National Freedman* 2 (May 1866): 146–47; letter of W. T. Richardson, Superintendent of Schools for the Cleveland Aid Commission, July 1, 1867, *American Missionary* 11 (September 1867): 206.

5. Letter of Colonel O. Brown to the Overseer of the Poor, November 20, 1865, Richmond City Council Minutes, November 27, 1865, Archives Division of the Virginia State

Such negotiations were repeated elsewhere. The bureau had to prod Nashville officials by giving one thousand dollars for the care of the sick in return for a guarantee that Negroes would be admitted into the poorhouse. But while local authorities were being cajoled or forced into accepting blacks in their alms-houses, segregation had become a reality. Nor was this situation altered once municipalities assumed jurisdiction. As the first Negro paupers entered the old Nashville poorhouse in August 1866, the white paupers moved into new quarters. A similar situation occurred in Richmond two years later.[6]

In addition to permitting blacks in the almshouses, municipal administrations slowly came to provide other assistance. Out-relief in the form of fuel or food became available once the cities were forced to abandon reliance on the Freedmen's Bureau. An 1866 Atlanta ordinance established a sliding scale of fees to be given the marshal or deputy marshal for distributing rations to whites, blacks, and black insane. During the same year the North Carolina legislature gave local justices of the peace the power to elect "two distinct and independent courts of wardens" for the poor, one for blacks and one for whites.[7]

The cities could not afford to neglect a second responsibility—the burial of black paupers. Since antebellum times three cities—Nashville, Raleigh, and Richmond—had by ordinance enforced racial segregation in their municipal cemeteries. Montgomery and Atlanta evidently had de facto rather than de jure segregation. With the end of the war, these practices continued, and much of the cities' aid to the Negroes consisted of burying their paupers. In Montgomery, for example, from December 1866 to April 1877, all but 6 of the 136 paupers interred in Potter's Field were black. In Atlanta five randomly chosen months of the years 1868–1872 disclose 21 white pauper burials as compared to 129 for blacks.[8]

Library, Richmond (cited hereafter as VSL; after 1866 the minutes are located in the Office of the City Clerk, Richmond City Hall); *Richmond Dispatch,* January 1, 1866; Richmond City Council Minutes, May 14, 1866; August 17, 1867; March 31, 1868. In July 1868 the council, due to "heavy drafts upon the City Treasury," was forced to ask the bureau to help in providing for the Negro destitute (Richmond City Council Minutes, July 1, 14, 1868). Money that had been earmarked for the blacks was not being used, however, and the bureau pressured the council into spending it (Richmond City Council Minutes, November 20, December 1, 1868).

6. Alrutheus Ambush Taylor, *The Negro in Tennessee, 1865–1880* (Washington, D.C.: Associated Publishers, 1941), 35; *Nashville Daily Press and Times,* August 6, 1866; Richmond City Council Minutes, March 31, 1868.

7. Atlanta, *Revised Code,* 1866, 61. See also the modification of this law, ibid., 1868, 74; North Carolina, *Public Laws,* 1866 (Raleigh, 1866), 102–3.

8. Montgomery, *Annual Message of the Mayor and Reports of the Various City Officers and Standing Committees of the City Council for the Term Ending April 30, 1877* (Montgomery, 1877), 52; Atlanta City Council Minutes, June 5, July 3, 1868; July 9, 1869; August

It is not surprising that there were so many Negro pauper deaths. There were more indigent among the race, and their living conditions produced appallingly high mortality rates. Whites pointed to a seeming degeneration among Negroes that proved the superiority of life in the country as a slave to life in the city as a free man. According to the *Montgomery Daily Ledger,* freedom was "prejudicial" to the health of Montgomery Negroes: "When slaves, they could be up early and late, labor hard, expose themselves in all kinds of weather and seldom complain or take to their beds. Now they seem unable to perform half the labor to which they have been accustomed, the least exposure throws them." Nor could the freedmen count on the supervision and help that they allegedly received as slaves. The newspaper later pointed to the case of a Negro mother who climbed into an abandoned dump cart after giving birth to a child on the ground. After she died from lack of care, hogs came along and ate her infant. The editor charged the Freedmen's Bureau with criminal negligence and claimed that such a thing would never have occurred under slavery. A black woman found dead of starvation in the streets of Richmond led the *Richmond Dispatch* to claim, "No such cases were known while the American citizens of African descent were in a state of servitude." A few days later the newspaper observed that the winter closing of the tobacco factories would especially hurt the black worker because, in contrast to the pre–Civil War days, "he is only employed when he is wanted."[9]

Ill Negroes may or may not have been able to count on their old friends in the countryside, but they could expect little from the Conservative governments that were brought into power by Presidential Reconstruction. Despite their need for medical care, blacks continued to be largely excluded from local hospitals. The public dispensary and system of city physicians inaugurated by Richmond officials in 1867, for example, was solely for the benefit of indigent whites. The Freedmen's Bureau and the army once again countered exclusionary policies with segregated facilities. Negroes had been treated in separate quarters of army hospitals during the war, and there seemed no reason to alter the previous practice. In Nashville, despite the opposition of neighbors, the bureau converted two buildings near the penitentiary into freedmen's hospitals. During an 1865 epidemic in Montgomery, the assistant superintendent of freedmen offered to receive into the army hospital "all cases of small pox without distinction of color, or treatment." This statement did not imply racial mixing, however, for he added, "Should tents be used, a separate tent will be assigned to white patients, and every effort made for their

---

4, 1871; August 3, 1872, Office of the City Clerk, Atlanta City Hall, Atlanta. Hereafter cited as *Annual Reports* with the appropriate year.

9. *Montgomery Daily Ledger,* October 3, 12–13, 1865; see also ibid., November 10, 1865; *Richmond Dispatch,* October 4, 17, 1866.

comfort." In Atlanta during the same year, a white woman and her two sick children were refused entrance to the army hospital because it was only for blacks. No other local facility was available, so they had to be sent to Chattanooga.[10]

Physical illnesses were not the only ones that plagued the former slaves, and in Virginia the bureau also ventured into the field of mental disease. Virginia, which alone among the five states considered in this study had provided for Negroes in its antebellum insane asylums, was one of two to admit them during Presidential Reconstruction. Before the war Negroes, or "as many of them as can be accommodated after all the white insane applying for admission," were assigned rooms in the basement of the Eastern Lunatic Asylum at Williamsburg. In 1865 the Freedmen's Bureau cared for sick and insane blacks in a former Confederate army hospital near Richmond. Four years later the state's military commander made the institution a state asylum. The bureau continued to pay its expenses through the following February, when control was turned over entirely to the reorganized state government. The few Negro insane in the Williamsburg asylum were transferred to the hospital, and nonresidents were sent to the Freedmen's Hospital in Washington, D.C.[11] The use of separate institutions was later strongly defended by the Redeemer president of the hospital's board of trustees on the ground that "the disposition, temper, and habits of the colored race are so different from those of the white and the management of the two classes so dissimilar."[12]

Health and Welfare Practices of the Radicals

A similar view was evidently shared by Republicans brought to power by Congressional Reconstruction. White Radicals, elected largely by Negro voters, were conscious of the need to improve the lives of their chief supporters; but, as was true of their northern predecessors, the major concern was with an end to exclusion. Integration was rarely considered, although blacks were promised

10. Richmond City Council Minutes, February 18, March 11, 1867; *Nashville Daily Press and Times,* April 13, 1867; letter of C. M. Buckley, September 30, 1865, Montgomery City Council Minutes; Atlanta City Council Minutes, September 29, 1865.

11. Dr. William Francis Drewy, *Historical Sketch of the Central State Hospital and the Care of the Colored Insane of Virginia, 1870–1905* (Richmond: Everett Waddey, 1905), unpaged. During the 1840s Dr. Francis T. Stribling, head of the Western Lunatic Asylum, had unsuccessfully called for an asylum exclusively for the Negro insane.

12. Virginia, *Reports of the Board of Directors and Medical Superintendent of the Central Lunatic Asylum of Virginia for the Months of July, August, September, and October, 1870* (Richmond, 1870), 6. Incorporated in June 1870, the institution remained in Richmond until transferred to Petersburg in 1888. See Drewy, *Historical Sketch.*

facilities equal to those of whites. Many Radicals were southerners who still believed in Negro inferiority, and, as has been demonstrated in a number of recent monographs, northerners had never been free from such prejudices either.[13] Nor were the realities of power lost on these men. Strongly anti-Negro mountain whites in North Carolina and Tennessee formed a major part of the Republican coalition, and integrated facilities would have constituted an obvious slight, probably costing many votes. Similarly, if the Republicans elsewhere were to stay in power, allies needed to be attracted from among independents, former Whigs, and even Democrats. The professed policy of separate but equal had the benefit of minimizing white hostility while still presenting the blacks with a significant improvement over their treatment at the hands of earlier administrations. Radicals did not seek to "Africanize" the South, but neither did they seek to perpetuate the old injustices.

Ignoring Virginia's conditional policy, Tennessee's leading Radical journal boasted in 1866, "Tennessee has the honor of being the first state to make special provision for her insane colored people." A Republican legislature had just authorized the Tennessee Hospital for the Insane to construct quarters for the Negro insane in Nashville "so as to keep them secure and safe, and yet separate and apart from the white patients." The first blacks moved into a three-story brick building near the structure for the whites in 1868. At about the same time the Radical-controlled North Carolina legislature set aside separate quarters for Negroes at the state insane asylum in Raleigh and founded the Negro department at the Institution for the Blind, Deaf and Dumb. Alabama Radicals were responsible for the separate wards at the Alabama Insane Hospital, where admittance procedures for both races were the same and blacks supposedly received "the same treatment and accommodation."[14]

There were fewer public facilities on the local level, but in those that existed, the same pattern was evident. Montgomery Radicals, for example, operated a city hospital divided into white and black wards. The segregated cemeteries the

---

13. See, for example, V. Jacque Voegeli, *Free but Not Equal: The Midwest and the Negro during the Civil War* (Chicago: University of Chicago Press, 1967) and Leon F. Litwack, *North of Slavery: The Negro in the Free States, 1790–1860* (Chicago: University of Chicago Press, 1961).

14. *Nashville Daily Press and Times,* August 6, 1866; Tennessee, *Acts,* 1865–1866, chapter 4, section 22; Tennessee, *Report of the Board of State Charities of Tennessee to the Fifty-third General Assembly* (Nashville, 1903), 22; *Raleigh Daily Sentinel,* March 18, 1875; L. L. Polk, comp., *Handbook of North Carolina Embracing Historical and Physiographical Sketches of the State with Statistical and Other Information Relating to Its Industries, Resources, and Political Conditions* (Raleigh: Raleigh News, 1879), 182; Alabama, *Seventh Annual Report of the Officers of the Alabama Insane Hospital for the Year 1867* (Tuscaloosa, 1867), 9.

Radicals found when they gained office were continued, and in Raleigh steps were taken to make the segregation even more pronounced. In 1868 the city council opened a separate city graveyard for Negroes. Blacks could still be buried in their section of the old cemetery, but lot prices were made lower in the new one so as to attract more customers.[15]

The Radicals had made an important break with past practice. Doors of public institutions were opened to blacks for the first time, but on a segregated basis. In other instances, such as the Richmond and Nashville almshouses or the Virginia insane asylum, the Radicals administered segregated institutions that the military had forced upon the postwar Conservative governments.[16] The justification, it must be remembered, was equal access. But the Radicals were in power for such a short period that they only had time to institute a small portion of the welfare apparatus needed by the freedmen. When the Radicals surrendered office, only Richmond and Montgomery had public hospitals; only Richmond provided for its Negro orphans. Certain state institutions continued to exclude Negroes, and relief and medical aid were still less available for blacks than for whites. Therefore, it was the Redeemers, many of them former slave owners and veterans of the Confederate army, who determined the quality and quantity of welfare facilities for blacks during the largest segment of the period.

The Policy of the Redeemers

Many of the Redeemers had taken part in the first postwar white governments that had excluded Negroes from health and welfare services. The conditions under

15. Montgomery City Council Minutes, October 5, 1868; March 18, 1872; Raleigh, *Amended Charter and Ordinances,* 1867, 46; 1873, 31–32. See also Richmond, *Amended Charter and Ordinances,* 1867, 91–92; Nashville, *Amended Charter, Acts of the General Assembly, and Ordinances,* 1868, 60. The segregation in Atlanta and Montgomery continued to be de facto.

16. Radicals seem to have played the same role in states and cities not selected for intensive examination. In Mississippi, Republican state governments in 1870 and 1871 maintained wards for Negroes in charity hospitals established in Vicksburg and Natchez; in 1870 the Radicals made provisions for separate and allegedly equal treatment of blacks in the state insane asylum; Radicals also opened the doors of the Institution for the Deaf and Dumb to blacks, evidently on a segregated basis. See Wharton, *The Negro in Mississippi,* 266–68. In South Carolina, Radicals provided segregated quarters for blacks in the state insane asylum and orphanage. They also admitted them to the Institution for the Deaf and Blind, but closed the facility when whites withdrew. See Williamson, *After Slavery,* 281, 290–91, and George Brown Tindall, *South Carolina Negroes, 1877–1900* (Columbia: University of South Carolina Press, 1952; reprint ed., Baton Rouge: Louisiana State University Press, 1966), 281.

which the blacks lived had grown even worse since 1867. Despite pleas by both whites and blacks that they would be better off in the countryside,[17] the blacks remained in the cities and each year saw their numbers increase. Democratic officials, seeking to account for high death rates among Negroes, frequently called attention to their miserable living conditions. Sometimes officials hedged and blamed the inherent weaknesses of the race, a subtle way of extolling the virtues of slavery. But the head of the Richmond Board of Health put the blame for the high mortality rate squarely where it belonged. It was not due to "race constitutional defects," he said. The main causes were poverty and overcrowding.[18]

The search for a solution to this problem of needy blacks divided the Redeemers. Some felt that to provide services would only encourage the influx of more Negroes to the cities, whereas if fewer services were provided, many of the blacks already there would return to the land. Few expressed such views openly, preferring instead to oppose new facilities because of lack of funds. Much of the opposition can only be inferred from the defeats suffered by proponents of greater aid to Negroes. In 1881 the president of the Richmond Board of Health urged city officials to provide more assistance, since "the care and the protection of the colored race now rests on us." Five years later he pointed to the "legion of old colored midwives" who practiced almost exclusively on the blacks. The resultant high Negro infant mortality, he said, "appeals to our liberality to furnish physicians to attend the indigent class."[19]

Nevertheless, the Redeemer city councils frequently reverted to the practice of excluding Negroes from poor relief or medical assistance. Sometimes public services were abolished, thus depriving whites as well as blacks of their benefits. In such instances, however, the Negroes were usually worse hit and the whites frequently found succor elsewhere. When Montgomery's Democrats won full control of the city government in 1875, the newly elected mayor closed the public hospital as part of his retrenchment program. The void was later filled for charity and paying white patients through the erection of the Montgomery Infirmary in 1888.[20] In Nashville, where the Democrats accused Republican mayor Thomas Kercheval of using poor relief as a device to attract Negro voters to his party, the Redeemers abolished the system of municipal out-relief. After Ker-

17. See, for example, *Nashville Union and American,* November 27, 1870; James S. Hinton, a Negro member of the Indiana Canal Commission, quoted in the *Nashville Daily American,* April 5, 1876.

18. See, for example, Report of the President of the Atlanta Board of Health, Atlanta City Council Minutes, January 1, 1883; *Nashville Daily American,* April 29, 1876; Richmond, *Annual Report of the Board of Health of the City of Richmond for the Year 1883,* 6.

19. Richmond, *Annual Report,* 1881, 6; 1886, 6–7.

20. Montgomery, *Annual Reports,* 1876–1877, 14; 1884–1885, 55–56; C. J. Allardt, comp., *Montgomery City Directory for 1888* (Montgomery: R. L. Polk and Co., 1888), 19.

cheval regained power, the Democratic-controlled council thwarted his efforts to reestablish the old system of public charity.[21] Throughout the rest of the period the city relied on the county asylum and private relief organizations to bear the welfare burden.

Concern over the possibility that undeserving blacks would benefit from public assistance was as much a factor as the political considerations. Newspapers were especially troubled by the allegedly great number of blacks who, though able to work, preferred to beg. "There are a number of trifling negroes who, constitutionally opposed to work, are commencing the winter campaign by the usual programme of living on charity," the *Nashville Banner* observed. Referring to a recent distribution of alms, the *Atlanta Constitution* noted that in the crowd were a number of blacks "in good health, strong of limb, and more comfortably dressed than some of the whites who were dispensing charity." The newspaper was happy to report that they "were properly dealt with," but it was upset that "the negroes . . . disgrace themselves by such exhibitions." In 1888 Atlanta abolished the office of Warden of the Poor and turned over the job of dispensing out-relief to a member of the police force to make certain that applicants would receive careful scrutiny.[22]

Not only were Negroes cut off from certain services they had previously received, but they continued to be excluded from many of the older welfare facilities. In addition, several new institutions that opened during Reconstruction, although supported by public funds, were only for whites. Perhaps because they had educational as well as welfare functions, orphanages, like schools, would not accept blacks even on a segregated basis. Davidson County (Nashville) supported three orphanages; Richmond had contributed to four since antebellum times; Fulton County (Atlanta) contributed to at least two others.[23] Despite receiving public tax money, all of them were restricted to whites. The same was true of the all-white state orphanages founded in Georgia in 1869 and in North Carolina in 1872.[24] Both the city and state governments went even further,

---

21. For a good summary of the Kercheval controversy, see, for example, *Nashville Daily American,* October 28, November 24, 1875.

22. *Nashville Banner,* November 23, 1882; *Atlanta Constitution,* January 9, 1884; Atlanta, Council Committee on Relief Report, *Annual Report of the Officers of the City of Atlanta for the Year Ending December 31, 1889* (Atlanta, 1890), 34.

23. On Davidson County, see, for example, *Nashville Republican Banner,* January 5, 1871; on Richmond, Jane Taylor Duke, "The Richmond Home for Boys, 1846–1855," manuscript (VSL), 16, 20; *Constitution and By-Laws of the Female Humane Association of the City of Richmond with a Sketch of the Association* (Richmond: J. C. Hill, 1898), passim; on Fulton County, *Atlanta Constitution,* February 12, 1889.

24. *Atlanta Constitution,* April 10, 1869; North Carolina, *Report of the Board of Public Charities of North Carolina for 1891* (Raleigh, 1891), 12–14.

however, and generally refused to provide public funds for Negro orphans even if they were housed in separate institutions. Two private facilities, Richmond's Colored Friends Orphanage and Atlanta's Carrie Steele Orphan Home, and the state-run North Carolina Colored Orphan Asylum, founded in 1887, were the sole exceptions.[25]

Officials were even more intransigent with regard to supporting Negro "fallen" or destitute women. Although Richmond, Nashville, and Atlanta made generous appropriations to private institutions that cared for white women, they made no provisions for blacks. Once again a minority of Redeemers attempted to broaden the scope of such concern. When a special committee of the Atlanta City Council advised that fifty dollars per month be given both to the Home for the Friendless and to the Woman's Christian Home, one member objected to the racially restricted character of the aid. The chairman of the committee replied, "Whenever the negroes get up a home of their own, I will be willing to help them."[26] The period closed without any such black facility.

Negroes also continued to be barred from most local hospitals. This was especially true of private institutions. All of those in Richmond during the 1870s and 1880s were strictly for whites. In Atlanta the city government paid private hospitals to take care of indigent patients. Finding facilities that would accept Negroes proved difficult, however, and for several years blacks did not receive similar benefits. "There has been no place for the sick of our colored population," wrote the mayor in 1881, "and I have been compelled to resort to private parties to furnish places and nurses for them." Sometimes the municipal officials contributed even more directly to exclusionary practices; the public hospital in Raleigh admitted only whites.[27]

Despite an occasional reversion to the policy of exclusion or its continuation where the Radicals had left it undisturbed, the Redeemers' most frequent response to the legacy of Radical rule was to endorse the shift from exclusion to segregation. It must be remembered, however, that the Redeemers were not a monolithic group, even within a given city or city council. Whether because of fear of northern intervention if Negroes did not receive adequate attention or because of paternalistic or political impulses, some Democrats argued that suffi-

25. *Charter and By Laws of the Friends Asylum for Colored Orphans* (Richmond: R. L. Hewlett and Bro., 1883), passim; Richmond City Council Minutes, July 1, 1866; July 8, 1867; December 31, 1868; *The Carrie Steele Orphan Home of the City of Atlanta* (Atlanta: Franklin Printing and Publishing Co., 1893), passim; Wiley Britton Sanders, *Negro Child Welfare in North Carolina* (Chapel Hill: University of North Carolina Press, 1933), 72.
26. *Atlanta Constitution*, April 2, 1889.
27. Valedictory of Mayor Calhoun, Atlanta City Council Minutes, January 3, 1881; Raleigh, *Annual Reports of the Mayor and Officers of the City of Raleigh for Fiscal Year Ending April 30, 1884* (Raleigh: Edwards and Broughton and Co., 1884), 12–13.

cient funds should be made available to help blacks. These men insisted, however, on segregated facilities. To them segregation was a satisfactory form of social control and was necessitated by the inferiority of Negroes and the fear that "race mixing" would produce amalgamation or racial warfare. Maintaining or increasing the number of separate facilities for blacks might attract more Negroes to the Democratic party and, in any case, would appease northern meddlers who had done no more for the freedmen. These Redeemers also publicly reaffirmed the Radical principle that separate treatment was to be equal treatment. When plans were made in 1876 for the opening of a Jim Crow institution for Georgia's Negro deaf and dumb, it was ordered by the legislature that "the present Board of Trustees [of the white institution] will act for this colored institution and conduct it, in all respects as the present one of the whites is conducted."[28] The annex of Atlanta Hospital to be completed in 1880 was for Negro patients "who will receive every attention bestowed on the whites." And the final justice: "Every grave which the keeper has dug," read a Richmond ordinance, "whether for the body of a white or colored person, shall be at least six feet deep."[29]

But the implementation of plans for Negro accommodations frequently met with delays and, in cases such as the Atlanta Hospital, never came to fruition. In explaining why Negroes were still barred from the Georgia Institution for the Deaf and Dumb in 1873, the board of commissioners stated, "It was incompatible with the general school law that blacks and whites should be educated together." They felt that it was now time to spend six thousand dollars for the separate accommodation of blacks. Money was finally appropriated in 1876 for a Negro department to be opened when there were ten or more applicants. The bill provided that the Negro division "shall, in all respects, be conducted separate from the other institution; . . . the funds appropriated for its use to be a separate fund; the teachers and all other employees to be as distinctly separate as though the two institutions were in different towns." Yet the school did not open until March 1882. Four months earlier the Negro department of the Georgia Academy for the Blind had opened in Macon in separate quarters far apart from the whites. The existence of the Macon facility was due in part to the urging of the superintendent of the academy, first expressed in 1880, that "all those rea-

28. Georgia, *Report of the Board of Commissioners of the Georgia Institution for the Education of the Deaf and Dumb for the Year Ending June 30, 1876* (Atlanta, 1876), 7. The possibility remains, however, that this injunction concerning the conduct of the institution was meant to apply merely to administrative procedures rather than being a call for equal treatment.

29. *Atlanta Constitution,* May 2, 1880; Richmond, *Amended Charter and Ordinances,* 1867, 93.

sons which move us to educate the blind of one race are equally strong in the case of the other."[30]

The exchanges between the state legislature and the principal of the Alabama Institution of the Deaf and Dumb and Blind even more graphically demonstrate the split among public officials and the reluctance of legislators to accept obligation for the care of black dependents. In his annual report for 1884, the principal sadly observed that he could "hardly see how the State can afford longer to *neglect entirely* the colored deaf and dumb and blind youth growing up in our midst." His pleas continued in subsequent reports, and his report for 1890 termed a Negro department *"a great public need"* and appealed for *"justice* [for] these unfortunate classes." Two years later the legislature finally responded with an appropriation of twelve thousand dollars. Placed in charge of the principal of the white school but with a separate staff of white teachers, the new department opened in January 1892.[31] In Virginia, care for this disadvantaged group was not seriously considered until 1896; and it was not until September 1909 that the Virginia School for the Colored Deaf and Blind Children belatedly opened outside Newport News.[32]

Whenever possible the Redeemers rigidified the separation initiated by the Radicals. Negroes who had occupied the six lower wards of the main building at the Alabama insane asylum during Reconstruction were moved by Redeemers into separate quarters nearby. North Carolina Redeemers sought immediately to transfer the blacks at the Raleigh asylum to one to be built in Wilmington. After delays due to a shortage of funds, the Negro institution was finally built in Goldsboro in 1880. And in both Raleigh and Atlanta, Redeemer councils passed stricter regulations regarding separation of the races in the cemeteries.[33]

Segregation was also present in new welfare services and institutions estab-

30. Georgia, *Report of the Institution for the Deaf and Dumb,* 1872–1873, 8–9; 1875–1876, 6; Georgia, *Report of the Board of Trustees of the Georgia Academy for the Blind for 1883* (Atlanta, 1884), 11; 1880, 14–18.

31. Alabama, *Annual Reports of the Alabama Institution for the Education of the Deaf and Dumb and Blind for 1883 and 1884* (Montgomery, 1884), 11–12; 1889–1890, 7–8 (italics in original); 1891–1892, 11. See also 1885–1886, 21–22; 1887–1888, 9.

32. Virginia, *First Annual Report of the State Board of Charities and Corrections to the Governor of Virginia for the Year Ending September 30, 1909* (Richmond, 1909), 169; Writers Program of the Works Progress Administration in the State of Virginia, comp., *The Negro in Virginia* (New York: Hastings House, 1940), 343.

33. Alabama, *Report of the Alabama Insane Hospital,* 1867, 9; 1871, 8; 1883–1884, 16; Polk, *Handbook of North Carolina,* 181–82; *Raleigh Daily Sentinel,* March 18, November 3, December 8, 1875; *Visitors Guide to the North Carolina Exposition and Raleigh, 1884* (Raleigh: Exposition Guide Publishing Co., 1884), 15; Raleigh, *Amended Charter and Ordinances,* 1876, 96–97; Atlanta City Council Minutes, September 13, 1867; January 3, 1873; April 2, 1877; Atlanta, *Code,* 1886, 156.

lished after Reconstruction. During the winter of 1874, for example, the Richmond office that handed out food and fuel to the poor was open to whites from
nine to noon in the morning and to blacks from two to five in the afternoon;
during the rest of the year, the hours for whites were ten to noon on Thursdays
and the same time on Fridays for blacks. In response to a serious outbreak of
smallpox in 1881, Atlanta officials instituted a system of compulsory free vaccinations with separate downtown offices for each race. The state of Tennessee
added a Negro department when it assumed direction of the privately run all-
white Tennessee Industrial School in 1887. And although most of Atlanta's hospitals would admit only indigent white patients referred by the city, the local
government finally convinced the Ivy Street Hospital and Providence Infirmary
to accept indigents of both races.[34] A possible reason for the change in policy of
these two hospitals was their connection with the Southern Medical College,
which used charity patients "for the promotion of medical teaching."[35] Whatever the reason, once admitted, the Negroes were treated in segregated wards.
Indeed, segregated facilities had been included in every plan for a public hospital in Atlanta since the early 1870s. One of the many reports issued by a group of
physicians in 1888 urged that while "equal provision" should be made for
whites and blacks, widely separated wards and entrances were required for each
race. The new institution, named after Henry Grady, opened with its segregated
wards and entrances in 1892. It followed by two years the opening of Nashville's
segregated municipal hospital.[36]

34. Richmond, *Annual Reports of the City Departments of Richmond, Virginia, for the
Year Ending January 31, 1874* (Richmond, 1874), 11; *Atlanta Constitution,* January 13,
1882; Tennessee, *Report of the Board of State Charities,* 1903, 33; Tennessee, *First Biennial Report of the Tennessee Industrial School for the Period 1887–1888* (Nashville, 1888),
22; Atlanta City Council Minutes, February 4, 1884; July 16, 1888; Atlanta, *Annual
Reports,* 1889, 35.
35. *Atlanta Constitution,* September 28, 1884. The Negro fear of medical schools was a
standing joke in southern newspapers. According to the *Atlanta Constitution,* January 2,
1880: "A medical student can do more to scare a negro than a score of policemen." The
January 8, 1880, issue added: "It is said that after dark, a darkey can't be found within a
mile of any medical college in the city." See also *Nashville Banner,* December 29, 1882.
36. Atlanta, *Annual Reports,* 1888, 41–45. See also *Atlanta Constitution,* January 27, 1872;
Writers Program of the Works Progress Administration in the State of Georgia, comp.,
Atlanta: A City of the Modern South, American Guide Series (New York: Smith and Durrell,
1942), 76. For a floor plan of the hospital, see *Atlanta Constitution,* December 7, 1890. For
the Nashville municipal hospital, see *Reports of the City of Nashville for the Year Ending
October 1, 1889* (Nashville, 1889), 33. Before the city hospital was opened, indigent blacks
received publicly supported treatment at the University Hospital and at the Hospital of the
Good Shepherd. As was true in Atlanta, both were affiliated with medical schools. See
Nashville, *Report of the Nashville Board of Health for the Two Years Ending December 31,
1878* (Nashville, 1879), 103; *Nashville Banner,* January 8, 14, 1888; March 30, 1889.

Negro Self-Help

The white Redeemers thus continued the policies practiced by the Freedmen's Bureau, the U.S. Army, and the Radicals; but as previously mentioned, Negroes were still often left to fend for themselves. Confronted by exclusion or insufficient attention, the Negroes sought to fill voids left by governmental neglect. Such attempts at self-help ironically further strengthened the system of segregated welfare care.

Negro benevolent societies were at the core of the self-help effort. Secret societies, including black lodges of Masons or Odd Fellows, performed welfare as well as social functions. Raleigh's Excelsior Lodge No. 21 of Colored Masons, for example, aided needy members, their widows, and their orphaned children. More important, however, were the numerous societies connected with local churches. In return for small monthly dues, members were entitled to sick benefits and, if necessary, burial fees. One of the first, the Nashville Colored Benevolent Society, was organized in 1865 by twelve Nashville blacks. Another, located in Atlanta, had as its motto: "We assist the needy: we relieve our sick; we bury our dead."[37]

As the years passed and the Negroes accumulated more money, the societies and their services to the black community multiplied. According to the *Republican Banner,* they proved invaluable during Nashville's cholera epidemic of 1873, although their treasuries were virtually depleted as a result. In that year the Colored Benevolent Society had twenty-seven branches throughout the state with a membership of two thousand. In its annual report of 1881, the Ladies' Benevolent Society No. 1 claimed 440 members, 207 of whom had been assisted and 11 buried; $1,528.25 had been paid for the sick, $330.00 for funerals, $30.50 for charity, and $96.00 for secretary and rent. Still left in the fund after these expenditures was $1,603.50.[38] Clearly the resources of such individual societies were not great, but when considered together, they helped to soften the impact of exclusionary practices.

The sick benefits were greatly welcomed by Negroes who could not afford the

37. Minutes of the Excelsior Lodge No. 21 of Colored Masons (Raleigh), 1875–86, North Carolina Department of Archives and History, Raleigh (cited hereafter as NCDAH). See, for example, entries for January 24 and September 25, 1876; Taylor, *Negro in Tennessee,* 157; *Atlanta Constitution,* June 13, 1871.

38. *Nashville Republican Banner,* July 20, April 13, 1873; *Nashville Banner,* September 9, 1881. For the role of benevolent societies in Atlanta, see *Atlanta Constitution,* November 13, 1883, and W. E. B. Du Bois, ed., *Economic Cooperation among Negro Americans,* Atlanta University Publications, ed. W. E. B. Du Bois, no. 12 (Atlanta: Atlanta University Press, 1907), 95.

premiums of large insurance companies (whose policies were in any case rarely made available to them) and who could expect little aid from the city governments. An even more important reason for the popularity of these organizations was the burial benefits. After his trip through the South, the Englishman William Hepworth Dixon concluded, "One thing only in the future weighs sufficiently on a Negro's mind to shape his action. He is very anxious about his funeral." Dixon was told by his hotel waiter in Richmond, "What makes us poor is de expens ob burin' us. . . . Every culled person is a member of two or three [burial] societies. He pay much money. When he die, dey have all big sights." The *Nashville Banner* marveled, "Singularly as it may appear the colored people have a great horror of being buried by the county, or even of receiving a coffin for that purpose. They will submit to all sorts of privations to bury their dead independently of the county." Although some were critical of the lavish funerals with brass bands, handsome hearses and coffins, and the spectacle of the society's members decked out in the finest uniforms, to the poor Negro and his family it was a brief time when he would be someone important. Faced with the alternatives of the involuntary donations of their bodies to the local medical school or paupers' burials in an unkempt potter's field where body snatchers preyed, many blacks not surprisingly contributed their pennies so that in places like Atlanta they could have funerals that ranged in price from $7.00 to $45.00 instead of the $1.83 burial accorded the indigent.[39]

Many of the societies had their own cemetery plots. In 1883, for example, Atlanta's Odd Fellow lodges claimed this benefit as one of their major attractions for prospective members. Nashville's Colored Benevolent Society went even further. All Negroes were buried in their portion of the municipal graveyard until the society, "feeling the great necessity that exists for a separate and properly enclosed burial place," founded the Mount Ararat Cemetery on the outskirts of the city in 1869. In Richmond, where blacks were excluded from the two best cemeteries and allotted an unfenced portion of Shockoe Cemetery, six private Negro cemeteries had been organized by 1880.[40]

Beginning in 1878, Atlanta Negroes had petitioned the city government to purchase a site for a black cemetery. In 1884 the sale of lots in the municipal

39. Dixon, *White Conquest,* 2 vols. (London: Chatto and Windus, 1876), 2:166; *Nashville Banner,* January 8, 1885; *Atlanta Constitution,* November 13, 1883. See also George Sala, *America Revisited: From the Bay of New York to the Gulf of Mexico and from Lake Michigan to the Pacific,* 5th ed. (London: Vizetelly and Co., 1885), 206–7.

40. *Atlanta Constitution,* November 13, 1883; *Nashville Daily Press and Times,* March 17, 1869; Richmond, *Amended Charter and Ordinances,* 1867, 91–92; U.S. Bureau of the Census, *Report on the Social Statistics of Cities,* comp. George E. Waring, Jr. (Washington, D.C.: Government Printing Office, 1887), part 2, 82.

graveyard was discontinued, and the private white-owned West View Cemetery was opened. In return for council approval of its charter, the company agreed to bury paupers of both races and guaranteed that separate ground would be set apart for the sale of lots to Negroes. The terms for the incorporation of West View convinced the blacks that the city had no intention of establishing a separate Negro cemetery; therefore, a black company founded South View Cemetery and petitioned the council for the right to bury Negro paupers. Finally in 1888, over the vigorous objections of West View's directors, who disliked losing the business, the city acceded to the demands of the Negro company.[41]

Aid to the Negro poor also came from black philanthropic organizations modeled after those of the white community. The Nashville Provident Association, which aided both blacks and whites, was organized by a group of black clergymen in 1865. On the first day they raised over five hundred dollars, with which they established a wood depot and later a soup kitchen. The Colored Home Mission Society No. 1 of East Nashville fulfilled a similar function of distributing supplies and clothing to the needy. The most important organization of this type was the Colored Ladies Relief Society, an offshoot of the Nashville Ladies Relief Society. The latter group had been formed by white women after the city discontinued its system of out-relief. It was especially active during the severe winter of 1884 in distributing food, fuel, and clothing to the city's poor. Yet its aid was highly selective. "You know we never help negroes," said one of its leaders in 1886, "unless they are very old people or sick."[42] And as a "scientific charity," it carefully distinguished between the deserving and undeserving poor. Soon after, the society decided "to let the colored people manage the taking care of their own people." In December 1886, the Colored Ladies Relief Society was organized with thirty members, each of whom paid dues of either three dollars per year or twenty-five cents per month.[43] The society intended to investigate the need of the applicants among the black poor in the same manner as the Nashville Ladies Relief Society did for the white community.

41. On the early demands for a Negro cemetery, see Atlanta City Council Minutes, February 18, March 14, 18, 1878; on South View, see Atlanta City Council Minutes, August 15, September 6, 1886; Atlanta, *Annual Reports,* 1888, 46. For the opening of West View, see Atlanta, *Annual Reports,* 1884, 18. For the reaction of its officials to South View, see Atlanta City Council Minutes, May 7 and 21, 1888. Among the officers of South View were two Negro undertakers, David T. Howard and Mitchell Cargile. *Atlanta Constitution,* March 17, 1886.

42. *Nashville Daily Press and Times,* December 16, 1865; *Nashville Banner,* January 28, 1888; Nashville Ladies Relief Society leader quoted in *Nashville Banner,* November 20, 1886. On earlier activities of the society, see *Nashville Banner,* January 11, 1884.

43. *Nashville Banner,* November 27, December 10, 1886;

In addition to individual donations from both blacks and whites, the Colored Society received $318.95 of the $1,000.00 appropriated to the Nashville Relief Society by the county court in 1887. Later in the year, however, the Colored Society's president told a reporter: "We have no money and no way to get it." Thanks to the support of white and black businessmen, the society continued to provide relief. Its April 1890 report of activities for the previous six months disclosed that between five hundred and one thousand people had received assistance, which included almost one thousand bushels of coal and other provisions.[44]

In two cities, Negroes resorted to private means to get the benefits denied them by the public hospitals. In 1885, seven years after the founding of the Hospital of St. John's Guild for destitute whites, the Leonard Medical Hospital opened in Raleigh under the management of Shaw Institute, a local black college. Raleigh Negroes received free medicine from the city, but the board and medicine of nonresidents had to be paid by their respective counties.[45] The black community of Montgomery, refused admittance to the Montgomery Infirmary, founded the James Hale Infirmary. Named after a prominent local black, financed largely by his widow, and run by Dr. C. N. Dorsette, the institution remained an indispensable service for blacks well into the twentieth century. Mrs. Hale fully supported the concept of self-help. Blacks should build not only churches and houses, she said, but "homes for the orphans, the poor and the aged of our race, and also infirmaries and hospitals where the lame, sick, and injured can be cared for."[46]

Negro orphaned and dependent children fared worst at the hands of public officials. When the facilities run by the Freedmen's Bureau and the northern societies closed, blacks were turned back on their own resources. Negro churches and benevolent societies supported many children and sought to place them with private families. Benefits such as one given in Nashville by the Centennial Singers brought in needed funds. But more was necessary, and blacks turned increasingly to the organization of their own asylums. Failure was often the result. In 1873 a group of Negroes organized the Colored Ladies House of Industry of Nashville to

44. Ibid., January 9, November 29, 1887; see also January 16, 1888. For statistics released in the April 1890 report, see April 8, 1890.

45. Raleigh, *Annual Reports,* 1883–1884, 12–13; "Circular Letter Addressed to Various Counties by President [Henry M.] Tupper of Shaw Institute," Raleigh, *Annual Reports,* 1884–1885, 16–17. Unlike the white hospital, the black hospital and its dispensary were open for only part of the year.

46. C. J. Allardt, comp., *Montgomery City Directory for 1891* (Montgomery: C. J. Allardt and Co., 1891), 16; Charles Octavius Boothe, *The Cyclopedia of the Colored Baptists of Alabama* (Birmingham: Alabama Publishing Co., 1895), 59; Mrs. Hale quoted in J. W. Gibson and W. H. Crogman, *Progress of a Race; or, The Remarkable Advancement of the American Negro,* rev. ed. (Atlanta: J. L. Nichols and Co., 1902), 480–81.

give "moral and religious instruction" to more than three hundred homeless black youths and to train them in "industrial habits and pursuits." The year before, another group had established the People's Orphan Association, but there is no evidence that either institution ever went into operation. Montgomery blacks were similarly thwarted in their efforts to start an orphanage.[47]

Two institutions for Negro girls were finally founded in Nashville and Montgomery,[48] but the greatest advances in the care of dependent black children came elsewhere. Continual requests from Richmond Negroes led the city council in 1867 to authorize the use of a lot for the erection of a black asylum. After much haggling, the city added $500 to the $6,250 raised by the Society of Friends, and the orphanage opened in 1869 as the Friends Asylum for Colored Orphans. Its trustees included five white Quakers and several representatives of local Negro churches. As with the five white institutions in Richmond, in return for yearly appropriations the orphanage accepted five children per year referred by the municipal government. Atlanta's Carrie Steele Orphan Home, built on land donated by the city, was founded in 1890 by Mrs. Carrie Steele Logan, a former slave who worked as a stewardess at the railway depot. Its board of trustees was composed entirely of religious, business, and educational leaders of black Atlanta. Some northerners and local whites contributed funds, but most of the support came from Negroes in the form of provisions or in amounts of money ranging from ten cents to fifty dollars. Whites were pleased, since, said a supporter, "an orphan's home would prove a blessing to the hundreds of negro children who are growing up in Atlanta without discipline or instruction and from whose ranks the chain gang is being filled." Besides, added another, "it is the intention of the people interested in the home to take the little negro waifs and make good servants of them."[49] To Negroes the asylum was a way of reducing suffering

47. *Nashville Daily American,* January 30, 1876; *Nashville Republican Banner,* November 5, 1873; August 8, 1872; for Montgomery blacks, see, for example, *Montgomery Daily Advertiser,* September 23, 1873; *Montgomery Herald,* September 25, October 16, 1886.

48. For the institution for dependent black girls in Nashville run by Julia G. Thomas, see William Wells Brown, *My Southern Home; or, The South and Its People* (Boston: A. G. Brown and Co., 1880), 219. For the Montgomery Industrial School for Negro Girls, see Ruth McAllister Vines, "The Contributions of Negroes in Providing School Facilities in the Montgomery, Alabama, City Schools" (M.A. thesis, Graduate Division, State Teachers College at Montgomery, 1943), 16, and William N. Hartshorn, *An Era of Progress and Promise, 1863–1910: The Religious, Moral, and Educational Development of the American Negro since His Emancipation* (Boston: Presrilla Publishing Co., 1910), 357.

49. *Charter and By Laws of the Friends Asylum for Colored Orphans,* passim; Richmond City Council Minutes, July 1, 1866; July 8, 1867; December 31, 1868; E. R. Carter, *The Black Side: A Partial History of the Business, Religious, and Educational Side of the Negro in Atlanta, Georgia* (Atlanta, 1894), 35–37. See also *Carrie Steele Orphan Home,* passim; first quote, *Atlanta Constitution,* March 16, 1887; second quote, Colonel Albert Howell in

among members of their race, but to whites it was a way of achieving social control over a new generation of blacks who lacked the ties with whites that had helped to keep their parents in their place.

Black Demands for Access to and Control of Public Social Services

The demands made to the city governments for Negro orphanages or cemeteries suggest that blacks were less concerned with encouraging integration than with ending exclusion. Indeed, Negro leaders for the most part left unchallenged the existence of segregation in welfare facilities.[50] This attitude did not indicate passivity, however. Where blacks were barred, they demanded the establishment of Negro departments or separate institutions. The petitions of black religious bodies for a Negro division at the Georgia Academy for the Blind played a key role in its formation, and it was a black legislator, Thomas A. Sykes, who introduced the bill that provided segregated accommodations for blacks at the Tennessee School for the Blind in Nashville and the School for the Deaf in Knoxville. W. H. Young, one of the two Negro justices on the Davidson County Court, took exception to appropriations for two white orphanages and a mission home for fallen white women because Negroes in similar circumstances were denied aid. He advocated a home for black fallen women and the construction of a Negro reformatory. He received encouragement from the *Nashville Banner,* which argued, "Public aid from the treasury of state, county, or city should be rendered to all alike."[51]

Atlanta Constitution, December 1, 1889. The Leonard Street Home for Negro female orphans was also founded in 1890, by an Englishwoman, Miss L. M. Lawson. The children were mainly from the Atlanta slums and had been abandoned by their parents. See Hartshorn, *Era of Progress and Promise,* 373–75; W. E. B. Du Bois, ed., *Efforts for Social Betterment among Negro Americans,* Atlanta University Publications, ed. W. E. B. Du Bois, no. 14 (Atlanta: Atlanta University Press, 1909), 78. Although both Du Bois and Hartshorn state that the home opened in 1890, the *Atlanta Constitution,* June 7, 1889, noted that a black orphan school was operating on Leonard Street with a Miss S. L. Grant (white) as matron. The roots of Miss Lawson's institution therefore probably go back at least to 1889.

50. Williamson suggests the same policy on the part of Negroes in South Carolina. See *After Slavery,* 281.

51. Georgia, *Report of the Academy for the Blind,* 1880, 18; Tennessee, General Assembly, *House Journal,* 42d session (Nashville, 1881), 5. For Young's argument, see *Nashville Banner,* January 9, 1884; for the *Nashville Banner*'s support of Young, see January 10, 1884. The newspaper correctly noted that Young had "objected to any discrimination in public favors." The support of black women and children, even if in separate institutions, would not have been seen by him as "discrimination," providing the appropriations were equal.

Once access to a service was attained, blacks demanded greater influence in its management. In response to conciliatory feelers from the local Democratic administration, the *Richmond Planet* called for black supervision of the Negro almshouse: "Let us have this done to start with. Let a colored physician attend to the wants of its inmates. . . . The glad tidings will be heralded that at last fair play and an era of good feeling has put in an appearance in the capital of Bourbonism." A group of Atlanta blacks petitioned the city council in 1889 to appoint a Negro named Ashbury as one of the city physicians and to turn over all black patients to him. In North Carolina James H. Harris, a Negro former state legislator and Raleigh councilman, insisted that blacks be appointed to the boards of all state institutions where blacks were housed. The reason was simple. "No one," he said, "can enter so fully into the sympathy of the negro's condition as the negro himself." In 1869, when Holland Thompson, one of Montgomery's two black aldermen, became dissatisfied with the portion of the city cemetery reserved for Negroes, he called for the establishment of an entirely separate graveyard for blacks.[52]

Demands for increased Negro participation bore little fruit. Their major impact was to convince whites that blacks were satisfied with the new status quo, that is, segregation. Despite opposition, however, there were a few Negro administrators. Alfred Menefee, a Nashville politician, served on the board of education in 1868 and as one of the county poorhouse commissioners in 1869. As late as 1877, James H. Harris was a member of the board of the North Carolina Institution for the Deaf and Dumb and Blind. Under the Readjusters in Virginia, a leading Richmond city councilman was selected as vice president of the board of directors of the Negro insane asylum. When the Tennessee Industrial School was opened in 1888, Thomas A. Sykes, a former North Carolina and Tennessee state legislator and Davidson County magistrate, was placed in charge of its Negro department. And in Alabama a board of six prominent blacks advised the all-white board of trustees of the Asylum for the Deaf and Dumb and Blind.[53] But such appointments were infrequently made, and for real control over their own welfare, the Negroes had to be content with their benevolent societies,

52. *Richmond Planet,* June 12, 1886; Petition of H. M. Turner et al., Atlanta City Council Minutes, February 4, 1889. A second petition was presented the following June and, like the first, was buried in committee. *Atlanta Constitution,* June 18, July 9, 1889; Harris quoted in *Raleigh Register,* March 27, 1878; Montgomery City Council Minutes, May 3, 1869.

53. *Nashville Union and Dispatch,* December 17, 1867; *Nashville Daily Press and Times,* January 8, 1869; State of North Carolina Appointment Certificate, June 1, 1875, James H. Harris Papers, NCDAH; Drewy, *Historical Sketch;* Tennessee, *Report of the Tennessee Industrial School,* 1887–1888, 22; Alabama, *Report of the Institution for the Deaf and Dumb and Blind,* 1890–1892, 22.

cemetery associations, and such institutions as the James Hale Infirmary, the Carrie Steele Orphan Home, and the Friends Asylum for Colored Orphans.

The Reality versus the Rhetoric of Separate but Equal

In seeking separate institutions, Negroes and their white allies evidently believed that such facilities could be made equal. The white Democrats who overthrew the Radicals proclaimed that the blacks would receive equal treatment. But how did the record of segregation square with the rhetoric of equality?

Occasionally whites and blacks did receive comparable treatment. The ideal came closest to realization in the institutions for the care of the blind, deaf, and dumb. Speaking before a Senate committee in 1880, James O'Hara, a black future congressman from North Carolina, compared the care given to both races in his state's institution: "They have the same kind of provisions, meats, vegetables, and fruits; the same bedding and furniture, carpets, pianos, etc., all the same in both institutions, without distinction at all."[54] In 1882 the trustees of the Georgia Asylum for Deaf and Dumb, in an evaluation of the program for Negroes, noted, "The quality of food and clothing furnished is the same as that supplied to the whites." As late as 1887, per capita expenditure for provisions at the Academy for the Blind was only five dollars greater for the white department.[55] City facilities sometimes also accorded Negroes a fair share of their services. Figures available for the Richmond municipal hospital, in-relief at the almshouse, and out-relief distribution indicate a rough parity in the numbers of both races being cared for.[56]

54. U.S. Congress, Senate, *Report of the Select Committee of the United States Senate to Investigate the Causes for the Removal of the Negroes from the Southern States to the Northern States*, 46th Congress, 2d session, 1880, part 1, 55. For the years 1872–1873, $5,000 was spent for repairs on each of the two buildings; during 1874–1876, $3,500 more was spent on the Negro than on the white building. Well into the 1890s whatever differences there were in the improvements favored the Negro department. See North Carolina, *A Statistical Record of the Progress of Public Education in North Carolina*, 1870–1906, comp. Charles L. Coon (Raleigh: Office of the State Superintendent of Public Instruction, 1907), 19–21.

55. Georgia, *Report of the Institution for the Deaf and Dumb*, 1881–1882, 7; Georgia, *Report of the Academy for the Blind*, 1886–1887, 8. The amounts were forty-two dollars for whites and thirty-seven dollars for blacks.

56. The Department of Out Door Poor Relief, for the year ending January 31, 1873, distributed an average of 173 bushels of meal per week to whites and 180 to blacks (Richmond, *Annual Reports*, 1872–1873, 322). During the following year the averages

Nevertheless, the principle of separate but equal flourished more in theory than in practice. Blacks still were not permitted in certain hospitals, state asylums, and orphanages. Even where public officials provided for their care, however, the belief in Negro inferiority that had once underwritten the policy of exclusion now led to an inequitable administration of separate facilities.

Discrimination was evident in admission policies. Destitute Negroes were more likely to receive hospital care than their more well-off brothers. The latter, unlike comparable whites, were not provided with facilities they could afford. Selectivity in the care of the insane posed a similar problem. In Alabama and Tennessee, for example, white patients at the state asylum were of three types—paying, indigent, and criminal—whereas only the latter two classes of blacks were present.[57] Despite a long list of Negroes waiting to get into the state asylums, local authorities paid more attention to the smaller number of needy whites. The Davidson County Poorhouse and Asylum for many years admitted only white insane. By the early 1880s it had begun to admit black lunatics, but in 1884, a typical year, there were sixty white inmates and only twenty-five black.[58] As elsewhere, the majority of black insane were confined in jails or left to wander the streets.

In other institutions as well, the number of white inmates grew while the Negro waiting lists mounted. The Tennessee Industrial School in 1890 had 25 black students and 165 whites; in the same year the Georgia Institution for the Deaf and Dumb had 26 Negroes and 75 whites; and in 1891 the Tennessee Hospital for the Insane had 291 whites and 95 Negroes.[59] Blacks had the same problem getting poor relief commensurate with their needs. In 1884 the Davidson County Asylum had 174 white inmates and 101 Negroes. Atlanta officials during 1887 gave out-relief to 310 whites and only 177 blacks. And although

---

were 333 and 297, respectively (Richmond, *Annual Reports,* 1873–1874, 38). For the year ending January 31, 1875, the figures were 431 for whites and 462 for blacks (Richmond, *Annual Reports,* 1874–1875, 40). From December, 1871, to January 31, 1873, 11 whites and 8 blacks were treated at the city hospital (Richmond, *Annual Reports,* 1872–1873, 325). The following year there were 10 whites and 26 blacks (Richmond, *Annual Reports,* 1873–1874, 44). During the year ending January 31, 1873, 226 whites and 204 blacks had been admitted to the almshouse (Richmond, *Annual Reports,* 1872–1873, 319).

57. See, for example, Alabama, *Report of the Alabama Insane Hospital,* 1888–1890, 11; Tennessee, *Report of the Central Tennessee Hospital for the Insane for the Two Years Ending January 1, 1875* (Nashville, 1875), 19.

58. Report of the Commissioners of the Asylum to the County Court, reprinted in *Nashville Banner,* July 7, 1884.

59. Tennessee, *Report of the Tennessee Industrial School,* 1889–1890, 26; Georgia, *Report of the Institution for the Deaf and Dumb,* 1890, 20–21; Tennessee, *Report of the Central Tennessee Hospital for the Insane,* 1889–1891, 14.

Richmond authorities dispensed equal amounts of out-relief to members of both races, many more black than white applicants were denied aid.[60]

Breakdowns of expenditures by race were seldom offered in reports but, when given, generally revealed inequality. In Virginia per capita expenditure at the all-Negro Central Lunatic Asylum in the mid-1870s was about $177 annually, as compared to $191 at the all-white Eastern Lunatic Asylum. By 1889 Central was receiving $127.91 per inmate, while appropriations at the three white asylums ranged from $151.20 to $236.04.[61] The North Carolina Asylum for the Negro Insane erected in 1881 cost $152,000; the older one for whites in Raleigh cost $350,000; and the new one in Morgantown, though still incomplete in 1884, was already in excess of the latter figure.[62]

Locally, the picture was the same. Although the Friends Asylum for Colored Orphans in Richmond received as much public money as the largest recipient among the white asylums, the total for the four white institutions was far larger.[63] During one month in 1869, Richmond officials on the basis of per capita expenditure spent more than three times as much on the white almshouse as they did on the one for Negroes. In 1885 white patients sent by the Atlanta City Council to Ivy Street Hospital cost the city seventy-five cents per day, while Negro patients cost less than twenty-five cents. And when Fulton County officials finally erected new poorhouse facilities in 1889, they expended $8,000 for a one-story brick building for whites, and $1,500 for six double wooden cottages for blacks on the other side of the woods.[64]

Insufficient funds meant poorer facilities. In many instances white accommoda-

60. Report of the Commissioners of the Asylum to the County Court, reprinted in *Nashville Banner,* July 7, 1884; Atlanta, *Annual Reports,* 1887, 35; Richmond, *Annual Reports,* 1876–1877, 45–47. By the mid-1880s a pattern emerged in which three to four times as many blacks as whites were annually being refused aid. The high rejection rate reflected the widespread belief that charity only encouraged idleness among blacks and led to their concentration in cities. See, for example, letter to the editor, *Richmond Dispatch,* October 24, 1874; interview with city warden of the poor, *Atlanta Constitution,* December 7, 1890; *Nashville Banner,* January 25, 1882; January 14, 1884.

61. Virginia, *Report of the Central Lunatic Asylum,* 1875–1876, 8; Virginia, *Annual Report of the Virginia Eastern Lunatic Asylum for the Year Ending September 30, 1877* (Richmond, 1877), 17; Virginia, *Report of the Central Lunatic Asylum,* 1888–1889, 38; Virginia, *Annual Report of the Board of Directors and of the Superintendent of the Western Lunatic Asylum of Virginia for the Fiscal Year 1889–1890* (Richmond, 1890), 18. A year later the figure for the Negro asylum had dropped to $115.65. Virginia, *Report of the Central Lunatic Asylum,* 1889–1890, 36.

62. Polk, *Handbook of North Carolina,* 181–82; *Visitors Guide to the North Carolina Exposition of 1884,* 15.

63. In 1876, for example, Friends and St. Joseph each got $1000; Richmond Male Asylum and the Female Humane Association, $750; and St. Paul's Church Home, $500. Richmond, *Annual Reports,* 1875–1876, 175.

64. Richmond City Council Minutes, January 10, 1870; Atlanta, *Annual Reports,* 1885, 54; *Atlanta Constitution,* April 12, 1889.

tions were also in unsatisfactory condition, but when money became available, they were the first to be rehabilitated or replaced. Many of the Jim Crow quarters were unsuited for their purposes, conveniences were lacking, and overcrowding was a constant problem. "Our colored department is in need of shop rooms and some repairs and extensions," complained the head of the Tennessee Industrial School in 1888. "The building now occupied by them [the Negroes] is too small, and we would respectfully recommend that in the early future a new and more substantial structure be erected." Two years later the director of the School for the Blind echoed: "The houses occupied by the colored pupils are ill adapted for a school—they were originally residences and are situated on a busy thorough-fare."[65]

The Negro insane were especially ill housed. In Georgia the Negroes were kept in a building described as "insecure and not adapted for the purposes for which . . . it is now used." The superintendent of the Alabama asylum reported in 1884 that while there was enough room for the white insane "for several years to come," the blacks were so crowded that a second story was immediately needed for each of their two small buildings. No action was taken by the legislature, however, and in 1885 he carried his fight in desperation to the *Atlanta Constitution.* He told one of its reporters that the newspaper could do much good by speaking "of one of the most important needs of the state . . . a comfortable building for the negro insane." Continuing his appeal, he noted: "None of the buildings erected for the insane of the state has been done for the negroes. We have saved enough from the current expenses to build two small buildings in which have been placed 90 negroes. We have brick and material accumulated at low prices for which to erect a new building when the state authorizes it. . . . It will only require a small appropriation, say of $30,000 to erect the suitable buildings." It was not until 1888, however, that a new structure for two hundred patients opened. In the interim two brick buildings had been erected to provide accommodations for an additional three hundred whites.[66]

The pattern found on the state level was duplicated in the cities: inferior accommodations, advocacy by certain whites of needed improvements, and a long lag in implementation. Conditions at the Richmond almshouse were typi-

65. Tennessee, *Report of the Tennessee Industrial School,* 1887–1888, 18; Tennessee, *Biennial Report of the Tennessee School for the Blind,* 1889–1891, 5.

66. Georgia, *Report of the Trustees, Superintendent, Resident Physician and Treasurer of the Lunatic Asylum of the State of Georgia from January 1, 1870 to October 1, 1871* (Atlanta, 1871), 5; Alabama, *Report of the Alabama Insane Hospital,* 1882–1884, 16; *Atlanta Constitution,* December 29, 1885; Alabama, *Report of the Alabama Insane Hospital,* 1886–1888, 23–24. By 1890 there were 913 white and 331 Negro patients. Alabama, *Report of the Alabama Insane Hospital,* 1888–1890, 11.

cal. The white almshouse was a three-story brick building; the Negro, though normally containing more inmates, was a smaller wooden structure. In 1876 the mayor drew attention to one of the results of this discrimination, the much higher mortality rate among Negro inmates. Although there were 35 more whites than blacks, 125 blacks had died but only 34 whites. In 1883 the superintendent of public charities pointed to the need for new quarters: "The building now used for the inmates . . . is totally unfit for the purpose, not having been erected for an almshouse and only selected for temporary use for the said institution, is therefore wanting in nearly every appliance and convenience; and I do not believe that it can be made suitable." In comparison to the steam-heated white almshouse, the Negro department was warmed by stoves; sexes were separated at the former, but not at the latter. To these and other inadequacies was added the deplorable condition of the Negro hospital, a facility that, though located in the almshouse, also served as the only hospital available to Negroes of all classes. "The general condition of the hospital is satisfactory, with the exception of the colored department which is defective," wrote the almshouse physician in 1887. "It is hoped that at an early day, we may be provided with one for the colored as well arranged as that for the white department." Despite such pleas, a new almshouse for the Negro paupers was not built until 1908.[67]

Blacks in Atlanta were no more fortunate. Not only did Negro paupers lack adequate poorhouse facilities, but they and their better-off brothers lacked equal hospital accommodations. In 1896 at a convention that met at Atlanta University to consider the problem of mortality among the Negroes in the cities, it was pointed out that in Atlanta,

> there is not a decent hospital where colored people can be cared for. At the Grady Hospital, which takes about $20,000 of the city's money annually to run it, is a small wooden annex down by the kitchen, in which may be crowded fifty or sixty beds, and that is all the hospital advantages 40,000 colored citizens have. But, on the other hand, our white friends, with a population of about 70,000, have all the wards and private rooms in the

67. Richmond, *Annual Reports,* 1875–1876, xiii; 1882–1883, 6–7. At the Montgomery City Hospital whites were also separated according to sex, but blacks were not. *Montgomery Alabama State Journal,* July 26, 1873; almshouse physician quoted in Richmond, *Annual Reports,* 1887, 6; Virginia, *Report of the State Board of Charities and Corrections,* 1908–1909, 107. Nashville Negroes were somewhat more fortunate. After a committee investigating the county poorhouse reported in 1874 that the black facilities were "inferior in every respect to the white quarters," authorities promptly prepared to build a new institution (*Nashville Republican Banner,* January 24, 1874). It was finally opened two years later, but even these new quarters were inferior to those of the whites.

entire brick building at this hospital, together with a very fine hospital here, known as St. Joseph's Infirmary.[68]

Equal treatment was missing in death as in life. Negro sections of municipal graveyards provided no support for claims by city boosters of the parklike beauty of their cemeteries. To an *Atlanta Constitution* reporter in 1884, the little hillside in Oakland Cemetery where the blacks were buried looked less like a burial ground than a newly planted potato patch, "a dreary spot, devoid of shrubbery" with graves so close together "that it is about impossible to step among them without stepping on" one. The area was littered with whiskey bottles, toys, iron bureaus, and other uncollected debris. In 1877 the superintendent of Richmond's Shockoe Cemetery complained about the portion allotted to the Negro poor. It was ill-fitted for a burial ground, he charged, being an unenclosed field, and "its now overcrowded condition renders it impossible to make any interment therein without disturbing some previous burial, thus making it both repulsive and inhumane."[69]

Conclusions

By 1890 white southerners had been forced to accept some responsibility for providing public and private welfare care for blacks. There were still many institutions that refused to accept Negroes, of course. Negro blind, deaf, and dumb were excluded from the Alabama and Virginia asylums; numerous local hospitals would accept white charity patients but not middle-class blacks; the black community was left to contend with the problem of its dependent children. New institutions like Richmond's Virginia Home for Incurables, opened in 1894, were still being founded "for whites only."[70] But Virginia and Alabama did finally provide for Negro deaf, dumb, and blind; hospitals like Richmond's Retreat for the Sick, opened only to whites since its founding in 1877, did eventu-

68. Quoted in Gibson and Crogman, *Progress of a Race,* 314. Blacks had long realized the need for adequate hospital facilities, but at least two efforts by Negroes to start a hospital failed. See *Atlanta Constitution,* December 23, 1887; May 21, 1890.

69. *Atlanta Constitution,* December 24, 1884; Richmond, *Annual Reports,* 1876–1877, 2–3.

70. [Charles Poindexter, ed.], *Richmond, Virginia: Her Advantages and Attractions* (Richmond: J. L. Hill, 1895), 122.

ally provide separate wards for black patients;[71] and Virginia in 1900 did accept support of the previously privately run Virginia Manual Labor School of the Negro Reformatory, eleven years after the state had opened the Laurel Industrial School for white boys.[72]

These facilities founded after 1890 were segregated, but such action marked a continuation of past practices. For in the years after the Civil War segregation became the norm in southern welfare policy. What it replaced was not integration, which rarely existed, but a policy of exclusion that had been formulated in antebellum times and was only reluctantly modified by the first postwar Conservative governments.

Contrary to current assumptions, therefore, segregation frequently signified an improvement in the position of the Negroes. It was neither a tactic invented by the Redeemers to punish blacks nor the result of a bargain between Democrats and Populists in the 1890s to forestall Negroes from becoming a pivotal force in southern politics.[73] It was the northerners, as represented by the U.S. Army, Freedmen's Bureau, and Radical politicians, who together with their southern allies inaugurated segregated welfare care. Negroes themselves favored this policy over exclusion and did not challenge it, as they did occasionally protest segregation in public accommodations, where from 1875 to 1883 at least they had the law on their side. As a result, they convinced any doubting whites that they too wanted segregation. Viewed in this light, the legacy of Reconstruction in health and welfare services, as in so many other facets of southern life, was the shift from exclusion to the principle of separate but equal treatment. The Redeemers, in coming to power, simply continued and extended a policy already in force. Nevertheless, given the belief in Negro inferiority and the lack of resources sufficient to operate an equitable set of dual institutions, it was inevitable that the practice would be one of separate and unequal.

71. The first mention of "two wards upon the grounds comfortably fitted up for such colored patients, male and female, as the Managers may consider it proper to receive" occurs in *Sixteenth Annual Report of the Retreat for the Sick, 1892–1893* (Richmond: Ezekiel and Bass, 1893). A black annex "furnished exactly like the white wards" was added to the Old Dominion Hospital around 1895 ([Poindexter], *Richmond, Virginia,* 124). The Richmond Eye, Ear and Throat Institute had separate quarters for blacks by 1885, as did the Medical College Free Dispensary by 1882. See *Richmond Dispatch,* March 22, 1885; *Richmond Virginia Star,* December 9, 1882.

72. Virginia, *Biennial Report of the Prison Association of Virginia for Years 1896–1897* (Richmond, 1897), 8; Virginia, *Report of the State Board of Charities and Corrections,* 1908–1909, 161.

73. See, for example, Woodward, *Strange Career,* 67–109 and passim.

Half a Loaf

The Shift from White to Black Teachers in the Negro Schools of the Urban South, 1865–1890

By 1890 four major decisions had been made concerning public education in the South. The first involved the very acceptance of state-supported public school systems. The second and third meant that blacks as well as whites were to be among the students, although the two races would be strictly segregated. And the final decision, well on its way to widespread implementation, was that blacks rather than whites would teach the black pupils.

It is common knowledge that by the end of the century education in the South was less advanced than in the rest of the country and that for blacks it was both separate and unequal.[1] Less attention, however, has been paid to the change from white to black teachers in the Negro public schools.[2] It is worth noting that

I wish to acknowledge assistance and criticism from Arthur Mann and financial aid from the University of Chicago Center for Urban Sudies.

1. See, for example, Louis R. Harlan, *Separate and Unequal: Public School Campaigns and Racism in the Southern Seaboard States, 1901–1915* (Chapel Hill: University of North Carolina Press, 1958) and Henry A. Bullock, *A History of Negro Education in the South from 1619 to the Present* (New York: Praeger Publishers, 1970).

2. The demand for black teachers in the colleges run by the northern societies, however, is ably covered in James M. McPherson, "White Liberals and Black Power in Negro Education, 1865–1915," *American Historical Review* 75 (June 1970): 1357–86. Only a few of the numerous state studies of Negroes during and after Reconstruction mention, and then only briefly, the interest of blacks in replacing white teachers. See, for example, George B. Tindall, *South Carolina Negroes, 1877–1900* (Columbia: University of South Carolina Press, 1952; reprint ed., Baton Rouge: Louisiana State University Press, 1966), 220–21; Charles E. Wynes, *Race Relations in Virginia, 1870–1902* (Charlottesville: University Press of Virginia, 1961), 126–28; Frenise A. Logan, *The Negro in North Carolina, 1876–1894* (Chapel Hill: University of North Carolina Press,

there was a shift to black faculties during the period 1865 to 1890 and that it was the blacks themselves who forced this change.

There was a pronounced succession in the kinds of people who taught blacks in the quarter century following the Civil War. First, there were the idealistic Yankee schoolmarms who came south as representatives of the northern missionary societies; they were replaced by southern whites unable to win positions in the white schools; they in turn were succeeded by black graduates of local colleges and normal schools. This progression and the reasons for it reveal much about the nature of Negro education in the urban South and the expectations and responses of both blacks and whites. Though occurring throughout the South this shift can be traced in the following cities: Atlanta, Georgia; Raleigh, North Carolina; Nashville, Tennessee; Montgomery, Alabama; and Richmond, Virginia. Educational developments in these cities mirrored those taking place elsewhere in the region, and together they provide an urban cross section in terms of the level of educational provisions for blacks, and in their size, location, and political background.

Geographically, the cities encompass the Atlantic seaboard, Deep South, and the border states. In attitudes toward blacks, the states they represent range from Virginia and North Carolina, commonly identified as moderate, to Alabama, usually considered more restrictive. Like the states, the cities were affected differently by so-called Radical Reconstruction. The Radicals never controlled Atlanta and enjoyed only a short hegemony in Nashville, Richmond, and Montgomery. In Raleigh, however, the city administration was in Radical hands from 1868 to 1875, one of the few instances in which a southern city remained under the Radicals for more than two municipal elections. Negroes were still serving on city councils in Richmond and Raleigh in 1890, while such black representation ended in Atlanta in 1871, Montgomery in 1875, and Nashville in 1885. In the matter of size, Montgomery and Raleigh were among the smaller southern cities, having populations of 21,883 and 12,678 respectively in 1890. Richmond and Nashville had already been relatively large cities before the war, and by 1890 the former had a population of 81,388 and the latter 76,168. Atlanta, with fewer than 10,000 in 1860, grew to 65,533 by 1890. All were distribution centers and, as befitted their roles as capitals, administrative centers as well; Richmond and, to a lesser extent, Nashville, also had manufacturing bases. The percentage of Negro population in 1890 for Atlanta was 43; Nashville, 39 percent; Raleigh, 50.1 percent; Richmond, 40 percent; and Montgomery, 59 percent. The provisions made for the education of blacks in Richmond were among the best in the South; those in Montgomery, among the worst.[3]

1964), 146; Lawrence D. Rice, *The Negro in Texas, 1874–1900* (Baton Rouge: Louisiana State University Press, 1971), 221–22.

3. U.S. Bureau of the Census, *Compendium of the Eleventh Census: 1890,* vol. 1,

As towns fell under the control of Union forces, representatives from northern philanthropic societies arrived to bring education and religion to the enthusiastic freedmen. Aided by the Freedmen's Bureau, these societies, particularly the American Missionary Association (AMA) and the American Freedmen's and Union Commission, played the leading role in educating blacks during the first five years after the war. It was a formidable task made even more difficult by the local hostility to their efforts.[4] To some extent the freedmen had prepared the way by establishing schools without outside support. The first three teachers sent to Raleigh by the AMA in July 1865 assumed control of a school for black children founded and taught by blacks at an African Methodist Episcopal church. The AMA teachers who arrived in Atlanta the same year found a small school organized by two ex-slaves in the basement of an old church. The blacks, however, had limited financial resources and soon came to rely primarily on the aid of their northern friends.[5]

With the Freedmen's Bureau supplying the buildings and the missionary societies paying the teachers, the number of blacks enrolled in classes mushroomed. Shortly after Nashville was occupied by Federal forces in 1863 there were 1,200 pupils in the freedmen schools. By 1867 schools run by four societies served approximately 3,000 students. In Montgomery the AMA's Swayne School had begun in October 1866 with an enrollment of 210; after eight months the number had grown to 700. By 1868, 700 of the 800 or 900 Negro children of school age in Raleigh were enrolled in the schools of the AMA and the American Baptist Home Mission Society.[6] Each city had lists of youngsters eager to attend but

---

Population (Washington, D.C.: Government Printing Office, 1892), 434, 448, 450, 667, 673, 719, 739, 743.

4. For local opposition to the education of blacks by northerners see *Richmond Dispatch,* May 8, 1866; *Atlanta Constitution,* May 1, 1869; see also the following letters from society officials and teachers: E. B. Adams, agent of the American Freedmen's and Union Commission for Georgia, *American Freedman* 1 (June 1866): 44; R. M. Manly, superintendent of freedmen's schools in Richmond, *American Freedman* 1 (August 1866): 75–76; Reverend W[illiam] G. Hawkins, Raleigh teacher, *National Freedman* 1 (September 15, 1865): 276; Anna F. Clarke, Raleigh teacher, *Freedmen's Record* 1 (November 1865): 181.

5. Letter of the Reverend W. G. Hawkins, *National Freedman* 1 (September 15, 1865): 276; Franklin M. Garrett, *Atlanta and Environs: A Chronicle of Its People and Events,* 3 vols. (New York: Lewis Historical Publishing Company, 1954), 1:741–42. Northerners paid the board of AMA teachers in Atlanta and contributed money to the fuel fund of the New England branch of the American Freedmen's and Union Commission school in Richmond. Appeal of the Reverend Mr. Ware, *American Missionary* 11 (October 1867): 224; letter of Horace W. Hovey, December 5, 1866, *Freedmen's Record* 3 (January 1867): 21. In all the schools students paid as much of the tuition as they could afford.

6. Reverend David Chapman, army chaplain stationed in Nashville, to George Whipple, November 18, 1863, American Missionary Association Archives, Amistad Research

denied admission because of lack of room or an insufficient number of in-structors.

Teachers in these schools were mostly white women from the Midwest and New England. Although they had a variety of reasons for coming, it seems clear that hostility toward the South or crass political motives carried little weight. The majority were imbued with strong antislavery beliefs, humanitarian impulses, and burning religious fervor.[7] Some, like a teacher at Atlanta's Storrs School, were perhaps atoning for past sins. "I am ashamed every day to think I was ever guilty of being a democrat," she wrote in 1870, "and [I] ask God [to] forgive me for ever having sympathy, in the least, with them who would keep these people in slavery." As for the typical reason, Raleigh's Lucy Dow expressed it best: "Our great hope lies in the children. They must be taught habits of industry, economy, personal and household cleanliness and much more besides book learning."[8]

Yet book learning was important, and the teachers hoped their pupils would go on to instruct others of their own race, especially in the countryside where the northern societies had not penetrated. An AMA teacher in Atlanta proudly told of a student who roomed in the city and walked six miles every day to teach in a rural school. In Raleigh the Washington and Lincoln schools of the AMA had produced five teachers by 1867. By 1871 fourteen of the students who had been educated by the New England branch of the Freedmen's and Union Commission in Richmond were teaching in the vicinity. The pioneer among the society's Negro teachers had been Peter H. Woolfolk, one of the handful of black instruc-tors employed by the northern societies. Given his own class after graduating from the society's normal school in 1868, he was frequently visited by officials who remarked favorably on his ability.[9]

Center, Dillard University, New Orleans; *Nashville Daily Press and Times,* June 14, 1867; letter of W[illiam] T. Richardson, superintendent of schools for the Cleveland Aid Com-mission, July 1, 1867, *American Missionary* 11 (September 1867): 205–6; Charles L. Coon, "The Beginnings of the North Carolina City Schools, 1867–1887," *South Atlantic Quar-terly* 12 (July 1913): 237.

7. This conclusion is drawn from an examination of letters in the American Missionary Association Archives and those reprinted in the *American Missionary,* the *Freedmen's Record,* the *American Freedman,* and the *National Freedman.* For a specific denial that the teachers came south "to fill the minds of our pupils with hatred," see letter of "MBS" [Mary B. Slade], *Freedmen's Record* 7 (January 1871): 98. Only two teachers played a prominent role in the political life of any of the five cities, John Silsby in Montgomery and R. M. Manly in Richmond. For a different view of the primary motivation of the teachers see Henry L. Swint, *The Northern Teacher in the South, 1862–1870* (Nashville: Vanderbilt University Press, 1941), 140–42 and passim.

8. First quote, unsigned letter, *American Missionary* 14 (January 1870): 7; second quote, letter, November 29, 1866, *Freedmen's Record* 3 (January 1867): 5.

9. Letter of "A Teacher," September 23, 1870, *American Missionary* 14 (November

Despite their normal-school divisions, however, the primary schools could not meet the pressing need for able black teachers. The societies realized this and soon founded more advanced schools. Though called colleges or universities, they were at first little more than high schools. Prior to 1870 most of them had primary and secondary departments, which permitted poorly prepared students to work their way up to collegiate or normal-school divisions. Some institutions were founded in rural areas or in smaller towns, but as with the primary schools, the benevolent societies concentrated most of their efforts in the larger cities, where the impact could be greater and more visible. The result was so successful that no city tour for important visitors was complete without an inspection of "the colored college." The two most influential schools were Fisk University in Nashville and Atlanta University. Others, however, included Central Tennessee College and the Nashville Normal and Theological Institute (later Roger Williams University) in the Tennessee capital; Shaw Collegiate Institute and St. Augustine's Normal School and Collegiate Institute in Raleigh; Clark University, Spelman College, and Atlanta Baptist Seminary (later Morehouse College) in the Georgia capital; and Richmond Institute.

By 1870 the missionary societies were thus shifting their priorities with the intention of improving their advanced schools and of turning over primary education to southern officials. From the beginning the societies had expected public authorities to assume responsibility in this area,[10] but the whites during Presidential Reconstruction had dragged their feet. Although prompted largely by anti-Negro attitudes, the delay was due partly to the disrepute in which public education had long been held in the South. Alone among the five cities providing the core of this study, Nashville had operated a public school system before the war, but its pupils were considered charity cases. On the state level only North Carolina had made any significant antebellum progress in the field of public education. Whatever had been done, of course, had been strictly for whites. After the war Negroes complicated the problem.

The initial southern response was to ignore the blacks and to move haltingly toward the education of white children at public expense. Under the administration of Governor Jonathan Worth, North Carolina initially abolished its state-

---

1870): 247; John W. Alvord, *Semi-annual Report on Schools and Finances of Freedmen* (Washington, D.C.: Government Printing Office, 1868), 17; letter of B[essie] L. Canedy, March 4, 1871, *Freedmen's Record* 7 (April 1871): 111; letter of "EDC," October 17, 1868, *Freedmen's Record* 4 (November 1868): 175–76. Woolfolk became a prominent figure in Negro political and economic life in the city.

10. See, for example, Reverend D[avid] Burt, superintendent of education of the Freedmen's Bureau in Tennessee, to the editor, *Nashville Union and Dispatch,* October 29, 1867.

supported public schools to prevent the enrollment of blacks.[11] Yet this policy could not be followed long in the face of the northern societies' success in educating Negroes. "The effort to educate the colored people of the State has given an impulse to education among all classes," wrote a Freedmen's Bureau official from Alabama in 1867. Similarly, a growing protest in North Carolina that Negroes had adequate schools while the whites allegedly had none forced the Conservatives in February 1867 to establish a system of public education for white children between the ages of six and twenty-one. No provision was made for blacks, thus continuing the antebellum policy of exclusion.[12]

Georgia had previously enacted legislation in December 1866 approving education for "any free white inhabitant" between six and twenty-one and any "disabled or indigent" soldier under thirty. The act merely permitted the education; it did nothing to make it possible. Frequent complaints by Atlantans that local whites went without schooling while blacks received excellent education from northern Invaders led the committee on public schools of the city council in November 1869 to urge the opening of public schools for whites. They admitted it would be wise for the board of education to provide for blacks as well, but provisions were already being made for them "through the aid of the Freedmen's Bureau and voluntary contributions from various sources." Clearly then, "the wants of the white children are more immediate and pressing." As late as February 1872 all twelve hundred pupils in Atlanta's public schools were white.[13]

11. North Carolina, *Public Laws,* 1866 (Raleigh, 1866), 87. For Worth's belief that "the Com. School system had better be discouraged, for a time, and thus avoid the question as to educating negroes," see letter to William A. Graham, January 12, 1866, in *The Correspondence of Jonathan Worth,* vol. 1, ed. J. G. de Roulhac Hamilton (Raleigh: Edwards and Broughton and Co., 1909), 467.

12. Excerpt from the report of the Freedmen's Bureau's superintendent of schools, *American Missionary* 11 (November 1867): 248; North Carolina, *Public Laws,* 1866–1867, 17–20. Among those objecting to the advantage that black children seemed to have over whites was the *Raleigh Daily Sentinel.* The October 29, 1866, issue, for example, estimated there were at least twice as many black children as white youngsters attending school in the city.

13. Georgia, *Acts,* 1866 (Macon, 1867), 59; Atlanta, *Report of the Committee on Public Schools to the City Council of Atlanta, Georgia* (Atlanta, 1869), 11. For complaints of the disregard for white education while blacks were in school see W. I. Mansfield to the editor, *Atlanta Constitution,* April 15, 1869; Elizabeth Sterchi to Bishop George F. Bannson, January 14, 1869, in "The Elizabeth Sterchi Letters," ed. Adelaide Fries, *Atlanta Historical Bulletin* 5 (July 1940): 202. For the reaction of teachers of white children to the advantage blacks had over whites in 1867 in a state not covered in this study see Joe M. Richardson, *The Negro in the Reconstruction of Florida, 1865–1877* (Tallahassee: Florida State University Press, 1965), 108. Even by the end of the period Georgians believed that Negroes had an unfair advantage over whites because of the support of northern philanthropists. See, for example, remarks of the chancellor of the University of Georgia, *Atlanta Constitution,* July 26, 1889; letter to the editor, *Atlanta Constitution,* August 25, 1889. For

Unlike other states, Tennessee early went on record in favor of schools for children of both races. An 1866 statute authorized public schools for all youngsters but required that the races be taught separately.[14] As elsewhere, passage of the law did not mean that the schools were built or that provisions were necessarily made for both races. Such action, although limited, was taken on the state level because at the time Tennessee was the only southern state in which the Republicans were in control of the government. Tennessee Republicans thus expressed the policy later to be followed by members of the party throughout the South in education as well as in many other spheres of life affecting blacks. The earlier policy of exclusion would be replaced, but by segregation rather than integration.

Nashville, however, was still in the hands of Conservatives who, while providing schools for the whites, used the existence of freedmen schools to defend the lack of facilities for Negroes. By the summer of 1867 the city fathers were ready to change their policy. Several factors, mostly negative, influenced this decision: the dislike of having blacks educated by northerners, the fear that impending Republican control of the council would result in integrated schools, and the possibility of noneducated Negroes becoming "thieves and scoundrels."[15] Soon afterward the board of education informed the assistant commissioner of the Freedmen's Bureau of the city's decision to educate blacks. Though the schools would be separate, selection and certification of teachers, grading of pupils, and the rest of the organization would be "in all the respects the same" as the whites received. In a sideswipe at the societies, the board also stated, "Nothing of a sectional, political or partisan nature in social or religious matters shall be included in these schools."[16] The authorities relied on the federal government and the benevolent societies to house these students. The two original schools, Bell View and Lincoln, which opened in September 1867, and the two that opened the following year, McKee and the Gun Factory Building, were either rented or purchased from the "northern invaders" and all had previously been used for freedmen schools.[17]

Elsewhere Negro public education was absent until Congressional Reconstruction brought Radical governments to power. In their Reconstruction consti-

---

white students in Atlanta public schools in 1872, see Atlanta Board of Education Minutes, January 30, 1872, Atlanta Board of Education Building, Atlanta.

14. Tennessee, *Laws,* 1865–1866 (Nashville, 1866), 65.

15. The debate over the issue is reported in full in the *Nashville Daily Press and Times,* June 14, 1867.

16. I. M. Hoyt, secretary of the board, to Major General William Passmore Carlin, July 27, 1867, Nashville Board of Education Minutes, July 27, 1867, box 25, James Emerick Nagy Nashville Public School Collection, Tennessee State Library and Archives, Nashville. These minutes will hereinafter be cited as such along with the appropriate box number.

17. Nashville Board of Education Minutes, September 4, 1867; April 1, 1868, box 25.

tutions Alabama, Virginia, North Carolina, and Georgia acknowledged for the first time the state's obligation to educate blacks. Although Negroes were to be educated at public expense, the Radicals, if indeed they desired otherwise, were careful not to go entirely against the grain of southern opinion. Negro education was to be equal to white education, but it was to be separate. Neither segregation nor integration was specified in the constitutions, but the position on this question was clarified in the laws passed by Radical-controlled legislatures. In North Carolina, for example, former provisional governor William Woods Holden sought to allay fears that the state constitutional convention had provided for the teaching of white children by black teachers. He voiced a view common among southern Radicals: "There will be schools for white children to themselves, with white teachers; and schools for the colored children to themselves, with colored teachers . . . but there will be no difference as to rights and responsibility. . . . If the white child gets a dollar for its education the colored child will get a dollar also. If the white child is provided with a good teacher, so will the colored child."[18]

On its concluding day members of the convention sought further to ease troubled minds. Part of the resolution proposed by a Negro member and unanimously adopted stated, "It is the sense of this Convention that . . . the interests and happiness of the two races would be best promoted by the establishment of separate schools." The school law drafted in 1869 clearly enunciated the principle of separate but equal education. Similarly, Georgia guaranteed separate schools in 1870, but its statute ordered that local officials "shall provide the same facilities for each [race], both as regards school houses and fixtures, and the attainments and abilities of teachers, length of term-time, etc." In Alabama, however, mixed schools with "the unanimous consent of the parents and guardians of such children" (an unlikely possibility) were permitted by an 1868 law.[19]

Individual cities proceeded at different speeds to make public education a reality. Everywhere, however, the Radicals prodded others to action, and the former missionary schools served as the nuclei for the new black systems. Richmond public schools actually antedated the beginning of the state system. Although the state constitution had made no mention of racial segregation in public education, the Radical-controlled Richmond City Council clearly spelled out its policy in an 1869 ordinance: ". . . the public schools herein provided for shall be kept separate and apart for white and colored children." In order to start

18. *Raleigh Daily Standard,* March 7, 1868.
19. Marcus C. S. Noble, *A History of the Public Schools of North Carolina* (Chapel Hill: University of North Carolina Press, 1930), 296, 314–15; Georgia, *Acts and Resolutions, 1870* (Atlanta, 1870), 57; Alabama, *Acts,* 1868 (Montgomery, 1868), 148.

the Negro schools the board of education relied heavily upon the Freedmen's Bureau and the northern societies. During the first year of operation the bureau contributed most of the buildings rent free and supplied without charge two-thirds of the furniture while the northern societies provided the teachers and paid half their salaries. The board of education appropriated fifteen thousand dollars each for the white and black schools. At the end of the year the bureau ceased paying the rent and sold all its property, much of it to the city.[20] Other freedmen schools such as the Bakery and Navy Hill properties were sold by the northern societies. Still others, like the Richmond Colored High and Normal School, were not turned over completely until 1876.[21]

It was not until 1877 that the Raleigh school system officially began. Prior to that date in the case of the Johnson School and until 1875 for the Washington School the city's two main Negro educational facilities received most of their funds from the AMA and remained under its direction. Once the system began the whites were taught in the old public schoolhouses while the Negroes continued to meet in churches and the buildings erected by the Freedmen's Bureau and benevolent societies.[22]

Frequently the system of dual support for the Negro public schools persisted several years after the initiation of the citywide school system. A source of continual dispute, however, was the composition of the teaching staffs. As late as 1882 the AMA was contributing almost three thousand dollars to the Montgomery Negro schools.[23] Until 1884 the society made available the Swayne School building and nominated the teachers, who were paid by the board of city school commissioners. Disagreements over hiring practices resulted in the school's

20. Richmond, *The Charter and Ordinances . . . with Amendments to the Charter* (Richmond, 1869), 251; Richmond Board of Education Minutes, September 30, 1869, Richmond Board of Education Building, Richmond; Richmond, Superintendent of the Public Schools, *Third Annual Report . . . for the Scholastic Year Ending July 31, 1871* (Richmond, 1871), 7. These published annual reports will hereinafter be cited as Richmond, *Annual Report of the Public Schools,* with the appropriate years.

21. Richmond Board of Education Minutes, January 16, May 22, 1871; Richmond, *Annual Report of the Public Schools,* 1876–1877 (Richmond, 1878), 222–23; 1875–1876 (Richmond, 1877), 68–70.

22. Raleigh, *Annual Reports of the Mayor and Officers of the City of Raleigh for Fiscal Year Ending April 30, 1877* (Raleigh, 1877), 222–23. For background of the 1877 state act that provided for a system of city graded schools supported by special local taxes see Coon, "Beginnings of the North Carolina City Schools," 239, 243. Until 1877 the only public revenue given local schools came from a statewide common-school fund.

23. Ruth McAllister Vines, "The Contributions of Negroes in Providing School Facilities in the Montgomery, Alabama, City Schools" (M.A. thesis, Graduate Division, State Teachers College at Montgomery, 1943), 21.

finally being turned over to the city.[24] In Atlanta, Radicals led by former Negro councilman William Finch finally secured black schools in February 1872. One school, Summer Hill, was rented free of charge from the Northern Methodist Missionary Society, with the city assuming the cost of its support. This arrangement continued until the board of education voted to purchase the building and the lot in 1876. The other school, Storrs, was also rented free of charge from the AMA, which nominated the teachers whose salaries were paid by the board.[25] As in Montgomery, however, disputes raged over who would have the final authority in hiring the faculty, and in 1878 the agreement was terminated. Storrs then became a private school that enjoyed an excellent reputation among members of the black community.[26] Although the schools themselves did not always provide a continuity with the original period of missionary fervor, some of the teachers did. Lizzie Stevenson in Atlanta, Louise L. Dorr in Raleigh, Lizzie Knoles in Richmond, and Teresa McKeon in Nashville were only a few of the many who stayed to teach in the public schools after the phasing out of the missionary endeavors.[27]

The continuation of the link with the northern societies was greeted with mixed emotion by the Redeemers when they replaced the Radical city administrations. On the one hand the supply of rent-free buildings was attractive to officials chronically plagued with monetary worries; on the other, as long as this tie persisted, whether through teachers or money, there would exist a formidable alternative to southern white control over the minds of the Negroes. One of the first orders of business for the Redeemers, therefore, was to hire only local residents as teachers. In addition to weeding out the northerners, this action would supply jobs to local whites who were unable to secure positions in the

24. See, for example, Montgomery Board of City School Commissioners Minutes, September 16, 1879; June 5, 1882, Montgomery County Board of Education Building, Montgomery. The transfer of control to the city is mentioned in H. G. McCall, *A Sketch, Historical and Statistical of the City of Montgomery* (Montgomery, 1885), 20.

25. Atlanta Board of Education Minutes, December 30, 1871; January 25, 30, 1872; December 13, 1876.

26. For friction between the Atlanta Board of Education and the American Missionary Association see ibid., July 5, 1872; July 24, August 28, 1873; July 27, 1876; July 1, 3, August 22, 1878. On the school's later history under a corps of American Missionary Association veterans who still went north during the summer see *Atlanta Constitution,* June 28, 1879; untitled article by Ella E. Roper, *American Missionary* 44 (July 1890): 212–14; American Missionary Association, *44th Annual Report . . . and Proceedings of the Annual Meeting . . . 1890* (New York, 1890), 53.

27. All but Miss McKeon remained in the Negro schools. At first she taught in black schools, but by 1881 she was teaching fourth grade at the white Hume School. Eight years later she was one of the school's two principals. *Nashville Banner,* September 10, 1881; September 7, 1889. It would be profitable to know more about the post-Reconstruction lives of such teachers.

white schools.[28] John Watson Alvord, the Freedmen's Bureau superintendent of schools, reported that Nashville teachers had been told their schools might not resume after the 1869 Christmas vacation. "It was thought this would induce these devoted Northern ladies to leave," but most remained and about half were employed when classes resumed.[29] Having failed with subtlety, the following summer the city council overwhelmingly passed a bill requiring faculty members in public schools to reside permanently within the corporation limits of Nashville.[30] Shortly thereafter the Richmond City Council refused an offer of the Friends' Freedmen Association of New York to provide twelve instructors and pay one-fourth of their salaries. At the end of the school year the board of education resolved, "This board will employ no teachers who are not permanent residents of this city or State." One of the two dissenting votes came from Rabsa Morse Manly, head of the Richmond Education Association, which ran the Colored High and Normal School.[31]

But the Redeemers had to tread carefully. Upon their return to power they found the lines on education firmly drawn. They might trim at the edges, but they had to respect the ground rules of the basic Radical policy as expressed in state constitutions, educational statutes, and city ordinances. The threat of federal intervention still hung over their heads, and, conscious of this fact, they announced that the gains won by blacks would not be jeopardized. The shift from exclusion to segregation would be maintained, but more important, the Radical policy of separate but equal treatment would be continued.[32]

The Redeemers also made clear their determination to continue staffing the black schools with white teachers, although of course seeking to replace any remaining northerners with southerners. Increasingly, however, this policy was

28. When the Atlanta Board of Education terminated its agreement with the American Missionary Association, a letter from "Many Citizens" in the *Atlanta Constitution,* August 29, 1877, rejoiced: "It is neither just nor patriotic to tax southerners for the education of the colored people among us, and then employ northern teachers, while there are so many southern men and women who need the situations, who are amply qualified and better understand the idiosyncrasies of the African race."

29. Alvord to O[liver] O[tis] Howard, January 26, 1870, in John Watson Alvord, *Letters from the South Relating to the Condition of Freedmen Addressed to Major General O. O. Howard* (Washington, 1870), 21

30. Nashville Board of Aldermen Minutes, July 28, 1870, Davidson County Building and Nashville City Hall, Nashville. This motion had been tabled on June 23, 1870.

31. Richmond Board of Education Minutes, August 8, 1870; June 12, 1871.

32. See, for example, the report on the hygiene of the public schools, Nashville Board of Health *Third Annual Report,* 1878 (Nashville, 1879), 260–61; Atlanta Board of Education, *Seventh Annual Report,* 1878 (Atlanta, 1878), 7–8; *Atlanta Constitution,* September 3, 1878; Atlanta, *Annual Reports,* 1888, 13. The annual reports of the Atlanta Board of Education will hereinafter be cited as such with the appropriate years.

challenged by local blacks who pushed for the appointment of Negroes. In 1887 when Atlanta Negroes were seeking to get a black faculty at Summer Hill School, the last facility with white instructors, the *Atlanta Constitution* assured northerners "that the white people are not trying to force colored teachers upon them [the Negroes], for it is their own notion and desire . . . to put colored teachers in the Summer Hill school." The newspaper added that Nashville Negroes were making similar demands, as had those in Augusta, Athens, and other cities. As early as 1881 the Colored Press Association Convention in Louisville had gone on record calling for Negro staffs in Negro schools. The following year a black newspaper in Richmond, the *Virginia Star,* presented the case for control by blacks of their schools:

> The *Star* and all the better thinking people of our race in the city and the state are asking for a Normal School *proper.* One where boys and girls can be instructed by teachers of their own race, who could be able to fit them in every particular to fill their part in the great dance of life. Give us a High and Normal School where our young people may be instructed by those who have their interests at heart. We are tired of having the treadles of all the machines run by the whites. Noble descendants of Ham stand up for pride of race.[33]

In the same issue the editor reported favorably on his visit to the Navy Hill School, then run by an all-Negro staff. In the interest of "justice and common sense," he said, school authorities should note "that it is best for all concerned" to appoint blacks to teach members of their own race. The pleas were continued the next month and supported by references to the successful substitution of Negro teachers for whites in all the Virginia Negro schools of Lynchburg, Petersburg, Norfolk, Hampton, Danville, Charlottesville, and Manchester. More than racial pride was involved, since the editor argued that in all these places the experiment had shown great improvement over the old system. The few cases in Richmond offered further proof. According to the reports of the superintendent, "attendance, scholarship, punctuality and deportment in colored schools taught by colored teachers" were markedly better than in those taught by white instructors. In a subsequent letter to the editor "F" endorsed the newspaper's position. "The American colored man will never be satisfied until he has all the rights of any other American citizen," he wrote. "We want a good honest government

33. *Atlanta Constitution,* June 18, 1887; *Montgomery Advance,* September 3, 1881; *Richmond Virginia Star,* November 18, 1882 (italics in original). In a similar manner, the editor of the *Montgomery Alabama Guide* in the October 1884 issue recommended Tuskegee Institute because "if there is any place in the whole state that our people should patronize in the way of educating their children in the way of race pride, it is certainly at this point, for the school is managed and controlled by our race."

that does not make a difference on account of the color of the skin." His proposals imply that segregated schools were not necessarily seen as a betrayal of Negro rights. Although the writer called for the end of the ban against inter- marriage and the end of segregation in churches, he cited the major need in school policy as the hiring of black teachers in the black schools.[34] Negro faculty members were therefore seen as more than merely making the best of a bad situation.

The reasons for wanting black instructors varied. Racial pride, of course, was important, but still more so were the attitudes and qualifications of the white teachers. In cities such as Nashville, certain white teachers forbade their Negro pupils to recognize them in public.[35] Of greater consequence was the fact that after the northern societies surrendered their power to appoint the faculties, the Negro schools served as the dumping grounds for the rejects from the white institutions. For the 1871–1872 session, for example, the Richmond Board of Education needed twelve teachers for the white and fifteen for the Negro schools. The individuals with the highest scores on the teacher's examination were sent to the white schools. Those with the next highest scores were assigned to the black schools if they were willing to teach black children. Since many whites refused to work with blacks, the remaining positions had to be filled with applicants "whose standard was lower than heretofore enumerated." Throughout the pe- riod it seemed that any incompetent white teacher ended up in a Negro school. Mrs. M. C. P. Bennett, for example, having failed to get reappointment to the white schools, argued her case in a series of four letters to the Richmond Board in 1876 and was finally assigned to a black institution.[36]

But black teachers were seen by blacks as preferable even to qualified whites. Some blacks, including a group of preachers in Nashville, wanted Negro teachers because they would mingle socially with the families of the pupils, assisting in the elevation of the race. Others, agreeing with the northern visitor William Wells Brown, were upset that excellent black instructors were being produced by schools such as Fisk, Central Tennessee, Atlanta, and Howard and had no poten- tial employers. Most would have agreed with James H. Harris, Raleigh's leading Negro politician, who called for the hiring of black teachers because "no one can enter so fully into the sympathy of the negro's condition as the negro himself."[37]

34. *Richmond Virginia Star,* December 9, 16, 1882.

35. William Wells Brown, *My Southern Home; or, The South and Its People* (Boston: A. G. Brown and Co., 1880), 215; see also an interview with a white teacher, *Nashville Banner,* January 29, 1884.

36. Richmond Board of Education Minutes, September 5, 21, 26, 1871.

37. *Nashville Daily American,* April 7, 1877; Brown, *My Southern Home,* 215; *Raleigh Register,* March 27, 1878.

Whatever their reasons, Negroes sought to convince the authorities of the need for black instructors. More petitions were presented to boards of education and city councils on this matter than on any other of concern to Negroes. Although such petitions appeared as early as 1869 in Nashville and 1873 in Atlanta, the great increase in the movement for black faculties came after 1875. This was due in part to the failure of the Civil Rights Act of that year to forbid segregated schools. This omission convinced Negroes that segregated schools would be a long-term reality. Then, too, the growing number of graduates from black colleges provided a pool of candidates who were ready to teach other members of their race and who clearly had no chance of teaching white children.[38] Thus, less than five months after passage of the Civil Rights Act, four Negroes petitioned the Richmond School Board. After profusely thanking the board for maintaining public schools for blacks, they cited "the necessity of employing *more colored teachers in the colored schools.*" They pointed out that black teachers had been in the school system since its inception and that on numerous occasions their performances had been praised by the superintendent. Nevertheless, they said,

> of the thirty-three colored schools [classes] of the city of Richmond only seven are instructed by colored teachers while there is not one colored principle [*sic*] in the entire city. It does not appear to us that there is any valid reason for this small proportion of colored teachers in colored schools, we, therefore kindly petition you, as a matter of justice to us, as citizens of this Commonwealth to give us a more equitable proportion of teachers and principals in the colored schools of the city of Richmond.[39]

Similar declarations continued to be sent in Richmond and the other cities. In general the approach of this early petition was followed: the Negroes thanked whites for what good had been done but respectfully asked that further improvement be bestowed through the appointment of Negro teachers. In the words of an 1878 appeal presented to the Atlanta Board of Education by the Reverend Frank Quarles and a group of "leading citizens of the city":

> Our highest gratitude for the kindness you extended to us in the appointment of two colored teachers in one of the public schools in the year 1877.

38. See, for example, letters of the Reverend L. M. Hapgood to the editor, *Nashville Banner,* May 23, June 13, 1883; account of a black protest meeting, ibid., June 9, 1883; interview of the Reverend Wesley John Gaines, *Atlanta Constitution,* June 16, 1887.
39. Richmond Board of Education Minutes, June 24, 1875 (italics in original).

And as they have met the highest approbation of the parents of the children, and we believe have given satisfaction to all your requirements, we ask you for the appointment of colored teachers in all the colored public schools of the city, if they can be found competent in every respect.[40]

In 1877 a white veteran of the missionary movement in Raleigh complained to the governor that "there was an attempt made by certain of the colored people to throw out all the northern teachers from my school . . . and to put all colored teachers in."[41] The effort was thwarted, but there as elsewhere it did not signal any loss of Negro interest in the matter.

Individual school boards and city administrators reacted differently to the requests for black instructors. As already noted, from the beginning Richmond assigned Negro teachers to Navy Hill, a black school under the direction of a white principal. The other cities, however, proved more reluctant to hire blacks. One of the major obstacles was the possibility that this step would lead to integrated faculties. Even when the decision was made to permit the entry of Negroes into the system, qualification examinations and teacher preparation classes were held at different hours or even days for the two races.[42] By the end of the period only Raleigh still had integrated staffs in Negro schools. Montgomery had permitted this practice in the AMA Swayne School, but when the school became totally subject to public decisions in the mid-1880s only blacks were

40. Atlanta Board of Education Minutes, June 13, 1878. A petition of four job-seeking Negroes two years earlier had paved the way for the initial appointments. Speaking for themselves and others interested in a teaching career, they informed the board, "We have finished our studies, having passed through the preparatory and collegiate course. We had considerable experience in teaching during the summer months" (ibid., April 27, 1876).

41. Louise L. Dorr to Governor Zebulon B. Vance, August 17, 1877, Governors' Papers, North Carolina Division of Archives and History, Raleigh. The Reverend Wesley John Gaines, a prominent Atlanta Negro, also expressed dissatisfaction with his city's northern teachers. See interview in *Atlanta Constitution,* June 16, 1887; letter to the editor, *Atlanta Constitution,* June 21, 1887. For additional petitions requesting black teachers see Atlanta Board of Education Minutes, August 22, 1874; July 10, 1876; Nashville Board of Education Minutes, March 6, April 3, 1877; June 12, 1883, box 26. At the meeting called to draw up the Nashville petition of June 12, 1883, William H. Young, a black lawyer and politician, proposed that blacks should withdraw their children from the schools if the petition was rejected. More moderate leaders prevailed, however, and Nashville was spared what would have been one of the first southern school boycotts. *Nashville Banner,* June 12, 1883.

42. See, for example, Nashville Board of Education Minutes, June 15, 1887, box 26; Atlanta Board of Education, *Annual Report,* 1884 (Atlanta, 1885), 17; Atlanta Board of Education Minutes, October 9, 1877; Montgomery Board of City School Commissioners Minutes, August 19, 1882; Richmond Board of Education Minutes, September 7, 1870.

employed.[43] The other three cities avoided racial mixing with the exception of one year at Atlanta's Storrs School. Richmond, however, believed it was necessary to have white principals in control of the Negro teachers and continued this policy into the twentieth century. Atlanta and especially Nashville, on the other hand, made it clear that schools would be turned over to black faculties only when there were enough qualified applicants to fill all the positions, including that of principal:

> While it has been the purpose of the [Nashville] Board to organize a corps of colored teachers as early as practicable, the Board can not recommend the passage of the resolution [of the City Council calling for employment of black teachers] as the effect would be to make it compulsory upon the Board to employ all or even one colored teacher who might upon examination prove competent which would inevitably result in having a mixed corps of teachers, some white and some colored. This state of affairs, in the opinion of the Board, would lead to serious embarrassments and should by all means be avoided.[44]

The problem of securing a sufficient number of competent Negroes to staff an entire school was the most frequent of the many excuses offered to forestall black demands. Sometimes the boards simply explained that it was inadvisable to take such action at that time or that the plan constituted an unnecessary experiment. Unstated was the feared loss of control over the Negro students. On one occasion the Richmond Board refused on the unsupported grounds that most of the black parents preferred white teachers and that acquiescence would serve only to extend further the color line in race relations. Another consideration, whether explicit or implicit, was never absent from the minds of board members. "I am perfectly willing for colored teachers to have colored schools," said an Atlanta boardmember, "but the colored schools in Atlanta have been served faithfully by white ladies, all of whom, except one, are southern born. I am not willing to see them turned off without notice."[45]

By the time black instructors were finally given control of Negro schools, this problem of what to do with the white teachers had been settled by their retire-

43. Compare the lists of teachers in Joel Davis, comp., *Montgomery Directory, 1883–1884* (Montgomery, 1883), 22, and C. J. Allardt, comp., *Montgomery City Directory for 1888* (Montgomery: R. L. Polk and Co., 1888), 16.

44. Nashville Board of Education Minutes, November 5, 1878, box 26.

45. Richmond Board of Education Minutes, June 30, 1880; *Atlanta Constitution,* June 25, 1887; see also similar reasons given for the rejection of a Negro petition in Richmond Board of Education Minutes, June 30, 1880.

ment or reassignment to newly built white schools.[46] There were other factors as well that accounted for the final surrender of the city boards to the wishes of the Negroes. Clearly, the unending array of petitions played an important role as did the pressure brought by such Negro politicians as James Carroll Napier, the prominent lawyer and Nashville city councilman. Perhaps foremost in the minds of many whites was the matter of economy; as a member of the Atlanta Board of Education pointed out, it was cheaper to hire black teachers.[47] The comparative salaries of blacks and whites bore him out.

Even though it was sometimes unclear if the discrepancy between the salaries of whites and blacks was a reflection of differences in abilities or merely due to prejudice, every city by the end of the period showed a widening gap in the salaries paid to the two sets of instructors.[48] Due to the lingering influence of the missionary societies and the continued employment of whites in the Negro schools, the salaries for teachers in the respective schools were initially comparable and at least theoretically based on merit. As late as August 1874 the salaries of teachers (all of whom were Caucasian) in Atlanta's white and Negro schools were similar, although the staffs in the black schools were already earning somewhat less. By 1891, however, when all the principals and teachers in the Negro institutions were black, the gap in salaries became a chasm. Negro principals earned $650 annually; only one of the thirteen white principals received such a small amount, and all but three of the remainder were being paid more than $1,200. One teacher in each black school made $400 and the others, either $350 or $375; in the white schools the lowest salary was $500, and most of the instructors earned at least $550.[49]

This discrepancy in salaries was challenged in 1893 by the Reverend Edward R. Carter, a moderate Atlanta Negro leader. In his view, "This one fact makes a wide difference between the white and colored schools of Atlanta." No better example could be given than the Summer Hill School. In 1885, when it was the only Negro school staffed by whites, its teachers received $400, less than at

46. See, for example, the decision to turn over Nashville's Bell View School to black teachers. Nashville Board of Education Minutes, June 12, 1883, box 26.

47. See, for example, accounts of the Nashville Common Council meetings, *Nashville Daily American*, August 29, 1879; *Nashville Banner*, May 26, 1882; Atlanta Board of Education Minutes, July 26, 1877.

48. At the same time pupil-teacher ratios were higher in the black schools. Again the differences were least in Richmond and greatest in Montgomery. For the 1890–1891 school year the ratio in Richmond was 39:1 in the white schools and 43:1 in the black schools. Richmond, *Annual Report of the Public Schools,* 1890–1891 (Richmond, 1892), 5–6. For the 1885–1886 school year in Montgomery the ratios were 42:1 and 73:1 respectively. Montgomery, *Annual Message of the Mayor,* 1886 (Montgomery, 1886), 76–77.

49. Atlanta Board of Education, *Annual Report,* 1873–1874 (Atlanta, 1874), 6–7; ibid., 1891 (Atlanta, 1892), 267–71.

white schools but more than the high of $350 then being paid to Negro teachers at the other institutions. In 1887, when the school was turned over to black teachers, salaries dropped into the $300–$350 range.[50] A majority of the Negro faculty members were graduates of Atlanta University and were by no means unqualified to take over instruction of their race. Even if a number were poorly trained, however, it is inconceivable that the best among them were no better than the worst among the white teachers. The board of education saw an easy way to save money, regardless of whether or not the reductions were merited.

Atlanta seems to have been in the middle in its attitude toward salaries of black and white employees in Negro schools. The scant information available for Raleigh suggests that teachers of white pupils enjoyed a slight edge, though not as great as in Atlanta.[51] The more extensive data for Richmond suggests the same pattern. In its first discussion of the matter in 1874 the Richmond Board of Education set fixed salaries based on the level of instruction and length of time in service. During the next few years there was no indication of discriminatory compensation. However, when a board of education dominated by Readjusters took over in 1883 it passed a resolution ordering that salaries of teachers in the black schools be the same as those of similarly qualified instructors in the white schools. The only previous indication of distinctions came in a request from the white principal of the Colored High and Normal School in 1881 that her salary be raised from $75 to $100 per month. Since her duties and responsibilities were the same as other principals, she believed she deserved the same compensation. The board raised her salary to $90 and also raised those of her first and second assistants. The successor to the Readjuster board reiterated this ideal of equal pay for equal qualifications, and in 1888 the salary of principals in all schools was placed at $150 per month. By 1891 teachers in the white schools made slightly more than their black counterparts in the black institutions, but there was clearly an effort to reward on the basis of qualifications. Whereas 62.9 percent of the whites made $500 per year or less, the figure in the Negro schools was 63.4 percent. The principals of the primary schools, all of whom were white, were paid equally, as were the heads of the Negro and white high schools. The only significant difference in salaries actually favored the blacks. Only 10.8 percent of

---

50. Carter, *The Black Side: A Partial History of the Business, Religious, and Educational Side of the Negro in Atlanta, Georgia* (Atlanta, 1894), 235–36; for salary figures, see Atlanta Board of Education, *Annual Report*, 1885 (Atlanta, 1886), 5; ibid., 1887 (Atlanta, 1888), 148.

51. This was due primarily to the large number of whites teaching Negro pupils. In the white Centennial Graded School one teacher received fifty dollars per month and the others, forty dollars per month; in the Negro schools two teachers received thirty dollars and the rest, forty dollars. Raleigh, *Annual Reports*, 1883–1884 (Raleigh, 1884), 52–57.

the blacks were making the minimum monthly salary of $33 as compared to 14.3 percent of the whites.[52]

Nashville, which maintained a roughly equal pay scale throughout most of the 1880s, moved in the direction of inequality with the appearance of its first schedule of salaries for white schools in 1889. In September 1891 new schedules were made for both the white and Negro schools. They marked a severe decline in the status of the teachers and principals in the black schools, all of whom were Negroes. Whereas white instructors in grades one to seven were to receive from $35 to $55 monthly based on years of experience, the comparable range for blacks was $25 to $41 dollars. The highest figure for blacks was reached after eleven years, while a white teacher in his second year made $40. For eighth-grade teachers the range was $55 to $60 for whites and $25 to $45 for blacks. The same inequality characterized the salaries of administrators, where the monthly gap between equally qualified Negroes and whites was at no time less than $80. At times it was as great as $110. There was a strong reaction to these discrepancies, however, and in December 1891 the schedule for Negro schools was revised upward. Nevertheless, in all cases a minimum difference of at least $5 per month still reflected the dual standard for teachers; the monthly gap between white and black administrators now ranged from $40 to $100.[53]

Montgomery officials had no compunction against furthering the divergence of salaries in their two sets of schools. While the arrangement with the AMA was in force, the wages were approximately the same. By 1875, however, the white school principal was earning $150, and the staff members, between $50 and $75; the Negro school principal received $100, and his teachers, $35 to $60, with only one in the highest category. By 1880 the average white school teacher was making $60 a month, and his Negro school counterpart, $49. Ten years later the white teachers had maintained their earlier salary level, but individuals in black schools (by now all Negroes) had been reduced to $38. By 1893 no black teacher was making more than $320 per year, while the lowest salary for whites was $400.[54]

Ironically, the shift from white to black teachers was made easier by the earlier neglect of black facilities. When new schools for blacks were finally opened in the 1880s it seemed natural to appoint Negroes because of black demands, the

52. Richmond, *Annual Report of the Public Schools,* 1874–1875 (Richmond, 1876), 351; Richmond Board of Education Minutes, July 26, 1883; July 1, 1881; September 25, 1884; September 24, 1888; Richmond, *Annual Report of the Public Schools,* 1890–1891, 38–39.

53. Nashville, Salary Schedules, Nagy Collection, box 51.

54. Montgomery City Council Minutes, December 5, 1870, Alabama Department of Archives and History, Montgomery; Montgomery Board of Education Minutes, December 31, 1875; July 1, 1893; Alabama, Superintendent of Education, *Report,* 1880 (Montgomery, 1880), 19; ibid., 1890–1891 (Montgomery, 1891), 162.

absence of white teachers to be displaced, and the lower salaries of blacks. Such considerations, for example, accounted for the appointment of blacks in the Knowles School in Nashville and the East End School in Richmond. Yet the innovation would have still been impossible had there not been competent Negroes available to fill the positions. Favorable reports from other cities about the quality of black appointees led an Atlanta Board of Education member, for example, to base his support partly on the precedents set in Augusta, Savannah, and Macon. The growing numbers of such qualified individuals by the late 1880s thus nullified the charge that inexperienced or incompetent blacks would be replacing whites. Whereas in 1884 only five of the twenty-four Negro applicants passed Nashville's teacher examination, by 1887 this was true of nineteen of forty-two. More significantly, two of the top three scores, including the highest, were achieved by Negroes. Seventh in the city was a young Fisk student named William Edward Burghardt Du Bois.[55]

Despite such arguments in favor of the black demands, the transition was a slow process, usually spread over several years and confronted by staunch resistance. The Pearl School, the last black facility in Nashville to be staffed by Negroes, had to wait until 1887.[56] In that year Summer Hill School achieved the same distinction in Atlanta, thanks to the tie-breaking vote of the president of the board of education.[57] In Richmond black teachers were placed in all the Negro schools only after the Readjuster-controlled board of education was appointed. The new board hired Negro principals and teachers for every black school except the high school. When the Democrats returned to power they replaced the principals with whites but retained the black instructors. The Colored High and Normal School, however, remained entirely in the hands of whites until 1924.[58]

55. Nashville Board of Education Minutes, October 7, 1879, box 26; Richmond, *Annual Report of the Public Schools,* 1881–1882 (Richmond, 1883), 22; Atlanta Board of Education Minutes, July 26, 1877; Nashville Board of Education Minutes, May 26, 1884; May 30, 1887, box 26. The *Nashville Daily American* on May 26, 1880, exaggerating the achievements in Nashville and underestimating conditions elsewhere, had argued, "Nashville is the only Southern city where the colored schools are up to the same standard as the white schools in discipline, scholarship and attendance. Nearly all the other cities have colored teachers in the colored schools." The *Nashville Banner* of June 11, 1883, based part of its opposition to black teachers on the fact that only two of thirty-two black applicants had passed that year's teacher's examination.

56. Nashville Board of Education Minutes, June 14, 15, 1887, box 26. The change was made because the performance of blacks in that year's teacher's examination could not be ignored.

57. *Atlanta Constitution,* June 25, 1887. The next day, when the time came to elect the Negro teachers, two councilmen were still in opposition. One said he wanted "no niggers" in the school (ibid., June 28, 1887). The chief stumbling block was the absence of sufficient available positions for the white teachers.

58. Richmond Board of Education Minutes, March 7, June 28, 1883; June 26, 27, 1884.

Having finally acted, the boards of education seemed pleased with the performances of the black faculty members. "I believe the Board found the key to the
problem of the education of our colored population when competent colored
teachers were put in charge of Houston Street School," wrote the Atlanta superintendent of education in 1881. They "have demonstrated the fact that they
understand their own race, and can discipline and teach to the satisfaction of
their patrons." His counterpart in Montgomery reported that the Negro instructors "have done very well," although he modified his praise by observing, "It
would not be very easy to find teachers among the blacks that would succeed
better." Commenting on the recent change in Richmond whereby white principals and white teachers had been replaced by blacks, the superintendent noted
that while he had expected much trouble, "in justice to the principals and
teachers I must say the schools were conducted with good order and with few
complaints from patrons and pupils, and when it is taken into consideration that
the principals were inexperienced and had 27 teachers new to the system, the
conduct of the schools was very satisfactory."[59]

Satisfaction with the new system was partly due to the fact that most of the
new faculty members were considered "safe"; the boards and the white citizens
at large believed that the students would not be exposed to ideas that would
threaten the status quo in race relations. When the Atlanta Board of Education
initially considered the appointment of Negro teachers in 1877, one of the requirements was that they be natives of the South and residents of Georgia; ten
years later one of the main arguments in favor of turning the last school over to
black instructors was the existence of a sufficient number of competent graduates of southern institutions. In 1887 twenty-four of the Negro teachers employed
by the city had received their training at Atlanta University; by 1910 more than
three-quarters of the faculty members in the black schools were its alumni. A
Nashville newspaper applauded the appointment of two local graduates as that
city's first Negro teachers. "This is right," proclaimed the *Daily American.* "In
employing colored teachers the Board of Education could scarcely find any
better prepared than those trained from the beginning in the schools where they
are to teach."[60] Indeed, not only did most of the teachers graduate from neigh-

---

The Readjusters, however, were dedicated to the principle of separate (though equal)
schools. See ibid., March 7, 1883.

59. Atlanta Board of Education, *Annual Report,* 1880–1881 (Atlanta, 1882), 8; Mont-
gomery Board of City School Commissioners Minutes, June 8, 1889; Richmond Board of
Education Minutes, June 26, 1884; see also Richmond Board of Education Minutes,
October 26, 1885.

60. Atlanta Board of Education Minutes, October 2, 1877; June 25, 1887; *Atlanta
Constitution,* December 23, 1887; William N. Hartshorn, *An Era of Progress and Promise,*

borhood colleges or normal schools, but many came up through the local public school system. Consider Mabel Beatrice Johnson. Although born in rural Georgia, she grew up in Atlanta, where she attended three of the public schools and later graduated with honors from Spelman College. First selected as a supernumerary, she was finally chosen as a regular teacher in 1888 and was rapidly promoted. Of the 84 Negro instructors employed in 1890 by the Richmond school system 80 had attended the Negro high school, as compared to only 87 graduates of the white high school among the 154 teachers in the white schools.[61]

But what of the schools in which blacks now taught? Despite Redeemer assurances that education would be both separate and equal, an ever-widening gap in the distribution of funds for the two races came to replace the relatively equal treatment accorded by the Radicals. The differences ranged from the expenditure per enrolled child in Richmond during 1890–1891 of $10.25 for whites and $9.50 for blacks to the $5.58 per white child and $3.47 per black youngster in Montgomery in 1880, the last year for which figures are available. The sums for the Alabama capital represented an investment of $1.17 for each white of school age and only 44 cents for each school-age Negro.[62]

Conditions in the schools reflected these differences. In every city there was a

---

1863–1910: The Religious, Moral, and Educational Development of the American Negro since His Emancipation (Boston: Presrilla Publishing Co., 1910), 88–89; Nashville Daily American, October 10, 1879.

61. For Mabel Beatrice Johnson, see Carter, The Black Side, 101–3. In 1894 four of the black teachers in the city were former pupils of the Mitchell Street School (240); Richmond, Annual Report of the Public Schools, 1889–1890 (Richmond, 1891), 13. Even "home-grown" talent could prove difficult. See, for example, accounts of the disciplinary problems of the Colored High and Normal School in Richmond Board of Education Minutes, December 28, 1885; July 2, 1886. School officials also had difficulties with individual black teachers and principals. Antoine A. Graves, a graduate of Atlanta University and principal of Atlanta's Gate City School, resigned after school children were dismissed for a celebration to honor Jefferson Davis. Carter, The Black Side, 233–34. Graves's successor, L. M. Hershaw, was fired after making a speech in which he criticized southern educational policy toward Negroes and compared the region unfavorably to the North. He was reinstated after writing a contrite apology. See Atlanta Constitution, July 26, August 30, 1889. Daniel B. Williams, a Richmond teacher, was dismissed after a clash with his white principal over the school's promotion policy. He was encouraged to reapply for his position by the board of education and having done so, saw his request unanimously denied. Richmond Board of Education Minutes, February 22, March 22, 1883.

62. Richmond, Annual Report of the Public Schools, 1890–1891, 38–39; Alabama, Superintendent of Education, Report, 1879–1880 (Montgomery, 1880), 28. The sums for Richmond in 1880–1881 were $12.60 per white and $11.11 per black pupil. Richmond, Annual Report of the Public Schools, 1880–1881 (Richmond, 1882), 14. Under the Radicals in 1870–1871 Montgomery had spent $11.51 on each white and $11.44 on each black student. Montgomery City Council Minutes, September 4, 1871.

shortage of space for blacks wishing to attend school. During the 1875 academic year Richmond educators lacked accommodations for 117 more white than Negro students, but 600 Negroes and only 200 whites were denied entrance in 1888. Worse still from the standpoint of the blacks, the whites would soon have seats thanks to the opening of additional rooms in Springfield and Elba schools, but the blacks would have to wait for new facilities until funds were available "in the near future."[63]

Such assurances about finding accommodations for the Negroes "in the near future" came to have a hollow ring. When more room was planned for whites, it was sought through the erection of new buildings. When dealing with black needs, however, renting or subdividing older buildings was preferred; if new construction was decided upon, sites were carefully chosen so as to hinder the dispersal of Negroes. Improvements in space for blacks were often delayed while better provisions were made as quickly as financially possible for whites. With such occasional exceptions as the Moore Street School in Richmond or the Gray Street School in Atlanta, both built after 1887, the Negro schools were generally older, less favorably located, and of inferior construction.[64] In 1876 the Richmond superintendent recommended closing the Navy Hill School, since it was in very bad repair and "very unfit for school purposes"; in 1891 the building was still in use. By 1891 only two of the six Negro schools were in "good" or "very good" condition as compared to nine of the ten white schools. The Cemetery Hill School, completed in Montgomery in 1887, was a frame building that provided blacks with "greater school facilities and much more comfort than they have had heretofore." On the other hand, a white school opened the previous year was an "elegant and commodious brick building," with a capacity of 405 students, more than twice that of the Negro school. The Lawrence School, built for blacks in 1890, indicated Nashville's attitude toward black needs. In an age when wooden schools were anachronistic and when several hundred black students were without accommodations, the city erected a one-story, five-room frame structure with seats for only 214.[65]

63. Richmond Board of Education Minutes, November 25, 1875; September 24, 1888. The excess of rejected black over white applicants was already evident in the 1877–1878 school year when 150 white and 525 black children were initially denied admission to the public schools because of lack of room. It was expected that at least forty of the whites would be accepted later in the year. Ibid., September 27, 1877.

64. For an extended discussion of the Gray Street School see Carter, *The Black Side,* 224–26; on the Moore Street School see Richmond, *Annual Report of the Public Schools,* 1890–1891, 44.

65. Richmond, *Annual Report of the Public Schools,* 1875–1876, 367; 1890–1891, 84–85; Montgomery, *Annual Message of the Mayor,* 1887 (Montgomery, 1887), 57; Nashville, Lawrence School Notes, Nagy Collection, box 57. The way in which a new Negro school

The principle of separate but equal also went largely unheeded in the number of advanced grades provided for Negro pupils. With the exception of Raleigh, all the cities had high schools for their white children at an early date, but only Richmond and Nashville had established such facilities for their blacks by the end of the period. And in Nashville the black high school was organized by adding grades to a grammar school, thus seriously increasing overcrowding.[66] Even more damaging was the absence of completely graded grammar schools. In Raleigh in 1884 only Johnson offered classes in all seven grades as did the white institutions. After it was closed at the end of 1885 Negro students were limited to the first five grades.[67] Even in Richmond, where black students received the best treatment, progress was often blocked by insufficient provisions for more advanced work. In 1891 eight of the nine white elementary schools offered classes in one of the two highest grades as compared to four of their seven Negro counterparts.[68]

Groups of Negroes, many of whom had fought for black teachers, sought to spur local lawmakers to improve the quality of Negro education. Rather than pushing for an end to segregation, the blacks fought for the ideal of truly equal, though separate, Negro schools; and most of the limited improvements can be traced directly to these pressures. In January 1874 the Nashville Board of Education acknowledged, "The colored people are demanding more convenient accommodations in the central and western portions of the city." Nine months later the board's request for additional facilities for blacks in west Nashville was approved by the board of aldermen. Petitions from Atlanta Negroes in 1880 and 1888 led the board of education after a slight delay to construct the Houston Street and Gray Street schools.[69]

---

was furnished ten years earlier also demonstrated the attitude of whites and was perhaps a regular procedure for black schools. According to the *Nashville Daily American,* November 1, 1879, "All the furniture for it was obtained from the various other school buildings in the city, and has not cost the city a cent."

66. See, for example, Nashville Board of Education Minutes, September 29, 1884; June 29, 1885; September 15, 1886, box 26. In Richmond the high-school program of whites was more rigorous and extensive than that of blacks. For the schedule of students see Richmond, *Annual Report of the Public Schools,* 1879–1880 (Richmond, 1881), 41, 43; 1890–1891, 56, 61.

67. Raleigh, *Annual Reports,* 1885–1886 (Raleigh, 1886), 87.

68. Expressed another way, 7.6 percent of the enrolled white students and 4.5 percent of the blacks were in the two highest grammar-school grades. Richmond, *Annual Report of the Public Schools,* 1890–1891, 36–37. By the end of the period Richmond and Atlanta also operated night schools only for whites.

69. Nashville Board of Education Minutes, January 6, 1874, box 26; Nashville Board of Aldermen Minutes, October 20, 1874. Typically, the new accommodations were to be in a rented rather than a specially constructed building. Eight years later Negro councilman

More often the petitions were tabled, bottled up in committee, or rejected outright. Unlike black demands for black teachers, the crusade for better black schools found white and black aims in conflict. Rather than easing the financial burdens of the local boards, the building of new black schools and the improvement of old ones would require massive appropriations. Twice during 1873 Atlanta officials cited the lack of funds in rejecting black pleas for additional schools. A petition signed by seventy-seven Richmond Negroes in 1878 complained, "All the public schools of this city for the education of colored youth lie within a space of five blocks by fifteen . . . and that long since the seating capacity of these has been entirely exhausted." Students had to travel great distances to attend Valley School, which was practically inaccessible during the winter months. The board's proposal to enlarge Valley was therefore seen as unsatisfactory. Instead, the petitioners called for new schools in Church Hill and Rocketts "for the sake of . . . those who so anxiously desire and so urgently need the benefits of education." The board responded that it sympathized heartily with the desire for more accommodations but could take no action due to lack of funds.[70]

Two years later a different group of thirty-four Richmond Negroes reiterated the demand for increased accommodations in the eastern section of the city. The plans to enlarge Valley School still had not been implemented, and the petitioners took the opportunity to criticize the site further and to endorse again a policy of dispersal rather than concentration. Of particular concern was the location of the school, which was not only at a great distance from the prospective pupils but also "in a bottom near a creek into which the filth of the other side of the city is drained." The petition was tabled. Four months later the board also rejected a recommendation that the Nicholson School property in the east end be set aside for blacks. At the same meeting the members voted to purchase a lot in that area for construction of a white school. Shortly afterward the board had second thoughts and ordered the Nicholson property to be sold, with the proceeds going toward erection of Negro facilities. In the face of pressure from white parents, however, the board once again reversed itself. The Nicholson property was retained and used as a school for whites.[71] Montgomery Negroes,

---

J. C. Napier successfully led the fight to construct two new black schools after receiving numerous requests from blacks. "It is cheaper," he said, "to take care of colored children in schools than in prisons" (*Nashville Banner,* May 26, 1882); Atlanta Board of Education Minutes, April 29, September 3, 1880; March 22, November 22, 1888.

70. Atlanta Board of Education Minutes, January 3, October 28, 1873; for similar rejections see ibid., October 30, 1875; June 26, 1880. The petition and the board's response can be found in Richmond Board of Education Minutes, February 28, 1878.

71. Richmond Board of Education Minutes, March 25, June 30, September 23, October 6, 1880.

who underwent similar experiences with their petitions, finally got the board to erect a new building in 1888, but only after raising five hundred dollars toward its construction.[72]

Blacks were equally unsuccessful in securing appointments to boards of education. Demands such as those made in 1883 by two Atlanta Negroes, politician Columbus C. Wimbish and principal Richard H. Carter of the Houston Street School, at the Georgia State Educational Convention for Colored Men bore little fruit, nor were the numerous petitions any more effective.[73] Here again, the contrast with demands for black teachers was marked, for much more was at stake. As the *Richmond Dispatch* put it, blacks should not be allowed to exercise control over white children, teachers, and taxpayers. It also feared that mixed schools would result and besides, it said, "where and when did the negro become possessed of the notion that he was the equal of the white man." Only when Republicans or Readjusters, as in Richmond, were in power did Negroes have the opportunity to serve on local boards. Alfred Menefee served on Nashville's Board in 1867, Richmond G. Forrester and R. A. Paul on the Richmond Board in 1883, and Holland Thompson on the Montgomery Board from 1870 to 1873. Along with their white Republican colleagues, they lost their positions when the city councils reverted to Democratic control.[74] The boards on which these men served were the most favorable to the cause of Negro education. The Readjusters, during their brief hegemony in Richmond, for example, not only

72. For petitions of Negro churches to have their buildings used as public schools see Montgomery Board of City School Commissioners Minutes, February 7 and August 14, 1876. For the role of Negro contributions in 1888 see Vines, "The Contributions of Negroes," 21. For evidence of continued difficulty in getting positive responses to petitions in Nashville see W. H. Young to the editor, *Nashville Banner,* November 29, 1889.

73. See *Atlanta Constitution,* December 14, 1883, for the remarks of Wimbish and Carter. Petitions calling for black representation on boards of education are mentioned in Nashville Board of Aldermen Minutes, November 21, 1876; Atlanta City Council Minutes, December 5, 1887, Office of the City Clerk, Atlanta City Hall, Atlanta.

74. *Richmond Dispatch,* May 26, 1883; see also ibid., May 25, 1883; *Nashville Union and Dispatch,* December 17, 1867; Nashville Board of Aldermen Minutes, October 30, 1869; William A. Christian, *Richmond: Her Past and Present* (Richmond: L. H. Jenkins, 1912), 382, 387; Montgomery City Council Minutes, September 19, 1870; January 10, 1873. There may have been a second Negro who served on the Montgomery Board of City School Commissioners. W. J. Stevens was elected by a Republican-controlled council in January 1874 to represent the heavily Negro Fifth Ward. *Montgomery Alabama State Journal,* January 20, 1874. Although he is not identified by race, "Stevens" may actually have been Wash Stephens, a local black politician. A check of the voter registration list for the 1875 municipal election published in the *Montgomery Daily Advertiser,* April 18, 1875, found no Stevens or Stephens listed among the whites in the Fifth Ward, but Wash Stephens was listed among the blacks. When the Democrats regained control of the council a white Democrat replaced Stevens. *Montgomery Daily Advertiser,* January 4, 1876.

appointed black principals and teachers to all the Negro grammar schools but added needed classroom space by making Moore Street Industrial School, a previously private Negro institution, a part of the public system and by constructing a twelve-room building in the neglected eastern part of the city. In the long run the board probably had the greatest influence on the decision of its successors to accord blacks the best treatment of any of the five cities.[75] Of all the Negro members, however, the most influential in the five capitals and perhaps in the entire South was Holland Thompson. Montgomery's leading black politician, former delegate to the state constitutional convention, and four-term city councilman, Thompson was appointed to the city's first school board by the Republican council of which he was a prominent member. He was instrumental in helping to organize the system and in defending the right of Negro schools to equal appropriations.[76]

The protests from local blacks thus resulted primarily in the replacing of white instructors with blacks. This early display of black power had its cost, however. Blacks accommodated themselves to the system of segregated schools and produced a group with a vested interest in its continuation. Some blacks accepted the view of those white Radicals and Redeemers who said schools could be separate and equal; others no doubt decided that half a loaf in the form of black faculties was better than nothing; still others probably believed that black teachers were more important than integrated schools and saw this as a prelude to greater control over the education of their children. In the end, of course, the gap between white and black schools widened. And, ironically, by accepting segregation blacks had made it easier for whites to discriminate. Finally, by stressing the need for black instructors, black representatives on the boards of education, and better black schools rather than integration, Negroes helped to convince any doubting whites that the blacks themselves really did want segregation.

75. See, for example, Richmond Board of Education Minutes, September 23, 1883.
76. See, for example, Montgomery City Council Minutes, September 5, 1870.

From Reconstruction to Redemption
in the Urban South

Historians now realize that nineteenth- and twentieth-century southern cities provide a fertile field for investigation. So far, however, relatively little attention has been paid to urban life during the era of Reconstruction and Redemption, even though southern cities actively participated in the growing urbanization of the nation during these years.

Not only urban historians, but also scholars interested in the impact of Radical Reconstruction on race relations can benefit from attention to events on the local scene. The decisions made in Congress and the state legislatures had to be implemented on the local level, and it was there that the tension between law and custom was most evident. By illuminating the policies of Reconstruction and Redemption as they touched the lives of people, details can be provided to fill in gaps or to correct misconceptions in the broader interpretations of the era.

There are many topics in need of examination, among them the relationship between white Radicals and their black allies, the attitudes of white Democrats toward Negro voters, and the quality of government provided by the Radicals. This study, however, will concentrate on two other basic questions—What were the techniques of Redemption in the urban South, and What difference did it make to urban blacks whether the Radicals or Redeemers controlled municipal governments?

Just as it is incorrect to talk of "the South," it is unwise to refer to "the urban South." Generalizations about the course of Reconstruction in the cities are especially hazardous. Like the states, each locality followed its own separate

I want to thank Professor Arthur Mann for reading an earlier version of this essay, and the University of Chicago Center for Urban Studies for financial assistance.

script in playing out the drama of the postwar period. Five cities, therefore, have been selected for intensive examination in the belief that together they reflect the variety of the Reconstruction experience. They are Atlanta, Georgia; Montgomery, Alabama; Richmond, Virginia; Nashville, Tennessee; and Raleigh, North Carolina. They present a cross section of the urban South with regard to the length and impact of Radical control; they also provide a mix in geographical location, size, percentage of black residents, and, with the exception of seaports, economic function.

The most significant difference among them was the varied tenure of Radical domination. The Radicals never controlled Atlanta; brief periods of hegemony ended in Nashville in June 1869 and in Richmond in March 1870. On the other hand, between 1868 and 1875 Montgomery had a Republican mayor and, except for 1872 and 1873, a Republican city council. Radicals were even more entrenched in Raleigh, where they controlled the council and the mayoralty from 1868 to 1875, one of the few instances in which a southern city remained fully under the radicals for more than two consecutive elections.[1] Republican influence also differed after Redemption was accomplished. In Atlanta and Montgomery Republicans were no longer elected to city government, while in Richmond, Raleigh, and Nashville, Republicans continued to serve on city councils into the 1890s. Nashville also had a Republican mayor for all but three years between 1872 and 1887.

As in the rest of the South then, Democrats (or, as they sometimes called themselves, Conservatives) rarely needed more than a few years to bring about Redemption. But before examining the strategies for Redemption, we must consider what was at stake for the urban blacks. That is, what benefits had they received from the Radical administrations during their brief tenure, and what did the Redeemers hope to undo? It should be emphasized that not even while the Radicals had control were the cities under Negro rule or menaced by a policy of "Africanization." Although the Radicals enjoyed success thanks to the solid support of the freedmen, at no time were more than a few of the local offices in black hands. Nonetheless, the limited period of Radical influence did permit a number of blacks to hold elective and appointive office. And as a result, the black population benefitted in a variety of ways.

Montgomery's James Rapier was the only black to represent these cities in Congress, but several served in state legislatures. Three were elected from Wake County (Raleigh), and between 1868 and 1876 ten black legislators were chosen

1. Others included Petersburg, Virginia; Jackson, Mississippi; Chattanooga, Tennessee; and Charleston, South Carolina.

1

Population Statistics 1850–1890

	1850	*1860*	*1870*	*1880*	*1890*
Nashville					
White	7,626	13,043	16,147	27,005	46,773
Black	2,539	3,945	9,709	16,337	29,395
% Black	25%	23%	38%	38%	39%
Atlanta					
White	2,060	7,615	11,860	21,079	39,416
Black	512	1,939	9,929	16,330	28,098
% Black	20%	20%	46%	44%	43%
Richmond					
White	15,274	23,635	27,928	35,765	49,034
Black	12,296	14,275	23,110	27,835	32,330
% Black	44%	38%	45%	44%	40%
Montgomery					
White	6,511	4,341	5,402	6,782	8,892
Black	2,217	4,502	5,183	9,931	12,987
% Black	25%	53%	49%	59%	59%
Raleigh					
White	2,253	2,693	3,696	4,911	6,327
Black	2,263	2,087	4,094	4,354	6,348
% Black	50.1%	44%	53%	47%	50.1%

Compiled from U.S. Bureau of the Census, *Ninth Census of the United States: 1870,* vol. 1, *Population* (Washington, D.C.: Government Printing Office, 1872), 81, 102, 225, 262, 280; *Eleventh Census of the United States: 1890,* vol. 1, *Population* (Washington, D.C.: Government Printing Office, 1893), part 1, 524, 527, 546, 555, 557.

from Montgomery, four of them for more than two terms.[2] When the Radicals controlled the county governments in Nashville, Montgomery, and Raleigh, Negroes served as commissioners and justices of the peace; in Nashville they also held the position of county jailer.

2. Rapier was elected in 1872 with an almost three-thousand vote majority, but was narrowly defeated for reelection in 1874. *Montgomery Alabama State Journal,* November 16, 1872; November 14, 1874; Elaine Joan Nowaczyk, "The North Carolina Negro in Politics, 1865–1876" (Master's thesis, University of North Carolina, 1957), 199–200; John W. Beverly, *History of Alabama* (Montgomery: privately printed, 1901), 203, 205–6.

But it was in the city councils that blacks made their greatest impact during their few years of ascendancy. Two of the four Radical councilmen elected in Atlanta in 1870 were black, including a successful tailor named William Finch who led the fight for equal rights.[3] Four blacks, but never more than two at a time, served on the Montgomery Council between 1868 and 1875. The most noteworthy, a grocer named Holland Thompson, was one of three aldermen chosen for the board of school commissioners, one of three appointed to fix rates of assessment on personal property, and one of two who prepared the new city code.[4] The sole Negro elected to the Nashville Board of Aldermen during Mayor A. E. Alden's victorious campaign in 1867 was disqualified because of Tennessee's bar on Negro officeholding; following its repeal, however, one of the ten new aldermen and at least six of the twenty council members chosen during Alden's reelection bid in 1868 were black. Two of the nine-man Raleigh Board of Commissioners appointed by military authorities in 1868 were also Negro.[5] From the first municipal election in 1869 through 1875 (when the board was increased to seventeen members), blacks won no less than three and as many as five of the commission seats.

Along with their white allies, black politicians made certain that blacks enjoyed patronage appointments ranging from municipal offices to jobs as common laborers. At one of its first meetings, the Radical council in Nashville unanimously resolved at the urging of Mayor Alden's spokesman that "in electing officers of the Corporation of Nashville, this Board will recognize no distinction in color, race or previous condition." One week later the mayor removed the white guards at the almshouse and replaced them with three Negroes. Other blacks were appointed city sexton and assistant street overseer, the latter job created especially for a Negro. Raleigh blacks fared best in patronage largely because of the length of Radical control and its secure base. Doc Chavis was city pump contractor during the period of great expansion in the town's waterworks. Norfleet Dunston, a shoemaker by trade and a politician by profession who served several terms as alderman and county justice of the peace, was appointed township tax receiver in 1872 and often drew extra pay as a registrar. Positions as election officials meant an extra three to eight dollars per day and were rarely

3. *Atlanta Constitution*, December 9, 1870. For Finch's background, see E. R. Carter, *The Black Side: A Partial History of the Business, Religious, and Educational Side of the Negro in Atlanta, Georgia* (Atlanta, 1894), 74–77, and Clarence A. Bacote, "William Finch, Negro Councilman and Political Activities in Atlanta during Early Reconstruction," *Journal of Negro History* 40 (January 1955): 341–64.

4. Montgomery City Council Minutes, January 1, 1872; August 1, 1870; February 6 1871, Alabama Department of Archives and History, Montgomery.

5. *Nashville Union and Dispatch*, September 29, October 2, 12, 1867; *Nashville Daily Press and Times*, October 2, 1868; *Raleigh Daily Standard*, July 14, 1868.

awarded to blacks, but exceptions occasionally were made also in Montgomery and Nashville.[6] In all the cities when the Radicals were in power, the mass of blacks benefitted from increased employment in construction work.

The most noteworthy form of patronage was the appointment of Negroes to the fire and police departments. Even here, however, regular black policemen were found only in Montgomery and Raleigh, the two cities where Radical influence was greatest.[7] Atlanta and Richmond, in which Radicals exercised the least power, not only refused to appoint black policemen but rejected black firemen as well. Nashville's Alden administration, while turning down Negro requests for appointment to the police department, did accept Negro firemen. The Radicals authorized an all-Negro Hook and Ladder Company, although it had a lower status than the five all-white units. Raleigh Radicals were responsible for not one but two all-Negro companies in their city. Meanwhile, in Montgomery the Radicals kept the segregated companies that existed when they came to power.[8]

Republican interest in segregated treatment for blacks extended to other spheres as well. In each of the five cities segregation was seen as the alternative to the generally accepted antebellum policy of exclusion of blacks and was supported by Republicans of both races. Usually, however, there was an insistence upon separate but equal treatment. In Nashville Mayor Alden continued the system of segregated schools begun by the Conservatives. In Atlanta the Radicals forced the admittance of blacks to the previously all-white system, although in separate facilities. In Richmond, Raleigh, and Montgomery the Radicals organized the first public school systems, but segregation was enforced from the beginning. At the height of Radical Reconstruction in Richmond and Nashville, blacks were cared for in separate almshouses, seated in segregated portions of the theaters, and assigned special seats on streetcars. Blacks continued to

6. Nashville Board of Aldermen Minutes, October 22, 1867, Nashville City Hall and Davidson County Building, Nashville; *Nashville Union and Dispatch,* October 29, 1867; Nashville Board of Aldermen Minutes, May 21, June 17, 1868; *Nashville Union and Dispatch,* October 29, 1867; L. Branson, ed., *The North Carolina Business Directory,* 1869 (Raleigh, 1869), 152; *Raleigh Daily News,* March 25, 1872; Wake County Board of Commissioners Minutes, August 19, 1870; August 18, 1871, North Carolina Department of Archives and History, Raleigh; *Montgomery Weekly Advertiser,* May 28, 1867; *Nashville Daily Press and Times,* May 8, 1868.

7. See my essay "The Conflict Between Blacks and the Police in the Urban South, 1865–1900," reprinted below.

8. *Nashville Union and Dispatch,* October 23–25, 1867. Nashville was the only city which by state law had previously restricted positions as firemen to whites. Nashville, *Digest of General Laws,* 1865, 41; Branson, *North Carolina Business Directory,* 1869, 152; ibid., 1872, 230; Montgomery City Council Minutes, December 3, 1866; February 18, 1867; January 4, 1869; *Montgomery Weekly Advertiser,* June 18, 1867.

be buried in segregated sections of cemeteries, and in Raleigh the Radicals even built a new municipal cemetery for them. And in each city there were black counterparts to white militia units.[9]

Clearly, then, the Radicals were not color-blind. Still, they were determined to replace the old policy of exclusion of blacks with segregation in the areas of education, welfare, militia service, and public accommodations. Many of the Conservatives had opposed this shift, but even more important in accounting for their determination to overthrow the Radicals was the specter of the Negro voter and officeholder and the fear that in the future far greater changes would be forced upon the southern white majority. If there could be Negroes arresting whites, the white Radicals and their black henchmen might be capable of anything.

In seeking to rid the cities of Radical control, local Conservatives and Democrats depended upon support from the newly redeemed state governments. Indeed, favorable action on the part of state legislators was the single most important factor in the triumph of urban Redeemers. The cities were the creation of the states and in the political sphere, as in so many other aspects of urban life, final power rested with the legislators. And since the five cities under discussion were all capitals, state officials had a special interest in them. Forced to spend part or all of the year in those cities, the officials were greatly concerned with controlling their Negro populations. While in other cities the primary thrust for enlisting the state government in ousting the Radicals came from the permanent residents, in these five cases the impetus came from both residents and the legislature.

Assisted by sympathetic governors, the state legislators arranged for the direct removal of opposition officeholders, altered the ways in which local officials were elected, rearranged political boundaries through judicious gerrymandering, and legislated new requirements for voting. These maneuvers gave the local Conservatives and Democrats great leverage. For this reason, there was less need to resort to the more generally publicized tactics of fraud, intimidation, and violence. Not that these illegal measures were not employed. Especially good use was made of them in Richmond and Montgomery, for example; but even in these cities they complemented the legal tactics of Redemption.

The most blatant lawful technique was simply to remove Radicals from office and either to appoint their replacements or to provide for new elections. Iron-

9. See my essays "Half a Loaf: The Shift from White to Black Teachers in the Negro Schools of the Urban South, 1865–1890," "From Exclusion to Segregation: Health and Welfare Services for Southern Blacks, 1865–1890," and "From Exclusion to Segregation: Southern Race Relations, 1865–1890," all reprinted in this volume.

ically, the precedent for such action was established by the military authorities during Congressional Reconstruction. In 1868 Commanding General John Schofield had appointed George Chahoon mayor of Richmond along with an all-white and largely Republican city council. They served until March 1870, when the newly elected Conservative state legislature, at the request of a Richmond Conservative, declared vacant all municipal offices. Under the terms of the act, moderate Republican governor Gilbert Walker appointed Conservatives to the city council. The council in turn chose as mayor Henry K. Ellyson, publisher of the rabidly Democratic *Richmond Dispatch.* Chahoon and his colleagues refused to acknowledge the legality of the legislation and barricaded themselves inside the police station. Special police chosen by Ellyson laid siege to the station, and federal troops were finally brought in after pitched battles between Ellyson and Chahoon supporters. The turmoil ended with the army in control and the opposing claimants agreeing to let the state supreme court of appeals settle the matter. In the interim both parties were given access to public buildings. For more than a month the city had a dual government: one recognized by U.S. Circuit Judge John Underwood, a staunch Radical, and the other by Governor Walker. Not unexpectantly the state court, composed entirely of Conservatives, held the Enabling Act to be constitutional and declared Ellyson the rightful mayor.[10]

Tennessee state officials played a similar role in disposing of Nashville's Radical mayor, A. E. Alden. On the strength of a four-to-one margin of black over white registrants, Alden and his entire ticket had been elected in September 1867. Representing the wing of the Republican party controlled largely by northerners supported by federal patronage, Alden was opposed by a band of "home-grown" Radicals led by his mayoralty opponent, H. S. Scovel, and S. R. Mercer of the *Nashville Daily Press and Times.* Both wings of the Republican party actively courted the Negro vote, although Alden was far more successful. "While many of our race and color 'entered devious paths and fainted by the wayside,'" Alden told the council in his inaugural address, "our colored friends with a true unflinching patriotism worthy of imitation, declared their loyalty at the ballot box almost unanimously."[11]

Alden continued to court Negro voters through adroit use of patronage. As his reelection campaign approached, he allegedly brought in Negroes from as far

10. *Richmond Dispatch,* March 16–18, April 1, 11, 30, 1870; William Asbury Christian, *Richmond: Her Past and Present* (Richmond: L. H. Jenkins, 1912), 314–24; Jack Maddex, Jr., *The Virginia Conservatives, 1867–1879: A Study in Reconstruction Politics* (Chapel Hill: University of North Carolina Press, 1970), 89–90.

11. *Nashville Daily Press and Times,* August 3, 1867; *Nashville Union and Dispatch,* September 29, 1867; Alden quoted in *Nashville Union and Dispatch,* October 11, 1867.

away as Kentucky to cast votes for him in return for money or jobs. Again Alden defeated a native Republican, this time by a vote of 1,839 to 1,336, an increase in the total number of ballots cast of over 500 despite a decline in the city's population. Though its charges must be weighed carefully, the opposition press seems to have been correct in attributing victory to the flagrant use of repeaters, the denial of the suffrage to legal voters, and other fraudulent practices. Helping also to assure victory was the appointment by Alden of all the election judges and clerks, many of them city employees with a clear stake in an Alden win. Whether legal or illegal, the Negro voters were the key to victory. And it seemed that Nashville could expect several more years of Alden rule. Yet because of alleged excessive spending ascribed to corruption, local citizens succeeded in getting the Conservative legislature to place the city in receivership. Alden was removed from office in June 1869, and in the subsequent municipal campaign the Conservatives swept every ward.[12]

A second technique employed by Redeemer legislatures to undermine local Radical strength was to change the procedures for selecting officials. Democratic strength in Atlanta, for example, was due in part to the greater number of white than black voters, even under the stringent registration requirements of the Reconstruction acts.[13] Even more important was the method used to elect members of the city council. During the first two municipal elections in which blacks were permitted to vote, the mayor and each of the ten councilmen (two from each ward) were chosen by the entire electorate. Despite splits in their party, the Democrats won complete victories in both elections. In October 1870, the Republican state legislature replaced the general ticket arrangement with a ward elections system. This change, while doing little to improve the prospects of electing a Republican mayor, helped the Republicans in council races due to their slim majorities in the Third and Fourth wards, where Negroes were concentrated. The tactic bore fruit two months later when the Republi-

12. *Nashville Union and American,* November 4, 1868; *Nashville Republican Banner,* September 27, 26, 1868. See also *Nashville Union and American,* November 5, 1868; *Nashville Republican Banner,* September 26, 1868; *Nashville Daily Press and Times,* September 29, 1868. *Nashville Daily Press and Times,* June 29, 1869; *Nashville Republican Banner,* September 26, 1869. For a defense of Alden's administration, see Gary L. Kornell, "Reconstruction in Nashville, 1867–1869," *Tennessee Historical Quarterly* 30 (Fall 1971): 277–87.

13. For the election of delegates to the 1867 Constitutional Convention, white registrants outnumbered blacks by 1,765 to 1,621. Franklin M. Garrett, *Atlanta and Environs: A Chronicle of Its People and Events,* 3 vols. (New York: Lewis Historical Publishing Company, 1954), 1:739. Atlanta was the only one of Georgia's five largest cities to have more white than black registrants. C. Mildred Thompson, *Reconstruction in Georgia: Economic, Social, Political, 1865–1872* (New York: Columbia University Press, 1915), 187.

cans elected four of the ten aldermen, including two blacks from the Third and Fourth wards.[14]

The *Atlanta Constitution* made the usual complaints about "the stupendous Radical frauds," including the use of illegal Negro voters made possible by both a weak registration law and the practice of allowing voters to cast ballots in any ward. The Republican *Daily New Era,* on the other hand, claimed with more evidence that the key to the council races was the change in the election law that ended citywide selection of aldermen.[15] Without it all the Radicals would have been defeated since Democrats who voted for the Independent mayoral candidate would not have supported Radical councilmen.

In light of these facts, the *Constitution* concluded that "the necessity of changing back is therefore apparent." Soon after the Democrats regained control of the legislature, the new law was indeed repealed and Atlanta reverted to the old system. In December 1871, the entire Democratic municipal ticket was swept into office, ending Atlanta's brief flirtation with Radical and Negro officeholders. According to the *Constitution,* the victory was "largely due" to the Fulton County (Atlanta) delegation in the legislature, which changed the voting procedure. Although President U. S. Grant carried the city in 1872, the Republican party had been destroyed as a major contender in local elections. The Republican challenger for mayor in that year was soundly defeated, and in 1873 the Democratic candidate ran unopposed, as was largely true of the Democratic slate of aldermen.[16] In future years black aldermanic candidates occasionally were the leading vote-getters in their home wards but were smothered by the white Democratic votes gathered by their opponents in other wards.[17]

The Tennessee and North Carolina legislatures also interceded to rob Radicals of their local gains. Nine weeks after the Conservatives in Nashville swept the city in the 1869 municipal election, the transfer of power was completed. The new Conservative state legislature abolished the Republican-controlled board of county commissioners and replaced it with the old General Court made up of locally elected justices of the peace. The court, dominated by Conservatives, discharged all Radical appointees of the commissioners and reinstated previous

14. *Atlanta Constitution,* December 3, 1868; December 3, 1869; Atlanta, *Code,* 1870, 41; *Atlanta Constitution,* December 9, 1870.

15. *Atlanta Constitution,* December 8–9, 1870; *Atlanta Daily New Era,* December 8, 1870.

16. *Atlanta Constitution,* December 9, 1870; November 11, December 7, 1871; November 7, December 5, 1872; December 4, 1873.

17. See, for example, ibid., December 5, 1879; December 2, 1880. For the reaction of a prominent black politician, see ibid., March 24, 1884.

officeholders. County government in Raleigh's Wake County was likewise redeemed by the North Carolina legislature. Empowered by the 1875 Redeemer
Constitution, the legislature transferred the right of electing justices of the peace
for counties, cities, and towns from the people to itself. The county commissioners, who had been popularly elected in the past (always Republicans in
Wake), were now to be appointed by the justices of the peace, removing still
other offices from the grasp of the Negro and white Republicans. Earlier the
legislature had helped to redeem the city of Raleigh itself. By an act of February
16, 1875, the election of the mayor was transferred from the people to a dras-
tically altered board of aldermen.[18]

What made the election of the mayor by the Raleigh aldermen such a victory
for the Democrats was the use of a third device employed by state legislatures
to provide sympathetic councils—gerrymandering. Indeed, gerrymandering in
its various forms was the most effective tactic used by sympathetic legislatures
both to redeem the cities and to keep them in the hands of white Democrats.
Without this technique, Redemption of Raleigh would have taken many more
years. The tenacity of Raleigh Radicalism was due to the presence of a significant number of white Republicans (as in Nashville) plus the relative parity in
the number of white and Negro voters (as in pre-1875 Montgomery). Then, too,
the white Conservatives were less inclined to use the tactics of violence and
fraud employed by Richmonders and, due to Radical strength in the state
government, they were unable, as had Atlanta, to count on help from that
sector until 1875.

In their frustrating attempts to oust the Radicals between 1869 and 1875, the
Democrats raised the specter of black rule and tried to rally the "good" whites to
throw out the "bad" scalawags, carpetbaggers, and Negroes. Despite this tactic,
in 1872 when there were more white than Negro registered voters for the first
time since the war, the Republicans again won the office of mayor and captured
seven of the nine positions on the board of commissioners. The Democratic
Daily News conceded that the party neither campaigned hard nor got out the
vote in contrast to the Republicans, who did both. As opposed to the other cities,
there was no cry of fraud or intimidation. Charges of Democratic apathy were
again leveled by the *Daily Sentinel* when the Negroes regained the lead in
registered voters the next year. The Republicans achieved a complete sweep in
the election, and the newspaper sadly concluded that "the white people are
satisfied with things as they are."[19]

18. *Nashville Union and American,* November 2, 1869; North Carolina, *Public Laws,*
1876–1877, 228; Raleigh, *Amended Charter,* 1876, 10.
19. *Raleigh Daily News,* May 7, 1872; *Raleigh Daily Sentinel,* April 26, 1873.

The Democrats returned stronger in 1874 and elected four of the nine commissioners, but still lost the mayoralty by three hundred votes. One of the four Democrats narrowly won election, while the five Republicans won handily. The following year, despite an all-out attack based on the racial issue by the two Democratic newspapers, the county Republican slate of delegates to the constitutional convention was overwhelmingly elected with Raleigh again leading the way.[20]

In short, Raleigh Democrats simply did not have enough white votes. Nor did their feeble attempts to attract black voters make much headway against the Radical tide. It was at this point that salvation came instead from a deus ex machina in the form of the new election law for the city passed by the legislature. Until February 1875, Raleigh had been divided into three wards: Eastern, Middle, and Western. The Middle Ward included the business district and many of the city's finest homes; it was the Conservative stronghold from 1865 to 1875. After the enfranchisement of Negroes, the two other wards were solidly Republican. With the exception of the Republican sweep in 1873, when a black was narrowly returned as one of the Middle Ward's aldermen, all of the Negro aldermen came from the Western and Eastern wards.

The same 1875 act that gave the aldermen power to elect the mayor divided the city into five wards.[21] Even though the Middle Ward contained less than one-third of the population of either of the other wards under the old system, its southern boundary was shortened in order to exclude a large number of Negroes. Despite the fact that the ratio of its population and voters to those of the Eastern and Western wards had been declining each year, the ward, now called the Third, was to be represented by five aldermen, whereas each of the other four was to have only three delegates. The Eastern Ward was irregularly divided into two wards, the First and Second, so as to assure Conservative control of the former. Under the old system the Republicans invariably sent three commissioners from the eastern part of the city; after redistricting, the Democrats and Republicans each sent three aldermen. A similar arrangement was made for the city's western sector. In 1874 the Western Ward contained 295 registered whites and 369 registered Negroes. As was true of the Eastern Ward, the whites were concentrated in the north and the blacks in the south. Judiciously separated into the Fourth and Fifth wards in 1875 with no regard to size of population or geographical boundaries, the old Republican ascendancy was now destroyed. For the 1875 elections the Fourth Ward had 47 white and 221 black voters; the Fifth had 299 white and 242 black.[22] The latter Negro figure is misleading,

20. *Raleigh Daily Sentinel,* May 5, 1874; August 5, 1875.
21. Raleigh, *Amended Charter,* 1876, 8–10.
22. *Raleigh Daily Sentinel,* April 22, 1874; April 23, 1875; U.S. Bureau of the Census,

however, since many of the blacks flooded the ward to register after the new lines had been drawn.[23]

Assured of five votes from the Third Ward and three from the First, Democrats needed to capture only one of the aldermanic races in the sole contested ward, the Fifth, to control the council and therefore elect the mayor. In fact, the Democrats were never caught napping and always returned the full slate. Even though the Republicans could count on electing six aldermen (at least half of them black), they had no chance of recapturing control of the city. They continued to receive a majority of the votes cast in local elections—Hayes and Garfield carried the city as well—but the Democrats had finally found a way to cope with the Negro vote. No wonder when announcing the return of eleven Democrats and six Republican aldermen in May 1875, the *Daily Sentinel* could gloat that "the long looked for time has come at last and Raleigh is in the hands of her good and true."[24]

In three of the remaining cities (Atlanta did not need much assistance), gerrymandering was also employed to keep the capitals free from Radical control. Closest to the Raleigh model was Richmond's similar attempt to nullify the Negro vote by isolating it within a portion of the city. Such action was necessitated by earlier Radical gerrymandering. During Mayor Chahoon's tenure, two heavily Negro areas on the outskirts of Richmond were annexed and the city was carved into five wards—Monroe, Clay, Jefferson, Marshall, and Madison— replacing the previous three-ward alignment. In drawing the boundaries care was taken to include large segments of black voters in each ward.[25] Thus, although Conservatives retained control of the council in the municipal election of May 1870, the first since the Radicals had been removed from office, all fifteen victorious Conservatives had been involved in close campaigns, the largest margin of victory being 45 votes. At that time in only one ward did the whites outnumber the blacks by more than three hundred voters, and even there the edge was only 1,701 to 1,330.[26]

Eleventh Census of the United States: 1890, vol. 1, *Population* (Washington, D.C.: Government Printing Office, 1893), part 1, 261; *Raleigh Daily Sentinel,* April 22, 1874; April 23, 1875.

23. See, for example, *Raleigh Daily Sentinel,* March 25, 27, 1875.

24. Ibid., November 12, 1876; *Raleigh News and Observer,* November 6, 1880; *Raleigh Daily Sentinel,* May 3, 1875.

25. Richmond City Council Minutes, December 30, 1867, Office of the City Clerk, Richmond City Hall, Richmond. In January 1868, the lines were slightly altered, evidently to reduce the overly high concentration of Negroes in Monroe Ward. The ward gained some whites and in turn gave some of its blacks to neighboring Clay. Ibid., January 13, 1868.

26. U.S. Bureau of the Census, *Ninth Census of the United States: 1870,* vol. 1, *Population* (Washington, D.C.: Government Printing Office, 1872), 280.

Taking advantage of the concentration of black population in the northern portion of the city, the new council created a sixth ward irregularly carved out of the upper area of four of the original five. This became the famous Jackson Ward, the center of black Richmond for the remainder of the century. Although the charter required that each ward have as nearly as possible an equal number of voters, by 1874 Jackson had a population of 11,806 while only two of the other wards had more than 9,100. More to the point, 70 percent of Jackson was black as compared to 44 percent of the ward with the next highest concentration.[27] In effect the Conservatives gave the Radicals and Negroes five seats on the council and three positions as justices of the peace in return for guaranteed possession of the remaining twenty-five seats and fifteen justiceships. In succeeding years Conservatives were free to offer occasional challenges in Jackson Ward, while the Republicans rarely contested elections in Conservative bailiwicks. After the charter was altered to establish a bicameral city legislature in 1874, white Conservatives or Democrats always held at least twenty-five of the thirty council posts and fifteen of the eighteen aldermanic seats.

The Tennessee legislature likewise endorsed Nashville's plans to limit the number of black council candidates. Local Democrats proved incapable of preventing the Republican leader, Thomas A. Kercheval, from winning two one-year and six two-year terms as mayor between 1872 and 1887. Nevertheless, in none of his terms did he ever have with him a majority of either of the city's two legislative bodies. Taking advantage of Kercheval's first defeat in 1874, the new mayor and city council pushed through a redistricting bill approved by the state legislature that made it all but impossible for the Republicans to elect representatives from any but two or three wards.[28]

But it was in Montgomery that the technique of gerrymandering was used to its fullest advantage. Rather than seeking to confine Republican and Negro influence, local Democrats and their friends in the legislature sought to eliminate it altogether. Not until 1875, after a hiatus of seven years, did Montgomery elect an entire Democratic slate of mayor and city council. Even then several of the races were close, and victory was due to a crippling split among white Republicans and the defection of an estimated 450 blacks. The Republicans had rebounded from an 1871 defeat to regain control of the

27. Richmond, *Charter,* 1870, 3; Richmond Board of Health Census, 1874, reprinted in *Richmond Dispatch,* January 1, 1875. As of 1890, Jackson contained 3,274 eligible black and 998 eligible white voters. Three of the other five wards had less than 3,050 males of voting age. Bureau of the Census, *Census: 1890,* vol. 1, part 1, 823.

28. *Biographical Directory, Tennessee General Assembly, 1796–1969* (Preliminary No. 21), Lincoln County, 28; the fight over redistricting can be followed in the *Nashville Republican Banner,* July 4, 8, 25, August 18, 26–28, 1875.

council, and drastic action was required in 1875 if the Democrats were to prevent another comeback. Allegedly as part of a retrenchment program, the new mayor called upon the Redeemer legislature to reduce the boundaries of the city to exclude an "unprofitable portion of its territory" where the city spent far more in providing services than it received from taxes. The resulting legislation, however, extended the police jurisdiction of the city one mile beyond its limits to include these retroceded areas, and it also guaranteed the former residents all privileges to Swayne School that they had previously enjoyed.[29]

It is at this point that the mayor's intent becomes clear, for Swayne was one of the city's two Negro schools. Nowhere else is there any indication that the excluded inhabitants were primarily black, but in fact the area was taken from the solidly Negro portions of the Fourth and Fifth wards, the two staunchest sections of Radical support. What was presented as an economy measure was actually a thinly veiled effort to minimize the effects of black suffrage. And it was successful. After the 1877 municipal election when the law became effective, the Radicals never seriously challenged for control of the city and no more blacks sat on the city council. As the *Daily Advertiser* stated, the victory "wipes out Radicalism entirely from our city politics."[30]

Gerrymandering was clearly the most effective technique in controlling the Radicals, yet it was made even more effective by legislative changes in the requirements for voting. Although this fourth legal device in support of the Conservatives became most significant later in the century, it was already being put to good use in the earlier period, especially in Montgomery. In 1871 the Democrats had captured nine of the twelve council seats, although the Radicals had elected their mayoralty candidate. The Democratic council immediately sought to tighten voting practices. Under the Republicans little effort had been made to maintain strict standards for voting. State law permitted the voter to cast his ballot at any polling place within his county of residence, and according to a staunch Democrat, "negroes soon began to tramp from place to place to cast their ballots at different boxes on the same day." Another law

29. *Montgomery Daily Advertiser,* May 5–6, 1875; *Montgomery Alabama State Journal,* April 20, May 5, 1875; August 6, 1876; Montgomery, *Annual Message of the Mayor of Montgomery and Reports of the Various City Officers and Standing Committees of the City Council for the Year Ending April 30, 1877* (Montgomery, 1877), 8; Alabama, *Acts,* 1876–1877, 254–57.

30. *Montgomery Daily Advertiser,* April 26, May 5, 1875; April 8, May 2, 1877. For Democratic endorsement of reduced city limits, see ibid., December 22, 1875; February 4, 1877. For Republican opposition, see *Montgomery Alabama State Journal,* December 31, 1875. For unsuccessful attempts by Republicans to enlarge the city limits in order to bring in more Negro voters, see *Montgomery Daily Advertiser,* April 4, December 3, 1873.

made it a crime punishable by a fine of not less than one thousand dollars to challenge voters.[31]

A new charter secured by the Democrats in February 1872 dealt a severe blow to Republicans. The registration book for each ward was required to be closed ten days before an election. In order to vote in a local election a person had to be a resident of the state for six months, the city for three months, and the ward for fifteen days.[32] Despite such obstacles, the Republicans managed to win back control of the council and reelect their mayor in the next election. In March 1875, therefore, even tighter restrictions were added after the *Montgomery Daily Advertiser,* speaking for local Democrats, pleaded: "If the Legislature does not come to the aid of the negro dominated communities then there is no help for this portion of Alabama."[33] The residency requirement was increased to five months in the city and three months in the ward. And in order to vote, a certificate of registration had to be surrendered at the polling place, which, thanks to another new section, had to be in the voter's home precinct. Throughout the process, both at registration and voting, officials (generally Democrats) had the right to challenge voters. Further undermining the Republicans, a provision shifted election day to May 1875 from the regularly scheduled December date, although victorious candidates were not to take office until December 1875. The Redeemers thus hoped to capitalize on the momentum generated by their statewide victories in the 1874 fall elections and more importantly sought to prevent nonresident Republicans from meeting the residency requirements in time for the municipal election.[34] One of the effects of the laws was immediately obvious to the English author Charles Nordhoff, who passed through Montgomery during the election swept by the Democrats. He noted: "In this place Democrats bought up, at two dollars a piece, the registration certificates of [over two hundred] colored men . . . and these were carefully retained, except in cases where it was quite certain that the original holder would vote the Democratic ticket."[35]

31. *Montgomery Daily Advertiser,* December 5, 1871; Hilary A. Herbert, "Grandfather's Talks about His Life under Two Flags," unpublished autobiography, 1917, 277–78, Southern Historical Collection, University of North Carolina, Chapel Hill.

32. Montgomery, *City Code,* 1875, 31–35.

33. *Montgomery Alabama State Journal,* December 2, 1873; *Montgomery Daily Advertiser,* February 6, 1875. See also *Montgomery Daily Advertiser,* January 27, 1875.

34. Montgomery, *City Code,* 1875, 39–40. The Republican *Alabama State Journal,* which had endorsed earlier election bills, strongly condemned the new measure, especially the change in election day. See, for example, January 31, February 2, 28, 1875. Registration dropped from 2,779 in 1873 to 2,131 two years later. *Alabama State Journal,* November 21, 1873; *Montgomery Daily Advertiser,* April 26, 1875.

35. Nordhoff, *The Cotton States in the Spring and Summer of 1875* (New York, 1876), 92. For Republican charges that Democrats were buying certificates, see *Montgomery Alabama State Journal,* April 7–9, 28, 1875. By manipulating the voting requirements after

In most of the five cities, and generally in the rest of the urban South, the legal techniques already described were sufficient to discipline the white Republicans and the new black voters. Yet Democrats and Conservatives in each city relied to varying degrees on the extralegal tactics of intimidation, fraud, and violence to obtain or hold power.[36] Nowhere, however, were they employed as consistently as in Richmond.

As already noted, Richmond Conservatives secured office through the removal of Chahoon's Radical administration by the state government, and once in power the city was gerrymandered to ensure their domination of the city council. Yet without the resort to illegal activities they would not have triumphed in the critical municipal elections in 1870 nor would they have continued their firm hold on the office of mayor.

In May 1870, a month after Chahoon had been removed from office, the contest between him and Mayor Ellyson was renewed in another municipal election. Other city officials and the entire city council were to be elected at the same time. Realizing the importance of the Negro vote, the Conservatives sought to neutralize it. This, of course, was nothing new. During the 1867 Constitutional Convention, for example, blacks had been threatened with the loss of their jobs for voting independently.[37] For the 1870 municipal election the *Richmond Dispatch,* in an editorial entitled "The Great Evil," warned blacks against being used by designing whites and called for an end to bloc voting by the freedmen.

The newspaper was most disconcerted by the registration figures, which revealed approximately 6,800 white and 6,200 black voters; it feared that if 300 whites voted with the blacks, the latter group would control the city. The Conservatives had done their best to increase their margin. In order to encourage whites to register there were separate places for the two races in each precinct. Committees of young white men were appointed to canvass the city and to weed out instances of fraudulent registration by blacks. They frequently

Mayor Alden was removed from office, Tennessee Redeemers were able to add twenty-seven hundred whites to Nashville's voting rolls. *Nashville Union and American,* July 27, 1869; Thomas B. Alexander, "Political Reconstruction in Tennessee, 1865–1870," in Richard O. Curry, ed., *Radicalism, Racism, and Party Realignment: The Border States during Reconstruction* (Baltimore: Johns Hopkins University Press, 1969), 72–73.

36. In Nashville, for example, after Alden won reelection, the *Republican Banner* urged that Negroes who had supported him be "instantly turned adrift" and their jobs given to "decent negroes" who had backed Alden's opponent (September 27, 1868). For the counting out of Montgomery Negroes, see Herbert, "Grandfather's Talks," 278–79.

37. *Richmond Enquirer,* October 26, 25, 1867; letter of B. L. Canedy, October 26, 1867, *Freedmen's Record* 3 (November 1867): 173. See also letter of M. L. Kellogg, December 25, 1867, *American Missionary* 12 (February 1868): 25.

had Negro and white Radicals arrested for allegedly giving false information or interfering with officers in the conduct of their duty. Invariably the charges were later dismissed but often not until after the election, thus costing the Radicals needed votes.[38]

On election day separate voting lines again were used for each race, a practice that, though inherited from the military authorities, was now used to limit the number of Negro voters. The predominantly Conservative officials at the polls also harassed many blacks. Although Richmond's Conservatives were clearly better organized than their counterparts in the other four cities—in addition to their fraudulent voting inspectors, they enjoyed formidable press support, used primaries to select their candidates, held nightly ward club meetings, had poll watchers, and provided transportation to the polls— Chahoon won by a majority of 283 votes and carried with him the rest of the general ticket. The Conservatives, however, captured fifteen of the twenty-five council seats. The *Richmond Dispatch* was consoled by the Conservative council victories and the fact that Republicans had elected justices of the peace in only two wards.[39]

The Conservatives, however, were not ready to settle for a partial victory. Despite the fact that even the *Dispatch* did not question the validity of Chahoon's triumph, the official count of the ballots by the Conservative-dominated board of election commissioners reversed the original tabulation and declared Ellyson the winner by a slim margin of 29 votes with the rest of the Conservative general ticket winning by 33 to 172 vote majorities. The action followed the disclosure that the ballots from the third precinct of Jefferson Ward allegedly had been removed from their box by a group of "ruffians" who attacked the person carrying them to City Hall for the official count. Although the tally had been placed on the poll books, the commissioners decided to throw out the precinct's results.[40]

The Radicals had been "counted out." Alone among the four precincts in the ward, the third had more black than white voters; indeed, it had the largest number of Negro voters of any precinct in the city. Whereas in the first count Chahoon had carried Jefferson Ward by 1,916 to 1,802, the official tabulation without the third precinct gave Ellyson the victory by 250 votes, sufficient to account for his margin in the entire city. The elimination of the precinct's votes also meant victory for the ward's five Conservative council candidates and their three running mates for justices of the peace. The Radical council delegation

38. *Richmond Dispatch,* May 28, 13, 1870; for examples of the arrests of Negroes and white Radicals, see ibid., May 23, 25, 28, 1870.
39. Ibid., November 26, May 28, 26, 1870.
40. Ibid., May 31, June 1, 1870.

was therefore reduced to the five from Monroe Ward and a sixth from Marshall Ward. Similarly, only three of the fifteen justices of the peace were Republican, compared to the original six. Another result was that all the justices and council-men were white.[41]

The Radicals challenged the right of the commissioners to throw out ballots in Jefferson Ward in the face of sworn statements by the judges that the poll books were correct.[42] To the dismay of the *Dispatch,* the Conservative judges on the Husting's Court agreed that the original vote total should have been accepted and acknowledged that had the votes from the Jefferson precinct been counted, the Republicans clearly would have won the election. As a result of numerous irregularities at the polling places, the judges ordered a new election. In the meantime, however, the recently sworn-in officials remained in office. Another concession to the Conservatives was even more significant. Despite the fact that the council race from Jefferson Ward was affected by the election commission's actions, only the race for citywide offices was to be repeated. Then, too, another registration drive held before the special election enabled the Conservatives to increase the white majority over black voters to 1,036.[43]

On election day Conservatives once again delayed and interfered with the casting of Negro votes, especially in Jefferson Ward. A Republican charged that although the second precinct in Jefferson Ward had approximately 900 registered voters, only a few more than 700 ballots were cast and at the time of closing more than 150 Negroes were awaiting to vote. In the third precinct over 300 blacks allegedly were left in a similar position. Thanks to the existence of separate lines for the races, white Conservatives sped through the polls. Even with such ploys and increased registration, the Democratic mayoral candidate won by only 189 votes. On the same day the incumbent Republican Congressman, C. H. Porter, was defeated by his Conservative opponent despite the presence of U.S. troops and federal deputy marshals, who arrested several Conservative judges for elec-tion irregularities. In future years the Conservatives and Democrats would use similar tactics to rule out the possibility of a Republican mayor, having already legally denied the opposition a chance to control the council.[44]

While urban blacks remained far better off than their rural counterparts, the

41. Ibid., May 18, 28, 31, 1870.
42. Ibid., June 6, 1870. They also challenged the elimination of part of the returns from a Marshall Ward precinct in which "irregularities" were discovered.
43. Ibid., July 21, 30, November 10, 1870.
44. Ibid., November 10, 26, 1870. For further examples of the tactics of Conservatives and Democrats, see, C. A. Bryce, "Good Old Days When Jackson Ward Was a Political Battleground," *Richmond Times Dispatch,* May 8, 1921; *Richmond Dispatch,* November 15–25, December 14–15, 1875; *Richmond Planet,* March 22, June 14, 1890.

triumphs of the Redeemers seriously undermined the gains made under the Radicals. Although blacks continued to exercise the franchise, their votes brought them much less. Most visibly the number of black officeholders declined greatly. Blacks continued to serve on city councils in Nashville, Richmond, and Raleigh, but their power was carefully contained. And with the return of the Redeemers, Raleigh and Montgomery lost their black policemen,[45] although black firemen remained in the three cities that had them. Patronage positions now depended almost entirely on Republican administrations in Washington. More significantly, although Redeemers adopted the Radical policy of segregation rather than returning to exclusion in such areas as welfare services and education, unequal treatment became the norm. In almost every category the loss was greatest in Atlanta and Montgomery where black political influence was weakest.[46] And blacks suffered as well at the bar of justice. Only in Montgomery and Raleigh had blacks seen more than limited service as jurors even during Reconstruction, but by 1890 they were largely gone from all local courts. By then black judges once found in Raleigh, Montgomery, Nashville, and Richmond were present only in Richmond. Unfortunately, unreliable or nonexistent statistics prevent any meaningful comparison of arrest and conviction patterns during Reconstruction and Redemption.[47]

Meanwhile white Democrats made only halfhearted attempts to attract the black vote. This was consistent with earlier policies of trying to block the enfranchisement of blacks and, these failing, to minimize the impact of the enfranchised blacks. Indeed, most Democrats preferred that Negroes remain Republicans. Blacks were already prevented from capturing control of any of the cities, and as Republicans they opened that party to the charge of being "the Negro party." It also would be divisive for factions of Democrats to compete against one another for the black vote.[48] Only by the end of the 1880s and the

45. *Raleigh Daily Sentinel,* August 21, 1875. The Negro policemen in Montgomery had actually been removed by the lame-duck Republican administration when the force was reduced for economic reasons. It was meant to be only a temporary measure. The new administration, however, restored the force to original size by hiring additional whites. *Montgomery Daily Advertiser,* June 15, September 7, 1875; January 11, 1876; Montgomery, *Annual Reports,* 1876–1877, 26.

46. See, for example, my essays "From Exclusion to Segregation: Health and Welfare Services" and "Half a Loaf," reprinted above.

47. Howard N. Rabinowitz, "The Search for Social Control: Race Relations in the Urban South, 1865–1890," 2 vols. (Ph.D. dissertation, University of Chicago, 1973), 2:559–73.

48. Appeals for the Negro vote and calls for white solidarity in the face of the "Negro dominated" Republican party alternated or even coexisted most graphically in two of the South's most influential newspapers. See, for example, *Richmond Dispatch,* December 9, 1870; March 9, 1875; May 25, 1876; *Atlanta Constitution,* November 21, 1875; October 23, December 8, 1881; October 22, 1890.

beginning of the 1890s with the decline of northern opposition and the frequency of local independent campaigns, especially the struggles over prohibition, would local Democrats become convinced that full-scale disfranchisement
was both necessary and safe to pursue. That decision would mark less of an
abrupt departure from earlier practice than is commonly acknowledged.[49] And
once again urban Democrats would look to the state legislatures to shape their
cities' political destinies.

49. On the pivotal role of the prohibition campaigns, see Rabinowitz, "Search for
Social Control," 2:773–83. For a different view of disfranchisement, see C. Vann Woodward, *The Strange Career of Jim Crow,* 3d rev. ed. (New York: Oxford University Press,
1974).

From Exclusion to Segregation

Southern Race Relations, 1865–1890

Since the appearance in 1955 of C. Vann Woodward's *Strange Career of Jim Crow,* extensive research has been devoted to uncovering the origins of racial segregation in the South. Woodward challenges the traditional view that the restrictive Jim Crow codes were the product of the immediate post-Reconstruction period. Emphasizing the legal side of segregation, he argues that the separation of the races grew out of forces operating in the last decade of the nineteenth and the first years of the twentieth centuries. He has modified his original position, but the existence of a law enforcing segregation remains the key variable in evaluating the nature of race relations. Because of the alleged absence of these statutes, Woodward contends that "forgotten alternatives" existed in the period between Redemption and the full-scale arrival of Jim Crow.[1]

Although George Tindall had in part anticipated Woodward's arguments, it is the "Woodward thesis" over which historians have chosen sides. Charles E. Wynes, Frenise A. Logan, and Henry C. Dethloff and Robert P. Jones explicitly declare their support for Woodward (even though much of their evidence seems to point in the opposite direction); and the same is true of the more recent implicit endorsements by John W. Blassingame and Dale A. Somers. In his study of South Carolina blacks, however, Joel Williamson, unlike Woodward, emphasizes customs rather than laws and sees segregation so entrenched in the state by the end of Reconstruction that he refers to the early appearance of a "duochromatic order." Vernon Lane Wharton's account of Mississippi blacks reaches a similar conclusion, and it has been used to support the arguments of Woodward's

---

1. *The Strange Career of Jim Crow,* 3d rev. ed. (New York: Oxford University Press, 1974), 65, 7, 3–109.

critics. Richard C. Wade's work on slavery in antebellum southern cities, Roger A. Fischer's studies of antebellum and postbellum New Orleans, and Ira Berlin's treatment of antebellum free Negroes also question Woodward's conclusions.[2]

The debate has been fruitful, shedding light on race relations in the postbellum South. But the emphasis on the alternatives of segregation or integration has obscured the obvious "forgotten alternative"—exclusion. The issue is not merely when segregation first appeared, but what it replaced. Before the Civil War, blacks were excluded from militia companies and schools, as well as most hospitals, asylums, and public accommodations. The first postwar governments during Presidential Reconstruction generally sought to continue the antebellum policy of exclusion. Nevertheless, by 1890—before the resort to widespread de jure segregation—de facto segregation had replaced exclusion as the norm in southern race relations. In the process the integration stage had been largely bypassed. This shift occurred because of the efforts of white Republicans who initiated it, blacks who supported and at times requested it, and Redeemers who accepted and expanded the new policy once they came to power.[3]

The first postwar governments, composed of Confederate veterans and elected by white male suffrage, saw little need to alter the prewar pattern of exclusion of blacks from most sectors of southern life.

2. Tindall, *South Carolina Negroes, 1877–1900* (Columbia: University of South Carolina Press, 1952; reprint ed., Baton Rouge: Louisiana State University Press, 1966); Wynes, *Race Relations in Virginia, 1870–1902* (Charlottesville: University Press of Virginia, 1961); Logan, *The Negro in North Carolina, 1876–1894* (Chapel Hill: University of North Carolina Press, 1964); Dethloff and Jones, "Race Relations in Louisiana, 1877–1898," *Louisiana History* 9 (Fall 1968): 301–23; Blassingame, *Black New Orleans, 1860–1880* (Chicago: University of Chicago Press, 1973); Somers, "Black and White in New Orleans: A Study in Urban Race Relations, 1865–1900," *Journal of Southern History* 40 (February 1974): 19–42; Williamson, *After Slavery: The Negro in South Carolina during Reconstruction, 1861–1877* (Chapel Hill: University of North Carolina Press, 1965); Wharton, *The Negro in Mississippi, 1865–1890* (Chapel Hill: University of North Carolina Press, 1947); Wade, *Slavery in the Cities: The South, 1820–1860* (New York: Oxford University Press, 1964); Fischer, "Racial Segregation in Ante Bellum New Orleans," *American Historical Review* 74 (February 1969): 926–37; Fischer, "The Post–Civil War Segregation Struggle," in *The Past as Prelude: New Orleans, 1718–1968,* ed. Hodding Carter et al. (New Orleans: Pelican Publishing House, 1968), 288–304; Fischer, *The Segregation Struggle in Louisiana, 1862–1877* (Urbana: University of Illinois Press, 1974); Berlin, *Slaves without Masters: The Free Negro in the Antebellum South* (New York: Pantheon, 1974).

3. Throughout this study *exclusion* refers to the policy by which blacks were not permitted to enjoy or benefit from the kinds of facilities available to whites. If, for example, only one insane asylum existed in a state and it barred blacks, this would constitute exclusion. But if provisions were made for blacks either in a separate wing of that asylum or in an entirely separate asylum, this would constitute segregation. By forming their own institutions after being excluded from comparable white ones, blacks contributed to the shift from exclusion to segregation.

During the period from 1865 to 1867 southern whites sought to limit admission to poorhouses, orphanages, insane asylums, and institutions for the blind, deaf, and dumb to whites. The states that established systems of public education, such as Georgia, Arkansas, and Texas, opened the schools to whites only. The North Carolina public school system, which dated from antebellum years, was initially closed because of fears that it would be forced to admit blacks. Savannah officials made the same decision about their city's parks.[4] Meanwhile, hotels, restaurants, and many theaters continued to exclude blacks.

Nevertheless, the policy of segregation rather than exclusion was already being forced upon the South. In Richmond and Nashville, for example, the United States Army and the Freedmen's Bureau made the local Conservative governments provide poorhouse facilities to indigent blacks. In both cases blacks were placed in quarters separate from whites. The Nashville Board of Education, fearing that it would be forced to integrate its newly opened school system, voluntarily set up separate schools for blacks in 1867. A year earlier the new Nashville Street Railway, which previously had excluded blacks, began running a separate car for them. On the state level, Alabama Conservatives admitted blacks for the first time on a segregated basis to the state insane asylum.[5]

Further undermining the policy of exclusion were the practices in those facilities that had experienced the shift from exclusion to segregation during earlier years. The use of separate streetcars for blacks in New Orleans, for example, superseded exclusion during the antebellum and war years. Steamboats and railroads had for many years segregated those few blacks who traveled as paying passengers. This practice continued, and Texas, Mississippi, and Florida strength-

4. Howard N. Rabinowitz, "From Exclusion to Segregation: Health and Welfare Services for Southern Blacks, 1865–1890," reprinted above; Georgia, *Acts*, 1866, 59; Arkansas, *Laws*, 1866–1867, 416; Texas, *General Laws*, 1866, 195. Tennessee was an exception. Because it was already in Republican hands, provision was made for the education of Negroes, though on a segregated basis. Tennessee, *Laws*, 1865–1866, 65; North Carolina, *Public Laws*, 1866, 87. In February 1867 a new system of public education was established in North Carolina for whites only. Ibid., 1866–1867, 117–20; Robert E. Perdue, *The Negro in Savannah, 1865–1900* (New York: Exposition Press, 1973), 22.

5. Richmond City Council Minutes, November 27, 1865; May 14, 1866; August 17, 1867; March 31, July 1, 14, November 20, Dec. 1, 1868, Archives Division of the Virginia State Library, Richmond; after 1866 the minutes are located in the Office of the City Clerk, Richmond City Hall; *Nashville Press and Times*, August 6, 1866; *Nashville Press and Times*, June 4, 1867; Letter of "A Colored Man" to the editor, ibid., June 26, 1866; Alabama, *Seventh Annual Report of the Officers of the Alabama Insane Hospital for the Year 1867* (Tuscaloosa, 1867), 9. Texas Conservatives appropriated ten thousand dollars to set up an asylum for Negroes, but evidently took no further action. Texas, *General Laws*, 1866, 207.

ened it through the passage of laws. Whatever exclusion there had been on boats and trains had not been forced; it had resulted from the absence of a large black clientele. Cemeteries suffered no such shortage. While most private cemeteries excluded all blacks except faithful servants, public cemeteries had by law or custom assigned blacks to special sections. This procedure continued after the war. Some places of amusement continued to exclude blacks; others retained their earlier pattern of segregated seating; still others, as in Nashville, opened their doors to freedmen for the first time, although on a segregated basis. Traveling circuses, especially popular with blacks, went so far in Montgomery as to establish separate entrances for the races. The Georgia Infirmary in Savannah and the Charity Hospital in New Orleans similarly continued as they had before the war to provide blacks with segregated medical care at city expense.[6]

Most white southerners remained committed to exclusion as the best racial policy. They were thwarted by the imposition of Congressional Reconstruction in March 1867 and thereafter were forced by military and civilian authorities to grant new privileges and services to blacks. Nonetheless, the net effect of the Radical measures on race relations in the southern states was to institutionalize the shift from exclusion to segregation.

The difference between the Republicans and their Conservative predecessors was particularly clear-cut in three areas: militia service, education, and welfare facilities. The former Confederates feared the arming of the freedmen and their enlistment in military companies; the Republicans quickly established black militia units, partly in the hopes that they would serve to support the governments. The Republicans, however, did not wish to antagonize local residents and so provided for segregated units under black officers. In a related area Radicals in Raleigh, North Carolina, and Nashville, Tennessee, established separate black fire companies.[7]

6. Roger A. Fischer, "A Pioneer Protest: The New Orleans Street-Car Controversy of 1867," *Journal of Negro History* 53 (July 1968): 219–33; Texas, *General Laws,* 1866, 97; Mississippi, *Laws,* 1865, 231–32; Florida, *Laws,* 1865, 24; Raleigh, *Charters Including Amendments Together with the Ordinances of the City for 1854* (Raleigh, 1854), 75; ibid., 1873, 31–32; Nashville, *A Digest of the Charter, Amendments and Acts of the General Assembly Pertaining to the City of Nashville with the Ordinances of the City in Force, June 1868* (Nashville, 1868), 60; Richmond, *Charter and Ordinances,* 1867 (Richmond, 1867), 91–92; Blassingame, *Black New Orleans,* 197; Fischer, "Post–Civil War Segregation Struggle," 296; Somers, "Black and White in New Orleans," 25; *Nashville Press and Times,* April 21, 1866; Whitelaw Reid, *After the War: A Southern Tour, May 1, 1865, to May 1, 1866* (London, 1866), 377; *Montgomery Ledger,* November 20, 1865. See also *Raleigh Standard,* March 3, 1866; *Richmond Dispatch,* October 6, November 7, 1866; *Nashville Press and Times,* April 3, 1865; Perdue, *Negro in Savannah,* 22; Blassingame, *Black New Orleans,* 197.

7. Otis A. Singletary, *Negro Militia and Reconstruction* (Austin: University of Texas

The public schools followed a similar policy. Under the Republicans, schools were opened to blacks for the first time. With the notable exceptions of South Carolina and Louisiana it was expected that there would be separate schools for each race. Only in New Orleans did a significant degree of integration take place, even during the height of Reconstruction.[8]

Much attention has been given to the Republicans' stand regarding the militia and public schools. This is not true of Republican welfare policy. It is commonly acknowledged that the Radical governments expanded the range of welfare services available to white and black southerners, but their private or public welfare facilities were rarely integrated. Blacks were provided for, but on a segregated basis. Republicans in Mississippi, North Carolina, and Virginia established either segregated quarters or entirely separate institutions for the Negro insane of their states. Facilities for the care of the Negro blind, deaf, and dumb in Mississippi and North Carolina were also segregated; the same would have been the case at the South Carolina Institution for the Deaf and Blind except that whites withdrew when blacks were admitted, thus forcing it to close. Segregated provision was also made for South Carolina's Negro orphans, although in most other states publicly supported orphanages remained for whites only. Montgomery, Alabama, Richmond, Virginia, Vicksburg and Natchez, Mississippi, and New Orleans, Louisiana, were among the many cities that provided new segregated dispensaries and hospitals for the Negro indigent.[9] But the poorhouses in Richmond and Nashville remained segregated, and in cities such as New Orleans, Raleigh, Richmond, and Nashville blacks were buried in segregated sections of the municipal cemeteries.

Press, 1957), 5, 11–15, 21; L. Branson, ed., *The North Carolina Business Directory,* 1869 (Raleigh, 1869), 152; *Nashville Union and Dispatch,* October 22–25, 1867.

8. North Carolina, *Public Laws,* 1868–1869, 471; Georgia, *Acts and Resolutions,* 1870, 57; Alabama, *Acts,* 1868, 148; Joe M. Richardson, *The Negro in the Reconstruction of Florida* (Tallahassee: Florida State University Press, 1965), 113–14; Wharton, *Negro in Mississippi,* 244; Williamson, *After Slavery,* 219–22; Louis R. Harlan, "Desegregation in New Orleans Public Schools during Reconstruction," *American Historical Review* 67 (April 1962): 663–75.

9. Wharton, *Negro in Mississippi,* 267; Williamson, *After Slavery,* 281; L. L. Polk, comp., *Handbook of North Carolina Embracing Historical and Physiographical Sketches of the State with Statistical and Other Information Relating to Its Industries, Resources, and Political Conditions* (Raleigh, 1879), 181–82; Dr. William Francis Drewy, *Historical Sketch of the Central State Hospital and the Care of the Colored Insane of Virginia* (Richmond: Everett Waddey, 1905); Wharton, *Negro in Mississippi,* 268; Polk, *Handbook of North Carolina,* 182; Tindall, *South Carolina Negroes,* 280–81, 278; Montgomery City Council Minutes, October 5, 1868, March 18, 1872, Alabama Department of Archives and History, Montgomery; Richmond, *Charter and Ordinances,* 1867, 130; Wharton, *Negro in Mississippi,* 266; Blassingame, *Black New Orleans,* 166.

The Republican-controlled legislature in North Carolina was so averse to the idea of forced integration that in 1870 it defeated a proposal to assure Negroes the same facilities as whites on steamboats and railroads. Even the spate of antidiscrimination laws passed elsewhere often over the objections of some white Republicans seem to have had little effect on the pattern of segregation in public conveyances. If they accomplished anything, the laws encouraged the railroad and steamboat companies to provide supposedly equal though separate accommodations for blacks. Despite the passage of the 1866 Civil Rights Act, a British traveler who toured the South during 1867–1868 concluded, "There are 'nigger cars' open, of course to white people, and often used as smoking cars, but to which all coloured passengers have to confine themselves." Wharton concluded about Mississippi's antidiscrimination railroad act passed in 1870: "In spite of its stringent provisions, the law had almost no effect." As demonstrated by the numerous suits by blacks against southern railroad companies, the best that blacks could hope for were segregated accommodations that equaled those provided the whites.[10]

The new governments had greater impact on traveling arrangements in streetcars. It is generally agreed that de jure segregation was a product of the 1890s.[11] The extent of prior de facto segregation remains uncertain, however, partly because of the character of the streetcar system itself. It would be a simple matter to determine if there had been different cars for the two races, either run sep-

10. "A Bill to Protect the Rights of Citizens Traveling in Public Conveyances," February 21, 1870, Legislative Papers no. 836, North Carolina Department of Archives and History, Raleigh; Williamson, *After Slavery,* 279–80, 357; Wharton, *Negro in Mississippi,* 230–31; *Cong. Globe,* 42d Congress, 2d session, 429–34 (January 17, 1872); David Macrae, *The Americans at Home: Pen-and-Ink Sketches of American Men, Manners, and Institutions,* 2 vols. (Edinburgh, 1870), 2:219. See also, Two Englishmen [Alexander Rivington and Harris Rivington], *Reminiscences of America in 1869* (London, 1870), 220; Wharton, *Negro in Mississippi,* 231. Louisiana's law was equally ineffective with regard to steamboats and railroads. Significant integration in trains, however, may have been secured through the use during the chartering process of written and verbal pledges to provide "equal accommodations" to members of both races. Blassingame, *Black New Orleans,* 190–94; for suits by blacks, see *Atlanta Constitution,* April 12, May 19, 1871; January 28, 1876; *Richmond Dispatch,* May 24, 1876; *Nashville American,* May 16, 1879; letter to the editor, *Montgomery Advertiser,* November 8, 1871.

11. Fischer, "A Pioneer Protest," 232–33; Marjorie M. Norris, "An Early Instance of Non-Violence: The Louisville Demonstrations of 1870–1871," *Journal of Southern History* 32 (November 1966): 487–504; August Meier and Elliott Rudwick, "A Strange Chapter in the Career of 'Jim Crow,'" in *The Black Community in Modern America,* 14–19, vol. 2 of *The Making of Black America: Essays in Negro Life & History,* 2 vols., ed. Meier and Rudwick (New York: Atheneum, 1969); August Meier and Elliott Rudwick, "Negro Boycotts of Jim Crow Street Cars in Tennessee," *American Quarterly* 21 (Winter 1969), 755–63; August Meier and Elliott Rudwick, "The Boycott Movement against Jim Crow Streetcars in the South, 1900–1906," *Journal of American History* 55 (March 1969), 756–75.

arately or in tandem, but the presence of one car without racial designation might still mean that either blacks had been excluded or had been segregated within that car.

Another difficulty in considering streetcars arises from their staggered appearance in southern cities. The New Orleans system, for example, dates from the antebellum period, while Richmond's began operating in 1865, Atlanta's in 1871, and Raleigh's in 1886. Each line might have been segregated from its inception, and thus it cannot be assumed that because Louisville or New Orleans apparently desegregated their cars before 1870, subsequent lines in other cities followed their example. The same is true within each city—because segregation was discontinued on one line does not necessarily mean that it was not resumed until the appearance of Jim Crow legislation. Nor does it mean that other companies in the city might not have initiated de facto segregation.

What is clear is that in many cities the initial Republican contribution was to force streetcar companies to admit black riders. Richmond, Virginia, provides an early example of the change in streetcar policy. Prior to May 1867, Richmond initially excluded Negroes from the cars and then permitted them to ride on the outside. In April 1867, four blacks staged a sit-in and were forcibly ejected from a car by a policeman. City officials ruled that as a private concern the railway company could establish its own regulations, but they were overruled by federal military authorities who directed that the cars must carry all passengers able to pay the fare. Nevertheless, General John Schofield permitted the substitution of segregation for exclusion. Sources differ as to whether there were alternate cars for each race with the Negro car distinguished by a black ball on its roof or whether those cars with a white ball were solely for white women and their escorts.[12]

This transition from exclusion to segregation with perhaps an intermediary stage of riding on the platforms of the cars was repeated in other cities. Negroes in Nashville, Charleston, and Mobile were among the many who won the right to ride in the streetcars under civilian Republican or military authorities. Maria Waterbury, however, a northern teacher, found that as late as 1871 a Mobile streetcar contained an iron latticework dividing the car racially. When a woman took her servant into the wrong end of the car, the conductor stopped the vehicle and moved the black woman into her "proper place." In cities such as New Orleans the question remains as to the presence of segregation when blacks finally rode in the same cars as whites.[13]

12. Writers Program of the Works Progress Administration in the State of Virginia, comp., *The Negro in Virginia* (New York: Hastings House, 1940), 241–42; Alexander Wilbourne Weddell, *Richmond, Virginia, in Old Prints 1737–1887* (Richmond: Johnson Publishing Co., 1932), 234; *Richmond Dispatch*, May 9, 1867; January 29, 1870.

13. *Nashville Press and Times*, June 26, 1866; June 18, 25, 28, 1867; *Mobile National-*

In a variety of public accommodations the Reconstruction governments proved unable or unwilling to push for integration. Exclusion remained the rule in the best restaurants and hotels as well as in many theaters. Judging from the recurring use in newspaper advertisements of "gentlemen" and "ladies" to describe the patrons of skating rinks, this new craze was another form of recreation initially denied blacks.[14]

Nevertheless, blacks did enjoy many forms of segregated recreation. Newspapers were filled with advertisements or news accounts about "negro barrooms," "negro brothels," and "negro billiard parlors." Montgomery boasted a "colored skating rink," Nashville had a "colored fairgrounds," and New Orleans and Nashville had Negro grandstands at the local racetracks. Negroes in Montgomery went to picnics at Lambert Springs and the Cypress Pond while whites went to Oak Grove and Pickett Springs. And most of the theaters, including many previously closed to blacks, provided segregated seating in the galleries.[15]

There is also evidence that Republican politicians observed the color line in official functions. At the 1868 Constitutional Convention in South Carolina, white delegates occupied the front rows while the blacks filled in the seats at the rear of the hall; in the courtroom of the Radical circuit court judge in Richmond, whites sat on the west side and blacks on the east; and in 1868, North Carolina Republicans divided the gallery of the senate into three sections: one for whites, one for blacks, and one for both races.[16] Republican governor Robert K. Scott of South Carolina sought to make amends to that state's blacks because none had

---

ist, May 9, July 25, 1867; April 29, 1870; Waterbury, *Seven Years among the Freedmen* (Chicago, 1891), 115–16; see Fischer, "A Pioneer Protest," 219–33. Fischer never confronts the basic distinction between exclusion and segregation.

14. Charles Dudley Warner, *Studies in the South and West with Comments on Canada* (New York, 1889), 14–15; *Montgomery Advertiser,* February 26, 1873; *Montgomery Alabama State Journal,* March 7, 1873; *Atlanta Constitution,* October 7, 1868; *Montgomery Advertiser,* March 12, 1870; *Montgomery Alabama State Journal,* April 9, 1872; *Atlanta Constitution,* December 21, 1869; October 18, 1871; *Nashville Union and American,* June 7, 1870.

15. *Atlanta Intelligencer,* July 14, 1870; *Nashville Press and Times,* February 1, 1868; *Montgomery State Sentinel,* July 3, 1867; *Montgomery Advertiser,* March 9, 1871; *Montgomery Republican Sentinel,* October 31, 1872; *Montgomery Alabama State Journal,* April 6, 1873; *Nashville Republican Banner,* March 2, 8, April 13, 1871; Blassingame, *Black New Orleans,* 185; *Montgomery Advertiser,* May 4, 29, June 3, July 6, 1869; May 28, 1870; *Montgomery Alabama State Journal,* July 5, 31, 1869; May 8, 17, June 11, 1872; for examples of seating in galleries, see advertisements in *Atlanta Constitution,* January 21, 1871; *Raleigh Standard,* October 15, 1869; *Richmond Dispatch,* May 3, 1869; *Nashville Union and American,* January 25, 1871; *Montgomery Advertiser,* January 30, 1872.

16. Williamson, *After Slavery,* 293–94; *Richmond Dispatch,* May 9, 1867; North Carolina, *Senate Journal* (July 1868), 41. Democrats also practiced segregation at their rallies. For the presence of separate speakers' stands and dinner tables at a Democratic barbecue, see *Montgomery Advertiser,* August 16, 1868.

been invited to the annual ball of the governor in 1869. He held open house every Thursday, but "only Negro politicians called at that time."[17]

It would seem, therefore, that the Republicans had little desire to "Africanize" the South. Indeed, with the exception of a few egalitarians, southern Republicans, whether during or after Reconstruction, did not seek to force integration on unwilling southern whites. Whether because of their own racial prejudice, the need to attract white voters to the party, or the belief that legislated integration was unconstitutional or simply could not succeed, the Negroes' white allies sought to replace exclusion with segregation. Ascribing motivation is always risky, but perhaps it was hoped that such a policy would appease blacks, while at the same time not frighten prospective white voters with the specter of miscegenation.

The Republicans stood for more than segregation. They called for separate but equal treatment for blacks. During debates on congressional civil rights legislation, for example, Senator Joshua Hill of Georgia and Representative Alexander White of Alabama argued that separate provisions for blacks in public carriers, places of amusement, or hotels and restaurants was not a violation of civil rights if the accommodations were equal to those of whites.[18] The Alabama Republican party in its 1874 platform declared, "The republican party does not desire mixed schools or accommodations for colored people, but they ask that in all these advantages they shall be equal. We want no social equality enforced by law." Tennessee's Republican governor signed a separate but equal accommodations measure in 1881, and a Georgia Republican legislature passed a similar bill in 1870. Alabama Republicans pushed for such a measure and congratulated those railroads that voluntarily provided separate but equal accommodations.[19] The Republican leg-

17. Williamson, *After Slavery,* 294.

18. *Congressional Globe,* 42d Congress, 2d session, 241 (December 20, 1871); *Congressional Record,* 43d Congress, 2d session, Appendix, 15 (February 4, 1875). For the opposition of Tennessee white Republicans to national civil rights legislation, see *Nashville Republican Banner,* May 8, September 10, October 1, 1874. For further support of the contention that, with the exception of a few Radicals, congressional Republicans sought to end exclusion and unequal treatment of blacks rather than segregation per se, see Alfred Avins, "Racial Segregation in Public Accommodations: Some Reflected Light on the Fourteenth Amendment From the Civil Rights Act of 1875," *Western Reserve Law Review* 18 (May 1967): 125–83.

19. *Montgomery Alabama State Journal,* August 23, 1874; Georgia, *Laws,* 1870, 398; Stanley J. Folmsbee, "The Origin of the First 'Jim Crow' Law," *Journal of Southern History* 15 (May 1949): 235–47; for the attempt to pass state civil rights legislation, see *Montgomery Alabama State Journal,* February 25, March 1, 7, 9, 10, April 8, August 14, 1873. For Republican support of separate but equal treatment, see ibid., January 27, 1872; May 29, June 6, 14, 30, July 11, 1874; *Alabama Weekly State Journal,* December 11, 1869; March 18, 1870; *Mobile Nationalist,* April 18, 1867.

acy to the Redeemers therefore consisted of the seemingly mutually exclusive policies of segregation and equality.

Given the opposition of southern whites it seems unlikely that the Republicans could have forced integration on the South. Conditions in the South at the end of Reconstruction were revealed in the reaction to the civil rights agitation that culminated in the Civil Rights Act of 1875. The *Atlanta Constitution,* though thankful for omission of cemeteries and schools from the final version of the law, concluded, "Its other provisions are all that the most revolutionary white villain or the densest negro brain could desire." After passage of the act, the *Raleigh Daily Sentinel* argued, "If the principles of the Republicans succeed, the negro will be forced upon . . . [the white man's] wife, and his daughter, on the cars, steamboats, in public inns, at hotel tables, and in theatres and other places of amusement."[20]

Once passions cooled the southern press reassured its readers that either the law quickly would be declared unconstitutional or else the Democrats would repeal it when they won their expected victories in the 1876 presidential and congressional elections. Referring to the statute as a "dead letter," the *Atlanta Constitution* pointed out, "It gets a judicial cuff whenever it appears in the courts, no matter whether the judge be a republican or democrat."[21] The paper was correct. Federal courts in Atlanta, Richmond, and Savannah upheld the right of railroads and steamboats to provide separate accommodations for the races just as they could for members of the two sexes.[22]

Bothered little by the 1875 Civil Rights Act even before its official demise in 1883, the Redeemers occasionally returned to exclusion or instituted segregation in those few cases where there had been integration. For example, the Montgomery city hospital, which was operated on a segregated basis under a Radical Republican administration, was closed by the Redeemer mayor; alternative provision was made for white patients but not for black. And although Hamilton Park

20. For earlier opposition to prospective state civil rights acts, see *Montgomery Advertiser,* August 13, 1868; December 7, 1869; July 4, 1873; Blassingame, *Black New Orleans,* 183–84, 190–91; Williamson, *After Slavery,* 280; *Atlanta Constitution,* February 6, 1875; *Raleigh Daily Sentinel,* August 2, 1875.

21. *Atlanta Constitution,* April 3, 1876; March 27, 1875; *Richmond Dispatch,* March 10, 1875; *Nashville Republican Banner,* March 2, 1875; *Nashville Banner,* October 18, 1883; *Montgomery Advertiser,* October 23, 1883. Even if the law did not alter southern life, the potential for more rigid enforcement always existed and whites therefore rejoiced when the United States Supreme Court declared it unconstitutional in 1883. *Richmond Dispatch,* October 14–21, 1883; *Atlanta Constitution,* October 16, 21, 1883.

22. *Atlanta Constitution,* January 28, 1876; *Richmond Dispatch,* May 24, 1876; *Nashville American,* May 16, 1879.

and Angelo's Hall in Jackson, Mississippi, had been used by whites and blacks on separate occasions under the Republicans, by 1890 both facilities were closed to blacks. The basic response of the Redeemers, however, was to continue already existing segregation. Frequently they sought to strengthen the barriers that had separated the races under the Republicans. Educational segregation previously enforced by school acts in Georgia, Tennessee, and North Carolina was now written into the new Redeemer constitutions.[23] Blacks in North Carolina and Alabama had been cared for in separate wards of white insane asylums; they were now moved into their own separate institutions. And in Raleigh, where the Radicals had given blacks the choice of being buried in the segregated portion of the old municipal cemetery or in a new cemetery built exclusively for them, the Redeemers prohibited the burial of blacks in the old cemetery.[24]

White opinion was not unified, but most Redeemers also adopted the rhetoric of the Republicans' separate but equal commitment. Despite the failure to honor this commitment, in several instances the Redeemers actually moved beyond their predecessors to provide segregated, if unequal, facilities in areas previously characterized by exclusion. Some whites distinguished between segregation and discrimination. Thus Tennessee law prohibited "discrimination" in any place of public amusement that charged a fee but nevertheless maintained that this provision did not outlaw "separate accommodations and seats for colored and white persons."[25]

Additional public institutions opened their doors to blacks for the first time under the Redeemers. Among those states making initial provision for Negro blind, deaf, and dumb were Texas, Georgia, Alabama, Tennessee, and South Carolina; and in 1887, the same year that Tennessee provided a Negro depart-

23. Montgomery, *Annual Message of the Mayor of Montgomery and Reports of the Various City Officers and Standing Committees of the City Council for the Year Ending April 30, 1877,* (Montgomery, 1877), 14; ibid., 1885, 55–56; C. J. Allardt, comp., *Montgomery City Directory for 1888* (Montgomery: R. L. Polk and Co., 1888), 19; Wharton, *Negro in Mississippi,* 232; Georgia Constitution (1877), art. 8, sec. 1; Tennessee Constitution (1870), art. 11, sec. 12; North Carolina Constitution (1875), art. 9, sec. 2.

24. Polk, *Handbook of North Carolina,* 181–82; *Raleigh Daily Sentinel,* March 18, November 3, December 8, 1875; North Carolina, *Annual Report of the Board of Directors and the Superintendent of the North Carolina Insane Asylum for 1877* (Raleigh, 1877), 30; Alabama, *Annual Report of Alabama Insane Hospital,* 1878, 45–46; ibid., 1880, 18; ibid., 1888, 24; Raleigh, *Charters and Ordinances,* 1876, 96–97. See also Wharton, *Negro in Mississippi,* 232.

25. For the Redeemers' failure to honor separate but equal treatment, see my essays "Health and Welfare Services for Southern Blacks" and "Half a Loaf: The Shift from White to Black Teachers in the Negro Schools of the Urban South, 1865–1890," reprinted above; Tennessee, *Laws,* 1885, 124–25. See also Henry W. Grady, *The New South* (New York, 1889), 246.

ment for the previously all-white and privately run Tennessee Industrial School, North Carolina opened its Colored Orphan Asylum.[26]

Segregation may have also replaced exclusion in other areas of southern life after Reconstruction rather than integration. As early as 1872, Atlanta's Union Passenger Depot had a "Freedmen's Saloon," and at least by 1885 Nashville's Union Depot had "a colored passenger room." In 1885 Austin, Texas, was among the Texas cities required by city ordinance to have separate waiting rooms for both races.[27] It is not known what facilities existed for blacks before the appearance of these Negro waiting rooms. The experiences of Montgomery, Alabama, and Raleigh, North Carolina, however, are instructive. The new Union Depot in Montgomery was described in 1877 as having "a ladies waiting room" and a "gents' waiting room"; the original plans for the Raleigh Union Depot in 1890 included a "ladies waiting room" and a "gentlemen's waiting room." Although there was no reference to a Negro waiting room, the use of the words *gents, gentlemen,* and *ladies* rather than *men* and *women* suggests the exclusion of blacks. The mention of three waiting rooms at the Montgomery Depot in 1885—one each for "ladies," "gentlemen," and "colored people"—and the revised plans for the Raleigh Depot that contained a separate waiting room for blacks suggest further evidence of the shift from exclusion to segregation.[28]

Segregation persisted or replaced exclusion in theaters. For the most part blacks were confined to separate galleries. In Richmond, however, because of

26. Lawrence D. Rice, *The Negro In Texas, 1874–1900* (Baton Rouge: Louisiana State University Press, 1971), 237–38; Georgia, *Report of the Institution for the Deaf and Dumb,* 1876 (Rome, Ga., 1876), 6; ibid., 1882, 7; Georgia, *Report of the Board of Trustees of the Georgia Academy for the Blind for 1883* (Macon, Ga., 1883), 11; Alabama, *Annual Reports of the Alabama Institution for the Education of the Deaf and Dumb and Blind for 1889 and 1890* (Montgomery, 1890), 7–8; 1891–1892, 11; Tennessee, *Acts,* 1881, 139; Tennessee, *Twenty-First Biennial Report of the Trustees and Superintendent of the Tennessee School of the Blind for 1885* (Nashville, 1885), 10; Tindall, *South Carolina Negroes,* 281; Tennessee, *First Biennial Report of the Tennessee Industrial School for the Period 1887–1888* (Nashville, 1888), 22; North Carolina, *Report of the Board of Public Charities of North Carolina for 1891* (Raleigh, 1891), 12–14. By 1887 the Arkansas Insane Asylum had separate wings for the races. In Kentucky, a southern but non-Confederate state, the legislature did not provide for the education of the Negro blind until 1884. Three years later the inmates of the Institution for the Blind were living in segregated quarters as was the case at the Industrial School of Reform. Warner, *Studies in the South and West,* 286.

27. *Atlanta Constitution,* January 25, 1872; *Nashville Banner,* December 15, 1885; Rice, *Negro in Texas,* 147. Segregation in Nashville waiting rooms was probably in force much earlier than 1885. The fact that in 1873 the city's Louisville Depot had a "gentlemen's sitting room" rather than a "men's" waiting room suggests the existence of a Negro waiting room or the absence of any provision for black passengers. *Nashville Republican Banner,* November 14, 1873.

28. *Montgomery Advertiser,* February 14, 1877; October 17, 1885; *Raleigh News and Observer,* April 24, October 31, 1890.

the 1875 Civil Rights Act blacks won access to a segregated portion of the once exclusively white dress circle.[29] Most restaurants and hotels continued to exclude blacks, as did the better barrooms. Some bars catering to whites charged blacks outrageous prices or provided poor service; less subtle was the sign over the bar of a Nashville saloon in 1884—No Drinks Sold to Colored Persons. In 1888 the *Atlanta Constitution* reported that of Atlanta's sixty-eight saloons, five served only blacks and only two catered to both blacks and whites.[30] On those instances when blacks were admitted to primarily white restaurants, bars, and hotels, the races were carefully segregated. A restaurant in the rear of a Nashville saloon served food to "responsible and well behaved colored people" in its kitchen; the Planters Hotel in Augusta, Georgia, seated blacks at separate tables in the dining room; the St. Charles, the only Richmond hotel to accept a black delegate to the 1886 Knights of Labor Convention, gave him second-class quarters and seated him at a table in the dining room farthest from the door and behind a screen; and in answer to the Civil Rights Act, Montgomery's Ruby Saloon set up "a small counter" apart from the main bar for black customers.[31] Such examples probably marked only a transitory stage on the way to total segregation.

29. *Atlanta Weekly Defiance,* October 8, 1881; *Atlanta Constitution,* September 23, 1874; *Nashville Republican Banner,* November 8, 1873; *Raleigh News and Observer,* January 11, 1891; *Richmond Dispatch,* December 9, 11, 1875. John Blassingame reports that after being confined to the Jim Crow section of the St. Charles Theatre following the war, New Orleans blacks finally gained the right to sit in the dress circle as a result of the Civil Rights Act of 1875. He does not mention if they were segregated as in Richmond. He also points out that after vacillating between segregation and integration, the New Orleans Opera House was finally forced to accept integration. There is no indication as to how long this policy persisted, but, whatever the length, it clearly departed from the provisions elsewhere in the South. Blassingame, *Black New Orleans,* 186–87.

30. *Nashville Union and American,* March 16, 1875; *Nashville Banner,* November 3, 1884; *Atlanta Constitution,* February 18, 1888. Under fear that the Civil Rights Act of 1875 would force black guests upon them, white hotels in Augusta, Georgia, and Chattanooga, Tennessee, gave up their public licenses and became private boarding houses. *Atlanta Constitution,* March 7, 9, 1875. A black who sought lodging at a Nashville boarding house was told by the proprietor, "I don't board your kind." *Nashville Union and American,* March 11, 1875. Blassingame concluded that even in New Orleans white hotel and restaurant owners were among the staunchest foes of the civil rights act. *Black New Orleans,* 196. See also Fischer, "Post–Civil War Segregation Struggle," 296–97; Wynes, *Race Relations in Virginia,* 76.

31. *Nashville American,* June 13, 1883; *Atlanta Constitution,* March 9, 1875; *Richmond Dispatch,* October 7, 1886; *Montgomery Advertiser,* May 12, 1875. The situation in New Orleans again seems to have been atypical in that a number of the leading restaurants were integrated. Even so, by 1874 former lieutenant governor P. B. S. Pinchback was refused service at Redwitz's Saloon. Blassingame, *Black New Orleans,* 188–89. White teachers at Negro colleges were severely criticized for eating at the same tables with their students. *American Missionary* 20 (February 1876): 36.

With the exception of New Orleans, athletic events in the South were rigidly segregated. Most cities had at least two black baseball teams. Militia companies similarly engaged in racially separated competition. Segregated places in parades and observances, usually in the rear, were provided for blacks as well.[32]

Prostitution also suffered the effects of segregation. Even in New Orleans, houses of prostitution offering white and black women to a mixed clientele had become a rarity by 1880. White and black prostitutes resided on separate blocks in Atlanta. When two well-dressed mulattoes sought admission to a brothel on Collins Street that served only whites, they were driven off by gunfire.[33] If taken to court, the prostitutes would likely have found the spectators racially separated, and perhaps, like the procedure in Savannah's mayor's court in 1876, they would have sworn on a Bible set aside for their particular race.[34]

The situation in parks was more complex. There were few formal parks and pleasure grounds in antebellum cities, and blacks were excluded from those that existed.[35] Indeed, it was not until the mid-1870s, in most cases after Republicans had relinquished control of local governments, that the park movement began to affect southern urban life. Most of these new parks were privately owned, often by streetcar companies that used them to encourage traffic on their lines, but municipally owned parks became common by the 1880s.

Increasingly blacks were barred from many parks. Sometimes this can be surmised only from the language of the local press.[36] In other cases speculation is unnecessary. Blacks taking the street railway to Atlanta's Ponce de Leon

32. *Atlanta Constitution,* May 31, 1886; August 11, 1887; *Nashville Press and Times,* March 24, 1868; *Nashville Banner,* July 6, 1881; September 2, 1887; Sarah McCulloh Lemmon, "Entertainment in Raleigh in 1890," *North Carolina Historical Review* 40 (October 1963): 334; *Atlanta Constitution,* July 6, 1884; Somers, "Black and White in New Orleans," 34–35, 39–41; *Richmond Dispatch,* October 17, 1885; *Atlanta Constitution,* August 23, 1883. White military companies from Atlanta, Savannah, and Montgomery withdrew from the national drill held in Washington, D.C., because black companies were to participate. *Savannah Tribune,* April 9, 1887. See also *Atlanta Constitution,* August 7, September 1, 1885; *Montgomery Alabama State Journal,* April 17–18, 1872; *Richmond Dispatch,* October 25, 1875; *Nashville Banner,* October 15, 1887.

33. Fischer, "Post–Civil War Segregation Struggle," 304; H. G. Saunders, comp., *Atlanta Directory,* 1891 (Atlanta, 1891), 150, 245; *Atlanta Constitution,* July 31, 1888. Nashville's Lone Star brothel had its ground and upper floors occupied by white prostitutes and its basement by blacks. It is not known whether or not the clientele was also mixed. *Nashville American,* March 28, 1877.

34. *Savannah Colored Tribune,* July 15, 1876. Jim Crow Bibles were present by 1868 in some courts in Virginia. Macrae, *Americans at Home* 1:146–47.

35. Wade, *Slavery in the Cities,* 267.

36. See, for example, *Nashville Banner,* June 16, July 7, 1883.

Springs in 1887 were informed "politely but forcibly" by policemen that they would not be admitted. Three years later blacks were excluded from the city's Inman Park. Already Atlanta blacks had begun to gravitate to the grounds and woods around Clark University, leading the *Atlanta Constitution* to call for construction of a park for them in that area.[37] Then, too, in most southern cities blacks and whites continued to frequent separate picnic groves while the large all-white cemeteries served as parks for whites.

Nevertheless, the existence of separate parks for whites and blacks as a general phenomenon seems to have been the product of the post-1890 period. As of 1882, Nashville's Watkins Park was visited by "persons of all shades and sizes." As late as 1890, blacks and whites were invited to watch a Negro militia company drill in Atlanta's Piedmont Park, and on Independence Day, blacks were among the mostly white crowd that enjoyed the facilities at the city's Grant Park. Montgomery's Highland and Raleigh's Pullen parks were apparently open to blacks and whites as well.[38]

In the absence of separate parks, segregation within the grounds became the norm. Although blacks enjoyed access to Atlanta's Ponce de Leon Springs until the late 1880s, the two races entertained themselves at separate dance halls and refreshment stands. Blacks attending the two free concerts given at Nashville's Glendale Park were barred from the new pavilion, while those visiting Raleigh's Brookside Park could not use the swimming pool. When a new zoo opened in Atlanta's Grant Park, it contained eight cages occupying the center of the building and stretching from end to end. An aisle was railed off on each side of the row of cages: one was for blacks, the other for whites. "There is no communication between them," the *Atlanta Constitution* observed, "and two large double doors at each end of the building serve as entrance and exit to the aisles."[39]

Segregation also seems to have been the rule at expositions and fairs. Nashville Negroes had fairgrounds purchased by a black organization. Blacks could

37. Letter to the editor, *Atlanta Constitution,* July 19, 1887; July 1, 1890; March 24, 1889.
38. *Nashville Banner,* October 16, 1882; *Atlanta Constitution,* July 5, 10, 1890; *Montgomery Advertiser,* June 3, 1890; *Raleigh News and Observer,* July 21, 1889. Highland Park had its name changed to Oak Park during the 1890s and was one of those affected by the trend toward separate parks for the races. A local Negro resident remembered that the only blacks admitted by that time were nurses with white children. Bertha Thomas McClain, *Montgomery Then and Now as I Remember* (Montgomery: Walker Printing Co., 1960), 23.
39. *Atlanta Constitution,* July 19, 1874; *Nashville Banner,* May 22, 1888; *Raleigh News and Observer,* May 4, June 13, 1890; *Atlanta Constitution,* April 4, 1890. It is not known if Negroes had been permitted in the old building and if so, under what conditions.

attend certain functions at the white fairgrounds but specifically which functions and when is not always clear. Negroes were barred, for example, from the interstate drill competition held in 1883. But again admittance of both races went hand in hand with segregation. There was a special gate provided for blacks in the exposition building at a Nashville fair in 1875; there was a "colored people's saloon" in addition to the main grandstand saloon at the 1871 Georgia State Fair in Macon; and at the Southern Exposition held in Montgomery in 1890 the two races ate in separate restaurants.[40]

Southern whites did not have the option of providing or not providing accommodations for Negro lawbreakers. Yet confinement of blacks in penitentiaries and local jails was largely a postwar development. In the antebellum years Negro criminals were more likely to be whipped than incarcerated.[41] As a result of the influx of black prisoners, racial contact became as much of a problem within the correctional institutions as in the outside world. As in the society at large, segregation was seen as the ideal solution for regulating contact between the races once exclusion became unfeasible.[42] A committee of the Georgia legislature recommended in 1866 that Negro and white convicts receive equal punishment, but hastened to add that "under no circumstances would a social equality be recognized—not even in the worst cases of felony." Nevertheless, segregation was possible only if there were sufficient space. When room was limited, blacks and whites were confined together despite the desires of law enforcement officials.[43]

One way to prevent the mixture of the races at small penitentiaries was to lease out black prisoners. This plan had the added advantages of providing favored employers with a source of cheap labor and the state government with

40. *Nashville Republican Banner,* March 2, 1871; *Nashville Banner,* May 25, 1883; *Nashville Republican Banner,* May 20, 1875; *Atlanta Constitution,* October 16, 19, 1871; *Montgomery Advertiser,* November 5, 1890.

41. Tennessee, *Message of John C. Brown, Governor of Tennessee, to the Thirty-ninth General Assembly of the State of Tennessee, January 4, 1875* (Nashville, 1875), 19; Georgia, *Reports of the Principal Keeper and Officers of the Georgia Penitentiary from April, 1872, to December 31, 1873* (Atlanta, 1874), 22.

42. This had been tried before the Civil War. Berlin, *Slaves without Masters,* 324.

43. *Atlanta New Era,* November 20, 1866. See also Williamson, *After Slavery,* 281; this was true during the post-1890 period when penal segregation is generally acknowledged to have become pervasive. The Code of Laws and Regulations for the Penitentiary System of Tennessee in 1896, for example, called for the separation of white and black convicts, but added that this should be done "only as far as practicable." Tennessee, *Report of the Warden, Superintendent, and Other Officers of the Tennessee Penitentiary for the Year Ending December 31, 1896* (Nashville, 1897), 13. See also Frank William Hoffer, Delbert Martin Mann, and Floyd Nelson House, *The Jails of Virginia: A Study of the Local Penal System* (New York: D. Appleton-Century, Co., 1933), 112.

extra revenue. Although some whites were leased, blacks suffered most from this inhumane and corrupt system.[44]

The need for segregation remained uppermost in the minds of Georgia officials who sought alternatives to the lease system. In 1876 the keeper of the penitentiary proposed substituting the islands off Savannah as penal colonies. "It would be my policy," he averred, "to separate the whites and blacks, working them on distinct farms." The lease system was kept, however, and after a trip to one of the camps, the keeper reported approvingly that in the barracks "the white men sleep to themselves on one side of the building." Most of the camps were in fact composed exclusively of Negroes so that intra-camp segregation was usually unnecessary. Laws passed in 1888 and 1890 decreed that white and black prisoners were not to work or be confined together, adding legal sanction to customs and attitudes already governing behavior.[45]

Although males were segregated in the Alabama prison camps by 1882, because of overcrowding, white women convicted of adultery with blacks occupied the same cells as Negro women. The warden complained, calling for the complete segregation of prisoners in one large prison. The two main prison camps for leased convicts had separate quarters for the races by 1884; in at least one of the camps two rows of tubs stood in the newly erected bathhouse—one side for blacks and the other for whites. Six years later Wetumpka Prison, where nonleased convicts were confined, had a different building for each race.[46]

Integration was probably more often present in local jails and workhouses. Chain gangs were instituted mainly for Negroes, but all prisoners had to be kept inside at night. Whether or not segregation existed depended mainly on the size of the facility; whether or not segregation appeared in descriptions of jails de-

44. Virginia used the system as early as 1858 as a substitute for exclusion. Berlin, *Slaves without Masters*, 323–24. See also Georgia, *Reports of the Penitentiary* (1888–1890), 3; North Carolina, *Biennial Report of the Board of Directors, Architect and Warden, Steward and Physician of the North Carolina State Penitentiary for the Two Years Ending November 30, 1890* (Raleigh, 1890), 40; Wharton, *Negro in Mississippi,* 239–40.

45. Georgia, *Reports of the Penitentiary* (1876), 10–12; ibid. (1878–1880), 4; Amanda Johnson, *Georgia as Colony and State* (Atlanta: Walter W. Brown, 1938), 668; Gilbert Thomas Stephenson, *Race Distinctions in American Law* (London: D. Appleton and Company, 1910), 146.

46. Alabama, *Biennial Report of the Inspectors of the Alabama Penitentiary for the Two Years Ending September 30, 1882* (Montgomery, 1882), 19–21; ibid., 1882–1884, 22, 27, 201, 264; Alabama, *First Biennial Report of the Inspectors of Convicts from October. 1, 1888 to October 1, 1890* (Montgomery, 1890), 5. For a call for the use of entirely separate prisons to prevent any contact between the races, see ibid. 1884–1886, 17. For segregated cells, hospitals, and prayer meetings in other state prisons, see North Carolina, *Reports of the Penitentiary,* 1878–1880, 46; ibid., 1882–1884, 17; Tennessee, *Reports of the Penitentiary,* 1878–1880, 15, 30; *Nashville Union and American,* December 15, 1870; *Nashville Banner,* April 3, 1885; Fischer, *Segregation Struggle,* 84.

pended on the observer. In Richmond to 1890, for example, neither the city council minutes nor the yearly reports of the various city departments concerning the jail mention racial separation, yet an inspection committee appointed by the Hustings Court in 1882 reported that the races occupied cells on the opposite sides of the building. Accounts for subsequent years continued to note this arrangement as well as the existence of Jim Crow bathtubs by 1889.[47] Questions remain about the nature of pre-1882 policy.

No matter how great the desire for segregated quarters, integration in small jails was often unavoidable. Not until the end of the period, for example, did the construction of larger jails in Atlanta and Nashville assure racial segregation.[48] In Montgomery, Alabama, where segregated quarters were assigned as early as 1865 and retained by a Radical jailer, racial mixing among convicts sometimes resulted from overcrowding. Even after the passage of a state law prohibiting the confining together of black and white prisoners, the *Montgomery Advertiser* complained in 1885 that at the county jail "the arrangements for keeping the races separate are far from what they should be." The shift from exclusion to segregation finally became complete that summer as plans were announced for a new jail, one that had solitary cells "for both male and female—whites and blacks separate."[49]

The situation in public conveyances is less discernible, and there seems to have been a greater divergence in practice. As under the Republicans, steamboats remained the most segregated form of travel. Although Virginia did not pass a law requiring the racial separation of passengers on steamboats until 1900, the *City of Richmond,* in service to Norfolk since 1880, had from its

47. Hustings Court Order Books, no. 13, 60, 367, Richmond City Hall; ibid., no. 16, 241: ibid., no. 24, 163.

48. Atlanta, *Annual Report of the Officers of the City of Atlanta for the Year Ending December 31, 1889* (Atlanta, 1889), 159; *Nashville Banner,* August 30, 1890. For complaints about the confining together of some black and white prisoners due to a lack of room, see *Nashville American,* October 13, 1887. By 1889 the Fulton County Jail as well as the Atlanta City Jail were segregated. *Atlanta Constitution,* June 11, 1889. During 1889, four years before the passage of a law requiring separation of young offenders, a group of Atlanta citizens proposed building a segregated reformatory. Ibid., December 21, 1889. Plans drawn the following year for a new stockade for county chain gang convicts included separate bathtubs for whites and blacks. Ibid., February 9, 1890. Raleigh, North Carolina, also may have followed the Atlanta and Nashville pattern. By 1890 it had a segregated jail, workhouse, and chain gang. *Raleigh News and Observer,* March 29, 1890.

49. *Montgomery Ledger,* August 29, 1865; *Montgomery State Sentinel,* July 22, 1867; *Montgomery Advertiser,* February 26, 1885, September 26, 1871; Stephenson, *Race Distinctions in American Law,* 146; *Montgomery Advertiser,* July 11, 1885. A similar progression had perhaps taken place by 1875 in Orleans Parish Prison in New Orleans. Fischer, *Segregation Struggle,* 84.

inception "a neat and comfortable dining room for colored passengers in the lower cabin." George Washington Cable discovered in 1887 that Louisiana Negroes had to confine themselves to a separate quarter of the boats called the "Freedman's bureau." And to Frederick Douglass it seemed ironic that the Negro had more freedom on steamboats as a slave since "he could ride anywhere, side by side with his white master. . . . [A]s a freeman, he was not allowed a cabin abaft the wheel."[50]

Although there was greater integration in train travel, blacks were generally confined to the smoking and second-class cars. Occasionally they were provided with separate first-class accommodations equal to those given to white passengers. During her trip through the United States in 1883, Iza Duffus Hardy was especially struck by the variety of methods used on trains to keep Negroes "in their place." On the train leaving Charleston, Negroes were in a separate second-class car although they did pay a lower fare than whites. At Savannah on the Florida Express, the Negroes rode in the forward part of the smoking car nearest the engine. Somewhat farther south Hardy found a car labeled For Coloured [sic] Passengers, which she discovered "was in every respect exactly like the car reserved for us 'white folk,' the same velvet seats, ice water tank; every comfort the same—and of course, the same fare." As opposed to this rare instance of a first-class car, the car assigned to Negroes in Charleston was described by her traveling companion, Lady Duffus Hardy, as "seedy looking." The association of Negroes with smoking cars was pronounced. While traveling on the Central Railroad in Georgia, Alexander Stephens and two other noted white Georgians were ejected from a first-class Negro car because they had seen blacks in it and had assumed it was a second-class car where they could smoke.[51]

The first-class cars for Negroes on the Central Railroad reflected an effort by certain railroads and sympathetic whites to provide separate but equal accommodations for blacks able to afford first-class rates. Noting the noncompliance with the 1881 statute requiring separate but equal accommodations for the races on Tennessee's railroads, the *Nashville American* observed in 1885:

50. Stephenson, *Race Distinctions in American Law,* 215; *Richmond Dispatch,* August 27, 1880; Cable, "The Negro Question," *The Negro Question: A Selection of Writings on Civil Rights in the South by George W. Cable,* ed. Arlin Turner (Garden City, N.Y.: Doubleday, 1958), 129; Douglass, "The Color Line," *North American Review* 132 (July 1881): 576. See also *Raleigh News and Observer,* May 4, 1890.

51. Iza Duffus Hardy, *Between Two Oceans or Sketches of American Travel* (London, 1884), 306–07; Lady Duffus Hardy [Mary McDowell], *Down South* (London, 1883), 85; *Nashville Republican Banner,* May 11, 1875. For further examples of the confinement of blacks to smoking cars, see *Nashville American,* March 23, 1879; W. H. Crogman, *Talks for the Times* (Atlanta, 1896), 191; *Atlanta Constitution,* April 10, 1889.

The blacks are forced into the smoking cars where they are subjected not only to all the annoyance of smoke and dirt, but often to the additional hardship of association with the roughest and most quarrelsome class of whites. . . . Now these things *should not be.* They are bad for the black race and they are equally bad for the white race. The law which provides for separate cars and equal accommodations is right. It is the only law which can be just to both of these classes of citizens, and at the same time prevent race conflicts, which would disturb the peace of the community.[52]

As early as 1870, the Orange Railroad passenger trains in Virginia had a special car exclusively for Negroes where smoking was prohibited. A regular smoking car was to be used by both blacks and whites. The Houston and Texas Central agreed in 1883 to provide "separate, exclusive, equal accommodations for colored patrons." Two years later a Louisville and Nashville train running between Montgomery and Mobile had a first-class coach "specially provided for colored people." In the opinion of the *Atlanta Constitution,* it "was as good in every sense as the [white] car. . . . There was no smoking or disorder permitted." In a case involving alleged discrimination on an Alabama railroad in 1887, the Interstate Commerce Commission held that different cars for the races could indeed be used provided that the accommodations were equal and that Negroes paying first-class fare received first-class facilities.[53]

In only one area of southern life was the shift to segregation relatively incomplete by 1890. Most southern streetcar systems initially excluded blacks; separate cars for the races followed. Once blacks gained entrance to the white cars, documenting the existence of segregation becomes difficult. August Meier and Elliott Rudwick argue that segregation "declined after being instituted in many places prior to and just after the Civil War." There is evidence to support the contention that streetcars were the most integrated southern facility. Referring to the color line, the *Nashville American* observed in 1880, "In Tennessee there is such a line, as every man, white and black, well knows, but on our street cars the races ride together without thought of it, or offensive exhibition, or attempt to isolate the colored passenger." Ten years later, when there was a rumor that the president of one of Richmond's street railways had been asked to provide separate cars for black passengers, the *Richmond Planet,* a Negro newspaper, expressed surprise

52. *Nashville American,* July 30, 1885. For additional examples of the concern shown by the Redeemer press for separate but equal accommodations, see *Montgomery Advertiser,* February 21, March 8, 1873; *Richmond Dispatch,* October 14, 1870; *Atlanta Constitution,* October 16, 1883; January 1, 1885; *Nashville American,* October 3, 1881.

53. *Lynchburg News,* quoted in *Richmond Dispatch,* April 8, 1870; *Houston Post,* quoted in David G. McComb, *Houston: The Bayou City* (Austin: University of Texas Press, 1969), 160; *Atlanta Constitution,* June 15, 1885; December 4, 1887.

and counseled against the plan since "we do not know of a city in the south in which discrimination is made on the street cars." In 1908 Ray Stannard Baker sadly concluded that "a few years ago the Negro came and went in the street cars in most cities and sat where he pleased, but gradually Jim Crow laws or local regulations were passed forcing him into certain seats at the back of the car."[54]

Segregation, however, may have been more prevalent than these accounts indicate. In Richmond and Savannah segregated streetcars persisted at least until the mid-1870s.[55] But segregation on horsecars could be inconvenient and expensive to maintain. Because the horses could pull only one rather small car at a time, the segregation of passengers required either the use of an entirely separate car and horse for blacks or limited them to a portion of the already crowded cars open to whites. This problem was remedied by the appearance on southern streets at the end of the 1880s of the dummy streetcar and the later electrification of the lines. The steam-driven dummy derived its name from the attempt to disguise the engine as a passenger car in order to cut down on noise and to avoid frightening horses. Since it had two cars or else a single car larger than that pulled by horses, segregation of the races was easier.

Montgomery initiated dummy service in 1886 with the forward cars reserved for whites and the rear cars for blacks. Two years later the dummy also made possible the first clear indication of segregation in Atlanta. The dummy service, begun by the Metropolitan Street Railway Company in September 1888, included two cars plus the engine—one painted yellow for whites, the other red for blacks. Likewise, the first documented case of segregation in a Nashville streetcar after 1867 was contained in an 1888 report about a Negro minister's sermon. It simply noted, "In a sermon Sunday night, [the minister] attacked the management of the dummy line for insisting that he should move to another car or get off." During the following two years, however, the newspapers reported additional instances of blacks being told to go to separate cars.[56]

The period of seeming flexibility came to an end with the passage of statutes

54. Meier and Rudwick, "A Strange Chapter in the Career of 'Jim Crow,'" 15; *Nashville American,* April 11, 1880; *Richmond Planet,* December 27, 1890; Baker, *Following the Color Line: An Account of Negro Citizenship in the American Democracy* (New York: Doubleday, Page and Company, 1908), 30.

55. *Congressional Record,* 43d Congress, 2d session, 955, 957 (February 3, 1875); Meier and Rudwick, "A Strange Chapter in the Career of 'Jim Crow,'" 16. See also Perdue, *Negro in Savannah,* 34; Nordhoff, *The Cotton States,* 106.

56. *Atlanta Constitution,* July 28, 1889; Franklin M. Garrett, *Atlanta and Environs: A Chronicle of Its People and Events,* 3 vols. (New York: Lewis Historical Publishing Company, 1954) 2:175; *Nashville Banner,* May 1, 1888; May 26, June 9, 1890. See also the statement by a white, W. F. Slaton, in which he remembered being ejected from the Negro car on the Nashville dummy even though there were only a few people in it while the white car was "packed full." *Atlanta Constitution,* August 6, 1889.

enforcing segregation. Both blacks and the streetcar companies often objected to Jim Crow measures. But what were they protesting? Was it segregation or legal segregation that blacks were against? Did the streetcar owners object to any form of racial separation or simply to one that made them supply additional cars, usually an unprofitable venture? The fact that many Nashville blacks would have settled for separate cars in 1905 as long as there were black fare collectors suggests that the boycotts were not simply against segregation. The twentieth-century practice of dividing streetcars into black and white sections lends credence to the view that white owners objected less to the initiation of segregation than to the law requiring more cars. As the *Richmond Planet* noted, southern managers realized that "separate cars would not pay and what was worse there would be more trouble on account of it."[57] Thanks to the cooperation of local officials the managers could handle the "trouble"; financial aspects were another matter.

Then, too, why would streetcars be immune from segregation, given its prevalence in most other areas of southern life? One answer would seem to rest less with the absence of white hostility than in the circumstances in which streetcars operated. The resistance of white managers might be a reason, but as important was the greater leverage blacks exercised over streetcar policy as compared, for example, to railroad policy. Clearly boycotts presented a more serious threat to local streetcar lines than they did to a railroad that drew passengers from many communities. In addition, boycotts could be better organized because of the existence of alternative means of transportation. Whether by using hacks, private carriages, or by simply walking, Negroes could go about their business without the streetcars.

This essay has been primarily concerned with the pervasiveness of segregation in the postbellum South as it came to replace exclusion as the dominant characteristic of race relations. It has been argued that both white Republicans and Redeemers came to embrace this new policy, though often for different reasons. But what helped to assure this shift was the attitude of the blacks themselves.

Blacks on occasion did challenge segregation. During Richmond's celebration of the passage of the Fifteenth Amendment, a Negro minister was accused by the *Richmond Dispatch* of saying, "The negroes must claim the right to sit with the whites in theatres, churches, and other public buildings, to ride with them on the cars, and to stay at the same hotels with them." Similarly after Tennessee passed its Jim Crow law in 1881, a minister from Nashville argued, "No man of color [should] ride in a car simply because it is set apart and *labeled* 'exclusively for

57. Meier and Rudwick, "Boycott Movement Against Jim Crow Streetcars in the South," 757; "Negro Boycotts in Tennessee," 761; *Richmond Planet,* December 27, 1890.

negroes,' but rather let every individual choose of the regular coaches the one in which to ride." And six years later when Charles Dudley Warner asked a group of leading black Nashville businessmen, "What do you want here in the way of civil rights that you have not?" the answer was, "We want to be treated like men, like anybody else regardless of color. . . . We want public conveyances open to us according to the fare we pay; we want the privilege to go to hotels and to theatres, operas and places of amusement. . . . [We] cannot go to the places assigned us in concerts and theatres without loss of self respect."[58]

Negroes opposed segregation by deeds as well as by words. By 1870, Charleston, New Orleans, Richmond, Mobile, and Nashville were among the cities to experience challenges to exclusion or segregation on their streetcars. Suits were brought also against offending railroad companies. Challenges to segregation were most pronounced after passage of the 1875 Civil Rights Act. For the most part, blacks failed to break down the racial barriers in theaters, hotels, restaurants, public conveyances, and bars. More isolated and equally unsuccessful attempts occurred with decreasing frequency in subsequent years.[59]

Despite this opposition to segregation, the majority of blacks, including their leaders, focused their attention elsewhere. The failure of a sustained attack on segregation perhaps resulted from the lack of support from white allies and the courts. There were other reasons as well. Five prominent Nashville blacks, for example, argued that Negroes would not use passage of the Civil Rights Act "to make themselves obnoxious" since they "had too much self respect to go where they were not wanted." Besides, they said, such actions would lead only to disturbances, and "colored people wanted peace and as little agitation as possible." Bishop Henry M. Turner echoed this view in 1889, telling a reporter that "I don't find much trouble in traveling at [sic] the south on account of my color, for the simple reason that I am not in the habit of pushing myself where I am not wanted." A similar attitude might have governed the response of "sev-

58. *Richmond Dispatch*, April 22, 1870. See also Savannah *Colored Tribune*, March 25, 1876. Letter of W. A. Sinclair to the editor, *Nashville American*, October 4, 1881; Warner, *Studies in the South and West*, 116–17.

59. *Nashville Union and Dispatch*, December 19, 1867; *Atlanta Constitution*, April 12, May 19, 1871; Blassingame, *Black New Orleans*, 191–92, 185–86; *Nashville Republican Banner*, March 13–14, 1875; *Nashville Union and American*, March 13–14, 1875; *Atlanta Constitution*, March 6, 9, 10, 1875; *Raleigh Sentinel*, March 6, 1875; *Richmond Dispatch*, March 9, 10, 1875; *Montgomery Advertiser*, March 6, 13, 14, 1875. For "testing" on railroads, see *Nashville American*, October 2, 3, 5, 1881; *Nashville Banner*, September 30, October 7, 1881; *Atlanta Constitution*, August 9, 1889. For an attempt to buy soda water at a Nashville shop that served only whites, see *Nashville Banner*, October 3, 1881. For attempts to sit in white sections of theaters, see *Atlanta Constitution*, September 28, 1881; *Nashville Republican Banner*, April 17, 1887. For an attempt to integrate a Nashville streetcar, see *Nashville American*, July 20, 1889.

eral really respectable colored persons" in Charleston to the attempt of a
Negro to buy a ticket for the orchestra or dress circle of the Academy of Music
in 1870. Calling the move a cheap political trick, they "avowed their willing-
ness to sit in the places provided for their own race when they visited the
Academy."[60]

Economic pressures also led blacks to accept segregation. Negroes who relied
on a white clientele were especially reluctant to serve members of both races.
Shortly after the passage of the Civil Rights Act two Negro barbers in Edgefield,
across the river from Nashville, refused to serve black customers. The previous
year a Negro delegation had been ejected when it demanded shaves at the shop
of a black barber in Chattanooga. Asked if their money were not as good as a
white man's, the barber, fearful of the loss of his white customers, answered,
"Yes just as good, but there is not enough of it." Both whites and blacks understood the locus of economic power. In 1875 the *Nashville Union and American*
listed twelve blacks who had been testing compliance to the Civil Rights Act.
The fact that "most of them got their reward by losing their situations" helps
explain why there were not more protestors.[61]

Other blacks sought to work out an equitable arrangement within the confines
of a segregated order. They accepted segregation because it was seen as an
improvement over exclusion and because they believed, or at least hoped, that
separate facilities could be equal. A rider in 1866 on the Nashville streetcar set
apart for blacks did not complain about the segregation, but threatened a boycott unless the company protected black passengers from abusive whites who
forced their way into the car and used obscene language in front of black
women. A Norfolk, Virginia, Negro observing that the city was building a new
opera house, suggested that "colored theatregoers . . . petition the managers to
give them a respectable place to sit, apart from those of a lewd character." To
one Atlanta citizen, writing during a period of racial tension in his city, it seemed

60. Quoted in *Atlanta Constitution,* March 6, 1875; January 7, 1889; *Charleston News,*
January 10, 1870. Implicit here is support for Fischer's contention that many blacks
accepted segregation out of a belief that the ultimate reward was not worth the effort
needed to secure it. Fischer, "Post–Civil War Segregation Struggle," 297.

61. *Nashville Union and American,* March 9, 1875; *Cincinnati Commercial,* quoted in
the *Nashville Republican Banner,* June 17, 1874; *Nashville Union and American,* March
11, 1875. For the threat of economic retaliation against protesters, see *Nashville Republican Banner,* March 11, 1875; *Montgomery Alabama State Journal,* March 13, 14, 1875;
Montgomery Advertiser, March 24, 1875. The fear of economic retaliation led Elias
Napier, a prosperous livery stable owner in Nashville, to announce publicly that he was
not one of a group of Negroes who had sought admission to a white restaurant. "I do not
wish myself on any man," he wrote, "and as for civil rights, I want all to know that I was
opposed to the passage of the civil rights bill from the first" *Nashville Republican Banner,*
March 11, 1875.

that whites and blacks should "travel each in their own distinct paths, steering clear of debatable ground, never forgetting to render one to the other that which equity and good conscience demands." And when the Negro principal of the Alabama State Normal School brought suit against the Western and Atlantic Railroad on the ground that despite his possession of a first-class ticket he was ejected from the first-class car and removed to the Negro car, he admitted the right of the company to classify passengers by race, but maintained it was the duty of the railroad to furnish equal facilities and conveniences for both races. This belief in the need to guarantee separate but equal treatment was expressed in a resolution offered in the Virginia senate by a Negro legislator in 1870. It provided that whites would be forbidden from traveling in portions of boats, trains, and streetcars reserved for blacks. In a letter to the *Richmond Dispatch,* the legislator attributed his action to the fact that there was little possibility of blacks being allowed to ride wherever they wanted and this would protect them, especially the women, from the intrusion of undesirable whites.[62]

In other areas, acceptance of segregation did not necessarily mean passivity on the part of blacks. Again, the targets of protest were exclusion and unequal treatment rather than segregation. For example, blacks placed more emphasis on securing better schools and welfare institutions than on achieving integrated institutions. Blacks went even further. They called for black control of separate facilities through the use of black staff or black directors of public institutions, such as penitentiaries and institutions for the blind, deaf, and dumb. The increase in the number of black colleges, like Tuskegee and Morris Brown, founded and run by blacks was another manifestation of this desire for control over separate institutions.[63]

When the white community persisted in its policy of exclusion, blacks responded by opening their own hospitals, orphanages, hotels, ice cream parlors, and skating rinks.[64] Part of this response was an accommodation to white preju-

62. *Nashville Press and Times,* June 26, 1866; *Richmond Virginia Star,* March 27, 1880; *Atlanta Constitution,* August 15, 1889; July 24, 1887; *Richmond Dispatch,* July 1, 4, 1870. For additional evidence of black interest in separate but equal accommodations in public conveyances, see *Montgomery Alabama State Journal,* July 26, 1869; *Alabama State Journal,* December 16, 1870; *Montgomery Advertiser,* June 2, 1885; Avins, "Racial Segregation," 1280.

63. See my essays "Half a Loaf" and "Health and Welfare Services for Southern Blacks." See also James M. McPherson, "White Liberals and Black Power in Negro Education, 1865–1915," *American Historical Review* 75 (June 1970): 1357–86; for the successful attempt of Morris Brown officials to secure the appropriation from the Georgia legislature that had previously gone to Atlanta University, see *Atlanta Constitution,* June 11, 12, July 19, 21, 1887; November 28, 1889.

64. Rabinowitz, "Health and Welfare Services for Southern Blacks"; Blassingame, *Black New Orleans,* 166–71; *Montgomery Advertiser,* August 16, 1885; J. H. Chataigne,

dice; but it was also related to the development of a group identity among blacks. Though it cannot be equated with the racism of whites, by moving in this direction blacks themselves contributed to the emergence of the separate black and white worlds that characterized southern life by 1890.

Although the sanction of law underwrote much of the system of parallel facilities, the separation of the races was accomplished largely without the aid of statutes for as long as both races accepted its existence. As early as 1866, an English traveler, William Hepworth Dixon, noted that the Negro in Richmond, Virginia, regardless of his legal rights, knew "how far he may go, and where he must stop." He knew also that "[h]abits are not changed by paper law." In 1880 two of the Negro witnesses testifying before a congressional committee pointed to this difference between the power of law and the power of custom. When asked if there were any laws in Alabama applied solely to one race, James T. Rapier answered: "Custom is law in our country now, and was before the war." Asked again if there were any discriminatory provisions in the constitution or state statutes, he replied: "None that I know of; but what we complain of is the administration of the law—the custom of the country." James O'Hara of North Carolina made a similar statement: "These are matters [segregation in public accommodations] that are and must be regulated purely by prejudice and feeling, and that the law cannot regulate."[65]

Though prejudice persisted during the quarter century after 1865, a profound change occurred in southern race relations. The policy of exclusion was largely discarded. Instead, by 1890 segregation had been extended to every major area of southern life. Doubts remained, however, as to the possibility of keeping Negroes fully "in their place" without resort to laws. During the last decade of the nineteenth and the first decade of the twentieth centuries, these doubts resulted in the legalization of practices in effect since the end of the war. As Gilbert Stephenson pointed out for train travel, "The 'Jim Crow' laws . . . coming later, did scarcely more than to legalize an existing and wide-spread custom."[66]

---

comp., *Chataigne's Directory of Richmond for 1891* (Richmond, 1891), 1031; *Richmond Virginia Star*, December 14, 1878; December 9, 23, 1882; *Richmond Planet*, June 12, 1886; *Atlanta Constitution*, March 10, 1882; *Nashville Union and American*, September 14, 1873; *Montgomery Citizen*, August 2, 1884; J. H. Chataigne, comp., *Raleigh City Directory*, 1875, 133; *Montgomery Herald*, July 23, 1887; *Fisk Herald* 7 (May 1890): 16; *Atlanta Defiance*, October 8, 1881; *Atlanta Constitution*, April 23, 1885; *Montgomery Alabama State Journal*, April 6, 1873.

65. William Hepworth Dixon, *New America*, 2 vols. (London, 1867), 2:332–33; U.S. Senate, *Report and Testimony of the Select Committee of the United States Senate to Investigate the Causes of the Removal of the Negroes from the Southern States to the Northern States* (Washington, 1880), part 2, 476–77; ibid., part 1, 57.

66. Part of the uncertainty as to the efficacy of de facto segregation may have been due

For whether under Radical Reconstruction or Redemption, the best that blacks could hope for in southern racial policy was separate but equal access. In fact, they usually met with either exclusion or separate but unequal treatment. Integration was rarely permitted. When it did occur, it was only at the initiation of whites and was confined as a rule to the least desirable facilities—cheap bars, inferior restaurants, second-class and smoking cars on trains. Whites were there because they chose to be; blacks were there because they had no choice.

---

to a more aggressive attitude on the part of younger educated blacks. Howard N. Rabino-witz, "Search for Social Control: Race Relations in the Urban South, 1865–1890," 2 vols. (Ph.D. diss., University of Chicago, 1973), 1:534–38, 2:887–90; Stephenson, *Race Distinctions in American Law,* 214. See also John Snyder, "Prejudice Against the Negro," *Forum* 8 (October 1889), 222.

Part Three

Reconstruction
and
Its
Legacy

The Conflict between Blacks and the Police in the Urban South, 1865–1900

The racial disturbances of the mid-1960s made Americans aware of the strained relations between segments of the black community and the police. Often overlooked is the fact that the sources of this friction are not of recent origin. They were already present in the urban South during the period from 1865 to 1900, when the recently emancipated slaves demanded the rights of free men. Very much in the news in those years were the issues of whether or not blacks should be appointed to police forces, what constituted the legitimate use of force against suspected black lawbreakers, and to what extent police authority was recognized and accepted by blacks.

Readers familiar with the growing literature on nineteenth-century law enforcement will recognize that these issues involved other groups besides southern blacks, particularly immigrants in northern cities.[1] Historians, however, have neglected southern cities during this period and thus have missed an important chapter not only in law enforcement but in urban and Negro history as well.

It is not surprising that concerns so common today should have surfaced in the postbellum South. Not only had blacks been freed, but the lure of the city led to

I want to thank Professor David R. Johnson for reading an earlier version of this essay.

1. See, for example, Roger Lane, *Policing the City: Boston, 1822–1885* (Cambridge: Harvard University Press, 1967); James F. Richardson, *The New York Police: Colonial Times to 1901* (New York: Oxford University Press, 1970); and David R. Johnson, "The Search for an Urban Discipline: Police Reform as a Response to Crime in American Cities, 1800–1875" (Ph.D. diss., University of Chicago, 1972). In many areas—housing, employment, and politics, in addition to problems relating to law and order—blacks were the southern counterparts of the northern immigrants. A comparison of policing in northern and southern cities would be quite valuable, but it is beyond the scope of this study. For a recent examination of the police in one southern city, see Eugene J. Watts, "The Police in Atlanta, 1890–1905," *Journal of Southern History* 39 (May 1973): 165–82.

a significant increase in the region's urban black population.[2] During the ante-bellum period whites had concluded that blacks and city life were not only incompatible but harmful to each other. The *Montgomery Daily Ledger* ex-pressed a common view when it asserted in the fall of 1865 that Negroes should "cultivate the soil, the employment God designed them for. . . . The city is no place for them; it was intended for white people." The former slaves, whites claimed, were needed in the countryside. Moreover, many southerners believed blacks had fled the farms to avoid work, and it was feared that jobless freedmen would turn to crime in the affluent urban environment. In the words of one Savannah resident: "Nothing is more demoralizing to the negro, than a town and city life. . . . They cannot obtain regular employment . . . and they will be tempted to pillage and steal . . . or . . . starve. . . . [And] it is ruinous to their health as well as morals. They crowd together in small and often filthy apartments, and disease and death follows." But even if the blacks did find work, they enraged whites with their demands for better schools, health care, protection of their civil rights, and, after 1867, by their exercise of the suffrage.[3]

To whites in the postbellum South the policeman stood as the first line of defense against the blacks. It was his responsibility to break up the black gam-bling and vice dens, to clear the streets of vagrants, to catch Negro lawbreakers, and on occasion to keep black voters in check. In the minds of most whites, blacks could not be trusted to fill this vital position. More important, black police might end up having authority over white citizens. For these reasons, the first

2. The percentage of blacks among the region's urban dwellers had declined during the antebellum period. In 1820, 37 percent of all town dwellers were black; by 1860, this was true of less than 17 percent. Richard C. Wade, *Slavery in the Cities: The South, 1820–1860* (New York: Oxford University Press, 1964), 243. Yet by 1890, almost a third of the South's urban population was black. U.S. Bureau of the Census, *Negro Population, 1790–1915* (Washington, D.C.: Government Printing Office, 1918), 92. Much of the increase came in the first years after the war. From 1860 to 1870, for example, the percentage of Negro population in Atlanta rose from 20 percent to 46 percent, in Nashville from 23 percent to 38 percent, and in Richmond from 38 percent to 45 percent. U.S. Bureau of the Census, *Ninth Census of the United States: 1870*, vol. 1, *Population* (Washington, D.C.: Govern-ment Printing Office, 1872), 102, 262, 280.

3. Wade, *Slavery in the Cities*, 244; *Montgomery Daily Ledger*, September 23, 1865; see also the September 4, 1865 issue; E. H. Bacon, as quoted in Zane L. Miller, "Black Communities in the Urban South: A Preliminary Analysis of Richmond, Savannah, New Orleans, Louisville, and Birmingham," paper read at the Southern Historical Convention, Houston, Texas, November 19, 1971, 1. For similar statements, see *Atlanta Constitution*, February 14, 1871; May 13, 1876; *Nashville Republican Banner*, February 19, 1873; August 20, 1875; *Nashville Daily Press and Times*, November 28, 1865; and *Raleigh Daily Sentinel*, April 24, 1866; for what whites considered the disruptive effects of black migra-tion to the cities, see my "The Search for Social Control: Race Relations in the Urban South, 1865–1890," 2 vols. (Ph.D. diss., University of Chicago, 1973).

postwar governments during Presidential Reconstruction hired only white policemen. Atlanta, Georgia, Negroes, for example, unsuccessfully petitioned the
city council in September 1867 to appoint one Negro from each ward to the
police department, since "justice demands that our color should be represented." White opposition remained strong, and subsequent efforts to place
blacks in the department also failed.[4]

The lack of Negro police in Atlanta, a city that avoided Radical domination,
bears witness to the close relationship between Republican control of city
governments and the hiring of black police. The coincidence of Republican
rule and black police was naturally greatest during Reconstruction. New Orleans blacks served on that city's metropolitan police until the overthrow of the
Radicals in 1877. In 1868, after a heated battle, Montgomery, Alabama, blacks
won almost half the positions in the police department under a Radical administration; but once the Conservatives regained power in 1875, black appointments ceased.[5]

A similar situation existed in Raleigh, North Carolina. The addition of Negro
police was the most striking innovation during the period of Republican rule
from 1868 to 1875. In July 1868, under the headline "The Mongrel Regime!!
Negro Police!!," the Conservative *Daily Sentinel* announced the appointment of
four Negroes and concluded, "This is the beginning of the end."[6] The Republican *Daily Standard*, however, defended the action by appealing to practical
politics, improved law enforcement, and principles of justice:

> If it is true . . . as obliged in certain quarters that a large portion of the thefts
> and burglaries are committed by the colored, the colored policemen will
> have means of information and consequently of bringing the perpetrator to
> justice, which never would have been extended to the former police. All
> classes will learn that the laws must be respected and the colored people

4. Atlanta City Council Minutes, September 6, 1867, Office of the City Clerk, Atlanta
City Hall, Atlanta. For later efforts, see *Atlanta Constitution,* April 2, 1885; March 26,
1889.

5. Writers Program of the Works Progress Administration for the City of New Orleans,
New Orleans City Guide, American Guide Series (Boston: Houghton Mifflin Co., 1938),
32; Montgomery City Council Minutes, August 15, 24, 1868, Alabama Department of
Archives and History, Montgomery; and Montgomery, *Message of the Mayor and Reports
of the Various City Officers and Standing Committees of the City Council for the Term
Ending April 30, 1877* (Montgomery, 1877), 26 (hereafter cited as *Annual Reports* with the
appropriate years). Negro policemen had actually been removed by the lame-duck Republican administration as a temporary measure when the force was reduced for economic
reasons. Conservative successors restored the force to its original size by hiring additional
whites. *Montgomery Daily Advertiser,* June 15, September 7, 1875; January 11, 1876.

6. *Raleigh Daily Sentinel,* July 25, 1868.

will not feel that it is an oppression on them or their race when tried and punished by a Republican mayor.[7]

Bryan Lunn, a Negro saloonkeeper, was appointed as one of the city's two assistants to the police chief. Although a black never became head of the force, there were always several black patrolmen and one assistant chief. In 1872, for example, in addition to the assistant chief of the day patrol, four of the nine members of the night police, including the sergeant, were Negroes. Despite the early opposition to Negro policemen, the Democrats on returning to power retained one black, whom the *Daily Sentinel* described as "a very efficient officer."[8] After 1877, however, he too was gone.

After Reconstruction, information for most cities is fragmentary. Occasionally, the Redeemers briefly retained black policemen, as in Raleigh, while in Memphis blacks served on the force until 1905. More often, black policemen were present only when Republicans exercised complete control or shared power as in the fusion governments of the late 1880s and early 1890s. Petersburg, Virginia, had black policemen from 1872 to 1874 as did Macon, Georgia, as late as 1879. Five Negro policemen were appointed by the new Republican city government in Chattanooga, Tennessee, in 1872. Charleston, South Carolina, had Negro policemen in 1885 and 1890, while the small town of Georgetown, South Carolina, had an entire black force in 1881, thanks to an alliance between Democrats and Negro Republicans. The Republican and Populist coalition in North Carolina during the 1890s resulted in the return of black policemen in Raleigh and their use in New Bern, Greenville, and Wilmington. And in Jacksonville, Florida, which had Negro police in 1873 under the Republicans, the victory in 1888 of a reform coalition heavily weighted with Negro and white Republicans resulted in the appointment of eleven blacks to the city's twenty-five man police force.[9]

But not even Republican victory always assured the hiring of black policemen.

7. *Raleigh Daily Standard,* July 27, 1868.

8. L. Branson, ed., *The North Carolina Business Directory,* 1872 (Raleigh, 1872), 219; *Raleigh Daily Sentinel,* August 21, 1875.

9. Gerald M. Capers, Jr., *The Biography of A River Town, Memphis: Its Heroic Age* (Chapel Hill: University of North Carolina Press, 1939), 180, 231; Luther Porter Jackson, *Negro Office-holders in Virginia, 1865–1895* (Norfolk: Guide Quality Press, 1945), 86; *Atlanta Constitution,* February 5, 1879; *Nashville Republican Banner,* December 5, 1872; George Brown Tindall, *South Carolina Negroes, 1877–1900* (Baton Rouge: Louisiana State University Press, 1966), 263, 306, 63; Helen G. Edmonds, *The Negro and Fusion Politics in North Carolina, 1894–1901* (Chapel Hill: University of North Carolina Press, 1951), 126, 130, 132; Wayne Flynt, *Duncan Upshaw Fletcher: Dixie's Reluctant Progressive* (Tallahassee: Florida State University Press, 1971), 16–17; *Atlanta Constitution,* March 29, 1873.

Soon after the Radical triumph in September 1867, Nashville Negroes petitioned the new city council "to make ample provision in all the corporate departments, including the city police—for the colored men of Nashville in common with the others." A resolution was prepared, but not offered, instructing the police department to make half of the appointments from the Negro population. When the force was chosen, it contained no blacks.[10] During ensuing years Negro councilmen and their white allies unsuccessfully sought to get the police commissioners to select blacks. In 1884, Negro leader James C. Napier succeeded in getting the Democratic council to pass a resolution supporting the principle of appointments without discrimination as to race, religion, or color. It was vetoed by the Democratic mayor, who argued it would be injurious and would aggravate, rather than allay, racial prejudices. Napier and the other black councilman were the only ones voting to override the veto.[11] A few Negroes did serve as law officers, though not on the regular city force. From 1871 to 1884, two Negroes alternated as one of two county constables elected from Nashville. Two others, chosen by a Republican mayor, acted as special detectives from the early 1870s to 1880.[12]

The number of Negro policemen was never very great. There seem to have been only five in the entire state of Florida in 1870. Most whites never accepted the view that blacks had a rightful claim to such positions. In 1889, the Democrats reacted to the presence of black police in Jacksonville as they had in New Orleans, Raleigh, Montgomery, and elsewhere. They pushed through the legislature a new charter that led to the removal of blacks after they had patrolled the streets for little more than a year. In Mississippi, the employment of Negro patrolmen helped to bring on the Meridian Riot in 1871 and, in Jackson, furnished the central theme of the successful challenge to the Republican government in 1889. And in Richmond, where Negro extras had been temporarily sworn in as policemen during the closing days of the Radical administration, the *Richmond Dispatch* never tired of warning local

10. *Nashville Union and Dispatch,* October 15, 1867.
11. *Nashville Banner,* February 15, 29, 1884. For earlier attempts to place Negroes on the force, see *Nashville Republican Banner,* November 29, 1873; *Nashville Daily American,* March 26, June 1, 1880.
12. For Negroes serving as city constables, see *Nashville Republican Banner,* August 3, 1872; July 1, 1881; *Nashville Daily American,* August 6, 1880; and *Nashville Banner,* August 8, 1882. For Negroes serving as special detectives, see *Nashville Daily American,* October 30, 1875; November 15, 1878. These two men were frequently charged with misconduct and finally were dismissed in 1880. *Nashville Daily American,* January 1, 1880. The closest that blacks got to service on the regular force was their selection as drivers of the patrol wagon, jobs more significant for their patronage than law enforcement implications. *Nashville Banner,* March 6, 1890.

whites that Democratic election defeats would mean the return of "insolent negro policemen."[13]

Even the Negroes' Radical allies often were opposed to giving blacks police jurisdiction over whites. Although the head of the Alabama Conservative party reported in 1871 that "negro police—great black fellows—[are] leading white girls around the streets of Montgomery and locking them in jail," the right to arrest whites was won only after a dramatic confrontation between the city council's two leading white and black Radicals.[14] In most other cities it seems that blacks were supposed to arrest only blacks. This was true of black detectives in Nashville as well as police in New Bern, and perhaps in Raleigh. The Republican mayor of Greenville, North Carolina, wrote: "I have expressly ordered Negro policemen not to arrest any white person, but to report any disturbance and the white policemen would make the arrest." This was evidently also the situation in Mobile, Alabama. Shortly after a new Republican police chief was appointed by the military following a bloody riot in 1867, five Negro policemen were appointed to the city's force. According to the *Mobile Nationalist,* they were to be "stationed on the outskirts of the city where the colored people predominate in numbers."[15]

The paucity of Negro policemen during most of the period served to exacerbate relations between Negroes and police. The only contact that most of the white policemen had with blacks was with the criminal element. Such conditions fostered feelings of mutual distrust and hostility. As the *Atlanta Constitution* observed, "A Negro with a bundle on his shoulders at the dead hour of the night is always an object of suspicion to a policeman." Blacks were often arrested on grounds of "suspicion." An Atlanta black named William Jones was arrested on "suspicion" after he sold a mule for what seemed to an officer to be too small an amount; another man was arrested on

13. Joe M. Richardson, *The Negro in the Reconstruction of Florida* (Tallahassee: Florida State University Press, 1965), 68; Flynt, *Duncan Upshaw Fletcher,* 18–19; Vernon Lane Wharton, *The Negro in Mississippi 1865–1890* (Chapel Hill: University of North Carolina Press, 1947), 168; Richmond, *Richmond Illustrated Police and Fire Department Directory* (Richmond, 1895), 22–25; *Richmond Dispatch,* October 11, 1875; May 6, 1880.

14. U.S. Congress, testimony of James H. Clanton, *Testimony Taken by the Joint Select Committee to Inquire Into the Condition of Affairs in the Late Insurrectionary States,* 42d Congress, 2d session, 1872, 8:244. For an incident in which a white man resisted arrest by two Negroes but peacefully submitted to a white policeman, see *Montgomery Daily Advertiser,* May 15, 1869; Montgomery City Council Minutes, August 15, 24, 1868. Several white Radicals were also among those councilmen who blocked an effort to assign one Negro and one white policeman to each beat. *Montgomery Daily Advertiser,* August 25–26, 1868.

15. *Nashville Daily American,* October 30, 1875; and Edmonds, *Negro and Fusion Politics,* 126, 130; *Mobile Nationalist,* July 4, 1867.

a similar charge for having a turnkey and a pair of shoes for which he could not establish ownership; a third had a handsome gold watch in his possession. A Richmond Negro, charged with being "a suspicious character," was sent to jail for thirty days.[16]

Periodic crackdowns aimed specifically at blacks heightened antagonisms. Shortly after a new administration entered office in 1867, the *Nashville Union and Dispatch* reported that the metropolitan police "are going for the darkies with a will." Ten years later the *Atlanta Constitution* similarly noted, "The police are determined to break up riotous negro dances." Richmond police often arrested large groups of Negroes on general warrants. Not only was this a method of Negro control, but, since sergeants and captains of the force received fees as county constables, it was a way of earning extra money as well. Although the mayor said in 1874 that he had put a stop to this "most vicious and unlawful practice," it continued after that date.[17]

While blacks sometimes complained that policemen ignored disorders involving only Negroes or in which Negroes were being abused, they complained more often of brutal treatment.[18] Throughout the period black citizens brought suits against white officers for using excessive force. They met with occasional success. In 1866, two Nashville policemen were charged with beating a Negro laborer without cause. One of them told his partner to "kill the God damned black son of a bitch," and when the Negro's wife pleaded that they stop the attack, she was told, "you God damned black bitch, I'll shoot your brains out." The city's Democratic mayor, supported by the captain of police, dismissed the men from the force after a brief hearing. In the same city in 1889, a longtime member of the force was dismissed after he accidentally shot and wounded a young Negro. The police commissioners ruled that he had violated the regulation prohibiting the use of a weapon except in self-defense. A similar regulation resulted in the suspension of an Atlanta policeman, described as "one of the best officers of the force," for firing at a black thief. Another Atlanta officer was suspended for thirty days "due to a lick [sic] which he gave a negro." In a third incident, an Atlanta

16. *Atlanta Constitution,* July 29, 1885; January 27, September 23, 1881; February 22, 1879; *Richmond Dispatch,* August 5, 1875. Most of the 120 persons arrested for "suspicion" in Montgomery, Alabama, in 1887 were undoubtedly black. Montgomery, *Annual Reports,* 1886–1887 (Montgomery, 1887), 31.

17. *Nashville Union and Dispatch,* October 22, 1867; and *Atlanta Constitution,* August 26, 1877; Richmond, *Annual Reports of the City Departments of Richmond, Virginia, for the Year Ending January 31, 1874* (Richmond, 1874), xiv.

18. See, for example, *Nashville Union and American,* October 15, 1869; *Nashville Republican Banner,* August 17, 1872. This conclusion is based upon a thorough examination of newspapers and public records in the cities of Nashville, Richmond, and Atlanta.

policeman was sentenced to three years in the penitentiary for killing a Negro who was allegedly resisting arrest.[19]

Despite these few cases of punishment, most of the officers charged with the use of undue force against blacks were found not guilty. In 1866, Richmond policeman Richard O'Dwyer, charged with kicking a Negro down the station house steps, was let off by the mayor with the admonition that he be less aggressive in the future. The following year the mayor presided over a case in which a city policeman allegedly struck a young Negro without provocation. After reminding those policemen present that they were given clubs to defend themselves from attack and not to use as offensive weapons, the mayor postponed the trial. The trial never resumed, indicating either that the charges were dropped or that a cash settlement was made out of court. The individual, nevertheless, remained on the force.[20] In 1885, an Atlanta policeman was acquitted in the seemingly unnecessary and coldblooded killing of a "bad negro." Another city officer was tried and found not guilty in the killing of a black who allegedly resisted arrest for the theft of a pair of shoes.[21] More significant is that most cases of irresponsible police behavior did not even result in the bringing of charges by the victim. The *Atlanta Constitution,* for example, mentioned two cases in 1890 of apparent police brutality. In one, a Negro was dragged through the streets by three policemen "as though he had been a brute." In another, a drunken Negro who had resisted arrest was brought by two officers from the Kimball House with his face and head "covered with blood, which flowed profusely from [a] wound." No charges were filed against any of the policemen.[22]

Incidents of brutality and harassment, the totally white composition of the force, and the natural antagonism between law enforcers and suspected law violators frequently led Negroes to challenge police authority. August Meier and Elliott Rudwick have chronicled the tendency by blacks toward retaliatory vio-

19. *Nashville Daily Press and Times,* June 17, 1866; *Nashville Banner,* March 14–15, 20, 1889; *Atlanta Constitution,* July 23, 1885, February 16, 1884; June 16, 1882.

20. *Richmond Dispatch,* May 28, 1866; May 9, 14, 1867.

21. For the circumstances of the first killing and subsequent accounts of the inquest and trial, see *Atlanta Constitution,* May 25, June 9, 24, December 17, 19, 1885; for details of the killing involving the theft of shoes, see ibid., June 20–21, 23–24, 1885.

22. Ibid., February 12, 1890. For additional cases in which policemen charged with brutality against blacks were exonerated, see Atlanta City Council Minutes, May 17, 1867; *Atlanta Constitution,* February 18, March 16, 1880; July 31, 1887. The Atlanta Negro newspaper, *Weekly Defiance,* October 22, 1881, unsuccessfully sought the dismissal of a local policeman who used for "rifle practice" a fleeing Negro arrested for disorderly conduct.

lence against police in the early twentieth century.[23] While lacking the intellectual defense made after the turn of the century, the pattern of such violence was already present in the postbellum years.

Antagonism surfaced especially when policemen sought to make arrests. Within months after the Civil War the *Montgomery Daily Ledger* noted that since local police had replaced military authority, "We have heard freedmen declare that they will not submit to overhauling or arrest by any damned rebel police!" After a series of stories about Negroes fighting with police or seeking to rescue prisoners, the *Richmond Dispatch* warned in 1866: "The negroes seem determined to try resistance to the police, but whenever they do so, they will find that they have begun a most unwise course. The laws of the State and city must be enforced, disorder and crime must be put down, if it takes every white man in the city to do it."[24] Despite the bravado, nine months later the newspaper reported another series of incidents between policemen and blacks. In one case, a crowd attempted to free a drunken Negro from three policemen. One policeman was thrown across a wagon wheel and choked; another was "roughly handled." Finally, the prisoner was put in a wagon and taken off to the station, but the officers "were followed by the negroes, who made all sorts of threats." A month later blacks rescued a prisoner from policemen at the door of the jail and officers throughout the city were pelted with rocks. A similar incident touched off large-scale disturbances that had to be quelled by soldiers. Nor were such occurrences limited to the chaotic early postwar years. During the 1876 political campaign, a bonfire in the largely Negro Jackson Ward started a fire in a nearby house. When a policeman sought to extinguish the fire, he was hit with a brick. A second officer came to his assistance and arrested two blacks. While bringing in their captives, "the officers were stoned as far as Leigh Street." After another political meeting in 1880, an officer was struck in the head by a large stone while seeking to arrest a Negro lad caught stealing a dry-goods box. Several other policemen were injured by sticks and stones when they came to his aid. One black was arrested and taken to the station, "notwithstanding the efforts made by some of . . . [his] friends to prevent the arrest."[25]

23. Meier and Rudwick, "Negro Retaliatory Violence in the Twentieth Century," *New Politics* 5 (Winter 1966): 41–51.

24. *Montgomery Daily Ledger,* October 4, 1865. For later attempts by Montgomery Negroes to rescue prisoners, see, for example, *Montgomery Daily Advertiser,* February 18, May 31, November 5, 1871. *Richmond Dispatch,* July 31, 1866. On June 25, 1866, the editor had stated, "The negroes are now growing insolent and unruly, and must be taught that they are still subject to the law, and are liable to be punished for committing a breach of the peace or for disturbing the quiet and order of the city. If a few of them are promptly and severely punished it will serve *pour encourager les autres.*"

25. *Richmond Dispatch,* April 1, May 10, 13, 1867; November 4, 1876; August 10, 1880.

Throughout the South numerous other cities experienced the same problems.[26] According to newspaper accounts, however, Atlanta was the city most
troubled by warfare between Negroes and the police. Meier and Rudwick specu-
late that the resistance by Atlanta Negroes during the famous riot of 1906 was
related to the local blacks' support of the militant Niagara Movement.[27] While
there is certainly a connection, this resistance was simply part of a pattern
established in the postwar years. One could argue that the Niagara Movement
benefitted from the spirit of resistance rather than being its cause.

Although an attempt by a group of blacks to rescue a prisoner from two
policemen in 1868 resulted in a riot that left a policeman injured, a Negro killed,
and two others wounded, such incidents were not common in Atlanta until the
1880s. Three years, in particular, of this decade witnessed enough conflicts to
lead the *Atlanta Constitution* to fear for the security of the city. In 1881, a Negro
allegedly pushed a white woman off the sidewalk in an effort to get into the
memorial service for President James Garfield. When he resisted arrest, he was
clubbed. A crowd of his friends gathered and prepared to free him. More police
were called. Since "there was a general resistance, . . . several bloody heads
were the result." Two hundred blacks followed the officer to the station, where
another fight ensued. Soon after the crowd dispersed, it attempted to free a
second Negro who had also been arrested. The *Constitution* took the occasion to
issue a stern reprimand: "Atlanta's colored population ought to learn that they
can make nothing by interfering with an officer in the discharge of his duty and
the sooner they learn it the better it will be for them." The newspaper, however,
did not blame all blacks for the incident: "The Negroes participating in the
difficulty were of that class which frequent every southern town. They are always
ready for a row and if one doesn't occur they are sure to make it. The affair is as
much regretted by the better class of colored people as by the whites." The
newspaper was especially sensitive to the outbreak because two months earlier a
large group of Negroes had stoned a policeman, and two of the blacks had
resisted arrest with drawn guns. Nor could the paper be cheered by the advice
given to local blacks by a Negro newspaper. After cataloging a list of grievances
against the police, the editor of the *Atlanta Weekly Defiance* asked, "Are we

26. See, for example, on Charleston, Joel Williamson, *After Slavery: The Negro in
South Carolina during Reconstruction, 1861–1877* (Chapel Hill: University of North Carolina Press, 1965), 271; on New Orleans, Joy J. Jackson, *New Orleans in the Gilded Age:
Politics and Urban Progress, 1880–1896* (Baton Rouge: Louisiana State University Press,
1969), 237, and Roger A. Fischer, *The Segregation Struggle in Louisiana, 1862–1877*
(Urbana: University of Illinois Press, 1974), 32–37; on Nashville, *Nashville Daily American,* August 7, 1878, *Nashville Banner,* July 10, 1888; on Savannah, *Atlanta Constitution,*
November 30, December 1, 1888.
27. "Negro Retaliatory Violence," 49.

going to be murdered like dogs right here in this community and not open our mouths?" The choice was either to leave Atlanta or insist that "something must be done and that soon."[28]

In August 1883, another series of incidents between Negroes and arresting officers led to renewed laments by the *Constitution.* A mob of blacks rescued a young boy from the police, who were taking him to the station house. The chief of police made it clear that this was not an isolated incident: "This thing is becoming too common. Almost every day something of the kind occurs. The negroes, whenever an arrest is made in an 'out of the way' part of the city, try every way to obstruct the officers. They even follow the officers all the way to the station house abusing them."[29] A week later, a black man accused of raping an elderly Negro woman was freed by his friends from the custody of a white man who had captured him. The *Constitution* attributed this action to the low class of Negroes who inhabited the region. The lesson was clear: "The affair shows how bold these negroes become at times." An editorial urged a tougher policy on the part of the police, arguing, "Those who lead in these demonstrations should be convinced by the shortest and surest arguments known to human experience that their action will not be tolerated in Atlanta anymore than it would be tolerated elsewhere." The newspaper contrasted the behavior of the white and Negro communities, this time not being careful to differentiate among blacks:

> When a white criminal is pursued and arrested, we never hear of the white people surrounding the officers of the law and attempting a rescue. But the conditions are all changed when the criminal is a negro. The moment that a negro steals, or robs, or commits some other crime, his person seems to become sacred in the eyes of his race, and he is harbored, protected and deified. If he is captured, resists an officer and is shot, as he should be, and as a white criminal would be, immediately the leading negroes drum up a mass meeting and proceed to pass a string of senseless but sympathetic resolutions, after a series of harangues that would be a disgrace to the Zulus.[30]

No attempt has been made to compare white and black attitudes on the subject, but, if the *Constitution* was correct about white deference toward the police, the

28. *Atlanta Constitution,* August 18–19, 1868; September 27–28, July 14, 1881; *Atlanta Weekly Defiance,* October 29, 1881. For claims of discrimination toward blacks in the courts, see ibid., October 22, 1881.

29. *Atlanta Constitution,* August 17, 25, 1883. The police commissioners responded by ordering policemen to arrest any persons, white or black, who might follow them when they were taking in a prisoner. Ibid., August 31, 1883.

30. Ibid., August 26, 1883.

reason might lie with the city's small immigrant population and the opening of the force to all whites. In any event, judging from coverage in the *Constitution,* relations between police and blacks improved during the next few years. By the summer and fall of 1888, however, confrontations once again had become common. After reporting several incidents which had almost resulted in riots on the Fourth of July, the *Constitution* noted, "The negroes had an idea that they owned the town yesterday and went just as far as they dared in their efforts to release almost every negro who was arrested." At the end of the month, another disturbance occurred when an escaped Negro was arrested on Decatur Street near Ivy, close to the notorious Willingham Building, the capitol of Atlanta's demiworld: "As usual, when arrests are made in this quarter, a number of negroes followed behind, the number increasing rapidly. Finally they became so bold as to shout at the officer and began pushing against him." The prisoner began struggling and the policeman summoned help. The mob continued to grow, and the police were forced to take refuge in the office of a coal yard. The crowd was finally dispersed through the arrest of two of its leaders and the appeals of Alonzo Burnett, editor of the *Weekly Defiance* and an unsuccessful aspirant for a position on the police force. A week later, a Negro cut a white man's face with a saber during an Odd Fellows procession. A policeman standing nearby served him with a warrant but did not make an arrest, since, according to the *Constitution,* "it might have provoked a riot, as the negro that did the cutting was inclined to be boisterous and his colored brothers were rather decided in their expressions of sympathy."[31]

This was not an isolated example of the effective use of intimidation by blacks against white policemen. In October 1888, a mob on Summer Hill freed a Negro arrested for drunkenness. Alonzo Burnett again calmed the crowd but was prevented from calling a patrol wagon. The police were thus isolated, and a compromise was reached when the brother of the prisoner said he would get him sober and produce him in court the following morning. By the next day, no arrest had been made and no one could find either the prisoner or his brother. Alleged members of the mob were later brought to trial but were freed for lack of evidence. Four years later, the *Constitution* observed that it was dangerous for an officer to go alone to Elbow Bend, an area "inhabited by negro workmen of the lowest and vilest sort," because "more than once policemen have been attacked" there. By 1895, the problem of Negro resistance to arrest was so serious that it was a subject during interviews of prospective policemen. An exchange reported in the *Atlanta Constitution* suggests not only the concern of the police

31. Ibid., July 5, August 1, 1888. For Burnett's interest in joining the force, see ibid., April 2, 1885.

over this matter but the extent to which Negro intimidation had been successful. One of the police commissioners asked an Irish applicant, "What would you do in case you tried to arrest a couple of niggers on Decatur Street and they started to fight you?" The Irishman replied: "What wud you do and what wud any sensible man do? Blow your gong and run like the virry divil!"[32]

Atlanta may have been exceptional in the frequency and intensity of its clashes between blacks and the police. No southern city, however, was without its share of incidents. The reasons lie as much with the changing patterns in housing as with the hostility between the contending parties. One result of emancipation in the cities was the emergence of Negro ghettos.[33] Some of the Negro areas had been settled in antebellum times by free Negroes and hired-out and fugitive slaves who congregated on the fringes of southern cities. The greater number, however, evolved after the occupation of federal forces. Freedmen camps were established that, though later officially disbanded, remained the nuclei for growing black communities. Still others resulted from the placement of key institutions such as colleges, public schools, meeting halls, and churches in parts of the city that already contained some blacks. Often these enclaves were the result of aggressive efforts of local white and Negro building associations or individual real estate agents. And while many of the clusters were the products of voluntary action, many others were due to the refusal of nearby white areas to permit black residents. Whatever the origin, these neighborhoods were in the worst sections of the city: in unkempt alleyways or low-lying ground near contaminated streams, slaughterhouses, flour mills, or other undesirable sites.

These, then, were what the *Atlanta Constitution* referred to as the "out of the way part" or "this quarter" of the city. Nashville had its Rocktown, Black Center, and Black Bottom; Montgomery, its Boguehoma and Peacock Tract; Raleigh, its Hungry Neck, Hayti Alley, and Hell's Half Acre; Atlanta, its Darktown, Peasville, and Jenningstown, where "the population consists chiefly of niggers, bobtailed dogs and babies."[34] By 1890, only 3,679 of Richmond's Jackson Ward population of 17,209 were white, and they were heavily concentrated in the eastern part

32. Ibid., October 22, November 13, 1888. It is unlikely that Burnett's second such intervention was due to coincidence. Either he was trying to prove to the police that he could be of use on the force or else he was already working for them in an undercover capacity. Ibid., June 24, 1892. Ibid., March 25, 1895, as quoted in Watts, "The Police in Atlanta," 176.

33. The following discussion of Negro residential patterns is based on Rabinowitz, "The Search for Social Control," 1:114–39.

34. *Atlanta Constitution,* September 25, 1875.

of the ward.[35] The 1876 riot had stopped at Leigh Street because it was the southern boundary of the ward.

It would seem, therefore, that while the large-scale race riots of the twentieth century will continue to interest scholars, more attention should be paid to the less visible day-to-day friction between the police and blacks. Already, at the end of the nineteenth century, resentment against the police and the system of local justice was a constant fact of life in the emerging southern ghettos, ready to be ignited by seemingly minor affronts. And once the blacks were driven to violence, the police were especially vulnerable because of the growing size and location of the Negro sections of the city and the police department's own deficiencies in organization and manpower.

35. Bureau of the Census, *Eleventh Census of the United States: 1890,* vol. 1, *Population,* pt. 1, 579.

Three Reconstruction Leaders

Blanche K. Bruce, Robert Brown Elliott, and Holland Thompson

The following essay first appeared in an anthology on nineteenth-century black leaders, which was directed at both an academic and general audience. Reflecting the editors' desire to appeal to nonspecialists, it was published without citations, but with a brief bibliographical essay. Although this reprinted version likewise omits the notes, it includes a more extensive but not updated bibliographical essay. For post-1986 secondary sources and the most comprehensive treatment of individual black politicians, see Eric Foner, *Freedom's Lawmakers: A Directory of Black Officeholders during Reconstruction* (New York: Oxford University Press, 1993).

Emancipation and Reconstruction transformed the nature of black leadership. To be sure, there was significant continuity between the antebellum and post-bellum years, symbolized by the continued predominance of the northern-based Frederick Douglass among black leaders. And, as before the war, many leaders did not hold either party or public office. This was true of some national figures and particularly so of local leaders, not only clergymen or prominent business-men, but often illiterate farmers in the countryside. Yet during Congressional (or Radical) Reconstruction initiated in 1867, black leadership became centered in the South rather than the North, and despite continued contributions by non-officeholders, public and party officials were now the most important figures.

I would like to thank Leon Litwack and August Meier for their comments on an earlier version of this essay.

Although there would not be a black congressman from the North until the 1920s, twenty-two southern blacks, including two senators, served in Congress between 1870 and 1901. Countless blacks served as state legislators and city councilmen and in other offices throughout the South.

Much controversy has surrounded black political leaders of the Reconstruction. Southern white opponents and even some northern whites at the time viewed them as illiterate, poverty-stricken, corrupt, and totally dependent on handouts from white Republicans, who allegedly controlled their votes. Early generations of scholars under the influence of Columbia University professor William Archibald Dunning and other critics of Reconstruction helped ingrain such views in history books. Woodrow Wilson, then a Princeton political scientist, concluded that during Reconstruction "unscrupulous adventurers" and plunderers, mostly from the North, manipulated "inexperienced blacks" in "an extraordinary carnival of public crime under the forms of law." Thirty-six years later, in 1929, Claude Bowers, in his best-selling book *The Tragic Era*, viewed black leaders as lazy, ignorant, and childlike, managed by carpetbaggers and scalawags who preached hate and distrust of the former Confederates. The Mississippi legislature was "one of the most grotesque bodies that ever assembled. A mulatto was Speaker of the House, a darker man was Lieutenant-Governor, the Negro Bruce had been sent to the Senate, a corrupt guardian was in charge of the public schools, a black, more fool than knave, was Commissioner of Immigration."

Yet a revision of this traditional approach was already underway. Begun by black participants in Reconstruction, the reevaluation of that era would include black and white liberal scholars and reflect the changing racial climate, capped by the civil rights movement of the 1950s and 1960s. It is now clear that no "Africanization" of southern politics occurred despite the unprecedented number of black officeholders at all levels of government. Even during the height of Reconstruction no black was elected governor or mayor of a major city, no large town had a black majority on its city council, and only in South Carolina did blacks constitute a majority in a state constitutional convention or legislative chamber. With regard to the backgrounds and qualifications of black leaders, the contrast with the traditional view is most vivid in places such as New Orleans and Charleston, South Carolina, which had contained significant antebellum free Negro communities; but throughout the South the first generation of Negro leaders was remarkably qualified for its new responsibilities.

On the basis of studies of individual congressmen, local leaders, and collective biographies it would seem that these black leaders tended to be relatively young, in their late twenties or early thirties, when the state constitutional conventions met in 1867 and 1868. Most were native-born and literate. One study of early Reconstruction leadership in New Orleans, for example, found that over 98 percent of these men were literate. The figures are about the same not only for the equally settled and cultured Charleston black community but for Raleigh, North Carolina, as well, where all twenty-five of the city's Negro councilmen between 1868 and 1901 were literate and all but one was born in North Carolina.

The leaders in Reconstruction were mostly artisans and petty tradesmen, with the addition, especially as the years passed, of an occasional lawyer or teacher, although ministers were especially important in Georgia. Significant numbers were property holders. In New Orleans 52.8 percent of the politicians had been skilled laborers, and another 44 percent were businessmen and professionals in 1860–1861; 25.3 percent of them had between $1,001 and $2,500 in assets. Few, if any, other groups of black leaders could match these figures, but the extent of property holding among them also was far greater than once acknowledged. For example, in 1870 the median wealth for the 174 delegates to the Reconstruction constitutional conventions of 1867–1869 for whom such information has been found was $650.

Although many of the leaders were dark skinned and most probably former slaves, there were disproportionate numbers of mulattoes and those with free antecedents. The latter two groups were again most significant in Louisiana and South Carolina, where there had been significant miscegenation involving upper-class white males and free and slave Negro females. In New Orleans over 91 percent of the leaders were mulattoes and over 97 percent had been free before the war; in Charleston the respective figures were 63 percent and 77 percent. More typical percentages were found among the delegates to constitutional conventions in which mulattoes and free Negroes had a slight majority, though individual conventions varied, with Louisiana and South Carolina having the largest number and Texas, Mississippi, and Georgia the fewest. Even in postconvention Georgia, however, where the influence of dark-skinned leaders and former slaves was perhaps the greatest in the South, among those state legislators for whom we have information, three of nineteen were mulatto and eight of twenty had been free before the war.

Southern black leaders were clearly an elite. Representing a largely unskilled, illiterate, rural constituency of dark-skinned former slaves, they were an ambitious group of young, skilled, educated men, often with urban connections, who were far more likely than their supporters to be mulattoes and to have free Negro antecedents. In his study of 255 Negroes elected to state and federal offices in South Carolina between 1868 and 1876, Thomas Holt concluded that most of them were literate, "a significant number" had been free before the Civil War, many owned property, and most worked in skilled or professional occupations.

The traditional view of black leadership concentrates on the alleged corruption, racism, and vindictiveness of black leaders and their manipulation by new white masters. The reality was quite different. Most black leaders supported amnesty for the former Confederates, opposed confiscation of rebel lands, and urged moderation in dealing with whites. Few of them called for "social equality" with whites. What they wanted for their people was land, education, and civil rights that included suffrage and equal access to public accommodations and public conveyances. Few black leaders called for integration. Initially, at least, they were satisfied to join their white allies in bringing about a shift from the exclusion that had characterized the previous policy toward blacks in schools, asylums, streetcars, and the like to a new policy of separate but equal access. By taking such stands, blacks helped produce the most democratic constitutions and responsible state and local governments ever found in the South. And while a few leaders came to favor black emigration as they began to despair over the undermining of Reconstruction by white economic intimidation, physical violence, and political fraud, most continued to seek the improvement of conditions for blacks within the South.

The relationship between the black leaders and their white allies was more complex. No doubt some were under the control of whites, whom they supported in return for jobs, money, or other favors; only a handful rose to power by defying whites of both parties; and few leaders were completely free from the need for white assistance. Nevertheless, black leaders followed their own instincts and sought to act in a way that would aid their people and also help their own careers. Although some leaders were placed in office by whites, most were elected or were attractive to whites because of their ties to the black community. Such basic institutions as the union leagues, churches, fraternal associations, and schools provided a training ground for black leaders that would be easily transformed into a power base.

White leaders who needed blacks as much as blacks needed them were often dismayed at black displays of independence. State and local Republican parties throughout the South were torn by factionalism that pitted white carpetbaggers, scalawags, and blacks against each other. But divisions were not simply on the basis of race, for blacks themselves were often divided. Sometimes divisions were based on color or antebellum status; at other times they were due to patronage or policy disputes, or simply competing ambition. In the end these divisions, as well as those between black and white Republicans and among white Republicans, made it easier for white Democrats to overthrow (or "redeem") the Reconstruction governments and severely restrict the power of those comparatively few blacks who remained in office.

The careers of three representative black leaders of the Reconstruction Era—

Blanche K. Bruce of Mississippi, Robert Brown Elliott of South Carolina, and Holland Thompson of Alabama—help to illustrate the diverse nature of southern black leadership. Although no small sample can do full justice to the spectrum of that leadership, together these three men provide a revealing cross section in terms of their backgrounds, policies, and levels of political participation.

Senator Blanche K. Bruce was the nation's most famous black officeholder. Although his less important fellow black Mississippian Hiram Revels had served briefly in the United States Senate in 1870, Bruce was the only black elected to a full term prior to the election of Edward Brooke of Massachusetts in 1966. Bruce owed his success to close ties with influential whites and his skill at political infighting. He was a compromiser, or accommodationist, who favored gradual change and sought to avoid taking strong stands on controversial issues.

Though born a slave in 1841, Bruce grew up in Virginia, Mississippi, and Missouri as the playmate of his master's only son. He was taught how to read and write, did little work in the fields, and was further set apart from the other slaves by his light skin. Despite the outbreak of civil war and the proximity of freedom, Bruce initially chose to remain with his master. He eventually fled, first to Lawrence, Kansas, where he founded a school for former slaves, and then in 1864 to Hannibal, Missouri, where he established the state's first school for blacks. In 1866, after briefly working in a local newspaper office, he left to attend Oberlin, but a lack of funds forced him to return to Missouri. Soon after Bruce returned to his native South in the hopes of benefiting from the implementation of Congressional plans for Reconstruction, which provided for Negro voting and officeholding. First he tried Arkansas, then Tennessee; with a friend he eventually moved to Mississippi, where blacks enjoyed a majority of some twenty thousand over whites at the polls. He found the Delta especially promising given the absence of an indigenous group of black leaders among its predominantly Negro population, coupled with the economic promise of the rich bottomlands.

Bruce first came to the attention of whites as a speaker during the 1869 elections and was appointed a voter registrar in Tallahatchie County following the wholesale Republican replacement of Conservative officials. But Bruce already had a higher office in mind. Journeying to Jackson for the inauguration of the new administration in 1870, he impressed Governor-elect James Alcorn with his dignified manner, eloquence, and knowledge of government. With Alcorn's support Bruce was selected sergeant at arms of the state senate over several white candidates. Office quickly followed office, usually because of white support. Alcorn appointed Bruce tax assessor of the Delta's Bolivar County. With the help of a white carpetbagger named H. T. Florey, the boss of Bolivar County, Bruce was elected sheriff and tax collector in 1871. Soon after, the Republican state board of education appointed him county superintendent of education. Now the only black in the state to be both sheriff and superintendent of education (few blacks held even one of the jobs), Bruce broadened his power when he was appointed to the board of levee commissioners for a three-county district.

The key to this rapid rise seems not to have been the support of the black masses with whom he had little contact but rather of the white planters who continued to dominate the economy and therefore the politics of the area. Bruce was considered safe—a dignified and educated mulatto who did not identify himself with threatening issues. He became even more palatable when he, too, became a landowner, first by buying several town lots in the new county seat and then by purchasing 640 acres of swampy but fertile land that he developed into a plantation. More land followed, and by the 1880s he was a wealthy man, raising cotton with black labor.

Bruce performed effectively in office. His decisions as sheriff and assessor met with general acceptance by local whites, and there was no taint of scandal or corruption. No doubt he kept the tax rates quite low, especially after he himself became a landowner. His most impressive contribution came as superintendent of schools, taking a faltering system and turning it into one of the healthiest in the state. By the end of 1872 the county had twenty-one schools with more than a thousand students. Shortly before his resignation the next year, Bruce reported, "There are no longer difficulties besetting my progress in the future administration of the school system in this county, which energy and time will not remove." He had accomplished much by following a policy that did not offend local whites. As elsewhere in Mississippi and almost everywhere in the South, the schools were segregated, expenditures were kept low, black teachers replaced potential "meddling" northern whites, and education was aimed at providing reliable workers and reducing crime. The prevailing attitudes and the continued power of the planter class over blacks and even white Republicans would have permitted little more. Still, by helping to establish the county's first school system and by assuring blacks a place within it, Bruce had furthered his own interests as well as those of his race.

At this point Bruce's relationship to his black constituents becomes clearer. Although he depended heavily on white allies, he was chosen for office to appeal to and provide recognition of a primarily black constituency. Black voters in turn could support Bruce for a number of reasons. Many blacks were grateful to him for giving them and their children an opportunity to get an education, no matter how limited. Others were thankful for patronage positions or personal favors that might range from an occasional small loan to a visit or a kind word. Still others no doubt voted for Bruce because they were paid to do so. But arguably the largest number of blacks supported him for symbolic reasons. To a certain extent they lived vicariously, taking pleasure in seeing one of their race, even though an "outsider," in positions of power and influence normally reserved for whites. What he did for them with that power was of less importance than its trappings.

Bruce's horizons continued to broaden as he now sought statewide office. In order to succeed he had to confront the white scalawags and carpetbaggers who controlled much of the patronage, as well as other ambitious blacks who sought to replace the recently deceased James Lynch as the state's most powerful black leader. It helped that Bruce was already known outside the Delta, having attended the state Republican Convention in 1871 and having served as secretary to the Mississippi delegation at the 1872 Republican National Convention. He was further aided by the fact that he had not aligned himself with either Republican faction—the Moderates led by Alcorn or the Radicals led by Senator Adelbert Ames—in their bitter struggle to control the state. His policies in Bolivar County made him attractive to the Alcorn wing, while his failure to support moderate opposition to a strong state law against racial discrimination in public accommodations left him acceptable to the Ames wing.

During the critical 1873 campaign Bruce finally had to chose between the factions. The Moderates under now-senator Alcorn and Governor Ridgley Powers were initially dominant, but their indifference to black rights and their cultivation of white southern Conservatives had alienated many Republicans. Courted by both wings at the state convention, Bruce was more receptive to Radical entreaties for his support because he wisely realized that the Moderates were losing influence. The Radicals offered him the position of lieutenant governor. Adelbert Ames had left the Senate to become the Republican party's gubernatorial nominee, but he planned to return after gaining control of the governorship for the Radicals, which meant that Bruce would soon move up to the governor's office. Nevertheless, he rejected the offer and instead asked for the Senate seat for himself. With Ames's support in the white-dominated legislature, Bruce subsequently defeated two white carpetbaggers by a comfortable margin and entered the Senate at the age of thirty-four, in March 1875. When his former patron, Senator Alcorn, refused to escort him for the swearing-in ceremony, Bruce fittingly attracted still another white sponsor in Senator Roscoe Conkling of New York, who stepped forward to do the honor. He repaid Conkling with his votes. And with the New Yorker's assistance Bruce was appointed to the standing committees on pensions, manufactures, and education and labor.

Bruce did not have an illustrious Senate career. Given the racist feeling in the chamber and the overthrow of Reconstruction in Mississippi in 1875 and throughout the South within two years, this should not be surprising. But he was a conscientious and capable representative of Mississippi and of his race. Like black officeholders at all levels of government he served constituents of both races in a number of mundane but necessary ways, such as introducing private relief bills. Bruce was also an especially strong advocate of Mississippi's interests as a member of the Senate Select Committee on River Improvements and as an ardent supporter of favorable railroad legislation.

His service in the Senate was most distinguished by his role as race spokesman. Although the first bill Bruce introduced called for desegregation of the U.S. Army, he normally took moderate stands and sought "to cultivate and exhibit . . . a courtesy that would inspire reciprocal courtesy." This time his strategy was less effective than it had been on the local level. Sometimes his low-profile approach frustrated him. Following the refusal of President Grant and the other Republicans to aid Mississippi Republicans during the infamous 1875 political campaign and the subsequent overthrow of Governor Ames's regime, Bruce uncharacteristically lashed out at the failure of the national Republican party to protect southern blacks against Conservative violence and intimidation. Similarly, he condemned fellow Republicans for not seating P. B. S. Pinchback, a former black lieutenant governor of Louisiana, who claimed victory after a contested senatorial election. Like other black leaders Bruce defended the granting of civil rights to blacks and warned that southern white violence would rob blacks of the benefits of Reconstruction. "Violence so unprovoked, inspired by such motives, and looking to such ends," he declared in his maiden speech, "is a spectacle not only discreditable to the country, but dangerous to the integrity of our free institutions."

Like most freshmen legislators Bruce became more active midway through his term. He argued against a Chinese exclusion bill and for a more humane Indian policy, no doubt mindful of the effects that exclusionary treatment of other minorities might have on policy toward blacks. Although he briefly chaired the committee on river improvements, his most visible role was as chairman of the committee that investigated the failure of the Freedmen's Bank, which had cost thousands of blacks much of their life savings. The committee report blamed mismanagement by its white directors, but Bruce failed to secure congressional reimbursement for black depositors. Finally, symbolizing his conservative inclinations and belief that blacks could in fact receive fair treatment in the South, he opposed the Exoduster migration of the late 1870s. Thousands of blacks, the largest numbers from Mississippi, were fleeing the South to seek a better life in Kansas. Although Bruce warned Conservatives of the need to treat blacks better, his own need for black laborers and voters, the desire of white planters, and an evidently sincere belief that blacks would suffer greater hardships by making the journey led him to side with the majority of black leaders who opposed the migration. Nevertheless, Bruce made a valiant though unsuccessful effort to secure direct federal aid to destitute migrants in Kansas. He expressed even stronger disapproval of a proposed back-to-Africa movement, claiming that since the antebellum period the Negro had secured personal, civil, and political rights. Furthermore, whites were so dependent on black labor and blacks were such a potent political force that if the black man had patience and worked hard, "he will live to rejoice over a condition of society in the communities of the South in which he can entertain independent political opinions without prejudice, and to assert and exercise all the rights without hindrance and without danger."

Such pronouncements were less important in assessing Bruce's effectiveness as a political leader than were his actions within Republican party politics. By 1878 Bruce, together with two other Mississippi Negroes, James Hill and John R. Lynch, had wrested control of the state Republican party from the white-dominated Moderate faction and had regained power following the "revolution of 1875." Hill, a former secretary of state under Ames, and Lynch, former speaker of the Mississippi House and three-term congressman, handled affairs in Mississippi while Bruce sought to protect the "triumvirate's" interests in Washington. The coalition's primary aim was patronage, which it retained responsibility for until the 1890s. Although Bruce succeeded in getting President Hayes to appoint Hill collector of internal revenue in the state, the three men trod carefully, recommending only a handful of blacks for office, thus assuring continued white acceptance of their power, which in turn encouraged Hayes to turn to them on patronage decisions.

Bruce had solidified his position within the state Republican party, but by the time his Senate term was over, Democrats controlled the legislature and there was no hope for reelection. While maintaining his interest in state politics, Bruce settled in Washington, where he shifted his attention to national Republican affairs and the pursuit of appointive office for himself. He supported Secretary of the Treasury John Sherman and later former president Grant in their unsuccessful quests for the Republican nomination in 1880 but then campaigned loyally for the nominee, James Garfield. As a reward he had hoped for a cabinet position; instead he was offered a post as minister to Brazil or as assistant to the postmaster general, both of which he declined. He asked instead to be appointed register of the treasury, and with the active support of his former Senate Democratic colleague L. Q. C. Lamar, he won Senate confirmation to the highest appointive position given a Negro up to that point. He lost the position when Cleveland was elected president. Before returning to politics in 1888 to campaign for Benjamin Harrison, Bruce went on a national lecture tour to promote racial harmony and better treatment for all minorities. In return for his part in Harrison's victory he was appointed recorder of deeds for the District of Columbia. Again out of office following Cleveland's victory in 1892, Bruce contented himself by supervising his more than one thousand acres of fertile Delta land, dabbling in state politics, serving as a trustee of Howard University and a member of the local school board, and awaiting the return of the Republicans to power. With McKinley's election in 1896 he was again made register of the treasury, which, since his initial appointment, had been reserved by Republicans for prominent blacks. Four months later Bruce died of diabetes at the age of fifty-seven.

Prominent men of both races attended his funeral. The *New York Times* called him next to Frederick Douglass "the foremost man of his race." The *Washington Post* was more perceptive, noting that he was not "especially beloved by the masses of his colored follow citizens" but "was admired by the judicious and respectable among the whites and blacks alike." In a sense Bruce had always been cut off from the black masses (ironically the very people white slate makers had used him to appeal to), first as a favored mulatto slave, then as a successful planter, and finally as a prominent national politician. Blacks voted for him for local office in large numbers, for reasons already noted, but there is no evidence that he was closely associated with any of the basic black institutions in Mississippi. And while black legislators helped elect him to the Senate, they made up a minority of the Mississippi state legislature. Even in Washington he lived in a largely white world, married to a wealthy mulatto, primarily entertaining white guests (in addition to leading blacks like Douglass and Lynch) and belonging to a white church, the First Congregational. Although he was not a "race-first man," like some leaders, he was not ashamed of being a Negro. Indeed, he was proud of it. "The Negro of America," he declared, "is not African, but American," and in his view assimilation into American society held the greatest prospects of success for him and his race. Like marginal people everywhere who are the products of a minority culture but feel equally or more comfortable within the dominant culture, Bruce served as an intermediary between the black and white worlds of nineteenth-century America, and in the end he came to prefer the latter.

For less fortunate blacks Bruce urged hard work, self-help, and the value of education. It was familiar and useful advice but increasingly less credible in the New South. Bruce knew that conditions did not favor black advancement. He protested the treatment of southern blacks and in 1890 urged federal aid to education and protection of black voting rights, but basically he believed that once southern whites came to appreciate the loyalty and ability of their black neighbors, conditions would improve. Meanwhile, Bruce discouraged emigration to Kansas and Africa, extolled black skills (as in his capacity as director of black exhibits at the Industrial Cotton Centennial Exposition in 1884–1885), urged patience, and held out the vague hope that blacks would be assimilated into American society on the basis of equal, if at times separate, treatment. Such hopes made sense to him. After all, he had flourished within American society despite his humble origins. Yet to the mass of blacks mired in poverty and losing their political and social rights, Bruce's lifestyle, opposition to the exodus, failure to help on the land issue, and entreaties to hard work and patience had little relevance. It was easier to identify with Booker T. Washington on the basis of his darker color, his decision to remain in the South, and above all, his more visible evidence of power among whites.

As a wealthy mulatto planter who had especially good relations with whites both within his state and the nation, thanks to his moderate policies and compromising nature, Blanche Bruce could not have been more different than Robert Brown Elliott, South Carolina's controversial black lawyer and congressman. The dark-skinned Elliott was a racial militant, anathema to most whites; though not above dealing with white politicians, he owed most of his success to a strong black base and his own forceful presence. Rather than a compromiser, he was an ardent practitioner of confrontational politics. And in whatever he did, neither he nor others ever forgot that he was a proud black man.

During Reconstruction, South Carolina offered more opportunities for black leadership than any other state. With 60 percent of its population black, it was the only state other than Mississippi with a black majority; and its blacks did a better job of capitalizing on their numbers than did those of Mississippi. Only in South Carolina did blacks make up a majority of the delegates to the conventions called to draft constitutions for the first Reconstruction governments. Although no black ever held the governorship, between 1868 and 1877 there were three black lieutenant governors, numerous other statewide officers, a two-to-one black majority in the House and a clear majority on joint ballot of the House and Senate. In short, South Carolina was just the kind of state to attract an ambitious carpetbagger like Elliott, even though, unlike Mississippi, it already had a cadre of indigenous leaders centered around the talented antebellum free Negro elite of Charleston.

Elliott was definitely an interloper, but his origins are shrouded in mystery. He claimed that he was born in Boston in 1842 of West Indian parents and had been educated in private schools in Boston, Jamaica, and England, including Eton College, from which he allegedly graduated with honors. He then briefly read law with a noted legal scholar before returning to the United States in 1861, soon after to join the Union army. Contemporaries and most historians have accepted his account, but his most recent biographer, Peggy Lamson, convincingly argues that except for the birth year it was all a fabrication. It seems instead that Elliott was actually born in England, educated in English schools (though certainly not Eton), trained as a typesetter, and served only in the Royal Navy. He might have jumped ship in Boston Harbor in 1866 or 1867 and decided to seek his fortune in America, without, however, taking out citizenship papers.

What is certain is that as of March 1867 Elliott was associate editor of Charleston's *South Carolina Leader,* a Republican newspaper edited by Richard Cain, a forty-two-year-old Negro clergyman from Brooklyn, New York, and a future state legislator and congressman, sent by the African Methodist Episcopal church to proselytize the freedpeople. One of Elliott's friends called Elliott "commanding in appearance," and Lamson describes him as "a full-blooded black of medium height and close-cropped hair and a neatly trimmed mustache." A *New York Times* reporter, however, provided a more common view among contemporary whites, describing him as "very black, very well spoken and bitter as gall." Indeed, throughout Reconstruction, whites would view Elliott as a talented orator and a forceful leader but also as a racial militant who personified black resentment of second-class treatment. Under his leadership Cain's paper rejected its gradualist approach and adopted the slogan Equality and Union, which Elliott championed throughout his short but spectacular political career, often to the dismay of allies and enemies of both races.

During the almost ten years of Radical rule in South Carolina, Elliott emerged as the major black spokesman in a state unsurpassed in the quantity and quality of its major black leaders. Elliott's importance and power is reflected in his impressive list of public and party offices. Although he arrived in South Carolina after the pivotal Colored People's Convention of 1865, which produced so many of the state's leaders, he was one of the seventy-one black delegates to the 1868 Constitutional Convention, which drafted the most democratic constitution in South Carolina's history. Though nominated for lieutenant governor at the Republican Convention of that year, he dropped out of the race after finishing third on the first ballot. The next month, when he was already the only black on the five-man board of commissioners in Barnwell County, Elliott was elected to the state House of Representatives, where he finished second in the balloting for speaker. Following his selection as chairman of the powerful committee on railroads and his appointment to the vital committee on privileges and elections, a Charleston paper claimed with some justification that he was one of eight men (four of them black) who controlled state government. Adding credence to this assessment was his appointment as assistant adjutant general of South Carolina, which placed him in charge of organizing a militia. In 1870 Elliott was elected to Congress over a white lawyer from a district that had only a slight black majority. He handily won reelection two years later but resigned near the end of the term to run again for the state House. Easily victorious, he served as speaker from 1874 to 1876. He was then elected state attorney general in 1876 but was among the five Republican officeholders removed following the Democratic triumph of that year. Elliott wielded even more power within the party itself. He attended three Republican national conventions (twice leading the delegation), served as state party chairman during much of the 1870s, and was usually permanent chairman of the state nominating conventions. In the latter two positions he played a decisive role in determining party policy and choosing candidates.

Whether in the constitutional convention, state legislature, or Congress, Elliott aligned himself with the Republican party's Radical faction. At the convention he successfully led the fight against articles requiring a literacy test for voters and a poll tax that would be used to fund public education. In each case he correctly predicted that the measure could be used by future hostile administrations to disfranchise blacks and undermine the gains of Reconstruction. He was equally adamant in calling for the invalidation of debts contracted for the purchase and sale of slaves. In the legislature he strongly supported a successful bill to ban discrimination in public accommodations and public conveyances. As a congressman he gave a celebrated speech in favor of federal suppression of the Ku Klux Klan, voted against the amnesty bill to remove political disabilities from former Confederates, and vigorously debated former Confederate vice-president Alexander Stephens over the merits of the proposed civil rights legislation that eventually became the Civil Rights Act of 1875. Fittingly, and as a sign of his growing national reputation, Boston blacks in 1874 invited Elliott to give the oration at ceremonies to honor the memory of the Radical U.S. Senator Charles Sumner.

Given Elliott's considerable power, visibility, and outspokenness on controversial issues, it is not surprising that he became the object of frequent Democratic attack and even opposition within his own party. What is surprising was the viciousness of the attacks and the extent to which he was singled out for abuse. There was, in fact, much in his record that Conservatives chose to ignore. Elliott occasionally lent support to white Democrats, in one instance supporting a Democrat for a circuit judgeship and in a second helping to remove the political liabilities of a Democrat who subsequently became his law partner. Despite his reputation as a racial militant, at the constitutional convention he coupled his support for a public school system and compulsory attendance with opposition to integration. Similarly, in a state so dependent on a black labor force, Elliott did little to threaten the economic status quo. Although he served as president of a state labor convention in 1869, he had favored a permanent halt to confiscation of planter land at the convention and never seriously interested himself in the plight of rural or urban black workers. And even some Democrats admitted that he took a more moderate view of the role of the militia than did Governor Robert Scott, who sought to use it as an offensive rather than a defensive force.

There was also the strong strain of self-help ideology that permeated Elliott's speeches. Like the more conservative Bruce, he was a firm believer in the value of public education. Then, too, he frequently reminded black audiences of the responsibility they had in South Carolina since they were the majority. In a nationally reported speech in 1874, following his triumphant civil rights speech in Congress, Elliott told a Columbia audience of the need to clean up state and party government because blacks were being judged by a different standard. Obsessed with fears about the fragility of the Reconstruction governments, conscious of the fact that "revolutions may go backward," Elliott called for federal support of southern blacks. But at the same time he argued that blacks themselves had their destiny within their own hands and should rise to the challenge.

Nevertheless, Democrats insisted upon seeing Elliott as an irresponsible hater of whites and a troublemaker. "Able, audacious and unscrupulous," one Democratic paper called him. To support such assessments white Carolinians, including some Republican enemies, claimed that Elliott was one of the state's major "corruptionists." This, of course, was a common charge against both black and white Radicals during Reconstruction. No doubt corruption existed, just as it did in the North, especially in such solidly Democratic cities as New York. Yet historians have amply demonstrated that even in the South white Democrats participated in much of this corruption during Reconstruction and often surpassed their Republican predecessors during the post-Reconstruction years. Among Republicans, South Carolina's white politicians, including carpetbaggers like governors Robert Scott and Daniel Chamberlain and U.S. Senator John Patterson, and scalawags like Governor Franklin Moses, Jr., engaged most often in financial irregularities and received the largest share of the spoils. Black politicians were generally left with the crumbs, often in the form of petty bribes. Contemporary and later critics of Elliott exaggerated the extent and seriousness of his alleged corruption; his recent liberal biographer minimized it in an effort to present a favorable picture of him, other black leaders, and Reconstruction itself. The record, in fact, is not all that clear, but it does seem that while Elliott was resistant to small bribes and other minor enticements, he was not above reproach. He benefitted financially from at least one suspect railroad deal, drew excessive legal fees as assistant adjutant general, received state and party funds for lobbying efforts (including six thousand dollars to prevent the impeachment of Governor Scott), and liberally distributed public and private money during election campaigns. As a result, despite a series of unprofitable law partnerships, he was able to live in fine style and purchase a number of city lots and an elegant three-story house in Columbia. But the corruption of a Moses or Scott was more blatant, and Elliott was never indicted for any crime, unlike several of his black and white contemporaries. The attention given to him seems to have been based on his considerable power and his color, not on any conclusive evidence.

Yet more than color, power, and positions were involved. Elliott was singled out in large measure because of his style and lack of deference toward whites, whether friend or foe. To one Democratic newspaper he was "as big a rascal as can be found anywhere within the ranks of Radicalism and is besides, *supremely insolent, arrogant* and *arbitrary*" (italics added). Sometimes blacks experienced his wrath or his acerbic tongue. During debate in the legislature, Elliott referred to future congressman Robert De Large as "a pigmy who was trying to play the part of a giant" and was "elocutionizing himself into a perspiration which stood out upon his skin like warts." It was more disturbing to Conservatives when he showed the same disrespect to whites. During debate on the civil rights bill, for example, Elliott sarcastically concluded that the Negro "aims at a higher degree of intellect than that exhibited . . . in this debate" by a Virginia congressman who had claimed that blacks were racially inferior. Elliott verbally attacked all three Republican governors, calling Chamberlain, who was admired by many Democrats, a liar and a crook. Elliott could also be vindictive, as when he led an unsuccessful attempt to impeach Chamberlain's leading black ally, state treasurer Francis Cardozo, and in his unremitting opposition to Chamberlain's renomination in 1876. While other blacks might object to segregation in public accommodations, only Elliott could boast that he had a white federal employee fired for noisily leaving a normally segregated Washington restaurant when Elliott was permitted to eat there. Blanche K. Bruce, of course, never gave whites such ammunition.

Elliott owed much of his reputation for being "uppity" and a "race-first man" to his key role in reversing the practice in South Carolina of blacks deferring to whites over nominations to major offices. At the 1868 nominating convention he had been reluctantly among those blacks who urged a go-slow policy that gave the four congressional seats to whites and settled for a black in only one state office. By 1870, however, as chairman of the nominating convention, Elliott was instrumental in placing blacks (all free before the war) in three of the four congressional seats, gaining the lieutenant governorship and in general expanding black influence in the party. Both white Republicans and Democrats seem never to have forgotten this. Nor did they overlook Elliott's continued role as a king maker in switching his support over the years from Governor Scott to Governor Moses and finally, and quite reluctantly, to Governor Chamberlain. The faction-ridden Republican politics of South Carolina, with its racially mixed slates of voters and constant friction even among regulars, defies description in a short essay. Suffice it to say that Elliott, as chairman of the nominating convention and party chairman, rarely backed a loser in nomination fights, and his influence, especially as the sole designator of credentials committees, was often decisive.

This did not mean that Elliott was all-powerful or even able to promote his own interests to the extent he desired. In 1872, for example, he lost his fight for the U.S. Senate nomination. Dismayed by the lack of patronage given to blacks by the incumbent senator Francis Sawyer, and no doubt impressed by his own considerable qualifications, Elliott sought to take the nomination from Sawyer. Despite his obvious strengths Elliott had a number of liabilities, which even in a fair fight might have meant defeat. Many whites were fearful and blacks envious, his sharp temper alienated others, and some simply believed that South Carolina's and the party's interests could be best served by a white man. When Sawyer dropped out of the contest the wealthy railroad magnate John Patterson emerged as the white frontrunner. Not taking any chances of being overlooked, Patterson liberally distributed bribes to legislators that allegedly averaged about three hundred dollars. The other white candidate, former governor Scott, averaged one hundred dollars a vote. Elliott, who had no funds, gave out no bribes, though he readily admitted he would have done so if he had had the money. Patterson even offered Elliott fifteen thousand dollars to remove himself from consideration. Elliott refused and Patterson won the nomination in the state Senate by offering two thousand dollars to a Scott man to switch his vote. Meanwhile, in the House, many blacks ignored appeals to vote their race and deserted Elliott, and so he lost by a count of twenty-seven to seventy-three. Clearly, whites rather than blacks tended to draw the color line, and with his liabilities and lack of resources Elliott had gone as high as he could.

Elliott hoped that his election as attorney general in 1876 would prove a stepping stone to the governorship, but time was running out for him and his party. As in Mississippi the previous year (and explicitly drawing on that example), white Democrats used violence, economic intimidation, and fraud to overthrow the Republican administration. Fraudulent returns from two northwestern counties produced a disputed election in which both sides claimed victory. For almost five months South Carolina had two state legislatures and both the Democrat Wade Hampton and the incumbent Daniel Chamberlain had themselves inaugurated as governor. Also in dispute were the state's electoral votes, which in 1876 assumed a critical importance. To win, Rutherford B. Hayes, the Republican presidential candidate, needed the votes of South Carolina, Florida, and Louisiana, the only southern states still in Republican hands. In the end the electoral votes went to Hayes; but in South Carolina, Democratic threats forced a favorable decision from the Republican-controlled state supreme court that produced a Democratic legislature and the installation of Hampton as governor. Chamberlain's fate was sealed when Hayes ordered federal troops, called out during the election, to return to their barracks. Elliott and five other executive officers who had been duly elected were subsequently removed by Hampton, an action upheld by the compliant supreme court. By the end of 1877 the Democrats had forced the resignation of numerous Republican legislators, a process made easier by the rifts within the Republican party.

As state chairman Elliott had been in charge of the 1876 campaign. Unlike the more cautious Bruce, who in Mississippi feared inciting whites as well as for his own safety, Elliott spoke throughout the state. He remained chairman, but in both 1878 and 1880 he successfully urged that the Republicans not run a statewide campaign. He believed that the lack of Republican opposition would lead to dissension among Democrats, just as the absence of Democratic challengers had earlier produced divisions among Republicans. By 1880, however, Elliott had become increasingly discouraged about prospects for the future. The following year he led a delegation of blacks to see President-elect James Garfield. Addressing Garfield, he listed the various examples of discrimination against southern blacks in the courts, voting precincts, schools, and public accommodations and warned that without federal help blacks would join the growing exodus. He was particularly interested in securing federal aid for education. Garfield answered with little more than platitudes.

Personal misfortunes fueled Elliott's despair. In 1879 dire financial straits forced him to close his law office. A minor patronage job as special inspector of the customs in Charleston at $144 a month helped, but he was soon required to sell his house to settle debts. His wife's medical problems and his first bout with malarial fever compounded his difficulties. He returned to the limelight as a delegate to the Republican National Convention in 1880, but he failed to see his choice, Secretary of the Treasury John Sherman, selected. Blanche K. Bruce remained optimistic about the Negro's eventual assimilation into American life because of his own experiences; Elliott, on the other hand, was pessimistic, particularly as his health, political power, and financial status declined. There followed other bouts of fever and an unwanted transfer to New Orleans, a move probably intended to separate a potential troublemaker from his power base. After eleven months in his new job as special agent of the treasury, Elliott's criticism of his boss and his decision to back a losing political faction cost him his job. A new law firm did not do well, his health worsened, and in August 1884 Elliott died of malarial fever at the age of forty-two.

Unlike Bruce, Elliott was not given an elaborate funeral, though his death was national news. Frederick Douglass penned a tribute, and some favorable obituaries appeared in northern and Negro newspapers. But the *Charleston News and Courier* more accurately represented the view of southern whites and most subsequent observers by headlining its report, "Another of the South Carolina Thieves Gone to His Account." Elliott was clearly a charismatic leader who provoked outrage among whites and enthusiasm among blacks—unlike Bruce, who did neither. He had his faults—among them a notorious temper, vindictive-ness, and, at best, amorality—but what outraged critics was his racial pride and insistence on *demanding,* not asking, for his rights and the rights of his people. By calling persistently for the unprecedented expansion of national power to guarantee the fruits of Reconstruction, while at the same time urging blacks to be more worthy of the freedom they had won, Elliott was a precursor of many twentieth-century black leaders. Yet despite the attention given to him as a proponent of racial politics, Elliott was always an ardent party man and, like Bruce, believed that a strong Republican party and Union were the blacks' best hope for equality. As a result, while whites such as Governor Chamberlain could attempt a rapprochement with Democrats and seek to deny office to black Republicans, Elliott, even after opposing men like Chamberlain within the party, could campaign vigorously for them in the general election. Had more South Carolinians, black and white, been as devoted to party unity and racial justice, perhaps the Republicans would not have been as easily ousted.

Despite differences in style and policy and Bruce's greater prominence, both Bruce and Elliott were nationally known black leaders. This was not true of Holland Thompson of Montgomery, Alabama. No one knew of him outside his state, historians have rarely mentioned him, and he has been almost totally forgotten in his hometown. Not a single Montgomery public facility immortal-izes his memory, his death went unrecorded in all but two local newspapers, and there were no tributes from national leaders. Information about him is more fragmentary than in the case of Elliott or Bruce, and there is no known photo-graph of him. He is thus representative of the large number of forgotten local black leaders; but more than that, a study of his career reminds us of the com-plexity of Reconstruction-era politics and the hazards of labeling politicians as militants or accommodationists, Radicals or Uncle Toms.

Thompson was born a slave in Montgomery in 1840. His parents had been brought from South Carolina in the 1830s by a South Carolinian named William Taylor, who became a moderately wealthy planter in Montgomery County. At the end of the Civil War, Taylor still owned Thompson, who was working as a waiter at a local hotel. After emancipation Thompson, who had learned to read and write as a slave, opened a grocery that became one of the most prosperous Negro firms in the city. By 1870 he owned city and rural real estate worth at least five hundred dollars and personal property worth two hundred dollars. Unlike Bruce and Elliott, Thompson depended for his living on a black clientele. Thompson was more firmly rooted in the black community in other ways as well. A fundamentalist Baptist who advocated temperance and Bible study, he was one of the founders of the First Colored Baptist Church and the Baptist State

Convention and head of the local and statewide Baptist Sunday School Association. He also served as president of the association appointed to oversee operation of Swayne School for blacks (run by northern white Congregationalist missionaries), as chairman of the Union League's Lincoln Council (an all-black political club that struggled for parity with the city's two all-white Republican clubs), and as a member of the advisory board of the local branch of the Freedmen's Bank. In these various capacities and others he made himself further known through a steady stream of speeches and letters to local newspapers.

Montgomery was a good place for a young, ambitious, and able former slave who was a fine orator and, as a local paper described him, physically impressive—a "pure African, nearly as black as they are ever made, six feet high and with a rather good natured expression." In 1870, 49 percent of the city was black, more than 55 percent in Thompson's home base of the Fifth Ward, site of his church and store. Although Republicans had only a tenuous hold on the Alabama state government, losing control temporarily between 1870 and 1872 before finally being permanently overthrown in 1874, few cities in the South could match Montgomery as a Republican stronghold. Between 1868 and 1875 its mayor was a Republican, and for all but two years Republicans controlled the council. Montgomery County was also under Republican rule until 1877, and no Democrats were sent to the state legislature until the following years. Blacks were especially well represented in the state legislative delegation, and there were always two blacks on the twelve-man city council.

Thompson was the city's most prominent black officeholder. Beginning in 1868 he served four terms as city councilman, three as board of education member, and two as state legislator. He was also one of the handful of blacks on the first state Republican Executive Committee. Although he clearly became a factor in Montgomery politics because of his work in black educational, religious, and political affairs, Thompson also benefitted from the support of several key white leaders, including scalawag mayor Thomas Glasscock and two carpetbaggers, Sheriff Paul Strobach and U.S. Senator George E. Spencer.

How did Thompson wield his power? On the one hand there is ample evidence to rank him as a Moderate or even a Conservative Republican. In the immediate aftermath of emancipation he urged blacks to help themselves rather than look to federal support, or as he told an 1866 Emancipation Day rally, "The colored race . . . must not stand waiting for others to push them along." Blacks, he argued in 1867, had to work industriously, educate their children, avoid whiskey, and cease "bickering" among themselves. He also asked blacks not to join military companies because such groups angered whites. He spoke out against confiscation of white-owned property, asked blacks to end hard feelings toward "our conservative friends," and called only for civil and political rights, since social rights "will work [themselves] out in good time." As councilman he was instrumental in setting up a segregated public school system. Rather than seeking to integrate the local cemetery, Thompson called for the establishment of a separate black graveyard; rather than seeking desegregation of the city hospital, he sought to improve facilities for black patients there. As a state legislator he accepted segregated railroad cars and a separate state agricultural school for blacks. On a personal level he seems to have named his oldest son after his former master.

There was another side to Thompson, however. He fought hard for several measures of special concern to blacks, including a branch of the Freedmen's Bank for Montgomery, equal pay for black streethands, a city public defender, city soup kitchens, and taxation that did not unfairly affect the poor. In August 1866, he called upon blacks to combat the conservative policies of Andrew Johnson's administration. Unlike many black leaders he placed the highest priority on making the new southern homestead law a more effective means of providing land for the freedpeople. Both as state legislator and councilman, Thompson unsuccessfully fought against efforts to limit black political power through laws requiring registration and other tightened voting procedures. And in another personal matter he named a second son after Wendell Phillips—the famous white abolitionist.

Particularly noteworthy was Thompson's success in getting black policemen appointed for the first time in the city's history and keeping roughly half the force black during most of Reconstruction. When a leading white Republican proposed that black police be appointed only if they were restricted to arresting blacks, Thompson said that that would be all right if white police could only arrest white criminals. The white Republican withdrew his proposal and—to the chagrin of many whites—interracial arrests became a fact of life in the city. Thompson unsuccessfully sought to end enforcement of a state law barring racial intermarriage, and he split with the Congregationalist missionaries over their failure to use black teachers in Swayne School. While accepting segregated access to schools, graveyards, agricultural colleges, and railroad cars, Thompson, like so many other black leaders, sought to move a resisting white South from the antebellum system of exclusion to segregation—and in Thompson's case, not simply segregation, but separate yet equal treatment, in those days by no means a conservative proposal. Indeed, as a councilman and school board member Thompson saw to it that throughout Reconstruction per capita expenditure for black and white schoolchildren was at least equal.

Nor did Thompson back away from challenging the white Republican incumbent in a race for Congress. This came in 1872, when at the age of thirty-two, with four years of experience in the state legislature and the city council and a strong base among urban blacks, Thompson felt it was time that the roughly one-half black district had a black congressman. Yet he faced two major obstacles: Charles Buckley, the white incumbent, and James T. Rapier, a black planter and a more formidable and popular member of the pro-Negro wing of the party. In the end, Rapier triumphed.

Thompson's failure reveals much about the recruitment of blacks for higher office and the interaction of white and black politicians. He was initially at a disadvantage because he had weakened his own position with potential supporters. In a recent nominating convention he had been chosen chairman since he was thought to be neutral in the intraparty strife between the forces aligned with carpetbaggers Strobach and Spencer and an opposing faction. When he sided with Strobach and Spencer on a number of critical decisions, he earned the enmity of the losers. This came at a time when he was taking increasingly militant stands in the state legislature. He had also become embroiled in church politics. Charged with financial irregularities, he was temporarily expelled from his church, something that no doubt seriously weakened his black base of support. One of the white Congregationalist missionaries who had done battle with Thompson over hiring Baptist as well as black teachers for his school gleefully reported, "Holland Thompson is rapidly losing his influence and a more generous and liberal spirit is coming in its stead." Unlike Blanche K. Bruce, Thompson failed to avoid involvement in factional disputes; unlike Robert Elliott, he had lost control of his black base.

Even if Thompson had not weakened his own case, there remained the redoubtable Rapier. Struggles among blacks for power were common in Montgomery and throughout the South, and Thompson was no stranger to such conflicts. During his rise he had, for example, withstood challenges from a successful black farmer named Hales Ellsworth, who represented the interests of country blacks in Montgomery County. He had also crossed swords before with Rapier, who had defeated him for the presidency of the state Colored Labor Convention. But this time the contest was clearly a mismatch. As a successful planter from Lauderdale County, Rapier commanded a larger following in the rural districts; he also enjoyed the support of several prominent Montgomery blacks. Although Thompson held two important elective offices, Rapier's position as assessor of internal revenue had much greater political impact in terms of the favors and patronage he could dispense. Finally, Rapier was less threatening to white leaders of the Spencer-Strobach faction and to whites in general. In vivid contrast to the slightly younger Thompson, Rapier was a former free Negro, a mulatto, and well educated in Canadian schools. The fact that his stands on racial issues were moderate buttressed the view that, if there had to be a Negro congressman, the more "refined" and "polished" Rapier was the man. In a state where white support was more critical than in Mississippi or South Carolina, the fact that Thompson was more a product of the local black community than someone like Bruce or Elliott actually proved to be a liability.

Thompson lost more than the congressional nomination. Shortly thereafter he was denied renomination to a third term in the legislature, evidently because of Strobach and Rapier, whom he had called thieves and fools. According to a Democratic newspaper the "carpetbag crew" wanted to destroy Thompson's influence among blacks because of his "independent ideas." Yet Thompson proved resilient. He repaired fences within his church and party, edited a Republican newspaper, and, with Senator Spencer's help, was appointed deputy collector of customs. In 1873 he was elected to a fourth term in the city council and was chosen orator of the day at the annual parade and banquet of Grey Eagle No. 3, the city's only black fire company. But the tide of change was apparent. In 1874 Democrats permanently returned to power in the state government; the next year a combination of fraud, intimidation, manipulation of voting requirements, and intraparty Republican strife enabled the Redeemers to triumph in Montgomery. Thompson did not stand for reelection and in the ensuing years participated only occasionally in party politics. He seems to have spent his time trying to bolster his declining grocery business, teaching young blacks to read, preaching, and helping to establish the Dexter Avenue Baptist Church, which Martin Luther King, Jr., would make famous. He also briefly served in 1881 as vice-president of the Industrial State Fair Association (Colored), which organized a Negro fair. Part of this withdrawal from politics was due to the limited opportunities for black political leadership following the overthrow of Reconstruction, but other black Montgomerians did remain active. More important in Thompson's case were a series of personal tragedies, including the death of his first wife in childbirth, the death of several of his children, and his own declining health. His last public appearance came in 1885 when he gave one of the eulogies at a service held to honor the memory of former president Grant. Two years later Thompson died of cancer at the age of forty-eight.

Thompson's political career had essentially ended in 1875 at the age of thirty-six. In a brief period that lasted no more than ten years he emerged from slavery to forge an impressive public career built on close association with the basic institutions of black life. He gained additional access to black voters through his relief activities as a councilman and the operation of his neighborhood grocery, traditionally a launching pad for ethnic politicians in nineteenth-century America. He reached still other blacks as newspaper editor, powerful orator, and inveterate writer of letters to the editor. And he was constantly visible to blacks as a city councilman and state legislator.

No doubt Thompson benefitted from the sponsorship of white men like Thomas

Glasscock, Paul Strobach, and George Spencer. He attracted their attention, however, because of his personal qualities and, even more important, because of the bloc of black voters he commanded. Throughout the South there were black leaders who were mere puppets manipulated by white masters, but this was not the case with Thompson or the more numerous men like him. After Thompson's victory and that of his black running mate in the city's first Reconstruction council election, a local paper reported, "The white rads . . . [were] awful mad because the black rads nominated . . . [them]." Neither was he, as some Democrats claimed, the force behind the throne, controlling white colleagues in a city that had been "Africanized." Rather, like Atlanta city councilman William Finch and his Raleigh counterpart James H. Harris, Thompson was a skillful politician who, despite the desires of white Republicans and Democrats, insisted on putting his own advancement and the advancement of his people ahead of injunctions to keep a low profile and stay in his place. He took stronger stands than did Bruce but in a less abrasive way than Elliott, so that at least one staunch Democrat could call him "a very respectable negro." But unlike Mississippi or South Carolina, Alabama did not have a black majority and secure Republican rule. Without the compromising skills of Bruce or the solid base and talent of Elliott, Thompson could go only so far up the political ladder.

In the end, both the black masses and the white leaders kept Thompson from rising to greater heights. His momentary loss of power within the church (it was never fully regained), along with the attractiveness to rural blacks and white Republicans of James T. Rapier (a Bruce-like figure), denied him any real chance to gain the congressional nomination he sought. The abuses of Redemption and the misfortunes of his personal life subsequently left him a political has-been at a remarkably young age. But Thompson was not unique, for a surprising number of black southern leaders, including Robert Brown Elliott, whether because of death, disillusionment, poor health, emigration, or other interests, ended their political careers prematurely, depriving other blacks of much-needed leadership.

In assessing the first generation of black officeholders, as represented by Bruce, Elliott, and Thompson, few scholars today would give much credence to the original Dunning-ite indictment. Even the corruption charge loses much of its significance when viewed in the context of Gilded Age society and the greater involvement of whites, both Republican and Democrat. Besides, black political participation per se, not corruption, was always the real issue for critics. Yet no single view has emerged to replace the old stereotypes. There is agreement on who these people were, what kind of qualifications they had, and what actions they took, but there are divergent assessments of their performance and legacy. Some historians, liberally inclined and explicitly reacting to the Dunning attack, have produced complimentary studies of these men that seek to rehabilitate their memory. While valuable in the effort to set the record straight, such works often gloss over the faults of their subjects in order to have them conform to what might be expected of race leaders today. Increasingly, however, other historians' more radical orientations have been more critical of these leaders, taking them to task for doing too little to help their race. Disparagingly referred to as "representative colored men" by Nell Painter, they are seen as having been out of touch with the black masses and more interested in their own careers and in white approval than in helping their people. Thomas Holt, in his study of South Carolina, argues that bitter infighting based on class and color differences led black legislators to ignore the land issue and other matters of importance to the masses and helped produce the divided party that proved no match for the Democratic counterrevolution. Still other historians view black politics as irrelevant and call instead for concentration on nonpolitical figures more firmly grounded in local communities.

Black leaders of the Reconstruction need to be studied on their own terms and viewed within the context of the times rather than judged by the greater commitment to racial progress and stronger means of implementation present in the late twentieth century. As typified by Bruce, Elliott, and Thompson, these politicians used a variety of strategies, drew on diverse constituencies that included white and black elements often at odds over objectives, and focused on different issues. Of the three, Thompson was the most representative black politician, not only because he rose no higher than the state legislature, but also because of his personal characteristics, political positions, and roots in the black community. Lacking the brilliance of the combative Elliott and the tactical skill of the more accommodating Bruce, Thompson sought out the middle ground of protest *and* accommodation in an effort to appeal to both his black base and his white sponsors. On less secure political turf and with less talent than Bruce or Elliott, he proved more vulnerable to the vicissitudes of Reconstruction politics.

On some levels black leaders were clearly inadequate. Bruce was not the only black who seemingly put his own interest and ambition before the needs of his race. Many, like Elliott, could have been more honest. They might have done more to help the poor and might have pressed harder for integration, or at least truly equal separate treatment. Some were too easily manipulated by whites. But these were men of their times, imbued with its values and attitudes. They were also politicians. The great majority of officeholders make no mark in office, produce no important legislation, and often act first to further their own careers and get reelected. They frequently engage in internecine combat based on both rational and irrational considerations. Why should these black politicians be judged by a different standard? Must there be only heroes or villains?

Even if a different standard is used, however, there is much that was positive about these men and ample reason to continue to emphasize their role in Reconstruction. They often functioned as the nation's conscience, and to a greater degree than any other component of the Republican coalition. To demand universal male suffrage, equal access to public accommodations, schools, and welfare facilities, and federal guarantees for such rights was to take a radical position in the mid-nineteenth century. Yet these men also delivered. The careers of Bruce, Elliott, and Thompson, for example, suggest they brought tangible benefits not only to their race but to their states and localities, particularly in the area of education. By doing so in an often eloquent, well-reasoned manner against white opposition, they themselves made a forceful case for racial equality. Such men, in fact, served as symbols for blacks and nonracist whites of what America might mean to the oppressed and of what blacks deserved. That these black leaders did not accomplish more was due in part to their own inadequacies but more to the opposition they faced from whites, Republicans and Democrats alike. That they were able, in the face of overwhelming odds, to help provide the foundation for the twentieth-century's Second Reconstruction was testimony to their courage, political skills, and persistent faith in the American ideals of freedom and equal opportunity.

Bibliographical Essay

The best sources for the study of Reconstruction leaders and the opposition they faced are the black conventions in the aftermath of emancipation, the state constitutional conventions of 1867–1868 in which blacks played a critical role, and several major congressional reports. See especially, Philip S. Foner and George Walker, eds., *Proceedings of the Black State Conventions, 1840–1865,* 2 vols. (Philadelphia: Temple University Press, 1979); *Proceedings of the Constitutional Convention of South Carolina* (Charleston, 1868); U.S. Congress, 39th Congress, 1st sess., *Report of the Joint Committee on Reconstruction* (Washington, D.C., 1866); U.S. Congress, 42d Congress, 2d sess., *Testimony Taken by the Joint Select Committee to Inquire into the Condition of Affairs in the Late Insurrectionary States* (Washington, D.C., 1872); and U.S. Senate, 46th Congress, 2d sess., *Report and Testimony of the Select Committee of the United States Senate to Investigate the Causes for the Removal of the Negroes from the Southern States to the Northern States* (Washington, D.C., 1880). John Hope Franklin, ed., *Reminiscences of an Active Life: The Autobiography of John Roy Lynch* (Chicago: University of Chicago Press, 1970), is a unique recollection by a black officeholder.

Howard N. Rabinowitz, ed., *Southern Black Leaders of the Reconstruction Era* (Urbana: University of Illinois Press, 1982), contains essays on separate individuals and groups of black leaders and extensive bibliographic citations. For this essay, I have drawn heavily on David Rankin's chapter on New Orleans black leaders, Richard Hume's on black convention delegates, and especially William C. Harris's study of Bruce and my own of Thompson. There are other essays on individual congressmen John Roy Lynch (Mississippi), Josiah T. Walls (Florida), James T. Rapier (Alabama), and James O'Hara (North Carolina); collective studies of black councilmen in Richmond, and state legislators in South Carolina; and studies of local leaders Aaron A. Bradley (Georgia low country), William Finch (Atlanta), Dr. Benjamin A. Boseman, Jr. (Charleston), and George T. Ruby (Texas). There is also an introductory essay on the changing image of black reconstructionists and an epilogue devoted to new perspectives on black political leadership in the Reconstruction era.

Numerous studies of prominent black Reconstruction leaders have been published (with many more on the way). Peggy Lamson, *The Glorious Failure: Black Congressman Robert Brown Elliott and Reconstruction in South Carolina* (New York: W. W. Norton and Co., 1973) was indispensable for the factual information about Elliott needed for my quite different interpretation of his career. See also, Melvyn I. Urofsky, "Blanche K. Bruce, United States Senator, 1875–1881," *Journal of Mississippi History* 29 (May 1967): 118–41; Russell Duncan, *Freedom's Shore: Tunis Campbell and the Georgia Freedmen* (Athens: University of Georgia Press, 1986); Euline W. Brock, "Thomas W. Cardozo: Fallible Black Reconstruction Leader," *Journal of Southern History* 47 (May 1981): 183–206; William C. Harris, "James Lynch: Black Leader in Southern Reconstruction," *The Historian* 34 (November 1971): 40–61; Okon Edet Uya, *From Slavery to Public Service: Robert Smalls, 1839–1915* (New York: Oxford University Press, 1971); Loren Schweninger, *James T. Rapier and Reconstruction* (Chicago: University of Chicago Press, 1978); and Peter D. Klingman, *Josiah Walls: Florida's Black Congressman of Reconstruction* (Gainesville: University Presses of Florida, 1976). For a more negative assessment of black leadership in this period, see Nell I. Painter, *Exodusters: Black Migration to Kansas after Reconstruction* (New York: Alfred A. Knopf, 1976).

Although ignored by historians when it first appeared, W. E. B. Du Bois, *Black Reconstruction: An Essay toward a History of the Part Which Black Folk Played in the Attempt to Reconstruct Democracy in America, 1860–1880* (New York: Harcourt Brace, 1935), is a classic account by a leading black intellectual. Studies of Reconstruction in individual states and localities further illuminate black political leadership. See, in particular, Peter Kolchin, *First Freedom: The Response of Alabama's Blacks to Emancipation and Reconstruction* (Westport, Conn.: Greenwood Press, 1972); Edmund L. Drago, *Black Politicians and Reconstruction in Georgia: A Splendid Failure* (Baton Rouge: Louisiana State University Press, 1982); Charles Vincent, *Black Legislators in Louisiana during Reconstruction* (Baton Rouge: Louisiana State University Press, 1976); Vernon L. Wharton, *The Negro in Mississippi, 1865–1890* (Chapel Hill: University of North Carolina Press, 1947); Joel Williamson, *After Slavery: The Negro in South Carolina during Reconstruction, 1861–1877* (Chapel Hill: University of North Carolina Press, 1965); Thomas C. Holt, *Black over White: Negro Political Leadership in South Carolina during Reconstruction* (Urbana: University of Illinois Press, 1977); William C. Hine, "Black Politicians in Reconstruction Charleston, South Carolina: A Collective Study," *Journal of Southern History* 49 (November 1983): 555–84; Elizabeth Balanoff, "Negro Legislators in the North Carolina General Assembly, July 1868–February 1872," *North Carolina Historical Review* 49 (January 1972): 22–55; Walter J. Fraser, Jr., "Black Reconstructionists in Tennessee," *Tennessee Historical Quarterly* 34 (Winter 1975): 362–82; Barry A. Crouch, "Self-Determination and Local Black Leaders in Texas," *Phylon* 39 (December 1978): 344–55; Luther P. Jackson, *Negro Office Holders in Virginia, 1865–1895* (Norfolk: Guide Quality Press, 1945); and my "A Comparative Perspective on Race Relations in Southern and Northern Cities, 1860–1900," reprinted below.

A Comparative Perspective on Race Relations in Southern and Northern Cities, 1860–1900

An invitation to participate in a conference on "Black Americans in North Carolina and the South," in Raleigh, North Carolina, in February 1981, gave me the opportunity to sum up the major findings of my first book, *Race Relations in the Urban South, 1865–1890,* particularly as they applied to Raleigh. I was also able for the first time to make some tentative comparisons between race relations in northern and southern cities. And finally, new research on Raleigh I did for the paper enabled me to correct some previous errors of commission and omission and to produce a chart on Raleigh black councilmen that extended my work on the city's black politicians beyond 1890. After some revision and further research, the paper was published together with the other conference presentations. Although it contains a good deal of the same information and themes found in essays reprinted earlier in this collection, I have reprinted it here in its entirety because I think it will make it easier for nonspecialists to integrate that material.

This essay seeks to do three things. First, and most important, it outlines in very general terms the basic developments in southern urban race relations between 1860 and 1900. Second, it shows how the black experience in Raleigh, North Carolina, reflected these broader trends. Finally, it suggests some possible similarities and differences between the experiences of blacks in northern and southern cities during the period.[1]

Like the rest of American cities in the latter part of the nineteenth century, southern cities grew in population largely as a result of migration. Elsewhere in

1. Unless otherwise noted citations and supporting evidence can be found in the relevant chapters of my *Race Relations in the Urban South, 1865–1890* (New York: Oxford University Press, 1978).

the country the migrants were either foreigners or rural whites; in the South large numbers of rural whites moved to the cities, but a more significant group was rural blacks. Like the Eastern Europeans in the North, the Chinese in the Far West, and the former farmers in the Midwest, these new urban dwellers in the South were a source of instability and social disruption. But blacks presented southern white urbanites with an even more serious problem. Not only were these newcomers poor, unaccustomed to the conditions and responsibilities of urban life, and of a different ethnic and racial background than a majority of the resident population, but they also were tainted by slavery. Unlike other migrants, blacks had long been assigned a role in the life of the region in which they settled. Their position had been one of subservience, as slaves controlled by the white race. A free Negro was an anomaly, someone whom southerners had sought to banish from their midst. North Carolina, for example, was among several states that considered formally expelling free Negroes, though in the end only Arkansas actually did so.[2] Now, as a result of the Civil War, all blacks were free.

By 1900, although only 17 percent of southern blacks lived in cities, they made up 31 percent of the region's urban population and 68 percent of the nation's Negro urban dwellers. Blacks were an even greater factor in North Carolina cities: 12.2 percent of the black population was urban, but blacks constituted 40.8 percent of all urban dwellers.[3] Better educated and more prosperous than their rural brothers, southern urban blacks played a major role in national Negro political, economic, and social affairs. Nevertheless, their imprint on urban society and the impact that city life had on them remain largely undocumented.

Urban historians, for example, have long slighted the South and have preferred to concentrate on a few large eastern and midwestern cities. Preoccupied with national policy-making and statewide trends, historians of the Reconstruction period have noted the urban scene only in passing. Students of black history have also tended to ignore the fate of these new migrants to southern towns and have viewed emancipation, as well as slavery, primarily within a rural context. Those interested in detailed descriptions of life in the postbellum years must turn to the growing number of monographs about black communities in the urban North, with a few recent exceptions.[4] As a result of these studies, it is commonly

2. Ira Berlin, *Slaves without Masters: The Free Negro in the Antebellum South* (New York: Pantheon, 1974), 371–80.

3. U.S. Bureau of the Census, *Negro Population, 1790–1915* (Washington, D.C.: Government Printing Office, 1918), 90–92.

4. For the urban South see my *Race Relations in the Urban South;* John W. Blassingame, *Black New Orleans, 1860–1880* (Chicago: University of Chicago Press, 1973); Robert E. Perdue, *The Negro in Savannah, 1865–1900* (New York: Exposition Press, 1973); Zane L.

agreed that it was in the North during the twentieth century that the modern Negro ghetto first appeared. Yet the experience of blacks in late-nineteenth-century southern cities suggests a different conclusion.

Any attempt to understand postbellum race relations in the urban South must begin by considering the tremendous increase in the number of black urban dwellers between 1860 and 1870, even though the great majority of blacks remained in the countryside. The antebellum trend toward the thinning out of black urban populations was reversed, and the pattern of absolute and often relative increases in the black urban population so common until 1900 was established. Between 1860 and 1870 Atlanta's black population, for example, grew from 1,939 to 9,929, and the black percentage of the population rose from 20 percent to 46 percent. Nashville's black population increased from 23 percent to 38 percent, New Orleans's from 14.3 percent to 26.4 percent, and Raleigh's from 44 percent to 53 percent. Because of the undercount of urban blacks in the 1870 census, the actual increases were greater still.

Rural blacks came to the cities for a variety of reasons. For some, the cities, which were headquarters for the federal forces, represented safety from the violence and intimidation of the countryside. Others came for the welfare and educational services provided by the army, the Freedmen's Bureau, and northern missionary societies. No doubt others were drawn by the attractions of city life and the simple desire to exercise their new freedom of movement. Whatever the motivation, most realized that in the antebellum period the cities had been better places for blacks than the rural areas.

The influx of blacks and the resultant problem of social control greatly troubled whites. In their view the Negroes "infested" the cities, "clogged" the streets, and threatened peace and prosperity. Writing in the fall of 1867, the editor of the *Raleigh Weekly Progress* complained:

Miller, "Urban Blacks in the South, 1865–1920: An Analysis of Some Quantitative Data on Richmond, Savannah, New Orleans, Louisville, and Birmingham," in *The New Urban History: Quantitative Explorations by American Historians,* ed. Leo F. Schnore (Princeton: Princeton University Press, 1974), 184–204; Robert Francis Engs, *Freedom's First Generation: Black Hampton, Virginia, 1861–1890* (Philadelphia: University of Pennsylvania Press, 1980); James Borchert, *Alley Life in Washington: Family, Community, Religion, and Folklife in the City, 1850–1970* (Urbana: University of Illinois Press, 1980); for the urban North see Gilbert Osofsky, *Harlem, the Making of a Ghetto: Negro New York, 1890–1930* (New York: Harper and Row, 1966); Allan H. Spear, *Black Chicago: The Making of a Negro Ghetto, 1890–1920* (Chicago: University of Chicago Press, 1969); David M. Katzman, *Before the Ghetto: Black Detroit in the Nineteenth Century* (Urbana: University of Illinois Press, 1973); Kenneth L. Kusmer, *A Ghetto Takes Shape: Black Cleveland, 1870–1930* (Urbana: University of Illinois Press, 1976); Harold X. Connolly, *A Ghetto Grows in Brooklyn* (New York: New York University Press, 1977); Elizabeth Hafkin Pleck, *Black Migration and Poverty: Boston, 1865–1900* (New York: Academic Press, 1979).

Table 1
Raleigh Population, 1850–1900

	1850	1860	1870	1880	1890	1900
White	2,253	2,693	3,696	4,911	6,327	7,922
Black	2,263	2,087	4,094	4,354	6,348	5,721
Percentage Black	50.1	44	53	47	50.1	41.9

Source: U.S. Censuses, 1850–1900.

> For nearly three years Raleigh has been to the great mobs of unbleached Americans in the western and contiguous counties of this state what Mecca is to the followers of Mohamet. . . . Caravan after caravan swarmed into the state capital—the immigrants being principally the idle and the desolate thus overcrowding our beautiful city with a population capable of at times being made a dangerous instrument in the hands of vicious men.[5]

To whites, God had ordained a rural existence for blacks, or as the *Montgomery Daily Ledger* put it most bluntly, "The city was intended for white people."[6] But while whites sought to reestablish the control weakened by the defeat of the Confederacy and the emancipation of the slaves, blacks sought to use the urban environment to fulfill their dreams of freedom. At times the interests of the whites and blacks coincided; more often, however, they were in conflict. Out of this interaction between whites and blacks there had evolved by 1900 a new pattern of race relations that contained elements of both continuity and change.

The economic status of blacks affected all other aspects of black urban life. As early as February 1867 a Raleigh newspaper noted, "Quite a number of colored people this year are embarking in business."[7] By 1900 in Raleigh and elsewhere there had emerged a small group of successful black caterers, contractors, undertakers, grocers, lawyers, and teachers. Some, like Raleigh livery business owner John O. Kelly, even employed whites. But the majority of blacks were mired in the lowest-paying jobs: the men were primarily employed as unskilled laborers and servants and the women (who made up a far larger segment of the Negro work force than did women among whites) worked almost entirely as domestics and washerwomen. It is true that most Negroes lacked the necessary

5. September 26, 1867.
6. September 23, 1865.
7. *Raleigh Weekly Progress,* February 7, 1867.

skills to get better-paying jobs, but many had been artisans either in antebellum cities or on the plantations. The fact that so few found work as cabinetmakers, machinists, or plumbers was due to the opposition of local whites, especially those in unions, from which blacks were often barred. Thus at the turn of the century a Raleigh resident reported that "the black artisan is losing here"; a key reason was that there were no Negroes in the local unions, and "it is doubtful they could get in."[8]

Many blacks who worked as servants, gardeners, and laundresses for their former masters lived in the old slave quarters behind their employer's house. But a combination of white hostility, economic constraints, and black desires increased segregation and soon altered the antebellum pattern of integrated neighborhoods. Community institutions, such as churches, schools, meeting halls, and, in some cases, businesses, were located in black areas, thus foreshadowing the appearance of the twentieth-century northern ghettos. Blacks concentrated in such areas as Atlanta's Shermantown or Summer Hill, Richmond's Jackson Ward, and Nashville's Black Bottom or Rocktown, which were located on the fringes of the still-compact cities near railroad tracks, industrial sites, and contaminated streams. By 1881 almost all of the 750 inhabitants of Oberlin, a mile northwest of Raleigh, were black. And by the end of the decade the predominantly Negro Second and Fourth wards in the southern part of the city contained Raleigh's two Negro grade schools, six of the nine black churches, the Institution for the Colored Blind and Deaf and Dumb, Shaw Institute, the Colored Masonic Hall, and most of the Negro hotels, boardinghouses, and businesses. The few whites in black neighborhoods throughout the South came primarily from three groups with limited mobility: laborers, widows, and grocers.

In an effort to discourage the urban migration whites initially sought to deny blacks municipal services. But thanks to the intervention of federal authorities and the governments established under congressional Reconstruction, the antebellum policy of exclusion of blacks from schools and welfare services was replaced by one of segregated access. For the first time in most cities blacks were admitted to poorhouses, insane asylums, hospitals, and public schools. In 1868 North Carolina blacks, for example, gained access to segregated quarters in the state institutions for the insane and the blind, deaf, and dumb located in the Raleigh area. City authorities, however, often dragged their feet when it came to educating blacks, as was the case in Raleigh, where northern missionary societies ran the Negro schools until the city incorporated them into a segregated system in 1877. Most blacks supported the shift from exclusion to segregation in the hope

8. Quoted in W. E. B. Du Bois, ed., *The Negro Artisan,* Atlanta University Publications, ed. W. E. B. Du Bois, no. 7 (Atlanta: Atlanta University Press, 1902), 136–37.

that segregated accommodations could be truly equal. Yet while the Redeemers accepted the Republican commitment to end exclusion, they pursued a policy of separate but unequal treatment of blacks. Calls by blacks for better services were usually rebuffed, though blacks did obtain black teachers for most of the black schools and gained admission to several facilities previously closed to them. In fact, Raleigh remained one of the few cities in the South in which racially mixed faculties could still be found in black schools as late as 1890.

The shift from exclusion to segregation was also evident in militia service, fire fighting, and a variety of public accommodations and public conveyances. Despite the Civil Rights Act of 1875 and Negro protests about its weak enforcement, de facto segregation quickly became the rule in steamships, railroads, hotels, restaurants, skating rinks, parks, and theaters. When Dan Castello's Grand Circus played Raleigh in 1866, accommodations for blacks were segregated, as was the case soon after in the city's Tucker Hall. A decade later James O'Hara, one of North Carolina's leading black politicians and soon to be congressman from the state's famous Second District, told a congressional committee: "I have gone to theatres in Raleigh frequently; and I have seen no exclusion on account of color. I suppose if a colored man should attempt to take a principle [sic] seat in a theatre in North Carolina he would have the same difficulty as in New York."[9]

Raleigh was also typical in that throughout the late nineteenth century racial intermingling was perhaps greatest in the parks. Pullen and Brookside parks remained open to blacks well into the twentieth century. Yet blacks visiting Brookside could not use the swimming pool, a fact representative of the internal segregation evident in parks elsewhere. When a new zoo opened in Atlanta's Grant Park in 1890, it contained eight cages occupying the center of the building and stretching from one end to the other. Aisles seven feet wide were railed off on each side of the row of cages, one for blacks, the other for whites, each with its own entrance and exit doors. (It is not known if the animals were told which way to face.) After 1890 this type of segregation was buttressed by laws, and whatever limited flexibility there had been in places such as streetcars soon disappeared.

Segregation also dominated the religious life of southern cities, though this was more an example of continuity rather than change. At the end of the war blacks, among them the members of Raleigh's First Baptist, left segregated white congregations and formed their own churches (by 1885 four black churches had sprung from the Colored First Baptist, although nine hundred to a thousand of the city's fifteen hundred Negro Baptists still belonged to the mother church).

9. U.S. Congress, Senate, testimony of James O'Hara, *Report and Testimony of the Select Committee of the United States Senate to Investigate the Causes for the Removal of the Negroes from the Southern States to the Northern States,* 46th Congress, 2d session, 1880, part 1, 57.

Other black congregations that had been organized before the war, including Raleigh's St. Paul AME, joined these new bodies to help make Sunday the most segregated day of the week.

The church occupied the central position in the black community. Not simply a religious institution, it had recreational, economic, and political functions as well. Only in church affairs could blacks exercise a significant degree of independent control. (Even in church, however, blacks often called upon whites for financial or other kinds of assistance and went so far as to provide segregated seating during fund-raising meetings.) The Negro pastors, who quickly replaced whites, such as the presidents of Raleigh's St. Augustine's College and Shaw Institute, in most of the pulpits, acted as intermediaries between the black and white worlds of the city. Active in most areas of community life, they functioned mainly as a force for accommodation, but to a surprising degree, as in campaigns for better schools and black teachers, they also served as agents of protest. As the period waned, the old uneducated slave preachers were followed in the major pulpits by young college-trained pastors. For black congregants, their appearance, and the building of impressive new edifices, testified to the great progress of the race.

In one area segregation was not enough. Despite white opposition blacks won the right to vote and hold office, the first time southern blacks had enjoyed political rights since the disfranchisement of Tennessee and North Carolina free Negroes in 1834 and 1835. Once this had been accomplished as a result of the Reconstruction acts, white southerners sought, as in all other areas of southern life, to develop a system that would minimize the effect of the Negroes' freedom. Not until after 1890 did southerners decide again on a path of wholesale de jure disfranchisement, and then only when they became convinced that northerners would not interfere. In North Carolina disfranchisement did not come until 1900, when through a constitutional amendment, the passage of which was assured by a discriminatory 1899 election law, voters were subjected to a literacy test and required to pay a poll tax.[10]

In the interim, however, the idea of controlling the black vote was the central consideration in southern politics, especially on the local level. Therefore, the important question for the political experience of urban Negroes was not merely whether or not they could vote but what power did their votes have. The answer, not surprisingly, was that their ballots were most influential during Reconstruction. Blacks sat on the city councils of most southern cities and worked with varying degrees of success for the equal treatment of their race. Once the Re-

10. J. Morgan Kousser, *The Shaping of Southern Politics: Suffrage Restriction and the Establishment of the One-Party South, 1880–1910* (New Haven: Yale University Press, 1974), 183–95 and passim; Helen G. Edmonds, *The Negro and Fusion Politics in North Carolina, 1894–1901* (Chapel Hill: University of North Carolina Press, 1951), 179–83.

deemers consolidated their power through an artful combination of gerrymandering, vote fraud, actual and threatened retribution, and rigged voting laws, black political influence was removed or effectively isolated. Meanwhile, the Democrats made only halfhearted attempts to woo the blacks away from their traditional allegiance to the Republicans. The blacks largely resisted, but the Democrats did not really mind. Without their black component, the Republicans would have been less of a target; with sizable black support competing factions of Democrats would have faced the unpopular task of vying for black votes.

Raleigh's experience with black suffrage and officeholding was in many ways typical. Two of the nine-man city council appointed by Governor William Holden in 1868 were Negro, including James H. Harris, an upholsterer by trade but a politician by profession and the city's most prominent black leader. Once municipal elections began in 1869, blacks held approximately one-third of the seats until Republicans lost control of the city in 1875. And though biographical information is incomplete and often unreliable, it would seem that Raleigh's twenty-five Negro councilmen resembled their counterparts throughout the South.[11] As the data in table 2 indicate, all but one were native grown and all were literate. They came generally from the ranks of artisans and petty tradesmen, with the addition, especially toward the end of the century, of an occasional lawyer or teacher. According to the 1870 census, at least five of the thirteen for whom such information is available owned property worth at least one thousand dollars. Many were black and most probably former slaves, but there were disproportionate numbers of mulattoes and persons with free antecedents.[12] For the most part, these were relatively young men, in their thirties or early forties when first elected.

Yet Raleigh differed politically in significant ways from most other southern cities in the years between the end of Reconstruction and disfranchisement. Most important, blacks remained on the new expanded council until the turn of the century, rather than being excluded as was the norm elsewhere. As was true of North Carolina as a whole, Raleigh also witnessed less voter intimidation and fraud both during and after Reconstruction. And the strength and persistence of Republican influence in the city and state set Raleigh apart from all but a few cities in states other than North Carolina, Tennessee, and Virginia. Yet after Redemption the Democrats controlled the gerrymandered seventeen- and later twelve-man

11. On black leadership elsewhere see Howard N. Rabinowitz, ed., *Southern Black Leaders of the Reconstruction Era* (Urbana: University of Illinois Press, 1982).

12. I want to thank Professor John Hope Franklin for permitting me to look at his files on North Carolina free blacks drawn from the 1860 census. A perusal of his records for sixteen counties in the Raleigh area produced two of the councilmen. A third, James Harris, is known from other sources to have been free. It is likely that an additional one or two were free, but the absence of more names in the 1860 census suggests that most of those whose antebellum status is listed as "not available" were indeed slaves.

Table 2
Raleigh Negro Councilmen, 1868–1901

Name	Black Mulatto	Born	Birth-place	Died	Occupation in Office
James Baker	M(1870–80) B (1900)	1840	NC	NA[a]	grocer
John H. Brown	M	1850	NC	NA	carpenter
Reuben Cole	M	1844	NC	1927	grocer
M. Nelson Dunstan	B	1855	NC	NA	barber
Norfleet Dunstan	M(1870) B (1880)	1835	NC	1919	shoemaker
Stewart Ellison	B	c. 1834	NC	NA	grocer, contractor
Albert Farrar	M(1860) B (1870)	1814	NC	NA	blacksmith
Bennett B. Goins	B	1854	NC	NA	teacher
James Hamlin	M	1859	Va.	1924	saloon-keeper, druggist
Andrew J. Harris	B?	1810?	NC	NA	porter
James H. Harris	M	c. 1832	NC	1891	supt. inst. for colored deaf, dumb & blind
Charles W. Hoover	M	1853	NC	NA	huckster, bar owner
Americus Hunter	M	1845	NC	NA	box mail collector
Edward A. Johnson	M	1860	NC	1944	lawyer
Henry C. Jones	B (1870) M(1880)	c. 1836	NC	NA	brickmason
James H. Jones	M	1832	NC	NA	bricklayer, tailor
Handy Lockhart	B	c. 1795	NC	1884	undertaker, carpenter
W. H. Mathews	B	c. 1828	NC	NA	brickmason

table 2

Property in 1870[b]	Council Service[c]	Literacy	Religion	Prewar Status[d]
$600 real $100 personal	1895–97 (1)	Yes	NA	NA
NA	1881–82 (1)	Yes	NA	NA
NA	1885–89 (2)	Yes	Baptist	NA
NA	1885–87 (1)	Yes	NA	NA
$700 real $300 personal	1869–72, 1877–83 (10)	Yes	NA	free
none listed	1869–76, 1877–79, 1880–84 (13)	Yes	NA	slave
$1,000 real	1869 (1)	Yes	NA	free
NA	1882–83 (1)	Yes	NA	NA
NA	1883–84, 1897–1901 (3)	Yes	Baptist (?)	NA
none listed	1887–89 (1)	Yes	NA	NA
$4,000 real $1,000 personal	1868, 1875–76, 1877–78, 1887–90 (4½)	Yes	Episcopalian	free
NA	1879–85, 1895–97 (7)	Yes	NA	NA
none listed	1883–84 (1)	Yes	NA	NA
NA	1893–95, 1897–99 (2)	Yes	Congrega-tionalist	slave
none listed	1875–76 (1)	Yes	NA	NA
none listed	1873–76, 1877–89 (10)	Yes	NA	slave
$1,500 real $300 personal	1868 (1)	Yes	NA	NA
$1,100 real	1887–89 (1)	Yes	NA	NA

Table 2 (continued)

Name	Black Mulatto	Born	Birth-place	Died	Occupation in Office
William Mitchell	M	1844	NC	1914	well digger, brickmason
Virgil Ricks	M	c. 1842	NC	NA	provision dealer
Nicholas F. Roberts	B	1849	NC	1934	college professor
B. J. Robinson	B	1860	NC	NA	grocer
Alfred Tate	M	1840	NC	NA	clerk
Charles Williams	B	1860	NC	NA	principal col. dept deaf, dumb, & blind inst.
James H. Young	M	1859	NC	1921	clerk in revenue dept.

Sources: U.S. Manuscript Census Schedules, 1860, 1870, 1880, 1900; Raleigh city directories, 1866–1901; miscellaneous biographical directories and newspapers; North Carolina Board of Health, Deaths, 1906–1929, North Carolina State Archives.
[a]Not available.
[b]As listed in the 1870 census. Several men for whom none was listed certainly owned property as well.
[c]Those appointed in 1868 served from July 15 to January 5, 1869; from then until 1885

council, and except for the brief period of fusion rule by Populists and Republicans during the mid-1890s the three or four blacks usually elected had little of the political leverage they had enjoyed during Reconstruction. School appropriations became increasingly unequal, black policemen were removed, and the new city hospital excluded blacks. Finally, the last Negroes, James Hamlin and Charles Williams, left the council in May 1901, shortly after North Carolina's George H. White became the last southern black to serve in Congress until 1972.[13]

13. For useful though often inaccurate discussions of Raleigh and North Carolina blacks after 1890, see Dorothy A. Gay, "Crisis of Identity: The Negro Community in Raleigh, 1890–1900," *North Carolina Historical Review* 50 (April 1973): 121–39; Frenise A. Logan, *The Negro in North Carolina, 1876–1894* (Chapel Hill: University of North Carolina Press, 1964); Edmonds, *Negro and Fusion Politics*.

Property in 1870[b]	Council Service[c]	Literacy	Religion	Prewar Status[d]
$325 real	1878–79 (1)	Yes	NA	free (?)
none listed	1873–74, 1879–80 (2)	Yes	Baptist (?)	NA
NA	1885–87 (1)	Yes	Baptist	NA
NA	1889–99 (5)	Yes	NA	NA
NA	1891–93 (1)	Yes	NA	NA
NA	1899–1901 (1)	Yes	Baptist (?)	NA
NA	1883–84 (1)	Yes	Baptist	NA

elected terms were for one year, the elections in 1869 and 1870 coming in January and the remainder in May. Two-year terms were initiated in 1885 with elections in May. There were three wards with a total of nine councilmen between 1868 and 1874; five wards and seventeen councilmen from 1875 to 1893; and four wards with twelve councilmen for the remainder of the period. Figures in parentheses indicate the number of terms served.
[d]See note 12.

Such a broad overview does not do justice to the variety of the southern urban experience or to the changes in the status of blacks over time. We can however, compare this general picture of race relations in the urban South with that of the North. The chief problem with such a comparison is not that meaningful distinctions between southern cities become blurred, but rather that the differences between northern cities prove so much greater than those between their southern counterparts.

In general the differences in patterns of race relations between northern and southern cities in this period are striking. Indeed, during no other period prior to the 1950s were these patterns in northern and southern cities more dissimilar than they were between 1860 and 1900. There were, of course, similarities, notably with regard to the central role in both sections of the Negro church and fraternal order. Yet even with these institutions there are differences, since in places like Cleveland, Detroit, and Boston and, to a lesser extent, in cities with larger black populations, members of the Negro elite could still be found in white churches, fraternal orders, and clubs.[14]

Differences are more evident in other areas. Most obviously, northern blacks were more heavily concentrated in cities, yet they constituted a small percentage of their region's urban population. In 1900, 70.5 percent of northern Negroes were urban, but they made up only 2.5 percent of the North's urban dwellers.[15] These demographic factors, and the presence of more whites committed to equal rights, greatly influenced northern urban race relations. At the same time that de jure segregation replaced de facto segregation in the South, for example, legal barriers between the races in the North came down. Whereas the Supreme Court decision in 1883 declaring the Civil Rights Act of 1875 unconstitutional added further support to existing discrimination in the South, it produced state legislation in the North that repealed most antimiscegenation statutes and banned segregated schools and public accommodations. Segregation often persisted, but it was now in clear violation of the law.[16] Similarly, while first piecemeal and then de jure disfranchisement lessened the political power of southern blacks, the competition for Negro votes between two evenly matched political parties in the North brought northern blacks their greatest power during the 1880s and 1890s.[17]

Economic comparisons are more difficult. As in the South, around 75 percent of northern urban black males were confined to the lowest-paying jobs. At least in some cities, however, their position improved or remained the same during the late nineteenth century, while conditions in the South deteriorated for those in similar circumstances. Northern female blacks certainly had more opportunities for advancement than their southern sisters. And the greater frequency of female-headed black families in the South further testifies to the stronger eco-

14. Katzman, *Before the Ghetto,* 136, 160–61; Kusmer, *A Ghetto Takes Shape,* 30, 92–93, 97; David A. Gerber, *Black Ohio and the Color Line, 1860–1915* (Urbana: University of Illinois Press, 1976), 56–57, 131–33.

15. Bureau of the Census, *Negro Population,* 90–91.

16. Gerber, *Black Ohio,* chapters 3, 7, 8; Spear, *Black Chicago,* 6–7; Katzman, *Before the Ghetto,* chapter 3; Kusmer, *A Ghetto Takes Shape,* 14–17 and chapter 3; Pleck, *Black Migration and Poverty,* 29; W. E. B. Du Bois, *The Philadelphia Negro: A Social Study* (Philadelphia: Published for the University of Pennsylvania, 1899), pp. 417–18; Osofsky, *Harlem,* pp. 36–37.

17. Gerber, *Black Ohio,* chapter 8; Katzman, *Before the Ghetto,* 33–37, 175–201; Du Bois, *Philadelphia Negro,* 368–83; Lawrence Grossman, *The Democratic Party and the Negro: Northern and National Politics, 1868–1892* (Urbana: University of Illinois Press, 1976).

nomic position of northern blacks.[18] Then, too, because of the relatively small number of blacks in most northern cities and the greater acceptance of integration, black businessmen and professionals could often rely on white clienteles, as their southern counterparts could not.[19] Although the matter is subject to debate, it would also appear that prior to 1900 residential segregation was less of a factor in northern than in southern cities, and members of the northern Negro elite had a far greater range of housing choices.[20]

The character of northern urban race relations would change after 1900 and especially after the so-called Great Migration.[21] Republican hegemony during the Fourth Party System (1894–1932) eliminated the incentive to woo northern Negro voters, and the growing number of black migrants (many of them from southern cities like Raleigh) alarmed whites at the same time that the massive influx of foreigners provided formidable competitors for blacks in the areas of housing and employment. But between 1860 and 1900, most notably after 1880, southern blacks who moved to northern cities usually enjoyed greater opportunities than those who remained behind. The last twenty years of the century witnessed a decline in the extent of legally enforced segregation and discrimination in the North, a greater role for blacks in politics, and perhaps an improvement in black prospects for economic success. After a more promising beginning, the social, political, and economic trends for blacks in the South ran in the opposite direction.

18. For differences in the percentage of female-headed households in selected northern and southern cities see Pleck, *Black Migration and Poverty,* 183–84. For the greater opportunities in northern cities for blacks especially as factory workers and clerks, see Kusmer, *A Ghetto Takes Shape,* 17–24; Gerber, *Black Ohio,* 60–80; Pleck, *Black Migration and Poverty,* 147–49.

19. Katzman, *Before the Ghetto,* 126–29; Gerber, *Black Ohio,* 80–92; Kusmer, *A Ghetto Takes Shape,* 98–103; Spear, *Black Chicago,* 54–70, 111.

20. Katzman, *Before the Ghetto,* chapter 2, especially, 77–78; Spear, *Black Chicago,* 6; Connolly, *A Ghetto Grows in Brooklyn,* 7–8, 21–22; Kusmer, *A Ghetto Takes Shape,* 12–13, and chapter 2, especially 47; Gerber, *Black Ohio,* 114–16.

21. See the books by Katzman, Kusmer, Spear, Osofsky, Connolly, and Gerber already cited.

Part Four

Jews
and
Other
Ethnics

Race, Ethnicity, and Cultural Pluralism
in American History

This essay originated in a January 1981 lecture that was part of a series of four nationwide workshops organized by the American Association for State and Local History to acquaint museum and historical agency professionals with the impact of the so-called new social history. Lecturers were asked to sum up the findings of this new approach to the past and assess their impact on a specific traditional field of American history, point out new sources that social historians were using so that workshop members would be alerted to their value for purposes of acquisition and exhibit preparation, and make suggestions for future research. Nine of the presenters were then asked to prepare written versions of their talks for a volume entitled *Ordinary People and Everyday Life: Perspectives on the New Social History*. Where appropriate, we were encouraged to retain the original informal and often highly personal character of our talks. In reprinting my contribution I have retained its tone but chosen to omit the annotated bibliography that originally accompanied it. My focus on the issue of assimilation accurately reflected the concerns of scholars in general as well as my own, circa the early 1980s. I continue to think that emphasis is warranted, but for more recent developments, updated bibliography, and a debate over the desirability of shifting the study of things ethnic to "ethnicization," that is, the process of creating ethnicity, see the special forum on ethnicity in *Journal of American Ethnic History* 12 (Fall 1992): 3–63.

The new social history has had perhaps its greatest impact on the study of race and ethnicity in American life. With the assistance of innovative approaches and methodological techniques, a new generation of social historians has at

I want to thank professors Anne Boylan and Arthur Mann for their comments on an earlier version of this essay.

times confirmed the assumptions of previous writers, but more often it has refined or totally revised long-accepted interpretations. In this essay, I want to examine the ways that these developments have affected our understanding of the role of race and ethnicity in American life. I will begin by indicating what I think the new social history is, especially what makes it different from the old, and why I think the subject of race and ethnicity has drawn so many of its practitioners. Then I want to examine some models for assimilation in American life before discussing the sources, approaches, and findings of the new social history as they apply to the five most commonly studied topics in the history of race and ethnicity.

There is no single definition of the new social history. Indeed, there is probably no common description of the old social history. For simplicity, however, I would argue that the old social history included a diverse group of topics not strictly political in the once common sense of applying to elections and political leaders—class structure, family life, but also clothing, recreation, religion, and architecture, which are now considered part of cultural history. Furthermore, as demonstrated in the *History of American Life* series (1927–1948), edited by Arthur Schlesinger, Sr., and Dixon Ryan Fox, the old social history did not approach its topics systematically, either in the use of evidence or in the application of theory.

The new social history is quite different. For one thing, it is the product of an underlying philosophy that calls for the study of "ordinary people," the "common folk," or the "masses." Sometimes social historians talk about studying the "inarticulate," which may refer occasionally to the middle and even upper classes. More often, they concentrate on the working class, in an attempt, as Stephan Thernstrom put it, to study history "from the bottom up."[1] Such an approach seeks to learn about the "people" rather than about their leaders— how working people lived, what they believed, how they interacted with each other and with the rest of society.

Second, the new social history has a new orientation or approach. It is interdisciplinary, with an emphasis on testing a theoretical framework, rather than simply reporting the details of everyday life. In the 1960s, pioneering scholars looked to sociology for their insights and methodology; more recently, there has been a shift of attention to the findings of anthropology and geography.

Finally, as befits a theoretically oriented subdiscipline interested in obscure people, the new social history has developed new research methods based on previously neglected sources. The most important of these sources—manuscript

---

1. Stephan Thernstrom, *Poverty and Progress: Social Mobility in a Nineteenth-Century City* (Cambridge: Harvard University Press, 1964), 7.

census schedules, wills, tax ledgers, organization records, and city directories—lend themselves especially well to quantitative techniques, which in many early monographs often seemed more important to the authors than the findings themselves. Thus the tools of the old social history, including diaries, letters, and newspapers, often have been neglected, because of their nonquantifiable nature and their inappropriateness for the study of semiliterate people.

The new social historians were naturally attracted to the field of race and ethnicity, where for so long an emphasis, often filiopietistic, on articulate or successful leaders had held sway. In part, the attractiveness of the new approach for historians of race and ethnicity was due to the influence of French and English scholars, but at least as important was the increased visibility of blacks, white ethnics, and other minorities during the 1960s. Thanks to the new sources and methodology, previous generations of ethnic or racial masses could now be examined and treated as subjects of history rather than merely as objects whose lives were determined by the assimilating forces in American life that plunged them into the nation's famous melting pot. As John W. Briggs expresses it in his examination of Italians in three American communities, "The Immigrants were not chameleons totally dependent on their surroundings for their character. They contributed to shaping their future rather than receiving their destinies wholly defined and packaged by others." Likewise, in his study of the Los Angeles Japanese community, John Modell rejects the tendency to view the Japanese in America as victims, accepting instead the new approach to ethnic history that argues, "Neither wholly autonomous nor simply passive recipients of the malign initiatives of majority Americans, minorities have evolved varied attitudes and institutions appropriate to their circumstances." Even slavery could not eliminate such options. According to John W. Blassingame, "The slave held onto many remnants of his African culture, gained a sense of worth in the quarters, spent most of his time free from surveillance by whites, controlled important aspects of his life, and did some personally meaningful things on his own volition."[2]

Many of the new social historians were primarily interested in seeing whether the forces of modernization and Americanization had indeed stripped immigrants and migrants of their basic values and institutions. The far-ranging impact of these forces is suggested by the title, if not always the content, of *The Uprooted,* Oscar Handlin's 1951 Pulitzer Prize–winning work on European immigration to the United States. In fact, Handlin's classic has become so much of a

2. Briggs, *An Italian Passage: Immigrants to Three American Cities, 1890–1930* (New Haven: Yale University Press, 1978), xx; Modell, *The Economics and Politics of Racial Accommodation: The Japanese of Los Angeles, 1900–1942* (Urbana: University of Illinois Press, 1977), vii; Blassingame, *The Slave Community: Plantation Life in the Antebellum South* (New York: Oxford University Press, 1972), viii.

target for the new social historians that at times it seems that their findings are almost as much the result of a revolt against *The Uprooted* as a revolt against the discredited idea of America as a melting pot. This is unfortunate. Such parasitic history not only lets someone else establish the questions, but also, because so many of the new generation have misread Handlin's extremely subtle book, leads to the creation of straw men. Furthermore, Handlin's critics ignore the extent to which he anticipated many of their own arguments, even though choosing to emphasize a different side of the immigrant experience. Finally, it is ironic that Handlin has not received the notice he deserves as the forerunner of the new social history. A student of Arthur Schlesinger's and the mentor of several leading new social historians, including Thernstrom, Handlin stands as a pivotal figure in the writing of social history, not only because of his status as student and teacher, but because his works, beginning in 1941 with *Boston's Immigrants,* have sought to reveal the lives of the very people that interest the new social historians.[3]

Before we examine the ways in which the new work in the field has revised or sought to revise *The Uprooted* and similar works, it is necessary to look briefly at possible models for the assimilation of racial and ethnic minorities—that is, the process through which foreign or racial outsiders become "Americanized." There are three major theories for the interaction between these groups and the host society. In each case, the view of assimilation contains an "is" and an "ought" dimension: each reflects not only its proponents' description of the assimilation process, but their desires concerning that process, as well.[4]

The most publicized model of assimilation is the traditional melting pot. The view of America as a melting pot is as old as the nation-state. A French visitor, J. Hector St. John de Crèvecoeur, wrote in 1782 of America: "Here individuals of

3. Handlin, *The Uprooted: The Epic Story of the Great Migrations that Made the American People,* 2d ed., enlarged (Boston: Little, Brown, 1973); Handlin, *Boston's Immigrants, 1790–1865: A Study in Acculturation* (Cambridge: Harvard University Press, 1941). For criticism of Handlin, see, for example, Virginia Yans-McLaughlin, *Family and Community: Italian Immigrants in Buffalo, 1880–1930* (Ithaca: Cornell University Press, 1977), 18, 26, 57, 62, 181; Briggs, *Italian Passage,* 118; Josef J. Barton, *Peasants and Strangers: Italians, Rumanians, and Slovaks in an American City, 1890–1950* (Cambridge: Harvard University Press, 1975), 2; Judith Fincher Laird, "Argentine, Kansas: The Evolution of a Mexican-American Community: 1905–1940," (Ph.D. diss., University of Kansas, 1975), 159.

4. The following treatment draws heavily on John Higham, *Send These to Me: Jews and Other Immigrants in Urban America* (New York: Atheneum, 1975), 196–230; Milton M. Gordon, *Assimilation in American Life: The Role of Race, Religion, and National Origins* (New York: Oxford University Press, 1964), chapters 4–6; Arthur Mann, *The One and the Many: Reflections on the American Identity* (Chicago: University of Chicago Press, 1979), chapters 5–6.

all nations are melted into a new race of men, whose labours and posterity will one day cause great changes in the world."[5] Dismayed by the rise of the Know-Nothing nativist movement during the mid-nineteenth century, Ralph Waldo Emerson subsequently echoed Crèvecoeur's assessment of the nation's uniqueness:

> Man is the most composite of all creatures . . . . As in the old burning of the Temple at Corinth, by the melting and intermixture of silver and gold and other metals a new compound more precious than any, called the Corinthian brass was formed, so in this continent,—asylum of all nations—the energy of Irish, Germans, Swedes, Poles and Cossacks, and all the European tribes,—of the Africans, and of the Polynesians,—will construct a new race, a new religion, a new state, a new literature, which will be as vigorous as the new Europe which came out of the smelting pot of the Dark Ages, or that which earlier emerged from the Pelasgic and Etruscan barbarism. *La Nature aime les croisements.*[6]

Nevertheless, as Arthur Mann reminds us, the phrase *melting pot* itself was unknown during most of American history. Webster's, for example, listed it for the first time in its 1934 edition.[7] No one knows who coined it, but it became a popular figure of speech only after Israel Zangwill's play by that title caught the public fancy in the years prior to World War I. Zangwill was a British Jew, whose play was first performed in 1908 and published in book form the following year. The author saw intermarriage as a key to the "immigrant problem," since it led to a little bit of everyone being mixed in the great melting pot. In his opinion, the best American was one of mixed ancestry. Such a view was denounced from different perspectives by many ethnic types and old-stock Americans, but it attracted widespread support, including that of President Theodore Roosevelt, who wrote the author: "I do not know when I have seen a play that stirred me as much."[8]

Another view of the melting pot had already emerged and would be expressed in the immigration laws of the 1920s. According to it, rather than having each group contribute to the melting pot, the immigrants would be Americanized, and their differences would melt away as they became Americans—that is, Anglo-Saxons, though perhaps with funny last names. That was allegedly what had happened to the so-called "old immigrants," who had come from northern and

5. *Letters from an American Farmer* (London, 1782; reprint ed., New York: Albert and Charles Boni, 1925), 55.

6. *Journals of Ralph Waldo Emerson,* 10 vols., ed. Edward Waldo Emerson and Waldo Emerson Forbes (Boston: Houghton Mifflin, 1909–1914), 7:115–16.

7. Mann, *One and the Many,* 97–98.

8. Israel Zangwill, *The Melting Pot* (New York: Macmillan, 1909); Roosevelt quoted in Mann, *One and the Many,* 100.

western Europe prior to the late nineteenth century. What emerged therefore was the doctrine of Anglo-Saxon supremacy or Anglo-conformity, which held that more recent newcomers had nothing to add to the values, virtues, institutions, and behavior of old-stock Americans. A response to the great influx of "new immigrants" from southern and eastern Europe between 1880 and 1914, it signaled, like all expressions of xenophobia in American history, a loss of confidence in the country's present and future prospects.

Many still defend that view, most notably in letters to the editor and calls to radio talk shows, but a third model is probably the most popular theory today. This is, of course, *cultural pluralism,* a phrase coined by Horace Kallen, an American Jew who took his degree at Harvard in philosophy. Writing in the teens and early twenties, most notably in *Culture and Democracy in the United States,*[9] Kallen proposed that every ethnic group live unto itself and retain its own language, religion, schools, clubs, history, customs, food, and other aspects of its culture. Because Kallen's ideas changed, over time, and exhibited a troublesome vagueness, they defy easy summary, but his theory was based on a number of assumptions that, as we shall see, did not always hold true. He assumed that immigration would continue; that claims of ancestry were irrepressible (men can change everything, Kallen wrote, except their grandfathers); that the "American creed" guaranteed the equality of all different kinds of men; and that the United States was strong in proportion to its diversity.

Kallen was confident, in the face of much evidence to the contrary, that ethnic pluralism was compatible with national unity. English would remain the official language, and everyone would accept and work within the democratic, capitalistic polity. Sociologist Milton Gordon has since labeled such an intersection of cultures cultural assimilation or acculturation. Kallen thus substituted for the melting pot the concept of America as an orchestra. Others, while changing the metaphor, have kept its meaning, as in Carl N. Degler's use of the term *salad bowl* to describe the nature of assimilation.[10] In any case, the constituent elements retain their special character, but blend together to form something greater than the sum of the parts.

Yet the end of large-scale European immigration, the impact of World War II, and other factors seemed by 1950 to have left ethnicity dissolved in the melting pot. Observers stressed the unity of American life; a so-called consensus school flourished among historians, who emphasized the shared values of Americans that cut across class, race, and regional boundaries; and Dwight Eisenhower

9. *Culture and Democracy in the United States* (New York: Boni and Liveright, 1924).
10. Gordon, *Assimilation,* 70–71; Degler, *Out of Our Past: The Forces that Shaped Modern America* (New York: Harper and Row, 1959), 296.

reigned over America's seemingly "affluent society." Works about *the* American character proliferated, and the new discipline of American Studies enjoyed rapid growth. Within that environment, neither academics nor laymen gave much attention to the presence of cultural diversity produced by racial and ethnic differences. Kallen's views nonetheless finally became fashionable as a result of the cold war, the founding of Israel, Third World revolutions, the civil rights movement, and especially the black power–ignited ethnic revival of the 1960s. The determination of individual groups to preserve their cultural heritage led pop and academic sociologists to pick up the cry, pointing to the persistence of ethnic attachment as a sign that something was clearly missing in the core American culture.

As a result, cultural pluralism is today used to describe the accommodation of American society to the diverse ethnic and racial groups in its midst. Indeed, the new social history uses cultural pluralism—that is, intergroup differences based on the persistence of older ethnic ties within the dominant culture—as a take-off point for American ethnic and racial history. Perhaps as important, since it colors so much of this work, the new social historians view such persistence quite favorably and treat it as something that should have happened. In other words, the new social history not only finds evidence of strong ethnic and racial identification, but usually celebrates it, as well, though often expressing dismay at the frequent examples of inequality among groups. And, as in the case of John Modell's sympathetic treatment of the first generation of Japanese Americans in their conflict with the more Americanization-oriented second generation, an author's preference for ethnic persistence does not necessarily depend upon membership in the group being discussed.[11]

So much for background. It is time to look at the extent to which the findings of the new social history have modified our understanding of five broad areas of ethnic and racial history: migration patterns, community formation, mobility, family structure, and politics. The primary point to keep in mind is that this body of work has revealed basic patterns of adjustment that cut across all ethnic and racial groups, while at the same time discovering attitudes, values, and forms of behavior distinctive to certain groups. The new social historians are dealing with shared *and* unique characteristics and trying to account for both the differences and similarities among groups. But whatever the final result, the migrants' personal preferences are central, reflecting a previously unacknowledged control over their own destiny. Even though an author like Richard Griswold del Castillo might acknowledge that "racial discrimination, cultural oppression, and outright violence have been major forces molding the Mexican-American experience," he

---

11. *Economics and Politics of Racial Accommodation,* passim, but especially 84–85.

typically emphasizes that "since the late nineteenth century, Mexican-American history has also been characterized by creative and constructive responses to changing circumstances."[12]

The first two areas—migration and community formation—are closely linked because they involve the extent of "uprootedness" and alienation produced by breaking away from an old, familiar environment and then having to adjust to new surroundings or even, as in the case of immigrants, a new country. In *The Uprooted,* Oscar Handlin argues that "the history of immigration is a history of alienation and its consequences." Though in this book Handlin was writing only of European immigrants, in his other works, including *The Newcomers* and *The American People in the Twentieth Century,* he extended that description to the internal migration of blacks and Hispanics.[13] For Handlin and most other scholars through the early 1960s, what was particularly significant was what was lost as migrants left settled, stable, rural communities in the Old World or the South and were transplanted as individuals to a hostile, strange, urban America. The ties with the past were weakened or even "snipped," as former values and behavior patterns came under attack from Americanizing or modernizing forces. Even if the first generation managed to hold onto the ancestral language, religion, and institutions, it did so in the face of a disorienting and destructive environment. The next generation, by contrast, was quickly assimilated. The struggle between the first and the second generations then made the degree of alienation even more frightening. Virginia Yans-McLaughlin has taken issue with this scenario and characterizes it as being "grounded in a conventional sociological model implying a clear dichotomy, as well as abrupt discontinuities between folk and urban societies."[14] Yans-McLaughlin and others maintain that the act of migration or emigration was not as wrenching as previously thought and that much of the earlier cultural patterns successfully weathered the migration, thus reducing the sense of alienation. Undergirding such assertions is a new interpretation of the migratory process itself.

As early as 1964, in an important and widely discussed article about southern Italians, Rudolph J. Vecoli drew attention to the extent of group migration, group settlement in the New World, and "chain migration," which allowed new migrants to join their former neighbors in the same cities or even in the same neighborhoods in America. More recently, Judith Fincher Laird, in a dissertation

12. *The Los Angeles Barrio, 1850–1890: A Social History* (Berkeley: University of California Press, 1979), xi.

13. *The Uprooted,* 4; *The Newcomers: Negroes and Puerto Ricans in a Changing Metropolis* (Cambridge: Harvard University Press, 1959); *The American People in the Twentieth Century* (Cambridge: Harvard University Press, 1954).

14. *Family and Community,* 18.

on a small Mexican community in Kansas, concludes in a similar vein, "Mexican immigration bore little resemblance to the 'uprooting' experience which Oscar Handlin depicted as characteristic of European immigration. Indeed, continuity rather than alienation, marginality and social disorganization, characterized Mexican immigration."[15]

The work of Josef Barton is especially significant in the development of this altered depiction of the effects of migration. It is also typical of the new emphasis given to the life of the immigrants in the Old World rather than simply focusing on the problems of assimilation in the New. In discussing the migration of Slovaks, Rumanians, and Italians to Cleveland around the turn of the century, Barton shows three stages of migrants—individual pioneers, followed by relatives and friends, and finally even whole villages. Barton also found that the migrants came from all classes and were not driven out of the Old World by destitution or persecution. They represented, instead, the more aggressive and ambitious individuals, who felt threatened by an increasingly unstable economic situation at home and who sought to better their situation in America. In Barton's hands, these migrants look more like the Puritan forefathers fleeing potential economic difficulty in East Anglia than like the starving Irish of the 1840s chronicled by Handlin in *Boston's Immigrants*. And unlike Handlin's late-nineteenth-century migrants in *The Uprooted*, they were highly self-selective.[16]

All recent authors join Barton in seeing individual desires for economic betterment based on the expectation of declining fortunes where they were as more important than religious persecution, hard times, and other crises in determining migration. Some see an even more selective process of chain migration. Using passport records of Italian towns and United States naturalization records, John Briggs stresses the importance of "small family-based migration chains." He reports the greeting given the Italian premier by a local mayor in the province of Potenza "in the name of the eight thousand under my administration, of which three thousand are emigrants in America and five thousand are preparing to join them." Briggs, however, is more impressed with the complexity of the chains than is Barton. He found that the migrants did not concentrate on a handful of destinations in the United States and once in America did not necessarily live

15. Vecoli, "*Contadini* in Chicago: A Critique of *The Uprooted*," *Journal of American History* 51 (December 1964): 404–17; Laird, "Argentine, Kansas," 159, as quoted with a muted endorsement in Mario T. Garcia, *Desert Immigrants: The Mexicans of El Paso, 1880–1920* (New Haven: Yale University Press, 1981), 197.

16. *Peasants and Strangers*, especially chapters 2–3. Barton's immigrants, however, have much in common with those described by Marcus Lee Hansen, whose pioneering work has been ignored by the new social historians. See, for example, Hansen, *The Immigrant in American History* (Cambridge: Harvard University Press, 1940).

only among those they had known back home; but the significant degree of linkage clearly reduced the sense of alienation. Chains were especially important in Mexican migration to southern California during the same period. "After one family situated itself," writes Albert Camarillo, "it would attract relatives and friends from the original home in Mexico: the familial migration network was very common." A Mexican resident who arrived in Santa Barbara in 1916 explained: "One family comes from Durango and establishes itself here. From here it writes there and says come! come! come over, it is good here. It brings others and others. Well, one was here . . . Juan Esparza—he brought twenty-eight families from Durango."[17]

The nature of the migration experience has critical implications for community formation. In the traditional view, the individual immigrant or migrant underwent a painful and isolated adjustment to the new conditions, with only a few voluntary associations unsuccessfully attempting to cushion the shock. But revisionists argue that chain migration and group settlement allowed the transference of premigration organizations and values. Even more suggestive of the remaining ties with the past was the surprising amount of reverse migration. That practice has long been known to have been common among the Chinese, but Thomas Kessner estimates that between 1907 and 1911 there was a yearly average of seventy-three repatriates for every one hundred Italian immigrants. Between 1908 and 1912, yearly repatriation for all "new immigrants," excluding Jews, was 42 percent (the Jews had a figure of only 7 percent, which Kessner attributes to greater economic success but which might also simply reflect the unattractive conditions back home.)[18]

The return home was often not the final act in the immigrant's saga, however. John Bodnar, in his study of a small community in Pennsylvania, uncovered evidence of significant numbers of Slavs moving back and forth between the United States and Europe. Given the proximity of their homeland, that phenomenon was most marked among Mexican Americans. Mario Garcia argues that most Mexicans who came to El Paso around the turn of the century fully intended to

17. Briggs, *Italian Passage,* chapters 1–5, quotation on 70; Camarillo, *Chicanos in a Changing Society: From Mexican Pueblos to American Barrios in Santa Barbara and Southern California, 1848–1930* (Cambridge: Harvard University Press, 1979), 144, 279, quotation on 146. See also Yans-McLaughlin, *Family and Community,* 58–64; Marc Lee Raphael, *Jews and Judaism in a Midwestern Community: Columbus, Ohio, 1840–1975* (Columbus: Ohio Historical Society, 1979), 16–17; John Bodnar, *Immigration and Industrialization: Ethnicity in an American Mill Town, 1870–1940* (Pittsburgh: University of Pittsburgh Press, 1977), 26–28; Elizabeth Hafkin Pleck, *Black Migration and Poverty: Boston 1865–1900* (New York: Academic Press, 1979), 63–67.

18. Thomas Kessner, *The Golden Door: Italian and Jewish Immigrant Mobility in New York City, 1880–1915* (New York: Oxford University Press, 1977), 28–31.

return south. Whether or not immigrants returned home, their primary loyalty often continued to be to the old country. Albert Camarillo found that, from 1910 to 1927, only 0.7 percent of the 849 naturalization petitions at the Santa Barbara Court House had been filed by Mexican immigrants, a pattern of nonnaturalization that continued throughout the 1930s. Unfortunately, it is not possible to trace the internal movements of American blacks, but I suspect that the use of oral history will reveal a constant two-way flow between northern cities and the Southern countryside—if not for the original migrants, then at least for their children.[19]

In other words, though some adjustment and change was obviously necessary, the migrants were far from being totally uprooted. The first generation especially joined churches and synagogues, mutual aid societies, and fraternal organizations based on town or district origins in the old country or in the South. Previous scholars, including Handlin, had allowed for such carryovers, but the new social historians see this behavior as seriously limiting the degree of alienation and sense of loss. Family patterns, about which I will have more to say later, were also transferred, and marriage was carried on within the ethnic group. The process of adjustment was made even easier by ethnically determined residential segregation. Like Barton's white ethnics, Modell's Japanese, and the Mexicans of Camarillo, Garcia, and Griswold del Castillo, blacks also used a high degree of residential segregation to good advantage. As I have argued elsewhere, blacks in the postwar urban South, for example, built in their sections of the cities churches, schools, and fraternal associations that eased the transition to urban life. Some caution is required here, however, as recent work demonstrates that individual groups of white ethnics were not as residentially isolated from each other as it was once believed, and their degree of segregation was certainly less than that experienced by Hispanics, blacks, and Asians.[20]

19. Bodnar, *Immigration and Industrialization,* 28–29, 55, 87–88; Garcia, *Desert Immigrants,* 106; Camarillo, *Chicanos,* 161. See also Griswold del Castillo, *Los Angeles Barrio,* 119–24. For evidence that proximity to the homeland stimulated similar behavior on the part of at least some French Canadians, see Tamara Hareven, "The Laborers of Manchester, New Hampshire, 1912–1922: The Role of Family and Adjustment to Industrial Life," *Labor History* 16 (Spring 1975): 249–65.

20. Barton, *Peasants and Strangers,* 18–22; Modell, *Economics and Politics of Racial Accommodation,* 32–33, 55–75; Camarillo, *Chicanos,* 10–13; Garcia, *Desert Immigrants,* 127–54; Griswold del Castillo, *Los Angeles Barrio,* chapter 5 (the name of the main barrio, Sonora Town, reflects the importance of chain migration); Howard N. Rabinowitz, *Race Relations in the Urban South, 1865–1890* (New York: Oxford University Press, 1978), parts 1 and 2. For the new view of "ghettoization" among white ethnics as compared to blacks, see Sam Bass Warner and Colin B. Burke, "Cultural Change in the Ghetto," *Journal of Contemporary History* 4 (October 1969): 173–87; Howard P. Chudacoff, *Mobile Americans: Residential and Social Mobility in Omaha, 1880–1920* (New York: Oxford University Press, 1972), 65–68, 75–83; Thomas Lee Philpott, *The Slum and the Ghetto: Neighbor-*

Nevertheless, the newcomers quickly established communities that nurtured old forms of behavior, while individuals started to adjust to their new environment. An ethnic group's core values and customs persisted at least until the second generation began the process of assimilation at the primary group level. Rather than simply learn English, adopt American dress, and accept the political and economic system, the "outsiders" now came to interact with members of the dominant society in organizations, forms of recreation, and even in marital relations. Termed *structural assimilation* by Milton Gordon, the extent of this process even today for some groups lags far behind the attainment of cultural assimilation. As John Briggs reminds us, the process of passing old values and identities from generation to generation, often in the absence of outside hostility, remains a major subject for future research.[21]

One historian, James Borchert, draws heavily on anthropological studies and photographs to carry the argument even further, in his discussion of Washington, D.C.'s black alley dwellers. Arguing that "urbanization does not necessarily void the importance of primary groups," he claims that southern black migrants withstood the modernizing and urbanizing forces of the dominant culture to the extent that successive generations maintained their values in terms of religious behavior, work habits, folklore, and family life. Borchert, however, goes too far in denying the obvious influence of the migratory trauma and new environment. Elizabeth Pleck's finding of a more limited persistence in terms of duration and degree of old habits among southern migrants to Boston seems more compelling; but Borchert's work serves as a valuable modifier of accepted wisdom concerning black America's move from plantation to ghetto.[22]

The discovery of relatively autonomous communities among post-1865 ethnic and racial groups echoes the findings of social historians who, during the past decade or so, have studied slave life. Indeed Borchert frequently cites the work of John Blassingame, Herbert Gutman, and Eugene Genovese to document the alleged continuity between the life-style of his alley dwellers and that of rural slaves. Much of this work on slavery was a reaction to Stanley Elkins's controversial landmark effort, *Slavery: A Problem in American Institutional and Intellectual Life* (1959). Because Elkins emphasizes the disintegrating impact of slavery

---

hood Deterioration and Middle-Class Reform, Chicago, 1880–1930 (New York: Oxford University Press, 1978), chapter 5; but see also Kathleen Neils Conzen, *Immigrant Milwaukee: Accommodation and Community in a Frontier City* (Cambridge: Harvard University Press, 1976), 127–36.

21. Gordon, *Assimilation*, 67, 70–71, 80–81, 110–11; Briggs, *Italian Passage*, 278.

22. James Borchert, *Alley Life in Washington: Family, Community, Religion, and Folklife in the City, 1850–1970* (Urbana: University of Illinois Press, 1980), passim, quotation on 240; Pleck, *Black Migration*, 3.

on the slave's psyche, his book has functioned for the current generation of scholars in black history as the counterpart of Handlin's *The Uprooted*. In both the study of slave and post-1865 minority life, the emphasis is on the ability of minority groups to preserve their cultural values and institutions in the face of a hostile, or at least different, dominant society. The individuals are thus not alienated or isolated, because they have each other and their "community."[23]

Both the new and older books would agree that there was both persistence and change in behavior, but the newer works are more impressed with the extent of the former. In their emphasis on continuity, these studies are part of a broader trend in the writing of American history. Another group of social historians, for example, now argues for the persistence of traditional ways of life long after settlement in colonial America.[24] Thus Borchert argues, "Although urbanization has clearly affected folk migrants, the change is more of degree than of kind. What is most impressive is not the extent of change, but the continuity, the persistence of traditional functions, forms, and outlooks." John Briggs writes of his Italian immigrants' "sense of continuity between past and present." And though more conscious of the examples of acculturation than most other younger scholars and thus demonstrating more affinity with Handlin, Mario Garcia concludes, "First generation immigrants and political refugees, through their re-establishment of spiritual societies common in Mexico as well as the re-enactment of native Mexican religious celebrations, successfully maintained cultural continuity and helped create a sense of community in the barrios." At first glance, it seems that Virginia Yans-McLaughlin's approach might be significantly different. She argues, "The relationship between modernity and tradition . . . is neither dichotomous nor linear but dialectical." In fact, she documents the forces of continuity, even where the clash between the new environment and tradition produced a blend of the old and the new.[25]

The persistence of older values has serious implications for the study of mobility in American history, the third broad topic. Social mobility studies have

23. Blassingame, *Slave Community;* Gutman, *The Black Family in Slavery and Freedom, 1750–1925* (New York: Pantheon, 1976); Genovese, *Roll, Jordan, Roll: The World the Slaves Made* (New York: Pantheon, 1974); Elkins, *Slavery: A Problem in American Institutional and Intellectual Life* (Chicago: University of Chicago Press, 1959).

24. See, for example, Kenneth Lockridge, *A New England Town: The First Hundred Years* (New York: Norton, 1970).

25. Borchert, *Alley Life in Washington,* 239; Briggs, *Italian Passage,* 272; Garcia, *Desert Immigrants,* 213; Yans-McLaughlin, *Family and Community,* 22. Two other works that, like Yans-McLaughlin's, emphasize a dialectical relationship between culture and environment, but nevertheless leave the reader more impressed with the high degree of cultural continuity and persistence, are Bodnar, *Immigration and Industrialization,* and Lawrence W. Levine, *Black Culture and Black Consciousness: Afro-American Folk Thought from Slavery to Freedom* (New York: Oxford University Press, 1977).

become practically a cottage industry since the publication, in 1964, of Stephan Thernstrom's *Poverty and Progress,* a study of mobility in Newburyport, Massachusetts, between 1840 and 1880. Indeed, from the mid-1960s to the mid-1970s, social mobility studies were practically *the* new social history. Characterized by increasingly sophisticated theoretical and methodological techniques, which now employ computers, these efforts have relied on manuscript census schedules and city directories. All have found little support for the old idea of rags-to-riches mobility, but neither have they found the static situation more common in Europe. They have documented, instead, limited upward movement throughout the social system, not only for individuals, but between generations—unskilled to semiskilled, upper-blue-collar to lower-white-collar, etc. Such studies also have demonstrated that high rates of geographic mobility have been the rule throughout American history and not the result of the automobile or the emergence of national corporations. Indeed, rates of geographic mobility as well as rates of economic mobility have changed remarkably little over the years.[26]

Not surprisingly, these studies have found differences among various ethnic groups and between natives and immigrants. Thernstrom's *The Other Bostonians* found a pattern echoed in other accounts for different cities and periods. Yankees did better than immigrants, Jews and Protestants better than Catholics, the sons of the middle class better than those of the poor, Russian Jews and English better than Irish and Italian, but all enjoyed a marked degree of upward mobility. Only for blacks has this not been the case, but at least since 1940, in Boston— and no doubt elsewhere—they too have begun to enjoy the fruits of a fluid social system. Subsequent studies of Mexican Americans have revealed not only a pattern of group immobility similar to that of blacks but also a notable amount of individual downward mobility, explained by the fact that in the Southwest and southern California the Mexicans were the original settlers caught in the midst of a changing society that left only menial jobs for them.[27]

Yet there are serious problems with the works on mobility. Due to the availability of manuscript census schedules and more manageable samples, they are best suited to the nineteenth century and for smaller cities. What is more, the significance of their findings is complicated by a number of factors, including reliance on occupational change as a substitute for other measures of mobility; alteration in job categories, over time; the omission of women; and discrimina-

26. Thernstrom, *Poverty and Progress.* See also Chudacoff, *Mobile Americans;* Kessner, *The Golden Door;* Peter Knights, *The Plain People of Boston, 1830–1860: A Study in City Growth* (New York: Oxford University Press, 1971).

27. Thernstrom, *The Other Bostonians: Poverty and Progress in the American Metropolis, 1880–1970* (Cambridge: Harvard University Press, 1973); Camarillo, *Chicanos,* 217–25; Griswold del Castillo, *Los Angeles Barrio,* 51–61. See also sources cited in note 26.

tion against transients, blacks, and the poor. Even more troubling, since it is more subtle, is the prior assumption that mobility is something that all groups sought. In fact, the absence of mobility may be seen by some groups as a "good thing," rather than a sign of failure.[28] Stephan Thernstrom's attempt to deal with problems in the data by claiming that "data that are not perfectly comparable seem to me better than no data at all," is not reassuring.[29] Worse still, while we know the patterns of mobility (many of which have long been suspected from impressionistic evidence), there is much disagreement in accounting for differences among groups. Barton found Italians more upwardly mobile than Slovaks because they placed a higher value on secular education and ambition, but Rumanians did better than both, because education was even more important to them, family size smaller, and their culture more secularly oriented. Kessner found Italians lagging behind Jews, because they were less concerned with education and social mobility, yet John Briggs argues that his Italians were quite interested in these factors, an interest that Briggs claims was brought over from the old country. Thernstrom believes blacks suffered in part because of their lack of skills, but Elizabeth Pleck in her study of Boston blacks identifies white racism as the culprit.[30] The major point, however, is that for whatever reasons, though ethnicity clearly intersects with class, social mobility has a basic ethnic component that must not be ignored.

Ethnicity and race also have a strong though even less well understood impact on the nature of family structure and family life, the fourth area of historical concern. I do not want to devote much space to the family, since Maris Vinovskis and Elizabeth Pleck analyze the contributions of recent research in their essays (elsewhere in *Ordinary People*), but two points must be noted. First, there is a great similarity among groups as far as family structure is concerned. The supposed shift from an extended to a nuclear family, a process at the heart of ideas about the impact of industrialization and modernization, was not a product of migration. In fact, the nuclear family (husband and wife, with or without children) has been the norm in western society since the Middle Ages. Herbert Gutman's work, for

28. See, for example, James A. Henretta, "Social History as Lived and Written," *American Historical Review* 84 (December 1979): 1315–16; Henretta, "The Study of Social Mobility: Ideological Assumptions and Conceptual Bias," *Labor History* 18 (Spring 1977): 165–78; Yans-McLaughlin, *Family and Community,* 34–36.

29. *Other Bostonians,* 330.

30. Barton, *Peasants and Strangers,* chapters 5–6; Kessner, *Golden Door,* passim; Briggs, *Italian Passage,* passim; Thernstrom, *Other Bostonians* 217–18; Pleck, *Black Migration,* chapter 5. For the most successful attempt to confront the problems inherent in the social mobility studies, see Clyde and Sally Griffen, *Natives and Newcomers: The Ordering of Opportunity in Mid-Nineteenth-Century Poughkeepsie* (Cambridge: Harvard University Press, 1978).

example, reveals that even in the alleged matrifocal world of blacks under slavery and freedom, two-parent households were in the majority. There are serious problems with Gutman's work—common sense tells us that slavery must have had a greater impact on the black family than he allows, and his nonlongitudinal "snapshot" research technique and presentist orientation are serious drawbacks—but he provides a needed corrective to previous assumptions about both the nature of American slavery and the status of the black family within it.[31]

The second point worth emphasizing has to do with the effect of the American urban environment on immigrant family life. Here we find some significant evidence of change tending toward homogenization. All recent work on Mexicans, for example, points to the expanded role of women within the family and especially to their greater representation in the labor market in the United States than in Mexico. Nevertheless, authors once again emphasize the degree of continuity between pre- and post-migration life and, especially during the first years after migration, carryovers from the place of origin clearly led to differences among ethnic, racial, and perhaps class groupings with regard to family values and functions. Despite the increased presence of their wives in the work force, for example, Italian and Mexican men retained their traditional power and authority within the family, even when out of work themselves.[32]

Although more research needs to be done, there seem to be pronounced differences in family size and attitudes, though, as in the case of blacks, class lines produce major variations within groups. Mexicans married young to protect virginity and to promote family growth; Irish and French Canadians married later, so that, though they also were Catholic and established big families, the families are not so large as those among Mexicans. Italians proved more hesitant than Jews to allow their girls and even boys to pursue an education; Barton's Slovaks sought parochial school education for their children, while Italians and Rumanians preferred secular schools; New York's Italian Catholics were more likely than the Irish to send their children to public schools and colleges. Then, too, although the nuclear family is now acknowledged as the dominant form, there are indications that certain ethnic groups, while arranged in nuclear households, had members of the extended family living in separate households nearby, as in the case of French Canadians studied by Tamara Hareven and as with Josef Barton's Slovaks.[33]

    31. *Black Family,* passim.
    32. Yans-McLaughlin, *Family and Community,* 20 and passim; Griswold del Castillo, *Los Angeles Barrio,* chapter 3; Garcia, *Desert Immigrants,* 117–18, 123–24, 201–4. For a somewhat different view, see Camarillo, *Chicanos,* 120, 137.
    33. Griswold del Castillo, *Los Angeles Barrio,* chapter 3; Barton, *Peasants and Strangers,* chapter 6; Kessner, *The Golden Door,* chapter 4; Nathan Glazer and Daniel Patrick

We also need to know more about marriage patterns. It seems that members of the first generation most frequently married within the ethnic group. The second generation, however, often married outside the group, indicating significant strides toward structural assimilation. Nevertheless, when deserting the ethnic group, most individuals evidently married within the same religion. Thus, in 1955, in an influential book entitled *Protestant, Catholic, and Jew,* the theologian Will Herberg argued for the declining significance in America of ethnicity versus religion. Herberg and others saw a "triple melting pot," in which Italian Catholics married Irish or Polish Catholics, German Protestants married Swedish and English Protestants, and German and East European Jews intermarried.[34] Yet, as in so much else in ethnic history, blacks were left out. Even if the extent of such white ethnic intermarriage by religion is as widespread as claimed, given the resistance to racial intermarriage, it would still make more sense, as David M. Heer reminds us, to talk of a "double melting pot."[35] But the triple-melting-pot idea held sway until the ethnic revival of the 1960s and 1970s.

One final subject, though technically a part of still another of the proliferating new versions of old subdisciplines, is politics. The new political history shares much with the new social history. In an effort to break away from the traditional emphasis on presidential politics, major leaders, and the centrality of such national issues as slavery, the tariff, and the bloody shirt, political historians, especially for the nineteenth century, have attempted to explain much of voting behavior in terms of ethnic and religious loyalties and values. Of course, we have long known that throughout our history the Irish have been Democrats and that Negroes were wedded to the Republicans from emancipation until the New Deal, when they switched to the Democrats. But by using manuscript census data, city directories, precinct registration records, and, in some cases, actual polling books, the new political historians have made far

Moynihan, *Beyond the Melting Pot: The Negroes, Puerto Ricans, Jews, Italians, and Irish of New York City,* 2d ed. (Cambridge: M.I.T. Press, 1970), 201–3. Laurence A. Glasco, "The Life Cycles and Household Structure of American Ethnic Groups: Irish, Germans, and Native-born Whites in Buffalo, New York, 1855," *Journal of Urban History* 1 (May 1975): 339–64; Tamara Hareven, "Family Time and Industrial Time: Family and Work in a Planned Corporation Town, 1900–1924," *Journal of Urban History* 1 (May 1975): 365–89; Myfanwy Morgan and Hilda A. Golden, "Immigrant Families in an Industrial City: A Study of Households in Holyoke, 1880," *Journal of Family History* 4 (Spring 1979): 59–68.

34. *Protestant, Catholic, and Jew: An Essay in American Religious Sociology* (Garden City, N.Y.: Doubleday, 1955). See also Ruby Jo Reeves Kennedy, "Single or Triple Melting Pot? Intermarriage Trends in New Haven, 1870–1940," *American Journal of Sociology* 49 (January 1944): 331–39.

35. "Intermarriage," in *Harvard Encyclopedia of American Ethnic Groups,* ed. Stephan Thernstrom (Cambridge: Harvard University Press, 1980), 521.

sharper distinctions than ever before and have drawn attention to the importance of such local issues as parochial school attendance, temperance, and
Sabbatarianism. They have sought to divide the electorate, not along class
lines, but rather according to whether or not they were "pietists" or "ritual-
ists," "evangelicals" or "liturgicals." Proponents argue that those whose religious commitment was confined to churchgoing opposed political parties that
took strong moral stands, while the evangelicals or pietists endorsed such
efforts.[36] In other words, ethnicity and religious affiliation influenced voting
behavior long before the creation of the moral majority, the state of Israel, or
Poland's Solidarity union.

However, the ethnoculturalists, as they are often called, do not command
complete control of the field. Nor should they. After all, the history of southern
politics and much of twentieth-century politics does not conform to their model.
Then, too, they often ignore the splits within ethnic groups based on class,
nativity, and degree of assimilation.[37] The battle between proponents of the
importance of cultural as opposed to economic factors or local over national
issues in determining voting preference can therefore be expected to continue
with ever-escalating sophistication in weaponry.

So much for what has been done by social historians in the treatment of race,
ethnicity, and cultural pluralism. I would like to conclude by offering a few
suggestions for the possible direction of future work.

First, I think we need more comparative studies. On the one hand, this work
should compare the experiences of a single ethnic group in different locations.
That might consist of focusing on different cities or even neighborhoods, as is
already being done. More ambitiously, however, we need to compare American
Italians, for example, with Italians in Argentina or Germany. A common variant
would be the comparison of two or more American ethnic groups. The value of
the comparative dimension should be obvious. Once we have discerned patterns within a group with respect to family life, migration, social mobility, community formation, or politics, how can we be certain of causative factors without
having available control groups? The temptation, for example, to ascribe lan-

36. See, for example, Frederick C. Luebke, *Immigrants and Politics: The Germans of
Nebraska, 1880–1900* (Lincoln: University of Nebraska Press, 1969); Paul Kleppner, *The
Cross of Culture: A Social Analysis of Midwestern Politics, 1850–1900* (New York: Free
Press, 1970) and *The Third Electoral System, 1853–1892: Parties, Voters, and Political
Cultures* (Chapel Hill: University of North Carolina Press, 1979). Richard J. Jensen, *The
Winning of the Midwest: Social and Political Conflict, 1888–1896* (Chicago: University of
Chicago Press, 1971); Ronald Formisano, *The Birth of Mass Political Parties: Michigan,
1827–1861* (Princeton: Princeton University Press, 1971).
37. For a corrective, see, for example, Arthur Mann, *LaGuardia Comes to Power, 1933*
(Philadelphia: Lippincott, 1965).

guage problems as the major source of limited mobility for Hispanics is tempered when we study the language problems of eastern and southern Europeans at the turn of the century. Similarly, color or race as a factor in limiting black mobility seems less important once the remarkable success of Chinese, Japanese, and Vietnamese Americans is noted. And how can we understand the persistence of old values and patterns of behavior in America without seeing whether or not those characteristics hold for immigrants outside the United States? Daniel Patrick Moynihan, for example, asserts that the Irish development of the boss system in America resulted from their "Irishness," based on conditions in the old country; yet the Irish who went to England and Australia failed to build the same kind of system. Such comparative work will of necessity depend heavily on secondary sources to support primary research on the main target group, but, as in the case of a recent study of Poles, blacks, and Italians in Pittsburgh by three authors, multiauthor monographs can be based on primary research for all groups involved.[38]

This kind of comparative work will naturally depend on continued borrowing from other disciplines, which—as I have noted earlier   is a hallmark of the new social history. Just as we need to lower the barriers that divide disciplines, however, we must begin to end the unnatural division between black history and immigrant history, for in the end we cannot fully understand the history of one minority group without knowing the history of the others. Though probably politically untenable on most campuses today, one positive step in this direction would be the merger of separate ethnic studies programs into a single unit that would put a premium on comparative study.

I also believe that it is time to reexamine our infatuation with the concept of cultural pluralism. After all, things did not work out as Horace Kallen had planned—immigration restriction became national policy, the ancestral language has been transmitted to only a minority of the second and especially the third generation, and increased intermarriage means that, while you cannot change your grandfather, you can change the grandfathers of your posterity. More important, however, Kallen and most defenders of cultural pluralism (or, in its current simplistic incarnation, multiculturalism) today overlook the obvious fact that each ethnic group is itself pluralistic. Thus, in his otherwise excellent study, Josef Barton confined his examination of ethnic persistence to those who had already qualified as ethnics through intermarriage and parish or club membership. We learn much about the people who retained their ethnic identity, but,

---

38. Glazer and Moynihan, *Beyond the Melting Pot,* 223–26; John Bodnar, Roger Simon, and Michael Weber, *Lives of Their Own: Blacks, Italians, and Poles in Pittsburgh, 1900–1960* (Urbana: University of Illinois Press, 1982).

because of the author's filtering process, nothing about those who had in fact already become part of the melting pot. Even when authors such as John Briggs acknowledge the differences within groups, the emphasis remains on shared values, institutions, and behavior. Many authors who describe the splits within a group then proceed to treat the group as a single "community."

Similarly, most new social historians take the discrimination and oppression encountered by their group as a given factor. Only the studies on Mexican Americans tend toward the oppression model once so common in the treatment of blacks and white ethnics, though there are, of course, concessions to what can be termed the new orthodoxy in ethnic history. The revisionists are correct to emphasize the resistance of migrants and immigrants to the forces of American-ization or modernization; but in redressing the balance, they come close to claiming true autonomy for the individuals and ignoring the considerable impact of the new environment in which they had to function. Even among those who claim they are merely arguing for the existence of dialectical rather than dichot-omous relationships between culture and environment, once the studies get under way the authors often lose sight of those outside pressures. If not careful, the reader of some works on slavery might get the impression that slavery was at worst a minor annoyance that at times restricted the slave's freedom of move-ment or limited his earning power. The new social historians have shown that both slavery and immigrant life consisted of more than debasing disorganization and oppression; but, though in many respects going beyond Handlin and Elkins, they have not as yet produced a compelling mix of oppression and resistance, defeat and triumph that might enable us to treat *The Uprooted* and *Slavery* merely as period pieces. Perhaps that is not surprising, given the desire to write corrective history, a history that often fails to acknowledge fully the insights of previous authors.

It is only common sense that the forces of modernization and Americanization must have had some impact on at least some of the migrants. Even those who resisted the total remaking of their lives must have made some accommodation to the new ways, while many others must have shed more significant aspects of their cultures. Divisions within the Mexican, Japanese, and black communities studied by Camarillo, Griswold del Castillo, Modell, and Pleck suggest the value of that approach. Yet John Bodnar, Virginia Yans-McLaughlin, and Lawrence Levine are the only ones to use such interaction as an organizing principle, and, as I have noted, the emphasis still remains on continuity.[39] Perhaps, then, it is

---

39. See, for example, Camarillo, *Chicanos,* 187–91; Griswold del Castillo, *Los Angeles Barrio,* 171–72; Modell, *Economics and Politics of Racial Accommodation,* passim; Pleck, *Black Migration,* 77ff., 118; Bodnar, *Immigration and Industrialization,* passim; Yans-

time to begin to analyze the ethnic map of America by looking at individuals instead of at groups. Possibly drawing on the underdeveloped insights of Milton Gordon, Arthur Mann has provided a useful typology of individual responses to ethnic identity.[40]

The first group Mann calls the "total identifiers," who live out their lives within the ethnic group. They are the classic cultural pluralists. They eat with, live with, worship with, and marry their own kind. At present, total identifiers are a fraction of the population, but their extent at various times in the past is subject to debate. Perhaps Mexican Americans, for whom immigration is a continuing process and the homeland so close, provide the closest current approximation for the kind of cultural identity so many of the social historians have found in previous generations of immigrants.

"Partial identifiers" are those who regard ethnic attachment as important, but not all-inclusive. Milton Gordon would see them as having undergone acculturation, but resisted structural assimilation by keeping alive contacts at the primary group level, whether with respect to associational, religious, and recreational activities, or with marriage partners.

"Disaffiliates" grew up in an ethnic or ethno-religious environment, but have chosen to deviate. They are often found in the world of academia, the news media, and show business. Most can be termed intellectuals who form a separate group with their own values, rituals, dress, heroes, fears, and ways of bringing up children. Unlike the partial or total identifiers, however, the disaffiliates are not tied by a common ancestry. More of a factor than in earlier years, their number figures to increase with the expansion of the college-educated population.

"Hybrids" are those of mixed ancestry unable to identify themselves as a single stock. The product of much intermarriage, they are the children of the melting pot. Perhaps they are like the college professor who took the columnist Abigail Van Buren to task for saying that a letter-writer's children were one-quarter Italian. "Abby," wrote Professor Joseph V. Ellis, "for nearly fifty years I have tried to get people to see themselves as Americans, not hyphenates. There is no such thing as 'Italian blood,' one-quarter or otherwise. . . . So let's begin to see people as people, four quarters' worth all the time."[41]

I think that Mann's model is appropriate, as long as we remember that individ-

---

McLaughlin, *Family and Community,* passim; Levine, *Black Culture and Black Consciousness,* passim. For divisions among blacks, see also my *Race Relations in the Urban South,* especially parts 1 and 2.

40. Mann, *One and the Many,* chapter 8.

41. Letter of Joseph V. Ellis to "Dear Abby," *Albuquerque Journal,* January 26, 1982, A-8. Internal evidence suggests that Ellis is a hybrid, though the possibility remains that he might in fact be a disaffiliate.

uals can move between categories over the course of their lives, because it removes cultural pluralism as the norm, deviations from which merit rebuke. Among many people today, maintaining the values, language, and behavior of one's ethnic group is as critical as the melting pot was for the Founding Fathers or as Anglo-conformity was for the immigration restrictionists. Thus, Joel Williamson, in an examination of miscegenation and mulattoes in the United States, expresses concern, though he himself is white, that "the integrity of Negro life is . . . going to be damaged by the large numbers of talented Negroes being recruited into the great white way, where they will strive, consciously and unconsciously, to leave their blackness behind and to gain full membership in the sterile, materialistic club of middle-class America." Similarly, Michael Novak, in celebrating the "unmeltable ethnics," is dismayed by those who surrendered their heritage.[42]

I do not mean to condemn cultural pluralism. In fact, I think that cultural pluralism marks an advance over previous theories of assimilation both as a descriptive and as a prescriptive tool, though I would personally lean in the direction of its expression through the partial-identifier mode. Still, the issue of deviation is most important, especially for blacks, Hispanics, and Indians. It is crucial to remember that you cannot say blacks, Hispanics, or Indians are not like other ethnic groups, since other ethnic groups are not like each other and never were. Like other Americans, therefore, individual Negroes, Hispanics, and Indians have the right to choose whether they want to be total identifiers, partial identifiers, or disaffiliates, or whether they want to contribute to the ranks of hybrids. Neither the 100 percent Americans nor the ethnic purists deserve automatic praise or condemnation.

In the end, a critical matter for debate will be whose responsibility it is to further ethnic identification and what form that identification should take. Is it the job of the family and the ethnic community, or is it the responsibility of the public sector, through its schools, museums, preservation societies, and governments? And when does the desire of one group to perpetuate its way of life infringe on the opportunities sought by other groups for advancement? Historians have begun to pay more systematic attention to the effects and nature of intergroup ethnic conflict—certainly a subject worthy of greater study for both the present and the past.[43]

42. Williamson, *New People: Miscegenation and Mulattoes in the United States* (New York: Free Press, 1980), 194; Novak, *The Rise of the Unmeltable Ethnics* (New York: Macmillan, 1972).

43. See, for example, Ronald H. Bayor, *Neighbors in Conflict: The Irish, Germans, Jews, and Italians of New York City, 1929–1941* (Baltimore: Johns Hopkins University Press, 1978); Bodnar, Simon, and Weber, *Lives of Their Own;* Bodnar, *Immigration and*

I think that, in this regard, John Higham's concept of a system of "pluralistic integration" provides some guidelines. Such a system would "uphold the validity of a common culture, to which all individuals have access, while sustaining the efforts of minorities to preserve and enhance their own integrity." The key to such a dual commitment would be the distinction between "nuclei" and "boundaries." Boundaries would be understood to be permeable; ethnic nuclei would be respected as enduring centers of social action. Thus, "Both integration and ethnic cohesion are recognized as worthy goals, which different individuals will accept in different degrees." It is Higham's hope that such a system, which is already partly in place, "implies that invigoration of the nuclei can relieve the defense of ethnic boundaries."[44]

The problem is that it will not always be self-evident where the nucleus ends and the boundaries begin; but, of course, this gets at the whole issue of American nationality or identity and the rights of minorities. It is a problem that we tend to forget confronts all countries. Russia and Canada are only two examples. The problem is particularly great in a nation of immigrants such as ours. After all, as Arthur Mann and John Higham remind us, how much diversity can you encourage without undermining the very foundations of national unity and identity? This is as yet a question that the new social historians in their celebration of diversity have not asked about our ethnic and racial past.

Industrialization.
44. *Send These to Me,* 242–46, quotations on 242, 246.

Writing Jewish Community History

The broad outlines of the American Jewish experience are well known. From the colonial period down to the early nineteenth century, Sephardic and the first wave of German Jews contributed to the growth of the nation while prospering and gaining the acceptance of other Americans. Then came a second wave of German Jews who likewise prospered and secured the ascendancy of Reform Judaism. At the end of the nineteenth and the beginning of the twentieth century, the descendants of the earlier groups were overwhelmed by the massive influx of East European Jews who had lower economic and social status and more Orthodox religious beliefs than the resident Jewish population. The struggle between the Eastern Europeans and their predecessors dominated local and national Jewish affairs in the early twentieth century, but as the years passed the two groups merged into a relatively unified Jewish community as a result of the accelerating economic success of the newcomers and a common identification with the new state of Israel. Most of the details for this story have come from the major areas of Jewish settlement—New York, Boston, Philadelphia, and other large cities. In recent years, however, several studies of medium-sized Jewish communities outside the East have appeared, including Steven Hertzberg's *Strangers within the Gate City: The Jews of Atlanta, 1845–1915* and Mark H. Elovitz's *A Century of Jewish Life in Dixie: The Birmingham Experience.* Marc Lee Raphael's *Jews and Judaism in a Midwestern Community: Columbus, Ohio, 1840–1975* and Myron Berman's *Richmond's Jewry, 1769–1976: Shabbat in Shockoe* are part of this trend and are worth considering not only because of what they have to say about their respective communities, but also because they represent important differences in approach toward the chronicling of local

Jewish history and raise significant questions about the future direction of Jewish community studies.[1]

Myron Berman's study was funded by a grant from the Jewish Community Federation of Richmond and "authorized" by the city's conservative Jewish congregation, Temple Beth-El, of which Berman is the rabbi. Like Rabbi Elovitz of Birmingham's Temple Beth El, Berman holds a Ph.D. in history; unlike Elovitz, his work is not a revised Ph.D. dissertation, though it has a similar orientation. Berman maintains that his book "examines the gamut of Jewish history in Richmond from the arrival of its first Israelites in the colonial era to the outbreak of the Yom Kippur War."[2] Yet this claim is misleading, for Berman's approach causes him to focus on only part of the Jewish community and to emphasize certain periods at the expense of others. Like most traditional work in the field of local Jewish history and, I might add, in the case of other ethnic groups as well, Rabbi Berman's account concentrates on the positive aspects of the community's elite and gives relatively little space to recent developments. It devotes one hundred pages of its ten chronologically arranged chapters to the years before the beginning of large-scale Ashkenazic immigration in 1841, but only a total of fifty pages to the years since 1931, and only nine of those to the post-1956 period.

To a large extent, Berman is the prisoner of his sources. He relies heavily on memoirs, private papers, synagogue and temple records, interviews with prominent Jews, newspapers, and unpublished and published secondary sources, all of which magnify the role of the leading Jewish families—but his anecdotal style and desire to stress Richmond Jewry's contribution to the city's growth also lead him in the same direction. The result is a chatty, often lively account of changes in the nature of Jewish leadership and attitudes. It supplants Herbert T. Ezekiel and Gaston Lichtenstein, *The History of the Jews of Richmond from 1789–1917,*[3] but fails to deal thoroughly with the "gamut of Jewish history" in the city.

In 1790, only New York, Charleston, and Philadelphia had more Jews than the one hundred in Richmond, and the city's Beth Shalome congregation was the sixth oldest in the country. As elsewhere, the non-Sephardic settlers were in the majority, but the Sephardic tone of worship was followed well into the nineteenth

1. Hertzberg, *Strangers within the Gate City: The Jews of Atlanta, 1845–1915* (Philadelphia: The Jewish Publication Society of America, 1978); Elovitz, *A Century of Jewish Life in Dixie: The Birmingham Experience* (University: University of Alabama Press, 1974); Raphael, *Jews and Judaism in a Midwestern Community: Columbus, Ohio, 1840–1975* (Columbus: Ohio Historical Society, 1979); Berman, *Richmond's Jewry, 1769–1976: Shabbat in Shockoe* (Charlottesville: University Press of Virginia, 1979).

2. *Richmond's Jewry,* xix.

3. *The History of the Jews of Richmond from 1769 to 1917* (Richmond: privately published, 1917).

century. The early Richmond Jews were successful merchants, and the initial division within the Jewish community was not so much a gap between the Ashkenazim and Sephardim as "a chasm between colonial Jewry and the more recent immigrants." Many of the Jews married Gentiles and had close contacts with the city's elite. Berman raises the important question as to whether assimilation and the lack of anti-Semitism were due to the Jews' "low profile or the frontier nature of Southern society that dissolved religioethnic differences"; but as so often occurs in the book, he fails to seek an answer.[4] Instead he chronicles the activities, especially the marriages and business ventures, of the interrelated Myers, Marx, Mordecai, and Hayes families—unfortunately without the aid of genealogy charts, which would have made the discussion easier to follow.

In the middle of the nineteenth century, the city experienced an influx of German Jews, the majority of whom were from Bavaria. They founded their own social and fraternal societies and, in 1841, Beth Ahabah synagogue. A few years later, Polish Jews founded Kenesseth Israel, which became "the" Orthodox synagogue as Beth Shalome's Sephardic observance lost favor. Berman notes that the highly assimilated Richmond Jews responded very much as did other southerners to the issue of slavery and the outbreak of the Civil War. In the immediate postwar years the community moved gradually in the direction of Reform, and B'nai B'rith and assorted social and philanthropic societies were established. Jewish leaders maintained a high profile in business and civic affairs, with William Lovenstein serving in the state legislature for almost three decades and the Thalhimer brothers building the major department store. Thus the mantle of leadership passed from the pioneer families to members of the German second wave. Berman is at his best discussing the thought and activities of Reform rabbi Edward N. Calisch, who served Beth Ahabah for fifty-four years beginning in 1891. Americanization and the public image of Jews became the watchwords of Calisch's career as he transformed his temple from a conservative progressive one into the epitome of Classical Reform.

Richmond's assimilated elite provided a receptive audience for Calisch's message; it was less well received by the East Europeans who sought to cling to their traditional faith and rituals by joining Kenesseth Israel or the new synagogue of the Russian Jews, Sir Moses Montefiore. Berman treats the familiar sources of German-Russian conflict—disagreements over ritual, philanthropic matters, and support for Zionism—but does so within the context of Richmond's traditional division between older residents and newcomers. By 1930, the city's fifty-three

---

4. *Richmond's Jewry,* 63, 98.

hundred Jews constituted 3 percent of the population, and in subsequent years the appearance of new synagogues and the mergers of old ones gave Richmond vibrant examples of Reform, Conservative, and Modern Orthodox Jewry. Meanwhile Jewish community institutions expanded to include an old-age home, Jewish Center, Richmond Community Council, and in 1965, a Hebrew Day School. By the 1970s there were about ten thousand Jews, thanks in part to immigration from the North and abroad. Interest in Conservative practice increased to the point where Berman's temple is now the city's largest. And whether socially or in civic affairs, the scions of Eastern European families were fully integrated into the previously German-Sephardic leadership. In short, "The contemporary Jewish community has finally attained a feeling of unity, which had existed in the post-Revolutionary period also."[5]

Rabbi Berman's account will certainly be well received by the local Jewish community. Both recent and longtime residents will delight in his anecdotes and find the narrative useful in placing themselves within the history of Richmond Jewry. And non-Jews will find a helpful glossary of Jewish terms— including *Hanukkah, gefilte fish,* and *kosher.* Scholars will also find useful material here. But maps would have made it easier to follow the peregrinations of the individual congregations and would have clarified the location of successive Jewish neighborhoods. Historians will also lament some of the inconsequential chronicling and anecdotes and, above all, will regret the author's failure to treat the mass of East European Jews, or for that matter, the "common folk" in general.

Thus readers will find evidence for Professor Raphael's assertion that "studies of nineteenth-and twentieth-century American Jewish communities represent an overemphasis on elites and elite sources." In support of this charge, Raphael notes that the Columbus *Jewish Chronicle* in 1918 recorded the activities of only 9 percent of the city's Jews, and ignored more than 95 percent of the Russian Jewish immigrants. The same bias was evident in B'nai B'rith lodge and synagogue minutes, city and county histories, and the general as well as Anglo-Jewish press—the same sources Berman relies upon for his study of Richmond Jewry. How then is one to get at the "real" history of Columbus Jews? According to Raphael, we need to use the sources of the new urban and ethnic history— federal and state census schedules, passenger ship manifests, naturalization records, voting lists, tax returns, divorce registers, wills, marriage records, city directories, and school files. Also invaluable are more broadly based interviews and the use of survey research techniques and perspectives drawn from the other

5. Ibid., 330.

social sciences. Only through such means can we get at the "lives of the elite *and* the less articulate segments of society."[6]

Berman's work resembles Elovitz's. Raphael's approach, on the other hand, parallels that of Hertzberg, whose Atlanta study uses the same kind of methodology and an analytical rather than narrative framework. Yet Raphael's book is not a revised dissertation, like Hertzberg's; like Berman's, it reflects a Jewish community's desire to have a history of itself. Supported by the Ohio Historical Society, Columbus Jewish Federation, and the Ohio State University, the advisory board of the Columbus Jewish History Project commissioned Raphael, an associate professor of history at Ohio State, to write the history. In many respects, therefore, the book is a hybrid; it contains elements of a celebratory chronicle common to the work of Berman and Elovitz, but shares Hertzberg's interest in the questions and techniques of the new urban and ethnic history. Its theme is clearly expressed and thoroughly compatible with Berman's more implicit argument: "Like Jews everywhere in America, Columbus Jewry revealed a passion for entering American middle-class life—the 'middle' of the middle-class—created and joined attractive looking synagogues, and enjoyed abundant amounts of leisure time, travel, and family activity, as well as club and organizational membership. Columbus Jews have fully completed the process of embourgeoisement in America."[7]

Raphael divides his book into four parts: The Early Years, 1840–1880; Years of Growth, 1881–1925; Defining the Community, 1926–1950; and The Postwar Community, 1951–1975. There is also an interesting appendix on the problems and promise of oral history. An introduction to each part assays the development of Columbus, thus reflecting Raphael's desire to integrate community and Jewish history. Each section surveys the Jewish population's composition and its secular and religious activities and attitudes. Though there is more emphasis on the pre-1926 period, the last two parts comprise more than 40 percent of the book. Whereas Berman begins each chapter with an anecdote concerning a member of the elite, Raphael's chapters open with a conceptually oriented discussion of the issue to be considered. Not surprisingly, while the first photograph in Berman's book depicts a member of the Jewish elite, in Raphael's study it is of the store of a leading Jew.

Despite the differences in organization and approach, the story Raphael tells is quite similar to the one Berman relates. Columbus did not have a colonial past, however, so its initial Jewish elite consisted of members of that second wave of German immigrants who enjoyed remarkable success as merchants (especially in

6. *Jews and Judaism,* 1, 2 (italics added).
7. Ibid., 4.

the clothing business) between 1840 and 1880. Raphael perceptively traces their reasons for coming to the United States in general and Columbus in particular, accounts for their economic success, analyzes their family structure, looks at their neighborhoods, and charts their institution building, bringing both the leaders and masses into sharp focus. Synagogues, B'nai B'rith lodges, and women's clubs appear in great profusion. Raphael follows the same approach in analyzing the East European Jews while emphasizing the economic, social, and religious differences that separated them from the more prosperous and Reform-oriented German Jews. Russian Jews founded Agudas Achim Synagogue, and Hungarians established Tifereth Israel rather than associate with the dominant B'nai Israel Reform congregation. But thanks to a firm base in peddling, the new immigrants were soon able to improve themselves financially, and the years 1880 to 1925 "were a replay of an earlier period of Jewish immigrant history."[8] Only now the success stories featured names like Gilbert, Schottenstein, and Kobacker rather than Lazarus or Gundersheimer. And though the Reform German Jews continued to dominate community institutions, the two groups supported in varying degrees a plethora of organizations that included the Hillel at Ohio State, the Schonthal Center settlement house, Columbus Hebrew School, and the Federated Jewish Charities. Between 1930 and 1950 the city's Jewish population grew from seven thousand to around nine thousand. The increasingly assimilated and affluent community founded new organizations such as the Jewish Center (as in Richmond, used by both Jews and non-Jews), and Reform, Conservative, and Orthodox alike became committed to the creation and preservation of Israel.

In many ways the concluding section is the most useful and perhaps most controversial in the book. Raphael uses a sixty-question survey sent to six hundred of the more than nine thousand adult members of the Jewish community in 1975. Almost five hundred were returned. The responses reveal a primarily American-born community, liberal Democratic in political affiliation (despite a median income higher than in any other Jewish community ever surveyed and well above the national average), and likely to choose its friends and acquaintances from among other Jews. Unlike most other Jewish communities, the percentage of Orthodox affiliates, 35 percent, was high compared to 35 percent for Reform and 30 percent for Conservative. Raphael, nevertheless, believes the Orthodox strength will diminish, since three-fifths of the affiliates were over fifty-five years old. Despite a good deal of conflicting evidence, he concludes that, also unlike other Jewish communities, the pattern of religious beliefs was not converging into a nearly uniform observance. The survey and Raphael's own observations reveal a well-developed and well-supported array of Jewish institu-

8. Ibid., 167–68.

tions. Though much of the philanthropy centers around support for Israel, there has been in recent years a greater appreciation of the need to care for the less fortunate among Columbus's Jews. The author is especially good at discussing patterns in fund-raising and charity work, since Jewish philanthropy had been the subject of his Ph.D. dissertation. Columbus Jews have thus, in the view of Raphael, achieved a notable compromise between the middle American and traditional Jewish life-style: "Growing up Jewish and American in hospitable Columbus, Ohio was a pleasant experience."[9]

Raphael has produced a more comprehensive and informative study of his community than has Berman, especially for the years since the early twentieth century. The questions he asks and his superior organizational framework are relevant here, as are his broader range of documentation and innovative presentation. Scattered throughout the text and copious notes are maps and numerous charts and tables that contain valuable information on a variety of subjects, including housing patterns, fund-raising profiles, community leaders, economic mobility and even school records. Such material is totally missing from Berman's book, which uses illustrative matter more as decorative elements than as documentation. Occasionally, however, the line between the old social history and the new, or between the community study as new urban history and as filiopietistic chronicle, is blurred, as when Raphael presents exam questions given to seniors at Columbus High in 1880, charts the location of individual Jews in the cemetery, lists World War II Jewish servicemen killed or missing in action, and includes batting averages of Sunday Morning League baseball players in 1947. No doubt members of the Columbus Jewish community will enjoy these bits of trivia (though perhaps not M. Furman, whose .088 batting average is now immortalized), but they clash with the more scholarly objectives that set the tone for the volume.

It is this clash between the values of the new ethnic history and the old that raises questions about the future of Jewish community studies. Traditionally, community studies of ethnic groups written by group members have been celebratory, a display of individual and group success that proclaims to the members and the rest of society that they have arrived and contributed to the growth of the entire city and nation. Though better written and more thoughtful than most books of this type, Berman's work unabashedly belongs to the genre. Raphael's book, however, is clearly a transitional work, as the author has one foot in the Columbus Jewish community and the other in the academic world. Obviously there is still room for the traditional approach, yet we need to be aware of its limitations. Neither Berman nor Raphael devote much attention to the faults of

9. Ibid., 432.

the Jewish community or its leadership. Raphael is better here, in noting the lack of emphasis on Jewish education and the neglect of poor Jews, but even he presents a basically laudatory account. Both authors, for example, found little anti-Semitism in their respective cities (an assessment open to debate), but say nothing of possible prejudice by Jews against others, an especially important consideration in a southern city like Richmond. Nor is this surprising, as both works were financed by the Jewish community, which is the object of study. Berman seems oblivious to this potential conflict of interest, while Raphael assures us that he enjoyed "absolute scholarly independence." Yet when he comes to the modern period, Raphael explains: "I have consciously refrained from writing about living persons—especially those in positions of leadership—and from narrating the history of communal agencies, organizations, and religious institutions in the postwar decades." In part this is because of the abundance of sources, but in addition "the roles of many leaders and resolutions of many issues are so passionately felt in the community that interpreting them would have proven extremely sensitive."[10] This attitude is understandable in the old booster history, but not in the work of a self-proclaimed devotee of the new urban and ethnic history.

But more is involved than how community studies are funded. There is also the problem of whether or not scholars should be spending their time writing histories of individual Jewish communities from their founding to the present. After all, these studies simply fill in the details for an overall picture that already seems clear. The survey approach is not likely to turn up information that will be of interest to anyone but local residents. It is worth noting that the most significant treatments of local Jewish communities have taken a shorter time period and explored it in depth through a conceptual framework. I am thinking in particular of the work of Moses Rischin and Arthur Goren, as well as Hertzberg.[11] By identifying critical issues and treating them intensively, such scholars are more likely to enrich our understanding of the Jewish experience than by doing synoptic histories that inevitably, even when a scholar is as skilled and thorough as Raphael, tend to confirm what we already knew, with only the names changed to identify the successful. Raphael whets our appetite for the kind of studies we really need. What is required are examinations of individual congregations that stress the way they actually functioned, accounts of the less well off Jews and the reasons for their failure to succeed, analyses of the Orthodox Jews who withstood the assimilationist trend, and more detailed investigations of

10. Ibid., ix, 356.
11. Rischin, *The Promised City: New York's Jews, 1870–1914* (Cambridge: Harvard University Press, 1962); Goren, *New York Jews and the Quest for Community: The Kehillah Experiment, 1908–1922* (New York: Columbia University Press, 1970).

divisions within the community. We also need more comparative studies of Jews and other ethnic groups in a single city of the type Ronald Bayor and Thomas Kessner have given us, and we should begin to produce the kind of interurban study of different Jewish communities John Briggs has recently done for the Italians.[12] In the matter of southern Jews, for example, it would be valuable to know how different Jewish communities reacted to the civil rights movement and what accounted for similar or different responses.

It is also worth asking whether or not Jewish community history can really come of age as long as it is the sole province of Jews, be they scholars, rabbis, or laymen. After all, several of the best studies of other urban ethnic communities have been written by Jews;[13] yet it is difficult to think of an important study of a single Jewish community by a black, an Irishman, or any other non-Jew. This means a loss of insight that an outsider can bring. There is, of course, little that Jews can do about this phenomenon; but until American Jewish history is seen as fair game for Gentiles and Jews alike, we can start to ask more probing and perhaps more painful questions about our interaction with American society. Surely there is more to that experience than smooth assimilation, rapid economic progress, and noble behavior toward ourselves and others. By all means, we can emphasize those factors when present, but not at the expense of the more rich and complex experience that is often missing from even the best of such history.

12. Bayor, *Neighbors in Conflict: The Irish, Germans, Jews, and Italians of New York City, 1929–1941* (Baltimore: Johns Hopkins University Press, 1978); Kessner, *The Golden Door: Italian and Jewish Immigrant Mobility in New York City, 1880–1915* (New York: Oxford University Press, 1977); Briggs, *An Italian Passage: Immigrants to Three American Cities, 1890–1930* (New Haven: Yale University Press, 1978).

13. See, for example, David M. Katzman, *Before the Ghetto: Black Detroit in the Nineteenth Century* (Urbana: University of Illinois Press, 1973); Gilbert Osofsky, *Harlem, The Making of a Ghetto: Negro New York, 1890–1930* (New York: Harper and Row, 1966); Allan H. Spear, *Black Chicago: The Making of A Negro Ghetto, 1890–1920* (Chicago: University of Chicago Press, 1967); Oscar Handlin, *Boston's Immigrants, 1790–1880: A Study in Acculturation,* 2d ed. (Cambridge: Harvard University Press, 1968).

Nativism, Bigotry, and Anti-Semitism in the South

The following essay originated in a serendipitous phone call from the head of public programs at the Valentine Museum in Richmond, Virginia. She asked me to give a lecture in November 1986 on "Nativism and Bigotry" as part of a series of lectures held in conjunction with the Valentine's new exhibit on the history of Richmond Jewry. I initially thought of turning down the invitation because it was outside my area of expertise, but I began to wonder what, in fact, I thought about the treatment of Jews in the South as compared to elsewhere in the country. The reception from an enthusiastic but small audience at Congregation Beth Ahabah encouraged me to expand and restructure the talk and submit it for publication. As is true in the case of the other essays reprinted in this collection that originated in oral presentation, the written version retains much of my initial conversational tone.

The December 1986 issue of *American Jewish History* reflected the growing interest in the study of American anti-Semitism.[1] There are many reasons for this new attention to a neglected topic. Some of the interest has to do with the greater sophistication of American Jewish history, which has begun to transcend its filio-pietistic origins and celebration of the openness of American society. There is also the increasing awareness among historians of the similarities and differ-

---

1. See, for example, John Higham, *Send These to Me: Jews and Other Immigrants in Urban America* (New York: Atheneum, 1975); David A. Gerber, ed., *Anti-Semitism in American History* (Urbana: University of Illinois Press, 1986); Leonard Dinnerstein, *Uneasy at Home: Anti-Semitism and the American Jewish Experience* (New York: Columbia University Press, 1987). Among still useful older works are Carey McWilliams, *A Mask for Privilege: Anti-Semitism in America* (Boston: Little Brown and Company, 1949) and Leonard Dinnerstein, ed., *Anti-Semitism in the United States* (New York: Holt, Rinehart and Winston, 1971).

ences between the experiences of Jewish and non-Jewish immigrants. Finally, Jews, in general, have become more sensitive to this issue in recent years due to the alleged rise of anti-Semitism among blacks. Yet while covering a wide range of subjects, the *AJH*'s special issue also represents a current trend by neglecting the study of anti-Semitism in the South.[2]

Any study of southern anti-Semitism would also have to assess the impact of bigotry and nativism in general. For some people, of course, this would be a straightforward subject. On the one hand, conservatives might simply dismiss any evidence to the contrary and proclaim the absence of discrimination in the land of freedom, equality, and opportunity. Radicals, on the other hand, would condemn the entire nation and especially the South for a long history of prejudice, racism, and oppression directed against all outsiders. However, since I am a liberal, an academic, and a Jew, nothing is ever simple. In fact, this is truly a complicated subject because it relies so much on one's frame of reference. That is, questions about bigotry, nativism, and anti-Semitism have meaning only in terms of "compared to what?"

This article, therefore, will briefly chronicle the history of nativism, bigotry, and anti-Semitism in the nation as a whole and then assess the degree to which the South shared in this national pattern of behavior and examine the reasons for the similarities and differences. I make no claim to new research in primary sources. Instead I have drawn primarily on a number of articles, most of them conveniently gathered in a few anthologies, and the handful of monographs that consider aspects of southern Judaism. Several of these secondary sources have been only recently published and have not been included in previous analyses of anti-Semitism. More importantly, in using these and other sources, I have often imposed my own perspective. Thus, in accounting for the degree of southern anti-Semitism, I will emphasize a previously unrecognized blend of structural and nonstructural factors that centers on the critical role of Jewish southerners' acceptance of racial discrimination and a special set of historical circumstances that made southern Jews different from both other Jews and other southerners.

Before doing so, however, it is necessary to make clear my basic point of

2. I have referred to the "alleged rise" of anti-Semitism among blacks because it is not clear to me, despite extensive publicity, just how widespread or deep-seated that anti-Semitism is, or how different it might be from less visible past beliefs. For rare examples of interest in southern anti-Semitism, see some of the essays in *American Jewish Historical Quarterly* 62 (March 1973), which is a special issue devoted to "Jews in the South" and others in two collections of essays: Leonard Dinnerstein and Mary Dale Palsson, eds., *Jews in the South* (Baton Rouge: Louisiana State University Press, 1973) and Nathan M. Kaganoff and Melvin I. Urofsky, eds. *Turn to the South: Essays on Southern Jewry* (Charlottesville: University Press of Virginia, 1979).

departure. Whatever our assessment of the nature and extent of anti-Semitism in the nation and region, the fact is that American anti-Semitism pales next to that practiced elsewhere, whether in the past or present. Here we will find no equivalent of Russia's settlement laws, pogroms, Doctor's Purge, or bars against emigration; France's Dreyfus Case; Spain's Inquisition; or England's Parliamentary religious test; to say nothing of the Nazi horror or the rich Germanic intellectual anti-Semitism that nurtured it. This, of course, does not lessen the suffering of the victims of anti-Semitism in America, but it does enable us to keep that suffering within the proper perspective.

To begin with, it is important to remember that America historically has had the most generous emigration and immigration policy in the world. Throughout most of our history people have been free to enter and leave this country in unprecedented fashion. Even the late-eighteenth-century Alien and Sedition Acts and the mid-nineteenth-century Know-Nothing movement did not challenge our tradition of unrestricted immigration, and with the exception of Chinese and Japanese exclusion in the late nineteenth and early twentieth centuries, that policy remained in force until the institution of quotas aimed primarily at southern and eastern European immigrants in the 1920s.

Yet despite the image symbolized by the Statue of Liberty of America as a refuge for the world's tired and poor, Americans have always been ambivalent about being a Nation of Immigrants. The negative reaction to recent Asian, Mexican, Haitian, and Cuban migration is nothing new. Significant numbers of Americans reacted the same way to the influx of the Irish in the 1840s and 1850s and to Jews and Italians and other so-called New Immigrants in the late nineteenth and early twentieth centuries. American nativism and bigotry toward such outsiders or aliens has flourished especially during times of crisis, in which old-line Americans felt threatened by rapid economic and social change linked to industrialization and urbanization. The three most significant eras for such concerns were the 1840s and 1850s, 1880s and 1890s, and the 1920s. During all of these periods the rural, capitalist, democratic, and Anglo-Protestant values upon which the nation was allegedly founded were seen as under attack. As a result of the defensive nationalism we call nativism, immigrants were viewed sometimes as threatening because of their allegedly radical ideas, at other times because of different religious values, and at still other times for alleged racial differences. At all times, however, both justified and unjustified economic fears, whether from people at the top, middle, or bottom of society, magnified the nature of the alien threat.[3]

3. The work of John Higham remains the best introduction to the history of nativism in America. See especially his *Strangers in the Land: Patterns of American Nativism 1860–1925* (1955; paperback reprint; New York: Atheneum, 1963) and *Send These to Me*.

Sometimes Jews were a primary target of this nativism, at other times only secondary targets, and at still other times not singled out but victims of the general nativist thrust. In the 1850s, for example, Irish Catholics were the chief enemies of the Know-Nothings, who in New York actually ran a Jewish candidate for governor. Jews, however, were clearly a prime target of the nativists during the restrictionist movement of the early twentieth century.

Indeed, it would seem that until the late nineteenth century this country was remarkably free, at least relatively, of anti-Semitism. It is true as Martin Borden has noted in *Jews, Turks, and Infidels* that unlike the federal Constitution, almost all of the original state constitutions required officeholders to affirm their beliefs in Protestantism or Christianity, and that numerous efforts were made to amend the Constitution to indicate that the U.S. was a Christian nation. Yet the officeholding provisions for the most part were soon eliminated or not enforced, and the Christian-nation efforts failed. Similarly, Rabbi Bertram Wallace Korn was correct to note the marked increase in anti-Semitism during the Civil War aimed at alleged Jewish profiteering, capped by General Grant's infamous but widely supported 1863 order expelling all Jews "as a class" from the Department of the Tennessee within twenty-four hours.[4] But that proved to be a temporary outbreak and the birth of modern, systematic anti-Semitism in this country clearly dates from the late nineteenth century.

Three groups were in the forefront of this wave of modern anti-Semitism: Northeastern and primarily New England intellectuals, such as Henry and Brooks Adams; southern and midwestern rural radicals; and urban masses, themselves often of immigrant backgrounds. This anti-Semitism took primarily four forms: verbal or written criticisms of Jews that included the dissemination of vicious stereotypes; calls for laws restricting Jewish immigration or influence; violence against individual Jews; and de facto social and economic discrimination.[5]

It is important to note here, as historian John Higham reminds us, that anti-Semitic statements or beliefs did not necessarily result in anti-Semitic actions, and that the range of those actions could vary. In any event the years from 1880 to 1930 brought a broad-range attack on Jews that included, in addition to immigration restriction, harangues by New England intellectuals and Populist speakers; social discrimination, which included exclusion of Jews from resorts where they had previously enjoyed unrestricted access; the opening of restricted country clubs and residential districts; the establishment of quotas at the nation's major universities; economic discrimination by leading law firms and large cor-

4. Borden, *Jews, Turks, and Infidels* (Chapel Hill: University of North Carolina Press, 1984), 11–52, 58–74; Korn, "American Judaeophobia: Confederate Version," in *Jews in the South,* ed. Dinnerstein and Palsson, 153–69.
5. Higham, *Send These to Me,* chapters 7–8.

porations; and even frequent physical harassment, such as the attack of Irish workers and police on the funeral procession of Rabbi Jacob Joseph in New York City in 1902.[6]

Given this general pattern in the nation's response to its Jewish citizens, what can we say about the extent to which the South shared in this experience?

On the one hand, there is much support for the contention that while no worse than the rest of the country, the South at the least did not depart from the national pattern. After all, with the exception of Jefferson's Virginia (thanks to the Statute on Religious Liberty), all the original southern states joined their northern counterparts in having religious tests for voting or state officeholding that excluded Jews.[7] Several strongly resisted removing those restrictions, including North Carolina, which didn't do so until enactment of the Radical Republican constitution during Reconstruction in 1868. And even in Jefferson's Virginia, it took seven years to approve the Statute on Religious Liberty, and it was at his university that America's first Jewish professor, the English mathematician James Joseph Sylvester, was hounded out of his position in 1842, less than five months after his appointment. A physical assault by two anti-Semitic students was the direct cause of his departure, but further hastening it was a hostile environment in which the organ of the Presbyterian church could state, "The great body of people in this Commonwealth are by professions Christians and not heathen, nor musselmen, nor Jews, nor Atheists, nor Infidels. They are also Protestants and not Papists." As such, the paper continued, they had the right to require their professors to be adherents to a "pure morality based upon Christian principles," though, it added in a nice touch, "without fanaticism." After Sylvester's departure no foreign scholar was appointed for the remainder of the century, thus undermining Jefferson's dream for a cosmopolitan university, expressed in the composition of the first faculty, which included four Britons, one German, three southerners, and only one native of Virginia.[8]

Such insular thinking was reflected on a regionwide basis during the Civil War. As Rabbi Korn notes, southerners joined their northern counterparts in their suspicion and condemnation of Jews for their alleged profiteering, corruption, and disloyalty, an antagonism that focused in the South on the powerful Confederate cabinet member Judah P. Benjamin of Louisiana and led, among other things, to the expulsion of German Jews from Thomasville, Georgia, in 1862.

---

6. Ibid., chapters 7–9. On the funeral riot, see also Leonard Dinnerstein, "The Funeral of Rabbi Jacob Joseph," in *Anti-Semitism in American History,* ed. Gerber, 275–301.

7. Borden, *Jews, Turks and Infidels,* 36–50.

8. Ibid., 13–15; Lewis S. Feuer, "America's First Jewish Professor: James Joseph Sylvester at the University of Virginia," *American Jewish Archives* 36 (November 1984): 152–201, quote 156.

Thus one Jew could write to the *Richmond Sentinel* in 1864: "I have marked with sorrow and dismay the growing propensity in the Confederacy to denounce the Jew on all occasions and in all places. The press, the pulpit, and grave legislators, who have the destiny of a nation committed to their charge, all unite in this unholy and unjust denunciation."[9]

As elsewhere, anti-Semitism diminished with the end of the war, but the economic crisis of the late nineteenth century led many southern farmers to focus on international Jewish bankers and northern Jews as scapegoats for their problems and helped launch the Populist movement. Former Populists like Tom Watson of Georgia carried such thinking into the twentieth century, as he railed against Jews as editor of the ironically named *Jeffersonian* and eventually as a United States senator. And his words could lead to deeds, as in his stirring up passions that led in 1915 to the most dramatic expression of southern anti-Semitic feeling—the lynching for the murder of little Mary Phagan of northern-born pencil factory superintendent Leo Frank near Atlanta. Typically, Watson defended the lynching by claiming, "All over this broad land there are millions of good people, not duped by Jew money, and lies, that enthusiastically greet the triumph of law in Georgia."[10]

Meanwhile southern resorts and country clubs joined their northern counterparts in excluding Jews, leading to the profusion of Jewish clubs and resorts in the South. As late as the 1870s, when Richmond's most fashionable club, the Westmoreland, was organized, membership included several Jews, and the club once elected a Jewish president. Yet one study published in 1949 revealed that not only did the Westmoreland now exclude Jews, but so too did the Commonwealth Club, Country Club of Virginia, the Hermitage Country Club, the Junior League, and the most fashionable women's groups. It is not clear when this shift occurred, but it was likely around the turn of the century, as witnessed by the fact that the Richmond YMCA still accepted Jews as members in 1910 but not as lodgers.[11] The YMCA's policy might have reflected more concern about visiting

9. Korn, "American Judaeophobia," passim, quote 143.

10. C. Vann Woodward, *Tom Watson: Agrarian Rebel* (New York: The Macmillan Company, 1938), 434–49, quote 445; Leonard Dinnerstein, *The Leo Frank Case* (New York: Columbia University Press, 1968). Despite his well-earned reputation for Jew-baiting, in 1901 Watson, using very different rhetoric, had successfully defended a Jewish merchant unjustly charged with murder. See, Louis E. Schmier, "No Jew Can Murder: Memories of Tom Watson and the Lichtenstein Murder Case of 1901," *Georgia Historical Quarterly* 70 (Fall, 1986): 433–55.

11. David and Adele Bernstein, "Slow Revolution in Richmond, Va.: A New Pattern in the Making," *Commentary* 8 (December 1949): 539–46; for YMCA policy, see Arnold Shankman, "Friend or Foe? Southern Blacks View the Jew, 1880–1935," in *Turn to the South,* ed. Kaganoff and Urofsky, 118, 191.

rather than local Jews. If so, then it was echoed by the region's universities and colleges, which, like the University of Virginia, established quotas for Jewish students aimed primarily at nonresidents. As late as 1961, the dean of Emory Dental School, who had cut off admission of Jewish but not Gentile applicants from New Jersey, New York, and Connecticut, still required students on the application form to indicate their "race"—Caucasian, Jew, or Other. Exposed by the Atlanta Anti-Defamation League, the dean resigned but subsequently served as dean of the Medical University of South Carolina from 1964–1971.[12]

Southern politicians like Mississippi governor and senator Theodore Bilbo and Congressman John E. Rankin added their voices to the forces of the anti-Semitic tide. Rankin, for example, viewed Jews as dragging the nation into World War II, and during the cold war he summed up the issue facing America as "Yiddish Communism versus Christian civilization." For Rankin, as well as Bilbo, however, the real threat from Jews came in the area of civil rights. And though the chief enemy was the northern Jew, whom Bilbo referred to as "New York Jew 'Kikes' that are fraternizing and socializing with Negroes for selfish and political reasons," all Jews might suffer as a result of their actions.[13] And again such words led to deeds, first in the marches of the Ku Klux Klan during the 1920s and the revived Klan and White Citizen Council attacks on Jews and Jewish institutions in the 1950s and 1960s, which included cemetery desecrations, attempted economic boycotts, and synagogue bombings.

Yet despite such examples, those few historians who have looked at this subject, and especially southern Jews themselves, claim that in fact the South has been more receptive to Jews and has exhibited less anti-Semitism than the nation as a whole, and certainly less than the East and Midwest.[14] And indeed there is much evidence to suggest that aside from the West, the South has been the least anti-Semitic region in the country. Harry Golden, the late editor of the *Carolina Israelite*, wrote in 1955: "There is very little real anti-Semitism in the South. There is even a solid tradition of philo-Semitism, the explanation of which lies in the very character of southern Protestantism itself—in the Anglo-Calvinist devotion to the Old Testament and the Hebrew prophets and the lack of emphasis on the Easter story which has been so closely connected with European anti-Semitism." Golden, of course, was writing before the wave of synagogue bombings, and even he acknowledged what he called the "social apartheid" that existed be-

12. Marcia Graham Synnott, "Anti-Semitism and American Universities: Did Quotas Follow the Jews?" in *Anti-Semitism*, ed. Gerber, 262–63.

13. Edward S. Shapiro, "Anti-Semitism Mississippi Style," in *Anti-Semitism*, ed. Gerber, 129–51, quotes 135, 140.

14. See, for example, Higham, *Send These to Me*, 162–64, and most of the essays in Kaganoff and Urofsky, *Turn to the South.*

tween Gentile and Jew when the sun went down, especially in the largest cities; but the record provides much more support for Golden's contention, if not for the widespread existence of philo-Semitism, then at least for the relatively lesser amount of anti-Semitism.[15]

The tolerance of Jews has been especially evident in politics. The first Jew elected to the U.S. Senate was David L. Yulee (born Levy), who was instrumental in achieving statehood for Florida and was sent to the Senate in 1845. As was true of the second Jewish senator and future Confederate cabinet member Judah P. Benjamin, Yulee married outside the faith and was not a practicing Jew, but both men were identified in the press and by voters as Jews and elected nonetheless.[16] On the state level, during the early twentieth century Charles Jacobson was the second most powerful man in Arkansas state government as a result of his close association with the redneck governor, Jeff Davis. Jews were especially successful on the local level. Many Richmonders are familiar with the careers of the multiterm antebellum councilman Gustavus Myers and the postbellum state legislator William Lovenstein.[17] Elsewhere, Montgomery, Alabama, in 1875 was perhaps the only city in American history where both the Republican and Democratic candidates for mayor were Jewish, and by the 1870s there was already a Jewish seat on Atlanta's board of education.[18] And although there seems to have been a decline in the frequency of Jewish officeholding in the aftermath of the Frank lynching, much of it seems to have been at least partially voluntary on the part of Jews, as the Watsons, Bilbos, and Rankins of the South were always repudiated by the "respectable folk." Similarly, and as surprising as it might seem in today's environment, the nineteenth-century efforts to publicly proclaim the U.S. a Christian nation were centered in the Midwest and not in the South.[19]

15. Golden, "Jew and Gentile in the New South: Segregation at Sundown," *Commentary* 20 (November 1955): 403–412, quote 403.

16. Leon Huhner, "David L. Yulee, Florida's First Senator," in *Jews in the South,* ed. Dinnerstein and Palsson, 52–74; Benjamin Kaplan, "Judah Philip Benjamin," ibid., 75–88.

17. Raymond Arsenault, "Charles Jacobson of Arkansas: A Jewish Politician in the Land of the Razorbacks, 1891–1915," in *Turn to the South,* ed. Kaganoff and Urofsky, 55–75; Myron Berman, *Richmond's Jewry: Shabbat in Shockoe, 1769–1976* (Charlottesville: University Press of Virginia, 1979), 127–29, 235–36.

18. *Montgomery Alabama State Journal,* April 8, 1875; *Atlanta Constitution,* May 6, 1890. Savannah was another southern city in which Jews were prominent officeholders. Herman Myers, for example, served as mayor from 1895 to 1897 and 1899–1907. David J. Goldberg, "The Administration of Herman Myers as Mayor of Savannah, Georgia 1895–97 and 1899–1907" (Master's thesis, University of North Carolina, Chapel Hill, 1978).

19. Arsenault, "Charles Jacobson," 67; Borden, *Jews, Turks, and Infidels,* 58–74. The case for the South's relative lack of interest in proclaiming the U.S. a Christian nation is even stronger than Borden suggests, since he ignores what southerners did when they

Economic discrimination against Jews seemed to be much less than in the North, except perhaps in places such as Birmingham, Alabama, where northern corporate influence was especially pronounced.[20] No doubt individual Jews were denied jobs because of their religion, but there was little systematic discrimination. Jews did suffer from so-called blue laws or Sunday closing laws, but no more than in the rest of the country. In this area Richmond was especially enlightened, as during the 1840s Jewish merchant opposition to the state's Revolutionary Era Sunday closing law and similar new city ordinances aimed at slaves and free Negroes led future mayor Joseph Mayo to have the first law amended and the second rescinded.[21] Social discrimination, while present to a greater degree than commonly acknowledged, seems to have been less extensive than in the North, especially in the case of social relations in smaller towns and in the area of college admissions.

What we have then is a good deal of conflicting evidence about the relative importance of anti-Semitism in the South. Allowing, however, for the variety of experience within the South and indeed within all regions, it seems that with the possible exception of the use of violence, the South and southerners can justifiably claim to have exhibited less anti-Semitism and even nativism than certainly the East and Midwest. Perhaps Virginius Dabney's assessment in his introduction to Rabbi Myron Berman's *Richmond Jewry* holds for other communities as well: "Relations between the Jewish and gentile communities of Richmond are as cordial as can be found anywhere. The Ku Klux Klan has never been able to get a firm foothold here, and anti-Semitism is at a minimum."[22]

But if this is so, the important question still to be asked is: Why? After all, contrary to Harry Golden's claim, the South's commitment to evangelical Protestantism might have just as logically led to anti-Semitism, and the small town and rural nature of southern life that supported it might have been expected to produce heightened parochialism and suspicion of outsiders. We should not forget the writer to the *Richmond Enquirer* in 1864 who believed it blasphemous for a Jew to hold so high an office as secretary of state and thought the prayers of

---

wrote their own constitution. The preamble to the Confederate Constitution merely invokes "the favor and guidance of Almighty God" (not Jesus), and Article 6, Section 4 bars religious tests for qualifications for office or public trust under the Confederate States. See "The Constitution of the Confederate States of America, March 11, 1861," in *Documents of American History,* ed. Henry Steele Commager (New York: Appleton-Century-Crofts, 1968), 376, 384.

20. Mark Lowett, "Rabbi Morris Newfield and the Social Gospel: Theology and Societal Reform in the South," *American Jewish Archives* 34 (April 1982): 68.

21. Borden, *Jews, Turks, and Infidels,* 118–21.

22. *Richmond's Jewry,* xiii.

the Confederacy would have more effect if Judah Benjamin were dismissed from the Cabinet. Even more troubling have been figures such as President W. W. Thornton of the University of Virginia, who in 1890 told the editors of the *American Hebrew:* "All intelligent Christians deplore the fact that the historical evidences of Christianity have so little weight with your people." To him anti-Semitism could be explained by the "mere fact of difference."[23]

Although one cannot do justice to this complicated issue in a brief essay, there are three general reasons why the South, if not the least anti-Semitic region in the nation, can at least lay claim to being no worse than the norm. The first has to do with structural factors; the second with the presence of other targets for prejudice; and the third with the conscious actions of southern Jews themselves.

The structural factors are relatively clear-cut. There were simply not as many Jews in the South as elsewhere, and a larger percentage settled in rural areas. More than that, they tended to arrive early in the region's major cities, such as Charleston, Richmond, and Savannah—early enough, indeed, to be among some of the South's First Families. In addition to arriving early, they filled a needed economic role, not only in the major towns, but also, as Golden notes, in the small towns of the back country. It is also worth emphasizing, however, that these early migrants tended to be Sephardic or German Jews, and that for the most part the late nineteenth century influx of Eastern European Jews had much less of an impact on the South, thus keeping southern Jewish communities relatively settled and stable. Where the new immigrants did have an impact, such as in Richmond and Atlanta, it was still less than in New York, Philadelphia, and Chicago, and the resulting discrimination was therefore less. But more important than the origins or timing of the Jewish migration were the kinds of pursuits the southern Jews engaged in. They were less likely than their northern counterparts to try to enter the professions or large corporations and challenge already entrenched Gentile interests. Whether consciously or unconsciously, they were more likely to stay in the family business, usually mercantile, and thus pose less of a threat to their Gentile fellow residents.[24]

But even if southern Jews had been more threatening in terms of their

23. Korn, "American Judaeophobia," 137–38; Thornton quoted in Stephen J. Whitfield, "Jews and Other Southerners: Counterpoint and Paradox," in *Turn to the South,* ed. Kaganoff and Urofsky, 86. Whitfield's extremely well written and witty essay is the only previous scholarly attempt to engage the broad sweep of southern anti-Semitism; however, the author chose to alternate examples of positive and negative attitudes toward southern Jews without arriving at a firm conclusion about the extent, in either absolute or relative terms, of the region's anti-Semitism.

24. See, for example, Berman, *Richmond's Jewry;* Steven Hertzberg, *Strangers within the Gate City: the Jews of Atlanta 1845–1915* (Philadelphia: The Jewish Publication Society of America, 1978).

numbers, origins, or aspirations, their white southern contemporaries might still have not singled them out for special discrimination due to the presence of other, more threatening groups. As the Mississippi editor Hodding Carter put it: "It takes perseverance to hate Jews and Negroes and Catholics all at the same time." Protestant southerners had always feared Catholics even more than Jews. Alabama Senator Tom Heflin relished running against the Pope, the man Tom Watson called a "fat old dago." And of course, no one needs to be reminded of the nature of black-white relations in the South. As North Carolina journalist Jonathan Daniels wrote in 1938: "In most Southern towns, except where many Jews have recently come in, the direction of racial prejudice at the Negro frees the Jews from prejudice altogether—or nearly altogether."[25]

But potential white southern antagonism toward Jews would not have been deflected by their concentration on blacks had Jews not accepted the southern racial climate as it was. And here we get to the basic source of the relative acceptance of Jews in the South. For conscious decisions by southern Jews, together with the less conscious structural factors already noted, have enabled them to assimilate, not completely, but to a greater degree than their northern brethren. One Richmonder caught this desire to assimilate or blend in, noting that the city's "old Jews" believed "they ought to be as quiet and unostentatious as possible."[26] And nowhere have the effects of this assimilation been more evident than in the matter of race relations. It is not clear whether or not the southern Jew's public behavior reflects his private feelings, but publicly he has chosen implicitly or explicitly to support the status quo. This tendency was already present prior to the Civil War as southern Jews reacted to the institution of slavery in the same way as did their Gentile contemporaries. Not only were Jews slaveholders, but politicians such as David Yulee and Judah P. Benjamin strongly opposed abolition and helped lead their states out of the Union.[27]

In recent years, slavery, of course, was not the issue. But civil rights were, and here southern Jews sought to keep a low profile. Some went so far as to join the white citizens councils (something which helps explain why some councils were not more anti-Semitic), but as other southerners had come to expect, most simply chose to remain silent. Those who were visible tended to apologize for the actions of their more civil rights oriented northern brethren

25. Quoted in Whitfield, "Jews and Other Southerners," 86, 87.
26. Bernstein, "Slow Revolution in Richmond," 542.
27. Bertram Wallace Korn, *Jews and Negro Slavery in the Old South, 1789–1865* (Elkins Park, Pa.: Reform Congregation Keneseth Israel, 1961); Huhner, "David L. Yulee"; Kaplan, "Judah Philip Benjamin."

and to make clear that the latters' views were not those of southern Jews. Thus, when a group of northern rabbis was arrested in Birmingham for their racial protests, they were visited by a delegation of local Jews who urged them to go home; otherwise reprisals would follow against Birmingham Jews.[28] In Richmond in 1958, Jewish leaders, on similar grounds, implored the young, aggressive, northern-born head of the city's Anti-Defamation League office not to publicly challenge a threatening and perhaps anti-Semitic editorial by *Richmond News Leader* editor James J. Kilpatrick directed at the ADL's support for desegregation.[29] By taking such actions, southern Jews helped encourage a long-standing tradition in which even purveyors of anti-Semitism could distinguish between what John Higham has called the "evil Jew," far away, and the Jew next door.

Such incidents reveal two important points. First, they show that southern Jews realized the linkage between acceptance and conformity to southern values, particularly regarding blacks. Such conformity, of course, transcended race. Jews had for some time been trying to blend in. As Rabbi David Marx of Atlanta told his congregation in 1900, "In isolated instances there is no prejudice entertained for individual Jews, but there exists widespread and deep seated prejudice against Jews as an entire people."[30] In part to defuse such feelings, Reform rabbis such as Marx and Richmond's Edward N. Calisch abolished skull caps, initiated Sunday morning services, minimized Hebrew in the liturgy, and stressed close relations with their Christian counterparts. In the effort to disavow what made Jews, in Calisch's words, "aliens in occidental climes," Jewish services became more Christianized; through a similar process, Jewish attitudes on race became more southernized.[31]

It must be emphasized, however, that the meshing of southern Jewish and Gentile attitudes was never complete in any area, including race. Yet southern Jews were still different from those in the North. Indeed, southern Jews are classically marginal men. In the fragmentary survey data comparing southern Jewish attitudes with those of their Gentile contemporaries and

28. Lecture of Rabbi Richard Rubenstein, USS *Waterman,* June 1963. For similar reaction throughout the South see Allen Krause, "Rabbis and Negro Rights in the South, 1954–1967," in *Jews in the South,* ed. Dinnerstein and Palsson, 360–85, and Leonard Dinnerstein, "Southern Jewry and Desegregation, 1954–1970," *American Jewish Historical Quarterly* 62 (March 1973): 231–41.

29. Murray Friedman, "One Episode in Southern Jewry's Response to Desegregation: An Historical Memoir," *American Jewish Archives* 33 (November 1981): 170–83.

30. Quoted in Whitfield, "Jews and Other Southerners," 82.

31. Ibid., 89–90; Berman, *Richmond's Jewry,* Chapter 8, quote 250.

northern Jews, they end up somewhere in the middle—that is, more liberal than Gentile white southerners but less so than northern Jews.[32]

What helps account for this middle position is a second point about the southern Jewish reaction to the civil rights movement. The linkage between the acceptance of Jews and racial conformity reflected an appreciation of the region's penchant for violence and the frightening potential for latent anti-Semitism to become blatant. As one Mississippian put it:

We have to work quietly, secretly. We have to play ball. Anti-Semitism is always right around the corner. . . . We don't want to have our temple bombed. If we said out loud in Temple what most of us really think and believe, there just wouldn't be a Temple here anymore. They [the Gentile neighbors] let it alone because it seems to them like just another Mississippi church. And if it ever stops seeming like that, we won't have a Temple. We have to at least pretend to go along with things as they are.[33]

Synagogue bombings elsewhere in the South were not necessarily anti-Semitic in nature: the real targets were often the forces of change in southern race relations. But most Jews did not make such fine distinctions, and while some courageous rabbis like Jacob Rothschild of Atlanta, Norfolk native Charles Mantinband (who served in Alabama, Mississippi, and Texas), and Emmet Frank of Alexandria, Virginia, spoke out against segregation, most, like their congregants, kept their mouths shut despite whatever reservations they had.[34]

The lesson then is that southern Jews have paid a price for whatever greater acceptance they might have achieved. Jews, like blacks, had to know their place. This is, of course, easy for a northern or now western Jew to say, but it is not meant as criticism. After all, southern Jews, despite their environment, have had as a group more enlightened views on race relations than their Gentile neighbors and were right to fear the outrage of their fellow whites. And one can expect the differences between northern and southern Jews to be reduced in the coming years as regional characteristics in general continue to

32. Alfred O. Hero, Jr., "Southern Jews," in *Jews in the South,* ed. Dinnerstein and Palsson, 217–50; Hero, "Southern Jews and Public Policy," in *Turn to the South,* ed. Kaganoff and Urofsky, 143–50; Abraham D. Lavender, "Jewish Values in the Southern Milieu," in *Turn to the South,* ed. Kaganoff and Urofsky, 124–34; John Shelton Reed, "Ethnicity in the South: Some Observations on the Acculturation of Southern Jews," *Ethnicity* 6 (March 1979): 97–106.

33. Quoted in Marvin Braiterman, "Mississippi Marranos," in *Jews in the South,* ed. Dinnerstein and Palsson, 356.

34. See, for example, Krause, "Rabbis and Negro Rights," passim; Malcolm H. Stern, "The Role of the Rabbi in the South," in *Turn to the South,* ed. Kaganoff and Urofsky, 30–32.

weaken, northern Jews become more conservative, Jewish newcomers to the South bring a heightened ethnic awareness with them, and race becomes less important to southern whites. Until this happens, however, the situation of southern Jews will remain special, and any attempt to assess the nature of nativism, bigotry, and anti-Semitism in the South will have to take into account the fear of reprisal as the foundation of the region's allegedly cordial Jewish-Gentile relations.

Part Five

Continuity
and
Change

Continuity and Change

Southern Urban Development, 1860–1900

The following essay was written for a pioneering volume that contained five chronologically arranged chapters on the role of cities in southern history. The editors' aim was to carve out for southern cities their rightful place within the broader fields of southern and urban history. Most of the contributors, and especially the editors David Goldfield and Blaine Brownell, who, respectively, wrote the chapters which preceded and followed my own (1820–1860 and 1900–1940), emphasized the characteristics southern cities and their leaders shared with their northern counterparts. My contribution, however, emphasized the relative distinctiveness of the urban South. Since the mid-1970s, most urban historians, including Goldfield and Brownell, have taken a position closer to mine. For more on the development of this subfield, particularly with regard to the degree of distinctiveness and continuity in southern urbanization, and an updated set of secondary sources, see my "What Urban History Can Teach Us about the South and the South Can Teach Us about Urban History," *Georgia Historical Quarterly* 73 (Spring 1989): 54–66. For a fuller discussion of the impact of urbanization on the late nineteenth- and early twentieth-century South, see my *The First New South, 1865–1920* (Arlington Heights, Ill.: Harlan Davidson, 1992) and "The Origins of a Poststructural New South," *Journal of Southern History* 59 (August 1993): 505–15.

During the late nineteenth century northern cities were radically transformed. The wrenching experience of the Civil War and Reconstruction might have similarly affected their southern counterparts. Instead, continuity between ur-

I want to thank Professors Arthur Mann, David R. Johnson, and Walter B. Weare for their comments on earlier versions of this essay.

ban development in the Old South and the New was more noteworthy than change.[1]

The continuing efforts of urban boosters to alter the basic character of southern life and to bring their communities into line with those of the North met with only limited success. Economic realities, the pull of the past, and northern competition proved too great to overcome. This is not to say that there was no change, only that in most aspects the closing years of the century witnessed the playing out of old themes in new circumstances. First, though continuing to exercise a disproportionate influence in their region, southern cities still lagged behind those in the North in size, numbers, municipal services, and wealth. Second, manufacturing gained a greater place in local economies, but as in the antebellum period, commercial and administrative functions of cities remained more important than in the North. And third, urban dwellers remained preoccupied with disciplining their growing black populations, now free rather than slave.

The main difference between antebellum and postbellum urbanization was the filling in of the urban network through the growth of important interior southern cities, a development that considerably rearranged the rank order distribution of cities that had existed in 1860. Before the Civil War the ten largest cities in what soon would be the Confederate South were river or seaports located on the perimeter of the region east of the Mississippi River. By 1900, however, the top ten included Atlanta, San Antonio, and Houston, while Dallas and Birmingham ranked eleventh and twelfth. Whereas in 1860 Virginia had four of the twelve largest cities and Texas none, by 1900 Virginia had two and Texas three. These inland cities, unlike the Old South's largest towns, owed their growth not to a choice water location but rather to the postbellum expansion of the region's railroad system. Older river ports like Memphis, Richmond, and Nashville, and the ocean port of Norfolk, were able to keep pace because of their railroad connections, while New Orleans, Mobile, Savannah, and Charleston were among the established coastal cities that lost ground because of changes in transportation patterns. New Orleans, for example, remained the South's largest city throughout the period, but the sharply diminished gap between it and the next four largest cities in 1900 revealed the growing maturation of the urban system that had occurred since 1860.

1. As used in this essay, the term *South* refers primarily to the eleven states that comprised the Confederate States of America. I believe that the forces that led to secession, together with the impact of the war and Reconstruction, set these states apart from Kentucky and Oklahoma, the other two states that are normally included in discussions of the postbellum South.

Table 1
Largest Southern Cities, 1860–1900

1860		1870		1880	
New Orleans	168,675	New Orleans	191,418	New Orleans	216,090
Charleston	40,519	Richmond	51,038	Richmond	63,600
Richmond	37,910	Charleston	48,956	Charleston	49,984
Mobile	29,258	Memphis	40,226	Nashville	43,350
Memphis	22,623	Mobile	32,034	Atlanta	37,409
Savannah	22,292	Savannah	28,235	Memphis	33,592
Petersburg, Va.	18,266	Nashville	25,865	Savannah	30,709
Nashville	16,988	Atlanta	21,789	Mobile	29,132
Norfolk	14,620	Norfolk	19,229	Galveston	22,248
Alexandria	12,652	Petersburg, Va.	18,950	Norfolk	21,966

1890		1900	
New Orleans	242,039	New Orleans	287,104
Richmond	81,338	Memphis	102,320
Nashville	76,168	Atlanta	89,872
Atlanta	65,533	Richmond	85,050
Memphis	64,495	Nashville	80,865
Charleston	54,955	Charleston	55,807
Savannah	43,189	Savannah	54,244
Dallas	38,067	San Antonio	53,321
San Antonio	37,673	Norfolk	46,624
Norfolk	34,871	Houston	44,633

As suggested by table 1, individual cities might rise or fall in spectacular fashion, but there was no sudden change in the overall hierarchy. Gradual change also characterized internal developments, which included the expansion of municipal services and the control of urban blacks. Both the internal and external dimensions of southern urbanization can be divided into four chronological periods. From 1860 to 1865 wartime conditions determined the character of urban life. During the subsequent eight years southern cities, with varied degrees of success, sought to recover from the effects of the war. This effort was cut short by the panic of 1873, whose economic aftereffects restricted growth and progress until the end of the decade. The last twenty years of the century brought sustained urban expansion and prosperity, which was only briefly undercut by the panic of 1893 and the subsequent depression.

1860–1865

No event has received more attention among southern historians than the Civil War. Often termed a watershed in southern history, its impact has been seen as especially great on urban development. In his study of the South during Reconstruction, E. Merton Coulter emphasized the damage to southern cities during the war. In Columbia, South Carolina, "everything in the business district had been swept away and two thirds of the rest of the city was gone." Atlanta "was now as famous for its utter destruction as it had been for its rapid growth and Savannah would mourn six blocks of ruins." Richmond, Selma, Fredericksburg, Petersburg, and Charleston were also singled out—"And so the story went; towns and villages throughout the fought-over Confederacy had their scars to show." In similar fashion Thomas Wertenbaker concluded that at the end of the war Norfolk "like all Southern towns was prostrate." She had escaped complete destruction, "but her commerce was at a low ebb, her tributary railroads broken, her finances deranged, her streets out of repair, her citizens impoverished."[2]

At first glance, comparative census data for the North and South support the claim that the war seriously hindered postbellum southern urban growth. A closer look, however, buttresses T. Lynn Smith's view: "It is doubtful that the twenty years of war and reconstruction greatly retarded the development of urban centers in the South."[3] In 1860 the eleven states had 54, or 13.8 percent, of the nation's 392 urban centers; ten years later the same states had 67, or only 10.1 percent, of the 663 urban centers. Yet, this decline in the South's percentage of the nation's towns was part of a long-term decline that antedated the war. From a high point of 17.8 percent in 1830, that percentage had dropped to 16.8 percent in 1840, then 15.3 percent in 1850, and finally to the figure of 1860. The region's share of places with more than ten thousand people had dropped even more sharply, from 18.9 percent in 1840 to 11.8 percent in 1860.[4]

Five years of fighting accelerated the growing gap between the extent of urbanization in the North and the South, but it did not prevent the accretion of

2. Coulter, *The South during Reconstruction,* 1865–1877, vol. 8 of *A History of the South,* ed. Wendell Holmes Stephenson and E. Merton Coulter, 10 vols. (Baton Rouge: Louisiana State University Press, 1947), 3; Wertenbaker, *Norfolk: Historic Southern Port* (Durham: Duke University Press, 1931), 271.

3. "The Emergence of Cities," in *The Urban South,* ed. Rupert B. Vance and Nicholas J. Demerath (Chapel Hill: University of North Carolina Press, 1954), 28–29, 33.

4. Number of urban places and percentages computed from U.S. censuses 1830 to 1870, and Smith, "Emergence of Cities," 28. If Kentucky is included, the percentage of the South's share of urban places declines from 20 percent in 1830 to 19.1 percent in 1840, 17.4 percent in 1850, 15.8 percent in 1860, and 12.1 percent in 1870. The share of urban places with over 10,000 people drops from 21.5 percent to 14.3 percent.

the southern urban population. By 1870, 8.6 percent of the region's population was listed as urban, as compared to 7.1 percent in 1860. Because of the undercount of southern urban blacks in 1870, the actual increase was no doubt greater; but it was still far less than the jump in the national percentage from 19.8 percent to 25.7 percent.[5]

Many cities suffered because of the disruption of their traditional trade routes, damage to their agricultural hinterlands, ruinous inflation and speculation, decline of public services, and loss of men to the war effort. But for most there were offsetting benefits, and for many the war definitely contributed to urban growth. Generalizations about a "prostrate South" are risky. Galveston and Houston, for example, were hurt by the Union blockade, but San Antonio flourished as a result of its secure inland position and its role as a military and supply center for the Confederacy. Charleston, Savannah, and Mobile lost a major share of the cotton trade, but the occupation of New Orleans and Memphis by Union troops in 1862 allowed cotton merchants in those cities to prosper. As Gerald Capers concluded about Memphis: "Few Southern towns suffered as little from the four years of war."[6] Even some cities that experienced much destruction and disruption quickly recovered. The outstanding example was Atlanta. By 1864 the city had doubled its 1860 population to over twenty thousand. As a military headquarters and manufacturing, supply, and medical center, it was among the three most important Confederate cities. The much-publicized "destruction" of the city in 1864, immortalized in *Gone with the Wind,* did little to hinder its path to regional dominance, in part because the extent of the damage itself has been exaggerated. On arriving in the city in November 1865, Sidney Andrews, surprised to find less devastation than he had expected, wrote, "The City Hall and the Medical College and all the churches, and many of the handsomer and more stylish private dwellings and nearly all the houses of the middling and poorer classes were spared."[7]

5. Percentages computed from U.S. censuses 1860 and 1870, and Smith, "Emergence of Cities," 33. If Kentucky is included, the increase in the percentage of urban population is from 7.2 percent to 9.4 percent.

6. Kenneth W. Wheeler, *To Wear a City's Crown: The Beginnings of Urban Growth in Texas, 1836–1865* (Cambridge, Mass.: Harvard University Press, 1968), 150–60; Harold D. Woodman, *King Cotton and His Retainers: Financing and Marketing the Cotton Crop of the South, 1800–1925* (Lexington, Ky.: University of Kentucky Press, 1968), 219; Gerald M. Capers, Jr., *The Biography of a River Town: Memphis, Its Heroic Age* (Chapel Hill: University of North Carolina Press, 1939), 162. Raleigh and Augusta were two other cities that came through the war largely unscathed. See Richard Yates, "Governor Vance and the End of the War in North Carolina," *North Carolina Historical Review* 18 (October 1941): 328–31; Richard Henry Lee German, "The Queen City of the Savannah: Augusta, Georgia, during the Urban Progressive Era, 1890–1917" (Ph.D. diss., University of Florida, 1971), 1–7.

7. Grigsby Hart Wotton, Jr., "New City of the South: Atlanta, 1843–1873" (Ph.D. diss., Johns Hopkins University, 1973), 90; James M. Russell, "Atlanta, Gate City of the South,

1865–1873

The first postwar years are usually divided into the eras of Presidential Recon-struction (1865 to 1867) and Radical or Congressional Reconstruction (1867 to 1877), but in terms of urban development the years from 1865 to the onset of the panic of 1873 form a more natural unit. In all but their treatment of blacks, southern cities reacted very similarly, whether Radicals or former Confederates were in control.

The primary tasks of the first postwar years were to rebuild urban economies on a sound basis, to repair the damage of the war, and to cope with the increased number of rural migrants, especially blacks drawn to the cities by rural disloca-tion and urban prosperity.

The task of postwar recovery was greatest for the older port cities, especially New Orleans and Charleston. Even before the Civil War these two cities had seen their once lofty positions challenged by competing towns and especially by the intrusion of interior railroad development. Their comparative decline continued in the early postwar years. Along with Mobile, both cities were plagued by obstructions still blocking their harbors. Charleston also suffered from the destruction of the 104-mile rail link to Savannah that remained out of operation until March 1870. But these port cities were hurt most by changes in the cotton trade. As they had done during and before the war, postbellum cotton factors initially continued to sell the cotton of inland producers and to supply them with imported goods and credit. Already on the eve of the war, however, improved rail connections had threatened the traditional role of the seaport factor. Farmers in western Georgia and northern Alabama had new markets for their crops and could choose among Charleston, Savannah, and Norfolk on the Atlantic; Mobile, New Orleans, and Pensacola on the Gulf; or widely scattered interior towns like Augusta, Macon, Montgomery, and Mem-phis. And in the first decade after the war, new rail links, which greatly ex-panded the small overland trade to the North by way of Memphis, seriously hurt the Gulf ports. The growth of east-west railroads south of the Ohio River also drew cotton to the Atlantic ports. While Charleston and Savannah contin-ued to be destinations, they were already being challenged by Norfolk. Norfolk greatly benefitted by the swift repair of both the Seaboard and Roanoke and the

1847 to 1885" (Ph.D. diss., Princeton University, 1972), 126; Sidney Andrews, *The South since the War, As Shown by Fourteen Weeks of Travel and Observation in Georgia and the Carolinas* (Boston, 1866), 339.

Norfolk and Petersburg railroads, which by 1874 had made the city the third cotton port behind New Orleans and Galveston.[8]

As elsewhere in the United States during this period, the railroad meant success or failure for communities of all sizes. Equipment was worn out and thousands of "Sherman's hairpins" (rails twisted around trees) bore testimony to the numerous gaps in the system. Nonetheless, John Stover reports that between 1865 and 1870 the lines were rebuilt and placed in operation. As early as 1866 "southern rail recovery was so advanced that nearly every state had new railroad projects in mind and in some cases work had actually begun."[9]

This railroad recovery spurred the growth of interior towns and altered their economies. Between 1860 and 1870 Montgomery grew by 19.7 percent, Augusta by 23.2 percent, Macon by 31.1 percent, Natchez by 37 percent, Memphis by 77.8 percent, and Selma, Shreveport, Vicksburg, and Little Rock by whopping percentages of 104 percent, 110 percent, 171 percent, and 232 percent, respectively. Each of these attracted more merchants and bankers, who eventually took over the credit and supply functions of the port factor. Dallas, for example, opened its first bank in 1868; by 1872 Atlanta had ten banks, none of which had existed at the end of the war.[10] And of course, interior merchants like the Lehman brothers in Montgomery began to purchase local cotton themselves. They added cotton gins, storage facilities, and large compresses so that the cotton could be readied for market locally before being sent by rail directly to the North or to inland transhipment centers such as Dallas, Brimingham, or Atlanta, thus bypassing the port cities. The coastal factors still remained important, but their days were clearly numbered. To survive they would have to turn to new ways of doing business.[11]

Railroads had already begun to alter trade routes and determine urban growth in the antebellum period, but there was a major difference in the postwar period. Before the war extensive subscriptions of money by individual cities enabled many of them to control railroads. Augusta determined the policy of the Georgia Railroad; Savannah, the Central of Georgia; Charleston, the South Carolina; and Mobile, Richmond, Norfolk, and New Orleans each had a special railroad to

8. John A. Eisterhold, "Charleston: Lumber and Trade in a Declining Southern Port," *South Carolina Historical Magazine* 74 (April 1973): 61–72; Merl E. Reed, *New Orleans and the Railroads: The Struggle for Commercial Empire, 1830–1860* (Baton Rouge: Louisiana State University Press, 1966); John F. Stover, *The Railroads of the South, 1865–1900* (Chapel Hill: University of North Carolina Press, 1955): 39; Woodman, *King Cotton,* 270–72; Wertenbaker, *Norfolk,* 298–303.

9. *Railroads of the South,* 57–58.

10. Woodman, *King Cotton,* 328–29; A. C. Greene, *Dallas: The Deciding Years: A Historical Portrait* (Dallas: Encino Press, 1973): 18; Russell "Atlanta," 169–70.

11. Woodman, *King Cotton,* passim.

secure the western trade. James Russell has concluded, however, that "never again would Southern cities have such opportunities. . . . After the Civil War, the cost of building a railroad rose far beyond the means of most cities."[12] Until the panic of 1873 cities nonetheless sought to continue the earlier policy. Atlanta businessmen pressed the city council to subscribe to a number of railroads; the first postwar city government in Montgomery bought $500,000 worth of stock in the South and North Railroad.[13] In the first eight years after the war, most cities, though, were content to lure railroads to town with limited capital subscriptions, tax breaks, and free rights-of-way. And the tactic worked. In 1870 Dallas was a sleepy Texas town in the middle of nowhere with a population of 2,960. Then in 1872 the Houston and Texas Central Railroad came to town, followed the next year by the Texas and Pacific Railway. By 1880 the town had over 10,000 people.[14]

But it was Atlanta, "The Chicago of the South," that benefitted most from the railroad in the immediate postwar years. Again we can see the antebellum roots of postbellum developments. During the antebellum period Atlanta, originally called Terminus, had emerged as "an incidental byproduct of a railroad system constructed to promote the prosperity of other towns." By the eve of the war it was connected by five railroads to major cities of the North, West, and South. Less than a year after Sherman had left the city in flames, all five railroads were in active operation. A local editor could rightfully claim in the fall of 1866 that Atlanta "is the radiating point for Northern and Western trade coming Southward and is the gate through which passes Southern trade and travel going northward."[15] Trade with the Midwest quickly revived after the war, and the city was also one of those that profited from the changes in the nature of the cotton trade. Atlanta's prosperity was further stimulated by the influx of northerners and others interested in making money, and by an active trade with nearby country stores. Its designation as the headquarters of the Third Military District under Congressional Reconstruction in 1867 and as the state capital in 1868 also spurred growth.

Known for their fervent boosterism even then, Atlantans were not content to simply let prosperity come—they went out and grabbed it. In 1865 Whitelaw Reid compared Atlanta to the former capital of the Confederacy: "The burnt

12. Russell, "Atlanta," 30.

13. Ibid., 195–206; *Montgomery Daily State Sentinel,* April 10, 1868; *Montgomery Alabama State Journal,* November 24, 1868. For support of public and private subscription for the Montgomery County Railroad, see *Montgomery Daily Advertiser,* February 28, 1872.

14. Greene, *Dallas,* 22–24.

15. Russell, "Atlanta," 47; Stover, *Railroads of the South,* 58; *Atlanta Daily New Era,* October 23, 1866, quoted in Wotton, "New City of the South," 149.

district of Richmond was hardly more thoroughly destroyed than the central part of Atlanta, yet with all the advantages of proximity to the North, abundant capital, and the influx of business and money from above the Potomac, Richmond was not half so rebuilt as Atlanta." In order to attract the wagon trade of nearby farmers, Atlantans quickly rebuilt the public market in 1866; in order to secure the capital, they promised to provide, free of charge for ten years, any necessary state buildings. And flushed by their manufacturing success during the war, they actively sought to encourage industry. The Atlanta Rolling Mill was back in operation by 1866, and within five years after the war there were seventy-four manufacturing establishments, more than ever before, producing goods valued at over two million dollars annually. Sparked by an impressive construction boom, Atlanta real estate increased in value from $2,752,650 in 1860 to $5,328,450 in 1866 and then to $8,972,562 in 1870.[16]

Other southern cities drew on their wartime experiences and memory of the antebellum industrial crusade in the hope of diversifying their basically commercial economies. Augusta, which had prospered during the war as a supplier of cotton goods and weapons to the Confederate army, sought to capitalize on its water power, sufficient venture capital, close proximity to the cotton fields, and abundance of cheap labor. City officials and businessmen believed that their community could become the "Lowell of the South" if they enlarged the old canal used since 1845 to supply water power to local mills. A majority of the voters approved the project in October 1871, and the city purchased the necessary dredging equipment, awarded a contract to a private contractor, and arranged for the importation of several hundred Chinese laborers to assist in digging the canal. After several years of labor the project was completed in 1875 at a cost of almost one million dollars. With the aid of northern and local capital, cotton mills, a flour mill, an ice factory, a silk mill, an ironworks, and other major industries were built along the banks of the enlarged canal. The new establishments in turn stimulated additional growth.[17]

Nevertheless, during the years from 1865 to 1873, advances in manufacturing were less important than the massive effort to improve the quality of urban life by providing residents with needed municipal services. Spurred on by the local press, there came an unprecedented building program, which left in its wake new waterworks, streetcars, bridges, city halls, market houses, and paved streets.[18]

16. Reid, *After the War: A Southern Tour,* 1865–1866, ed. with an introduction by C. Vann Woodward (New York: Harper and Row, 1965), 355; Russell, "Atlanta," 153–54, 88.

17. German, "Queen City of the Savannah," 23–25, 365.

18. For examples of newspaper boosterism, see *Nashville Republican Banner,* August 8, 1871, and *Montgomery Alabama State Journal,* April 1872, passim.

Though still leaving southern cities behind their northern counterparts, this period of construction helped to close the gap and to prepare the way for further gains in the 1880s.

Much of this activity was financed directly by the cities. Prior to the war city income derived primarily from wharfage, license fees, bond issues, and special taxes. After 1860 the ad valorem tax on property was the chief source of regular income, although an increasing number of cities sought to fund major projects through the issuance of bonds. Between 1866 and 1873 Atlanta tax receipts grew from $80,000 to $300,000, thanks largely to the doubling in the value of city property. During roughly the same period the value of bonds issued by the city amounted to an estimated $100,000 more than the total revenue gained from taxes. This was part of a national trend. In fifteen principal American cities the city bonded debt increased 271 percent from 1866 to 1875. The larger part of the increase took place from 1870 to 1873.[19]

The cities used the money primarily to improve intraurban communication. The major expenses in Houston were for streets and bridges; in Atlanta, the same expenses consumed 32 percent of the budget between 1868 and 1873. Other large chunks of money went to new public buildings. Montgomery, Atlanta, and Houston were among the many cities that rebuilt or erected new public markets and city halls. Municipal waterworks were built in Norfolk, Montgomery, and Atlanta.[20] And by 1873 almost every southern city had inaugurated a public school system, a further contribution to local construction booms.

The private sector also contributed to the postwar building surge. In addition to impressive new commercial buildings, there were great hotels like Atlanta's six-story Kimball House and theaters like New Orleans's Grand Opera House. Everywhere private gas companies received charters and began tearing up the streets to lay their pipes. But most important to urban life was the appearance of horse-drawn streetcars. Only New Orleans and Mobile had had streetcars prior to 1861. The Civil War delayed the installation of systems in the other large cities, but did not seriously interfere with their subsequent adoption. In 1865 streetcars began operating in Richmond, Charleston, and Memphis, giving the former Confederate states a total of five of the nation's forty-eight cities with lines. All major cities had street railways by the early 1870s, most by 1866. Aside

19. Wotton, "New City of the South," 372, 374; Ernest S. Griffith, *The Modern Development of City Government in the United Kingdom and the United States* (London: Oxford University Press, 1927), 64.

20. David G. McComb, *Houston: The Bayou City* (Austin: University of Texas Press, 1969): 73; Wotton, "New City of the South," 377; *Montgomery Daily Advertiser,* August 8, 1873; Wertenbaker, *Norfolk,* 271–74; *Montgomery Alabama State Journal,* June 17, 1874; Russell, "Atlanta," 175, 282.

from the five already mentioned, the list includes Nashville (1866), Savannah (1869), Atlanta (1871), Norfolk (1870), Houston (1868), and Dallas (1873).[21] The streetcar systems not only provided needed construction work but also encouraged the extension of city boundaries, the creation of economic subcenters, and the sorting out of the population. Nevertheless, it was not until the appearance during the late 1880s of the steam dummy and the electric car that urban mass transit began to have its greatest effect on urban life.

On the eve of the panic of 1873, local boosters could take pride in the recovery and prosperity of their cities. There were still complaints about muddy streets, inadequate water, insufficient police protection, and high freight rates, but clearly there was much ground for optimism. By 1873 most white urban dwellers could also express satisfaction with the way in which they had handled their "Negro problem."

One of the consequences of emancipation and the end of the war was a marked cityward movement of large numbers of rural blacks, even though the great majority remained in the countryside. Whether seeking protection from the violence and intimidation of the countryside or drawn by the educational, relief, and recreational opportunities of the cities, such black migrants used urban destinations to test out their newfound freedom of movement. As a result, the antebellum trend toward the thinning out of black urban populations was reversed. According to U.S. Census data, between 1860 and 1870 Atlanta's black population grew from 1,939 to 9,929, and the percentage of the black population from 20 percent to 46 percent. In 1860 Richmond's 14,275 blacks constituted 38 percent of the city's population; in 1870, 23,110, or 45 percent, of the residents were black. Nor did federal censuses tell the true story of the immediate postwar years. The 1870 censuses greatly underestimated the number of urban black southerners, and by that date there had already been some exodus to the countryside. According to the *Nashville Dispatch,* for example, there were 10,744 freedmen in Nashville in 1865 as compared to the prewar figure of less than 4,000; the 1870 census, however, counted only 9,709 blacks, who nevertheless represented 38 percent of the city's population as compared to 23 percent in 1860. And in Atlanta local censuses conducted in 1867 and 1869 recorded 9,288 and 13,184 blacks.[22]

21. Arthur J. Krim, "The Innovation and Diffusion of the Street Railway in North America" (Master's thesis, University of Chicago, 1967), 103, 100.

22. U.S. Bureau of the Census, *Ninth Census of the United States: 1870,* vol. 1, *Population* (Washington, D.C.: Government Printing Office, 1872), 102, 262, 280; *Nashville Dispatch,* August 16, 1865; V. T. Barnwell, comp., *Barnwell's Atlanta City Directory and Stranger's Guide* (Atlanta, 1867), 16; W. R. Handleiter, comp., *Handleiter's Atlanta City Directory* (Atlanta, 1870): viii.

Local whites were horrified and dismayed by the influx of blacks. They believed that the blacks were needed in the countryside and that city life would be harmful to them. Most important, they felt that the blacks would constitute a threat to public order. "Our advice to them is to go into the country and cultivate the soil, the employment God designed them for and which they must do or starve," declared the *Montgomery Daily Ledger* in 1865. To the *Raleigh Daily Sentinel,* "Nothing can be more deleterious to the black race as their strong proclivity to congregate in the towns. The temptation to idleness, viciousness, and crime are tenfold what they are in the country."[23]

Such views were common in the antebellum period. But now the blacks, no longer slaves, were even more difficult to control. The first postwar local governments elected by white suffrage under Presidential Reconstruction consisted primarily of former Confederates, often members of the wartime administrations. Together with the help of the Freedmen's Bureau and the army, they sought to prevent additional migration or to export blacks to the countryside. When this policy had little effect, city officials did as little as possible for the blacks, preferring to concentrate on the needs of the whites. The antebellum policy of excluding blacks from schools and welfare services was initially continued. Increasingly, however, the federal authorities forced city governments to assume responsibility for needy blacks, though they were cared for in segregated facilities. Little else was done by local officials from 1865 to 1867 to ease the transition of the freedmen from slavery to freedom.[24]

With the onset of Congressional Reconstruction in 1867, conditions for urban blacks began to improve. In most areas the governments appointed by military commanders or elected by black and white suffrage replaced the old policy of exclusion with a new one of separate, though allegedly equal, treatment. Throughout the urban South separate black militia companies were formed; blacks were admitted to segregated almshouses, institutions for the blind, deaf, and dumb, insane asylums, and hospitals; and by 1873 Republican governments had either organized segregated public school systems or, as in Atlanta, provided separate accommodations for blacks in what had been all-white systems. Only in New Orleans was an effort made to "mix the races," but even there the extent of integration was never great.[25]

23. *Montgomery Daily Ledger,* September 23, 1865; *Raleigh Daily Sentinel,* April 24, 1866.
24. This discussion is based on examination of local newspapers, city reports, and board of education and city council minutes. For fuller documentation, see my essays "From Exclusion to Segregation: Health and Welfare Services for Southern Blacks, 1865–1890" and "Half a Loaf: The Shift from White to Black Teachers in the Negro Schools of the Urban South, 1865–1890," reprinted above.
25. Otis Singletary, *Negro Militia and Reconstruction* (Austin: University of Texas Press,

The shift from exclusion to segregation also affected black access to public accommodations. The new streetcar systems in Nashville and Richmond, for example, initially excluded blacks. By the early 1870s black protests in these two cities, New Orleans, Charleston, Mobile, and elsewhere had forced streetcar companies at first to permit blacks to ride on the platforms of the cars, then in separate cars, and finally in the same cars as whites.[26] The extent of integration within the cars, however, remains a subject of controversy. Recent research has also modified the views of C. Vann Woodward concerning the prevalence of integration in other forms of public accommodation. Rather than the flexible system of race relations portrayed by Woodward, it seems that by 1873 the urban landscape for blacks was dominated by segregated galleries in the theaters; exclusion from leading hotels, restaurants, and bars and segregated access in others; segregated or no waiting rooms in railroad stations; and second-class or smoking cars on the railroads.[27] It must be remembered, however, that contrary to current assumptions, segregation generally marked an improvement for blacks, for what it replaced was not integration but exclusion. Meanwhile, a combination of white hostility and black voluntary action produced separate Negro churches, fraternal and benevolent societies, and residential segregation, which by 1873 had helped to create separate black and white worlds within most southern communities. Black neighborhoods with their own institutions, such as Atlanta's Shermantown or Summer Hill and Nashville's Black Bottom or Rocktown, were located near railroad tracks, industrial sites, and contaminated

---

1957); Rabinowitz, "Health and Welfare Services" and "Half a Loaf"; Louis R. Harlan, "Desegregation in New Orleans Public Schools during Reconstruction," *American Historical Review* 67 (April 1962): 663–75.

26. Writers Program of the Works Progress Administration in the State of Virginia, comp., *The Negro in Virginia* (New York: Hastings House, 1940), 241–42; *Richmond Dispatch*, May 9, 1867; January 29, 1870; letter of "A Colored Man" to the editor, *Nashville Daily Press and Times*, June 26, 1866; June 18, 25, 28, 1867; *Mobile Nationalist*, July 25, 1867; April 29, 1870; for Charleston, see *Mobile Nationalist*, May 9, 1867; Roger A. Fischer, "A Pioneer Protest: The New Orleans Street Car Controversy of 1867," *Journal of Negro History* 53 (July 1968): 219–33.

27. For documentation and a discussion of the problems involved in determining the extent of segregation, see Rabinowitz, "From Exclusion to Segregation: Southern Race Relations 1865–1890," reprinted above. The system of race relations was most fluid in New Orleans, but even there widespread segregation existed by the early 1870s. Two studies of New Orleans that implicitly support the Woodward thesis are Dale A. Somers, "Black and White in New Orleans: A Study in Urban Race Relations, 1865–1900," *Journal of Southern History* 40 (February 1974): 19–42, and John W. Blassingame, *Black New Orleans, 1860–1880* (Chicago: University of Chicago Press, 1973). Cf. Roger A. Fischer, *The Segregation Struggle in Louisiana, 1862–1877* (Urbana: University of Illinois Press, 1974). For the "Woodward thesis" itself, see C. Vann Woodward, *The Strange Career of Jim Crow,* 3d rev. ed. (New York: Oxford University Press, 1974).

streams on the fringes of the still-compact cities, typically land considered unfit for white habitation.

The determination of whites to keep blacks "in their place" and the absence of nonagrarian skills among most blacks similarly produced a distinct occupational structure in which blacks were confined mainly to unskilled and semiskilled jobs. The low pay of these jobs and their scattered location contributed to the low quality and segregated character of Negro housing. Although the number of Atlanta blacks with property worth one thousand dollars or more increased from four in 1866 to forty-five by 1874, the mass of blacks were mired at the bottom of the economic ladder. In 1870 76.1 percent of the city's black males sixteen and over were classified as unskilled as compared to 16.8 percent of their white counterparts.[28] This concentration was repeated throughout the urban South and increased as the period waned.

Although most whites were willing to accept the shift from exclusion to segregation, they were less satisfied with the specter of Negro officeholders. During these early years native whites spent as much time, energy, and newspaper space on trying to "redeem" their local governments from the control of white "carpetbaggers," "scalawags," and their black allies as they did in trying to rebuild their cities. Often the two problems went together, as when the *Montgomery Daily Advertiser* urged the defeat of the local Radical administration for fear that otherwise the Democratic state government would move the Alabama capital to another city.[29]

Using gerrymandering, restrictive voting laws, and the less subtle means of vote fraud and intimidation, southern whites usually needed little time to redeem their cities. In the first popular elections under universal manhood suffrage, many cities, including Norfolk, Savannah, Memphis, and Richmond, immediately came under Conservative or Democratic control, while in Atlanta, an independent Democratic mayor elected with Radical support confronted a Democratic-controlled city council. In others, including New Orleans and Nashville, brief periods of Republican hegemony had ended by 1873. Redemption did not occur in Houston until 1874, and Raleigh and Montgomery until 1875. In only a handful of other cities, including Jackson, Mississippi, and Chattanooga, did Republicans continue in power until the late 1880s.[30]

28. Wotton, "New City of the South," 323, 218, 321.
29. *Montgomery Daily Advertiser,* October 25, 1871; April 21, 1875.
30. For the situation in Richmond, Nashville, Montgomery, Raleigh, and Atlanta, see Rabinowitz, "From Reconstruction to Redemption in the Urban South," reprinted above. For the experience of the other cities, see Wertenbaker, *Norfolk,* 268–70; Robert E. Perdue, *The Negro in Savannah, 1865–1900* (New York: Exposition Press, 1973), 43; Capers, *Biography of a River Town,* 173; Vernon Lane Wharton, *The Negro in Mississippi 1865–1890*

The extent of black officeholding varied. No black served as mayor of a major city, but with the exception of a few cities like Savannah, the Reconstruction city councils did include some blacks, though never a majority. Black councilmen like William Finch of Atlanta, Holland Thompson of Montgomery, and James H. Harris of Raleigh used their considerable influence to secure schools and greater relief aid for blacks and to provide improved services for Negro neighborhoods. Thompson and Harris also pressed successfully for the appointment of Negro police and the establishment of segregated fire companies.[31] Few other cities had Negro policemen during the period, but with the notable exceptions of Atlanta and Richmond, most cities had Negro firemen.

Redemption in places like New Orleans, Atlanta, and Montgomery meant the end of Negro officeholding in nonfederal jobs until the twentieth century. Elsewhere, as in Richmond's Jackson Ward and Raleigh's Second and Fourth wards, the gerrymandering that prevented Republican control of the cities permitted the election of Negro councilmen until the turn of the century. These black politicians, however, were no longer able to help their black constituents to the extent their counterparts had during Reconstruction.

1873–1879

The celebration over urban Redemption was quickly tempered by growing nationwide financial difficulties. Although the panic of 1873 and the subsequent six years of depression severely hurt the North, the South suffered more. In part, this was because southern cities were "traditionally low in capital with substantial credit advanced to the agricultural regions." More important was the crippling effect on the region's railroads and on the cities whose lifelines they had become. John Stover's survey of postbellum southern railroads concluded that as a result of their financial position on the eve of the panic, southern railroads

---

(Chapel Hill: University of North Carolina Press, 1947), 168; Joy J. Jackson, *New Orleans in the Gilded Age* (Baton Rouge: Louisiana State University Press, 1969), 28; for Chattanooga, see *Nashville Banner,* February 29, October 10, 1889; McComb, *Houston,* 77–81.

31. See, for example, Montgomery City Council Minutes, August 15, 24, October 19, November 2, 1868; May 3, 1869; September 5, 1870, Alabama Department of Archives and History, Montgomery; Clarence A. Bacote, "William Finch, Negro Councilman and Political Activities in Atlanta during Early Reconstruction," *Journal of Negro History* 40 (January 1955): 341–64; *Raleigh Daily Standard,* July 14, 1868; January 5, 1869; *Raleigh Register,* March 27, 1878; Elaine Joan Nowaczyk, "The North Carolina Negro in Politics, 1865–1876" (Master's thesis, University of North Carolina, Chapel Hill, 1957).

suffered more than northern lines.[32] Though Stover's subject states included Kentucky and excluded Texas and Arkansas, his findings apply to the conditions in the eleven states of the former Confederacy.

By November 1873, 55 railroads in Stover's ten states had defaulted on interest on their bonds. Within three years 45 percent of the 127 major southern lines were in default of their bond coupons, and the figure was 50 percent or more in Virginia, Florida, Alabama, and Louisiana; in the rest of the country less than one-fourth of the lines were in default. Default usually led to receivership, and together they greatly restricted the amount of new railroad construction. The depressed conditions of the 1870s thus accelerated the decline of the South's share in the nation's railroad mileage. That share had shrunk from nearly one-third of the total in 1861, to little more than one-fourth in 1865, and to one-fifth in 1873. By 1880 the 14,811 miles in the southern states constituted less than 16 percent of the national total. The shortage of funds also led to a decline in the quality of equipment, roadbeds, and service. And, finally, many of the bankrupt locally owned southern railroads fell into northern hands. Of the 45 major roads in Stover's ten states in 1870–1871, only 19 percent of the traceable members of the boards of directors came from the North, whereas in 1880–1881 37 percent of the directors were northerners and nearly half the companies had northern presidents, compared to less than one-sixth ten years before.[33]

Internally the period from 1873 to 1880 was one of belt tightening for southern cities in payment for the heady expansion of the early postwar years. The economic downturn made it increasingly difficult to maintain municipal services and pay interest on bonded debts. Collection of the newly levied property taxes became even more difficult than in the past.[34] In an unsuccessful effort at social pressure, newspapers listed the names of residents owing taxes, but even city officials such as Nashville mayor Thomas A. Kercheval could be found among the defaulters. The combination of national depression, overspending, and tax evasion forced Houston's officials to arrange compromises with that city's creditors in 1875, 1881, and 1888. They were able to fund a consolidated debt at a lower interest in return for cutting expenditures and raising taxes. In November 1873 Montgomery's Republican newspaper called upon the voters "who desire economy in city government" to turn out the Democratic-controlled council because it had allowed the floating debt to rise from twenty thousand to seventy thousand dollars. The voters answered the call, and the new Republican council,

32. Russell, "Atlanta," 209; Stover, *Railroads of the South,* 124.
33. Stover, *Railroads of the South,* 124, 125, 129, 153.
34. See, for example, Harold Lawrence Platt, "Urban Public Services and Private Enterprise: Aspects of the Legal and Economic History of Houston, Texas, 1865–1905" (Ph.D. diss., Rice University, 1974), 20–21, 29.

along with the reelected Republican mayor, cut city expenses from $180,887 in 1873 to $144,874 in 1874. Because revenue for 1874 was only $143,832, the call for retrenchment was renewed. In response, the council eliminated one city office, consolidated several others, and reduced most salaries.[35]

The little town of Greensboro lagged behind its larger counterparts in the timing of its expansion and contraction but provides an excellent example of what was happening in cities throughout the region during the 1870s. In 1874 Mayor Cyrus Mendenhall was elected to the first of three consecutive terms as mayor in response to pleas for better services. Under Mendenhall charter amendments were passed tripling the property tax rate and increasing the poll tax from two to three dollars. As other cities had done prior to 1873, the city under Mendenhall constructed a new market house, set up a mayor's court, improved the streets, gave free vaccinations, and levied new taxes to support a public school system. But by 1877 hard times had arrived in Greensboro, and a taxpayer revolt defeated Mendenhall. Silas Dodson was elected on a platform promising retrenchment and economy. Reelected annually from 1877 to 1882, Dodson cut taxes in half, causing city income to fall substantially and city services to decline greatly.[36]

For several cities the economic troubles of the 1870s were made even worse by the ravage of disease. In 1873, for example, epidemics of cholera in Nashville and yellow fever in Montgomery drained city finances and interfered with trade.[37] But hardest hit by the economic repercussions were New Orleans and Memphis. Though New Orleans remained the South's largest city throughout the period, its postbellum rate of growth was seriously slowed by a number of problems. Hurt most by the impact of the railroad, she also suffered from the absence of a populous local market area and the effects of the Civil War on the cotton trade. Throughout her history the epidemic-plagued Crescent City had also suffered from frequent quarantines that brought commerce to a standstill. After the war yellow fever visited the city in 1873 and more severely in 1878. In the latter year thousands fled for their lives, leaving behind 3,977 dead. Throughout the South cities closed their doors to New Orleans trade lest the disease be spread. Not until the late 1880s would there be an economic

35. See, for example, *Nashville Daily American,* December 7, 1875, which lists Kercheval as owing $11.75; Platt, "Urban Public Services," 17–22; *Montgomery Alabama State Journal,* November 30, 1873; January 6, 1875; *Montgomery Daily Advertiser,* December 22, 1874.

36. Samuel Millard Kipp III, "Urban Growth and Social Change in the South, 1870–1920: Greensboro, North Carolina, as a Case Study" (Ph.D. diss., Princeton University, 1974), 47–50, 56.

37. See, for example, *Nashville Republican Banner,* June 8–July 1, 1873; *Montgomery Alabama State Journal,* October 1873, passim.

revival, some eight years after the city's more healthful competitors again had begun to prosper.[38]

The importance of a healthy environment to urban growth was even more evident in Memphis, which, unlike New Orleans, had been prospering in the postwar period. Blessed by a choice river location and the coming of the railroads, the Bluff City became the largest inland cotton market with a population that grew from 22,623 in 1860 to 40,226 ten years later. Through the early 1870s it looked like nothing would impede the city's rise to regional dominance, but in 1878 its longtime disregard for sanitation and the poverty of its growing lower-class population finally took its toll. The city had endured frequent yellow fever epidemics, but in 1878–1879 the dreaded disease killed approximately 5,800 people, nearly half of them Irish. Meanwhile the wealthy fled, many of whom, especially Germans, settled permanently in St. Louis. Unable to meet its financial obligations, the battered city lost its corporate status, and its legal name was changed to "Taxing District of Shelby County." It was governed by two sets of commissioners made up equally of appointed and elected members, an arrangement which became a model for future commission governments. By 1880 the population had shrunk to 33,592. As Gerald Capers observed, there were "two cities . . . one which existed prior to the pestilence, and a second metropolis which sprang up like a fungus growth on the ruins of the first."[39]

While a few places such as Richmond, Atlanta, Nashville, and the young Texas towns did comparatively well during the 1870s, for most of the urban South the decade was a disaster. Without the prosperous first three years the debacle would have been even worse. Cursed by an unhealthy location, like New Orleans and Memphis, Mobile saw its population reduced from 32,034 to 29,132. Savannah grew by less than 2,500 and Knoxville by under 1,100. A slight increase in the South's urban population resulted in the percentage of urban dwellers rising from 8.6 percent in 1870 to 8.68 percent ten years later. Meanwhile, outside the South the urban population had grown by about four million people, and the percentage of the nation's urban dwellers had grown from 25.7 percent to 28.2 percent.[40]

38. C. Vann Woodward, *Origins of the New South, 1877–1913,* vol. 9 of *A History of the South,* ed. Wendell Holmes Stephenson and E. Merton Coulter, 10 vols. (Baton Rouge: Louisiana State University Press, 1951), 108; David Paul Bennetts, "Black and White Workers: New Orleans, 1880–1900" (Ph.D. diss., University of Illinois at Urbana-Champaign, 1972), 14–15.

39. Capers, *Biography of a River Town,* 182–205, quote, 204.

40. Individual city populations for 1870 and 1880 from the U.S. census. All future city population figures cited in this essay are derived from the federal census unless noted otherwise. Regional and nationwide figures computed from censuses and table in Smith, "Emergence of Cities," 33. If Kentucky is included, the percentage of urban dwellers in the South remains unchanged at 9.4 percent by 1880.

While slower population growth and rising unemployment weakened the tax base and forced city governments to cut basic services, private companies were also failing to live up to the requirements of their franchises. The chief victims were the poor and the middle class. In 1875 the Montgomery Street Railway Company discontinued service after less than a year in business; in 1876 two Nashville streetcar lines increased their fares from five to ten cents. By 1881 the Houston Gas Light Company had laid 10 miles of mains on the city's 200 miles of streets but only in the most lucrative areas.[41] Neither private nor municipal waterworks extended their lines into poorer neighborhoods, continuing instead to supply the central business districts and better residential areas. Most cities remained without any sewer systems, and the early efforts at street paving languished. In 1880 less than a third of Charleston and only 94 of New Orleans's 566 miles of streets were paved. Houstonians with no paving called Galvestonians "sandlappers"; the latter with half of their 200 miles of streets paved called their upstart rivals "mud turtles." To a northern visitor Mobile looked "dilapidated and hopeless," and the business district of Charleston remained in the ruins left by the war.[42] Even in Atlanta, where the decade of the 1870s had begun so favorably, the decline in municipal services took its toll, especially after local businessmen in 1874 pushed through a new charter framed so as to help pay off the city debt and not incur a new one. The value of trade and real estate rose very slightly, and as in other cities Retrenchment and Reform replaced Enterprise and Progress as the slogan of the day. Arriving in Atlanta in 1878, George Campbell was "disappointed to find that it is not at all a pretty or nice town; very inferior in amenities to all the other Southern towns I have seen. It is, in fact, a new brick town built with no trees in the streets, but abundant mud." By 1880 only 3 of Atlanta's 100 miles of streets were paved, all downtown. And by 1883 the less than 20 miles of water pipes proved inadequate to save from fire the city's most visible symbol of progress, the Kimball House hotel.[43] Only the city's mild climate and high elevation protected it from the ravage of disease, for as yet there was no adequate sewer system or sanitation service.

41. *Montgomery Alabama State Journal,* May 6, 1875; *Nashville Daily American,* June 30, 1876; Platt, "Urban Public Services," 41.

42. U.S. Bureau of the Census, *Report on the Social Statistics of Cities,* pt. 2, *The Southern and the Western States* (Washington, D. C., 1887), 99, 272; Coulter, *South during Reconstruction,* 263; Woodward, *Origins of the New South,* 107.

43. Russell, "Atlanta," 209–11, 278–87; Campbell, *White and Black: The Outcome of a Visit to the United States* (London, 1879), 369.

1879–1900

The trouble of the 1870s was largely forgotten in the boom years that followed. The period from 1880 to 1892 was one of rapid urban growth throughout
the country, and this time the South led the way. Whereas in 1880 8.6 percent of
southerners qualified as urban, by 1890, after an increase of 49 percent, the
figure stood at 12.8 percent. During the decade the national percentage had
climbed from 28.2 percent to 35.1 percent, a gain of only 25 percent. Urban
growth continued during the 1890s, though it was less marked because of the
panic of 1893 and the economic hard times that followed. By 1900 14.8 percent
of southerners were urban as compared to 39.7 percent of the nation as a
whole.[44]

An infusion of northern capital and capitalists helped pull the railroads out of
the depression and thus aided local merchants who had been suffering from
erratic service and high freight rates. Of crucial importance was the organization
in October 1875 of the Southern Railway and Steamship Association. Open to
any southern railroad south of the Ohio and Potomac rivers and east of the
Mississippi, it had twenty-seven members in 1877. Thanks to the efficiency of
this new pooling arrangement, freight rates to eastern cities declined from 1875
to 1887. Rates from New York, Boston, or Baltimore to Atlanta, for example,
were reduced roughly one-third between 1876 and 1884. As Stover concluded,
"The rationalization of the freight rate structure plus the mere passage of time
brought a degree of prosperity to the Southern railroads." There was no new
default among major railroads after 1878, and new construction increased in
1879 and 1880. As early as 1877 the northern press was noting the first indications of an economic recovery in the South.[45]

During the 1880s American railroads added more mileage than in any other
decade in history. This time the South outpaced the nationwide growth; while the
increase in mileage for the nation was 79 percent, Stover's ten southern states
increased their rail network by 98 percent. Had his sample included Texas rather
than Kentucky, the percentage increase would have been even greater. During the
decade the Lone Star State led the entire country in miles constructed with 5,934;
its 1880 total of 2,697 had already placed it first in the South in total mileage.
Georgia ranked second in miles added, while Alabama almost doubled her total
trackage, and Florida's almost quadrupled. Though Virginia, South Carolina, and

44. Percentages computed from the 1880, 1890, and 1900 U.S. censuses and the table
in Smith, "Emergence of Cities," 33. If Kentucky and Oklahoma are included, the percentage of urban dwellers rises to 13.4 percent in 1890 and 15.2 percent in 1900.
45. Stover, *Railroads of the South,* 150–52, 186.

Tennessee lagged behind, each of them still built more new lines in the decade than all of New England.[46] Some of this expansion was due to the construction of entirely new roads like the Georgia Pacific and the Louisville, New Orleans, and Texas, but most of it was due to the activities of the eleven largest companies of 1880. New construction slowed in the 1890s, especially after 1893, yet the southern rate of increase remained slightly greater than the national average, with Texas, Georgia, Louisiana, Florida, and Alabama in the forefront. By 1900 Florida had jumped from last in total trackage in the region to fifth.[47]

The last twenty years of the century also brought increased consolidation of the southern lines, first as a result of the prosperity of the 1880s, and then because of the numerous receiverships prompted by the economic downturn of the 1890s. Though coming later in the South than in the North, that process of consolidation was essentially completed by 1900. In 1890 there were fifty-eight lines over one hundred miles in length; by 1900 there were only thirty-one. By 1900 three-fourths of the mileage in the South outside of Texas was controlled by five corporations: Southern Railway, Louisville and Nashville, Atlantic Coast Line, Seaboard Air Line, and Illinois Central. All five were controlled by northern bankers. Indeed, the expansion and consolidation of southern railroads had been accomplished by a steady increase in northern capital and management. In 1880 37 percent of the directors of the forty-five major lines in Stover's ten states had come from the North. In 1890 fifty-eight major lines drew 47 percent of their board members from the North, and thirty-six of the presidents were northerners, including the heads of nine of the twelve longest lines. By 1900 over 60 percent of the directors of the major lines came from the North, as did 58 percent of the presidents. Throughout the period the extent of northern control was even greater than it seemed, for southerners operated only the shortest lines, over which the larger railroads, through leases, stock ownership, and other financial ties, exerted significant influence.[48]

The expansion, consolidation, and infusion of northern capital greatly improved the southern rail system. Certainly without consolidation and northern influence, the switch by southern railroads to the northern 4-foot, 8½-inch gauge in 1886 would have been delayed several years. By 1900 there was better service, more efficient interchange of traffic, better equipment, and lower rates than there had been in the past, although in none of these areas had the southern railroads attained parity with the North.

46. Ibid., 190; U.S. Bureau of the Census, *Eleventh Census of the United States: 1890: Report on Transportation Business in the United States*, pt. 1, *Transportation by Land* (Washington, D.C.: Government Printing Office, 1895), 4.

47. Stover, *Railroads of the South*, 196, 255.

48. Ibid., 207–8, 274–75, 279–80, 282.

The urban impact of these railroad developments cannot be overestimated. T. Lynn Smith concluded that the perfecting of rail transportation in the last quarter of the nineteenth century was probably the most important factor in determining the precise locations for concentrations of population in the South. As a result, "By 1900 important towns were aligned along the principal railways like beads on a string." Or, as John Stover concluded about the railroad boom of the 1880s, "Expansion and economic growth came most definitely to those cities such as Atlanta and Memphis, which were served by newly built railroads." Memphis, whose population rose 92 percent, from 33,592 in 1880 to 64,495 in 1890, added seven railroads in the dozen years after 1880, while new lines enhanced Atlanta's position as the South's major rail center and helped swell its population from 37,400 to 65,533.[49] With the aid of better railroad transportation, Chattanooga grew from 12,892 to 29,100; Knoxville from 9,693 to 22,535; Houston from 16,513 to 27,557; San Antonio from 20,550 to 37,673; and Dallas from 10,358 to 38,067. The expansion of the Norfolk and Western Railroad into the rich Virginia and West Virginia coal fields had by 1885 allowed coal to replace cotton as Norfolk's chief export and helped increase the population from 21,966 to 34,871, well above the percentage increase for other coastal cities.[50] By 1900 the penetration of Florida by rail had led to the founding of Miami in 1896 and almost quadrupled the population of Jacksonville from the 1880 figure of 7,650, and Tampa had grown from 720 to 15,839.

Most noteworthy was the growth of Birmingham, no more than a cornfield in 1870. Two northern real estate speculators, attracted by the rich iron deposits of northern Alabama's Jefferson County, founded the town in 1871. Realizing the site's potential, the Louisville and Nashville Railroad completed the South and North Alabama Railroad to Decatur, making a junction with the Alabama and Chattanooga near Birmingham. L and N officials invested in real estate and in the town's new iron mills, ran special trains for prospective investors, and provided lower rates for southern pig iron.[51] Because of a cholera epidemic and the effects of the panic of 1873, growth was slow: there were only 3,086 inhabitants in 1880. But the town was linked to Atlanta by the Georgia Pacific in 1883, and a plethora of new lines soon connected the once isolated community with the major cities of the North and South. By 1890 the population was 26,178, and ten years later it had climbed to 38,414, on its way to the almost unbelievable figure of 132,685 in 1910.

49. Smith, "Emergence of Cities," 36; Stover, *Railroads of the South,* 187. Atlanta, however, suffered throughout the period because of freight rate discrimination. Russell, "Atlanta," 39.
50. Wertenbaker, *Norfolk,* 308; Stover, *Railroads of the South,* 261–62.
51. Stover, *Railroads of the South,* 218.

After 1880 railroad penetration and industrial development went hand in hand. In 1880 the southern states produced approximately one-sixteenth of the nation's pig iron. By 1890, thanks to Birmingham and her sister towns of Anniston, Sheffield, and Bessemer, Alabama was producing nearly one-tenth of the nation's pig iron, and the South accounted for nearly one-fifth of the 10,307,000 tons in the country.[52] The iron mines and later the steel mills of Birmingham dominated the economic as well as the physical landscape of the community. By 1900 there were 282 manufacturing plants employing seven thousand workers who produced goods valued at more than twelve million dollars. Around the city there were numerous coke ovens, blast furnaces, rolling mills, iron foundries, and machine shops, in addition to the newly erected steel mill. The products of the mills went north on the city's eight railroad lines, which also helped distribute the products of the city's more than fifty different kinds of noniron related manufacturing enterprises.[53]

Of the ten largest cities in the South, only Memphis approached Birmingham in the debt owed to manufacturing. Here too the most spectacular phase of the city's industrialization coincided with the railroad expansion of the 1880s. In 1880 there was $2,313,975 invested in manufacturing establishments that turned out products valued at $4,413,422; by 1890 the respective figures were $9,357,821 and $13,244,538. The increase in invested capital from 1880 to 1890 was 304 percent, while the increases in Nashville, Atlanta, and Richmond were 154 percent, 285.2 percent, and 142.4 percent. Memphis experienced a similar comparative advantage in the growth of value of her manufactured goods. Though slowed by the panic of 1893, the rate of investment in manufacturing continued to increase. The city's major industry until the turn of the century was the production of lumber. Second largest was the manufacture of cottonseed products, which began in the 1880s. Additional manufacturing included beer, snuff, printing and publishing, drugs, and pharmaceutical supplies.[54]

Throughout the South other communities sought to build their post-1880 economies around industry. Richmond initially was the tobacco capital of the nation, with more than fifty factories in operation by 1880; its rich hinterland also provided resources for its flour mills and iron and steel foundries. Steamboats ran regularly between the city and Norfolk, New York, Baltimore, and

52. Ibid., 193–94.
53. Paul B. Worthman, "Working Class Mobility in Birmingham, Alabama, 1880–1914," in *Anonymous Americans: Explorations in Nineteenth-Century Social History*, ed. Tamara K. Hareven (Englewood Cliffs, N. J.: Prentice Hall, 1971), 174–75.
54. William D. Miller, *Memphis during the Progressive Era, 1900–1917* (Memphis: Memphis State University Press, 1957), 43–48.

Philadelphia. It was the terminus of six railroads, nearly all parts of trunk lines that connected Richmond with principal markets throughout the country.[55] But just as Birmingham took its place in the production of iron, and cities like Norfolk challenged its flour milling leadership, by the end of the century the new tobacco towns of North Carolina had replaced Richmond, using production of what King James I once called a "stinking weed" to catapult themselves from obscurity to urban prominence. From 1880 to 1900 Winston grew from 443 to 10,008, and the Dukes of Durham had pushed their town's population to 6,679 after it had been entirely omitted from the census of 1870. To the south Tampa had grown "from an isolated gulf coastal city town of sandbeds, small merchants and cattlemen to a thriving commercial port city" after the beginning of the cigar industry in 1885.[56]

Much local manufacturing centered around cotton. Memphis, for example, became the country's leading producer of cottonseed oil. Montgomery was typical of many of the medium-sized interior towns. One local firm produced cottonseed oil, another manufactured cotton presses and other machinery, and a third operated a cotton press.[57] Cotton presses were especially important to the economy of interior towns because newer and larger presses meant tighter packing of cotton, allowing more cotton to be sent by rail without transshipment in the port cities.

Montgomery also had a textile mill, a type of facility that southerners increasingly sought during the 1880s. In the 1870s the South had no more than 6 percent of the nation's cotton textile spindles and looms, and processed no more than one-tenth of the cotton manufactured in the nation; by 1890 the South had one-eighth of the nation's spindles, and southern mills were using nearly one-third as much cotton as northern mills.[58] The Atlanta International Cotton Exposition held in the fall of 1881 gave southern textile manufacturing a boost. In its wake there appeared a veritable cotton-mill crusade, allegedly aimed at providing jobs for needy white workers but with more than passing interest in profits and town building. The stimulus of the mills, often financed and controlled by northerners, helped increase the populations of numerous North Carolina towns: between 1880 and 1900 Greensboro grew from 2,105 to 10,035; Charlotte from 7,094 to 18,091; and Gastonia from 236 to 4,610. By employing as textile

55. Bureau of the Census, *Social Statistics of Cities,* pt. 2, *Southern and Western States,* 80–81.

56. Durward Long, "The Making of Modern Tampa: A City of the New South, 1865–1911," *Florida Historical Quarterly* 49 (April 1971): 333–45, quote, 334.

57. H. G. McCall, comp., *A Sketch, Historical and Statistical of the City of Montgomery* (Montgomery, 1885), 40, 51–60.

58. Stover, *Railroads of the South,* 192–93.

workers the wives of men who worked in the city's furniture factories, High Point, unlisted in 1870, grew to 4,163 by 1900.

The effort of Raleigh to get a textile mill indicates the importance of the facility as an element in urban rivalry and urban imperialism, but it also points out that not everyone was equally enthusiastic about the quest. "How about that cotton factory?" chided the *Raleigh Daily Constitution* in urging local businessmen to "awake from your lethargy" in 1875. "Wilmington has one, Charlotte is thinking about establishing one and Raleigh should not be behind the times." Thirteen years later civic leaders were still trying to bring a factory to the city. "What is to become of Raleigh unless we do something to increase its business?" bemoaned the *State Chronicle*.[59] Finally, in 1891 a mill began operating, soon followed by two others.

Southerners like Atlanta's Henry W. Grady pointed with pride to southern gains in manufacturing. Yet the gilt of New South imagery obscured the core of Old South realities. As C. Vann Woodward has demonstrated, the South, by running fast had, despite considerable progress, merely succeeded in standing still in its race with the North. In 1860 the South had 17.2 percent of the manufacturing establishments in the country and 11.5 percent of the capital; by 1904 the respective figures were 15.3 percent and 11 percent. The value of manufactures rose from 10.3 percent of the total value produced in the United States to 10.5 percent. In 1900 the proportion of people in southern states east of the Mississippi engaged in manufacturing was about the proportion in all the states east of the Mississippi in 1850.[60]

The antebellum dream of a balanced economy secured by a strong manufacturing base that would free the region from dependence upon the North remained unfulfilled. As before, commerce was the lifeblood of most southern cities, which continued to depend primarily on an exchange of goods with their agrarian hinterlands. Atlanta, for example, tried mightily to become a manufacturing center. In addition to hosting the exposition of 1881, city businessmen and officials supported construction of the Georgia Pacific to Birmingham in search of cheap fuel, and in 1886 had the city chosen as the site for the Georgia Institute of Technology. As a result, the city added about twenty new factories during the 1880s. Yet by 1890 the city's 410 industries employed 8,684 workers and had an annual value of products of only slightly more than thirteen million dollars.

59. *Raleigh Daily Constitution,* July 9, 1875, quoted in Sarah McCulloh Lemmon, "Raleigh: An Example of the New South," *North Carolina Historical Review* 43 (July 1966), 265; *Raleigh State Chronicle,* February 2, 1888, quoted in ibid., 266. Even a large city like Memphis resisted efforts to support a mill. See W. D. Miller, *Memphis during the Progressive Era,* 54.
60. *Origins of the New South,* 140.

Whereas in 1880 34 percent of the employed male workers were in trade and transportation and 28.5 percent in manufacturing, ten years later the respective figures were only 38.6 percent and 31.5 percent.[61] Manufacturing lagged in the city initially because of the absence of water power and later because of the inability to get cheap coal for steam power as a result of freight-rate discrimination. Above all, there was the lack of investment capital, as local businessmen preferred the rich rewards of commerce and railroad speculation.

Elsewhere the story was similar. In 1890 42 percent of the employed males in the fifty largest American cities worked in manufacturing, 30.3 percent in trade and transportation, and 24.9 percent in professional and personal services. Yet of the six cities of the former Confederacy in the sample, only Richmond, with 38.4 percent of its employed males in manufacturing, even approached the big-city mean; the other five cities ranged from 28.5 percent in New Orleans to 33.6 percent in Nashville. Each city naturally exceeded the mean for percentages of service and trade and transportation workers.[62] Cities like Memphis and Augusta used manufacturing to encourage growth, but their respective economies clearly depended on their positions as the first and second largest inland cotton markets in the country. The value of manufactured goods in Memphis, for example, had increased to $18 million by 1900, but during the 1890s the city's annual trade was estimated at $200 million. The production of cigars helped Tampa, but without the trade of its growing agricultural hinterland, the export of phosphate discovered nearby in 1883, and its role as the major embarkation and supply port during the Spanish-American War, its growth would have been minimal.[63] And, as in the case of sugar refining in New Orleans, tobacco manufacturing in Richmond, or furniture making in Memphis, manufacturing usually was itself commerce-related.

The extent to which commercial and service-oriented pursuits continued to dominate the life of southern cities is also evident in the pattern of political leadership. In northern cities during the last twenty years of the century, the old commercial elites that had governed throughout the nineteenth century were being replaced by professional politicians. And in major industrial centers like

61. Wotton, "New City of the South," 416; Russell, "Atlanta," 243–44; R. David Weber, "Urbanization, Ethnicity, and Occupational Status in the Rising American City, 1870–1900," paper delivered at the sixty-eighth annual meeting of the Pacific Coast Branch, American Historical Association, August 21, 1975, Berkeley, Calif., Miscellaneous Tables on Composition of the Work Force in the Largest American Cities.

62. Weber, "Urbanization, Ethnicity, and Occupational Status," table 3 and miscellaneous tables. Weber nevertheless emphasizes the similar composition of the work force in all major cities.

63. Capers, Biography of a River Town, 217–18; 224, German, "Queen City of the Savannah," 17; Long, "Making of Modern Tampa," passim.

Pittsburgh, manufacturers figured prominently in the nationwide urban reform opposition generally led by lawyers. But although cities like New Orleans and Augusta were controlled for many years by professional politicians, it was the merchants who generally ran the southern city governments or spearheaded the reformers. Nashville, for example, enjoyed a marked increase in the importance of manufacturing during the postbellum period, but only one manufacturer, the owner of a hardware firm, was elected mayor, and then not until 1898. Of the thirty members of the city council in 1878, only two were manufacturers; four years later there were none. In both years the majority of councilmen were merchants and petty tradesmen.[64] Not until 1902 did control of government in Houston shift from mercantile hands, and then the recipients were lawyers rather than manufacturers. Even in the mill town of Greensboro, the manufacturers had a minority share of the power. By the turn of the century political leadership "was in the hands of a small oligarchy of bankers, large merchants, industrialists, influential editors and professional men." Not until 1910 was there a definite shift of power from commercial elements to manufacturers. Surprisingly, Birmingham also fit the broader pattern: commercial interests controlled the government and eventually triumphed over industrialists whose power was concentrated outside the city.[65] Throughout the South merchant-dominated chambers of commerce and boards of trade were the most powerful institutions in urban life.

The success of trade, the stimulus of manufacturing, and the general return to prosperity in the nation after 1880 allowed the southern cities to resume the task of extending and modernizing municipal services. By the last decade of the century, however, it was evident that there was an important difference between this period of expansion and that of the 1870s. As Harold Platt has written about Houston, "Reconstruction officials possessed an unrestrained spending authority and an uncertain ability to collect revenues. Administrations in the 90s mainly faced decisions on how to allocate insufficient but predictable amounts of income."[66] Southern cities were clearly less inclined than northern cities to spend public funds for urban improvements. In 1902 every southern city over 25,000

---

64. Mayer N. Zald and Thomas A. Anderson, "Secular Trends and Historical Contingencies in the Recruitment of Mayors: Nashville as Compared to New Haven and Chicago," *Urban Affairs Quarterly* 3 (June 1968): 53–68; *Nashville Daily American,* October 11, 1878; October 2, 1882.

65. Platt, "Urban Public Services," 171; Kipp, "Urban Growth and Social Change in the South," 343; Carl V. Harris, "Annexation Struggles and Political Power in Birmingham, Alabama, 1890–1910," *Alabama Review* 27 (July 1974): 169. See also Eugene John Watts, "Characteristics of Candidates in City Politics: Atlanta, 1865–1903" (Ph.D. diss., Emory University, 1969).

66. "Urban Public Services," 117.

had a tax levy per capita below the national average of $12.89 for the 160 cities with that population. Only 7 of the 21 southern cities—New Orleans, Richmond, San Antonio, Houston, Dallas, Galveston, and Fort Worth—came within two dollars of that figure. And whereas the total debt per capita for the 160 cities was $62.04, only 8 of the southern cities—Richmond, Charleston, Norfolk, Houston, Mobile, Galveston, Fort Worth, and Montgomery—exceeded that average.[67] While some of the gap between public spending in the North and South was due to the great number of poor people, particularly blacks, in southern cities, it was due more to the twin desires to keep spending low and to give tax breaks to manufacturing concerns.

Within the confines of limited budgets, the municipal governments sought to improve their urban plants. By 1902 the high rates charged by electric light companies led five of the cities—Nashville, Little Rock, Jacksonville, Galveston, and Fort Worth—to join the fourteen northern cities with more than 25,000 people that had erected municipally owned electric light plants. Jacksonville, Galveston, and Fort Worth constructed municipal waterworks, while Dallas, Montgomery, New Orleans, and, in 1903, Memphis purchased private companies that had been poorly supplying their cities with water. In the case of Memphis, the result was a 20 percent decline in rates.[68] Nevertheless, by the end of the century water mains were still confined largely to the better sections of town and the downtown area, and most citizens relied on cisterns and wells. Often there was insufficient pressure with which to fight fires, and pure water did not become a reality until after 1900. Slaughterhouses and tanneries were inadequately regulated and, as was true of individuals, dumped their waste directly into the streams, wells, or rivers that furnished the water. A letter writer in Nashville described the town's drinking water in 1890 as "warm and thick," and visitors unaccustomed to it were advised to flee to the suburbs for a purer version.[69]

Prompted by the yellow fever epidemic of 1878, most cities sought to prevent contamination of their water supplies. Businessmen in towns like Mobile, Memphis, and New Orleans had learned the economic costs of disease and took the lead in urging improved sanitation measures. Their counterparts in healthier cities like Atlanta sought improvements in public health in order to maintain prosperity rather than to regain it. Memphis, Atlanta, and New Orleans had by 1879 greatly strengthened the powers of their boards of health. They also con-

67. U.S. Bureau of Census, *Statistics of Cities Having a Population of Over 25,000 in 1902 and 1903,* Bulletin 20 (Washington, D.C.: Government Printing Office, 1905), 443–45.

68. Ibid., 104–5; W. D. Miller, *Memphis during the Progressive Era,* 69.

69. Letter of "A. F." to a friend in Ohio, reprinted in *Nashville Banner,* July 10, 1890.

centrated on sewerage and waste disposal. But here again the better neighbor-hoods were the chief beneficiaries.[70] Memphis had the most ambitious program. Between 1878 and 1898 the city constructed approximately forty-five miles of sewers; from 1899 to 1901 an additional ninety-eight miles were added. In New Orleans, however, it took the deaths of almost four hundred people from yellow fever between 1897 and 1899 to force the city to purchase the franchise of the dormant sewage company and to begin laying sewer pipes in 1903.[71]

Together with the installation of sewers, the paving of streets received the bulk of municipal expenditures. The little town of Tampa, whose population went from 720 in 1880 to nearly 6,000 in 1890, approved bonds totaling $95,000 in 1889 for streets and sewers and then approved an additional $100,000 two years later. Despite significant advances in paving over the previous twenty years, by the turn of the century few southern cities had more than half their streets paved. By 1902 New Orleans had more than doubled its mileage of paved streets, but that still left almost 500 of the city's 700 miles of streets unpaved; Atlanta's paved street mileage had increased from 3 to 63.4, but that left 140 miles of streets unpaved; about one-tenth of Memphis streets were paved.[72] In each case it was the downtown and better residential areas that avoided the dust and mud that plagued most urban residents.

The urban South also continued to lag behind the rest of the country in the quality of education offered its children, though again significant gains occurred in the closing years of the century. The decade of the 1880s was especially noteworthy as the number of schools in Richmond rose from eleven to eighteen and Nashville added five to its previous total of nine. The number of Norfolk schools rose from six in 1874 to ten by 1893 and fifteen in 1902.[73] By 1902 almost all school buildings were owned by the cities rather than rented, as had been the case earlier in the period, and everyone of the towns over 25,000 had

70. John H. Ellis, "Business and Public Health in the Urban South during the Nine-teenth Century: New Orleans, Memphis, and Atlanta," *Bulletin of the History of Medicine* 44 (May–June 1970): 197–212; (July–August 1970): 346–71. See also Richard J. Hopkins, "Public Health in Atlanta: The Formative Years, 1865–1879," *Georgia Historical Quarterly* 53 (September 1969): 287–304.

71. W. D. Miller, *Memphis during the Progressive Era,* 68; J. J. Jackson, *New Orleans in the Gilded Age,* 153.

72. Long, "Making of Modern Tampa," 337; Bureau of the Census, *Statistics of Cities . . . 1902 and 1903,* 114.

73. Richmond, *Annual Report of the Superintendent of Public Schools of the City of Richmond, Virginia, for the Scholastic Year Ending July 31, 1881* (Richmond, 1882), 4; ibid., 1890–1891, 23; W. W. Clayton, *History of Davidson County, Tennessee* (Phila-delphia, 1880): 249–50; Nashville, *Annual Report of the Board of Education of Nashville for the Scholastic Year 1889–1890* (Nashville, 1890), 37; Wertenbaker, *Norfolk,* 280; Bureau of the Census, *Statistics of Cities . . . 1902 and 1903,* 93–94.

at least one high school. When compared to northern cities of comparable population, however, southern cities were still far behind in the percentage of children enrolled, number of schools and schoolrooms, and numbers and salaries of teachers. Whereas in 1902 the 160 cities with over 25,000 population spent an average of $4.37 per capita on their schools, New Orleans spent $1.74; Memphis, $1.61; Atlanta, $1.90; and Charleston, $1.41. Houston with $3.68 led the South, Fort Worth and Dallas being the only two others spending more than $3 per person. Nor were southern towns fertile ground for learning outside of the classroom. Of the twenty-nine cities with more than 25,000 people that had no public library in 1902, twelve were in the South; and those cities with libraries generally had fewer books in them than did northern cities of comparable size.[74]

Law enforcement and fire protection followed the same pattern. Important strides were made in professionalization, the integration of new technological advances, and numbers of men. By the 1870s police forces of the major cities were uniformed and more efficiently deployed, and by the early 1890s patrol wagons and modern communications systems, already common in the North, enjoyed widespread use. Throughout the South new city jails bore testimony both to the period's expensive public works efforts and the desire for greater security against lawbreakers. During the same period full-time paid firemen replaced the volunteer fire companies, though often, as in New Orleans, not until after 1890. Increasingly the new firemen benefitted from better alarm systems and fire-fighting equipment. Yet, as in the North, political favoritism greatly influenced police and fire department appointments.[75] And because of low funding, southern cities were probably less adequately protected than their northern counterparts.

City administrations had the most success in adding publicly owned parkland that provided aesthetic and recreational benefits to their communities. Though well underway in the North since the 1850s, the park movement had only slightly affected the South as late as the 1870s. As of 1880 there were no public parks in Norfolk, Chattanooga, or Montgomery; Charleston had 33 acres of parks; Memphis, 4 acres; and Atlanta, about 3 acres. Only New Orleans, with

74. Bureau of the Census, *Statistics of Cities . . . 1902 and 1903,* 93–94, 479–81, 101.
75. See, for example, Eugene J. Watts, "The Police in Atlanta, 1890–1905," *Journal of Southern History* 39 (May 1973): 165–82; *Souvenir History of the Richmond Police Department* (Richmond, 1901); *Souvenir History of the Montgomery Fire and Police Departments, 1819–1902* (Montgomery, 1902); Wertenbaker, *Norfolk,* 278, 280; *The Richmond, Virginia, Fire Department: Its Organization and Equipment, with an Account of Its Precursors* (Richmond, 1894); J. J. Jackson, *New Orleans in the Gilded Age,* 101–7; McComb, *Houston,* 80, 128. Compare, for example, Watts, "The Police in Atlanta," 176–82, and James F. Richardson, *The New York Police: Colonial Times to 1901* (New York: Oxford University Press, 1970).

659 acres, ranked with northern cities. Although the amount of parkland in New Orleans dropped to 522 acres during the subsequent two decades, other southern cities made remarkable gains. By 1902 Norfolk had 95 acres, much of it reclaimed from marshland; Atlanta, 155 acres; Charleston, 449 acres; and San Antonio, 294 acres. With a late spurt of acquisition, Memphis produced the most spectacular change. As of 1898 the city had only 30 acres of parks; by 1902 it had 782 acres, including the much publicized Riverside and Overton parks.[76]

After 1880 city governments also moved more aggressively to ensure that private companies provided needed services to residents. Unlike the financially troubled water companies, most utility and all traction operations remained in private hands. Exceptions included the municipally owned electric plants already mentioned and the gas works in Richmond, one of the five municipally owned in the entire country in 1902.[77] As in the rest of the nation, the service provided by these companies and the rates they charged were major issues in local politics. Because of the high stakes, franchise owners and seekers became actively involved in politics. In Houston between 1874 and 1888 twenty-one of the seventy mayors and aldermen were connected with a franchised corporation; in Greensboro, the head of the waterworks company was on the board of aldermen waterworks committee.[78] Elsewhere presidents of streetcar and gas companies chaired council franchise or streets committees, and their companies contributed generously to candidates for office. City administrations at first were hesitant to regulate closely these companies, but increasingly, especially after the panic of 1893, urban reformers in cities like Houston, New Orleans, and Augusta joined their northern counterparts in demanding greater regulation. The earlier policy of defending the public interest by liberally granting franchises to competing companies was replaced by the acceptance of supervised monopolies.[79]

This shift was aided, especially after 1893, by the kind of expansion and consolidation in privately owned municipal services that characterized the railroad system. Similarly, by 1900 northern capitalists owned most of the traction and utility corporations.

76. Bureau of the Census, *Statistics of Cities . . . 1880*, 67, 137, 201, 100, 144, 274–75; *Statistics of Cities . . . 1902 and 1903*, 114–19; W. D. Miller, *Memphis during the Progressive Era*, 79–83.

77. Bureau of the Census, *Statistics of Cities . . . 1902 and 1903*, 104–5.

78. Platt, "Urban Public Services," 238; Kipp, "Urban Growth and Social Change in the South," 368–69.

79. See, for example, Platt, "Urban Public Services," 54, 104–5, 124, 129–30; J. J. Jackson, *New Orleans in the Gilded Age*, 316–17; German, "Queen City of the Savannah," passim. For a similar shift in the North, see David Thelen, *The New Citizenship: Origins of Progressivism in Wisconsin, 1885–1900* (Columbia: University of Missouri Press, 1972).

By the turn of the century the "natural monopolies" of telegraph and tele-
phone that had arrived in most southern cities by the late 1870s were under the
control of Western Union and the Bell System. Likewise, the twenty-year competition within the gas and electric light industries had left one company in
each field in control of a given city. As in so many other areas of southern life,
the loser was frequently a local outfit; the winner, either northern-owned or
northern-financed. New Orleans, for example, chartered three electric light
companies, two of them owned by local residents. By 1897 the northern-
owned Edison Electric Company had absorbed one of its local rivals and had
driven the other out of business. In the early 1890s the economic difficulties of
two competing Houston electric light companies resulted in their merger into
Citizens Electric Company, financed by outside capitalists. Smaller towns exhibited the same tendency. The locally owned Tampa Electric Company, formed in 1887, was taken over in the 1890s by the Boston firm of Stone and
Webster.[80]

The most significant franchised enterprise of the closing twenty years of the
century was the street railway. Telephones remained very much the playthings of
the rich and successful (1,641 phones in New Orleans in 1898);[81] electric lights
illuminated the downtown areas and homes of the wealthy; even gas and water
left the lives of many urban residents unaffected. But for all but the very poor the
streetcar was an indispensable part of urban life. As in the rest of the country, the
period from the mid-1880s until the panic of 1893 witnessed a tremendous surge
in the installation of the first streetcar systems in cities like Raleigh, Natchez, and
Baton Rouge, or the reinstallation in cities like Montgomery, where previous
efforts had failed during the hard times of the 1870s. Installations were especially frequent in towns of less than ten thousand, for which streetcars became a
symbol of urban maturity. Furthermore, the South took the lead in the electrification of the lines. The first electric streetcar in regular operation appeared on
Montgomery streets in 1886, and two years later successful service on hilly
Richmond streets "proved, even more conclusively than Montgomery, that the
electric railway was practical." By 1890 several southern towns were among the
fifty-one cities with electrified lines, though New Orleans and Norfolk were
among those dragging their feet.[82]

80. J. J. Jackson, *New Orleans in the Gilded Age,* 165–67; Platt, "Urban Public Services," 136; Long, "Making of Modern Tampa," 337–38.
81. J. J. Jackson, *New Orleans in the Gilded Age,* 168.
82. Krim, "Innovation and Diffusion of the Street Railway," 93, 100; John Anderson
Miller, *Fares Please! A Popular History of Trolleys, Horsecars, Streetcars, Busses, Ele-
vateds, and Subways* (New York: D. Appleton Century Co., 1941), 55–69; J. J. Jackson,
New Orleans in the Gilded Age, 164; Wertenbaker, *Norfolk,* 318; the estimate of fifty-one

As with the other utilities, the rapid expansion of the streetcars during the 1880s and 1890s attracted northern financiers. During the 1890s the Memphis streetcar network expanded from thirty to seventy miles through the consolidation of the different lines into the Memphis Street Railway Company. Consolidation also meant a shift from mule to electricity. Then, in 1905, the system was sold to a northern syndicate. Representing associates in Omaha, Nebraska, E. A. Allen and O. M. Carter purchased Houston's two streetcar lines and converted them to electric power in 1891. Ten years later, after several receiverships, the Stone-Webster syndicate of Boston assumed control. In Tampa, where Stone and Webster owned the electric company, it was the New York–financed Light and Power Company that forced the locally owned Tampa Street Railway into bankruptcy in 1894.[83]

The electric streetcar and the steam dummies that also appeared on southern streets after the mid-1880s greatly affected the lives of city residents. As in the North, they contributed to the sorting out of the population by race and income and helped to usher in the golden age of the downtown area. The entry of the lines into previously isolated areas of the city sparked a housing construction boom. Housing advertisements now identified neighborhoods in terms of their proximity to the streetcars. In 1882 the *Nashville Banner* observed that the six-month-old Fatherland Streetrailway had "brought into prominence that hitherto comparatively inaccessible but most beautiful portion of the city known as the East End." The following year it noted that in North and East Nashville "immense numbers of small cottages are being built within a short walk of the 'tramways.'"[84] Even those too poor to ride the cars regularly to work could take them to pleasure grounds like Atlanta's Ponce de Leon Springs or Nashville's Glenwood Park that the lines operated to increase their ridership.

The streetcar's greatest impact was on the boundaries of the metropolitan area. The expansion of the lines resulted in the development of numerous communities on the rim of the city. In 1891 the *Richmond Dispatch* noted, "Men of means seeking villa sites; mechanics desiring cheap lots; people who delight in roominess and ample acreage have . . . encircled Richmond and Manchester with built up suburbs." The previous year the *Nashville Banner* carried a full-page advertisement for the sale of lots in "Waverly Place, the Suburban Gem." Located twenty or twenty-five miles from the heart of the city, Waverly offered to the "wealthy and professional classes" as well as the "man of moderate means"

---

cities with electric streetcars is from Arthur M. Schlesinger, *The Rise of the City* (New York: The Macmillan Company, 1933), 92.

83. W. D. Miller, *Memphis during the Progressive Era,* 72; McComb, *Houston,* 106–7; Long, "Making of Modern Tampa," 338.

84. *Nashville Banner,* August 31, 1882; June 18, 1883.

"all the quiet of the country with the advantage of proximity to the business center of a big city, by means of quick motor transportation." The streetcar was also responsible for the growth of Ghent outside Norfolk. In a short period of time it changed from farmland to "one of the most exclusive residential sections of Norfolk." Often operation of the street railway and suburban land development were directly connected. O. M. Carter and his American Loan and Trust Company of Omaha purchased the Houston City Railway in 1890 to ensure that his suburban community, Houston Heights, would be linked by rapid transit to the city.[85]

For the same reasons we hear today, cities sought to annex the surrounding areas. Proponents urged annexation so as to achieve better sanitation for the entire metropolitan area, raise the city tax base, and make suburbanites pay for the use of such city services as street maintenance and police protection. "In plain words tax dodging through the use of a trolley line should be abolished," said the *Birmingham Age-Herald* in 1900. "Suburbs should not be built up at the expense of cities. . . . If one avails himself of the advantages of a city in the earning of his daily bread, he should share the burdens of that city."[86] Urban boosters also called for annexation so that the federal census would show a great increase over the previous decade. It was no accident that annexation efforts usually appeared just before a new census was scheduled. In 1879 the *Nashville Daily American,* while stressing the sanitary advantages of annexation, noted the success of annexation in St. Louis and "the tendency of large cities" to prosper. Ten years later the *Nashville Banner* pointed to Chicago and Cincinnati to argue, "The bigger the town the stronger it draws people and capital." By taking in the "populous suburbs," Nashville would have "the population of a great city." The failure of annexation efforts in 1889 no doubt left Nashville boosters feeling like their unsuccessful counterparts in Birmingham in 1899. "The city," the *Age-Herald* said, pointing to the forthcoming census, "stands before the world belittled by cramped confines."[87]

Suburban dwellers were divided on the issue of annexation; but by the 1890s they were more attracted by improved city services—water, schools, sewage, etc.—than repelled by the expected increase in their taxes. Some annexations

85. *Richmond Dispatch,* January 1, 1891; *Nashville Banner,* March 30, 1889; Wertenbaker, *Norfolk,* 318; Platt, "Urban Public Services," 134. For the impact of the streetcar on a northern city, see Sam Bass Warner, Jr., *Streetcar Suburbs: The Process of Growth in Boston, 1870–1900* (Cambridge, Mass.: Harvard University Press, 1962).

86. *Birmingham Age-Herald,* September 26, 1900, quoted in Harris, "Annexation Struggles and Political Power," 163.

87. *Nashville Daily American,* December 17, 1879; *Nashville Banner,* March 30, 1889; *Birmingham Age-Herald,* October 14, 1900, quoted in Harris, "Annexation Struggles and Political Power," 172.

had already taken place. Nashville annexed Edgefield across from it on the Cumberland River in 1880; by that year Jefferson City, Lafayette, Carrollton, and Algiers, once suburbs, had been incorporated into New Orleans. The great surge in annexations, however, came after the mid-1880s. Norfolk annexed Brambleton in 1886 and Atlantic City in 1890. Houston added South Houston in 1890, Houston Heights in 1891, and Deer Park in 1893. After much resistance from the surrounding communities, Memphis enlarged its 4.5 square miles to 16 square miles and added thirty thousand people to its population through annexation in January 1899. Even towns like Greensboro, which added South Greensboro in 1891, kept pace with their bigger rivals. The big lure was city schools, and the end result was the quadrupling of Greensboro's area to four square miles and the addition of about three thousand people.[88] Meanwhile Birmingham, through a series of small annexations in 1873, 1883, and 1889, took in some adjacent residential areas so that the city limits had grown from 1.4 square miles in 1871 to 3 square miles. In 1895 the city added North and South Highlands, but opposition from the industrialists outside the city prevented annexation of the major furnaces and rolling mills. The industrialists continued to thwart the desire of city officials, downtown business interests, and city and suburban residents who supported the Greater Birmingham Movement organized in 1898. Unsuccessful at annexing all the surrounding suburbs in time for the 1900 census, the Greater Birmingham advocates finally got their wish in 1910. The city expanded to forty-eight square miles and added approximately 72,000 people.[89] Few cities made as spectacular use of annexation as Birmingham, but throughout the South these annexations contributed greatly to the growth in urban population.

The horizontal expansion of the cities, which kept pace with developments in the North, was not matched by a vertical expansion. The less expansive economies of southern cities and their relatively uncongested cores meant that downtown skylines were still of human scale. In 1900 the Memphis business district consisted mostly of old four-story brick buildings. The highest structures were the eight-story Randolph Building and the eleven-story Porter Building. Neither Nashville nor Norfolk had a building over seven stories, though plans were soon announced for a thirteen-story one in the former and a twelve-story edifice in the latter.[90] Significantly, they were to be banks. But in 1900 large

88. *Nashville Daily American,* February 8, 1880; Bennetts, "Black and White Workers," 6; Wertenbaker, *Norfolk,* 286–87; McComb, *Houston,* 143; Capers, *Biography of a River Town,* 214; Kipp, "Urban Growth and Social Change in the South," 294, 377.

89. Harris, "Annexation Struggles and Political Power," passim.

90. W. D. Miller, *Memphis during the Progressive Era,* 17; William Waller, ed., *Nashville, 1900 to 1910* (Nashville: Vanderbilt University Press, 1970), 10; Wertenbaker, *Norfolk,* 323.

office buildings did not dominate the urban landscape. Rather, the new Union railroad stations, hotels, theaters, YMCAs, government buildings, and churches were preeminent. On business streets such as Nashville's Second Avenue or Montgomery's Commerce Street, one could enjoy the finest period of American storefront architecture—two- and three-story commercial buildings erected after 1880 with concern for scale and design that was sorely lacking in subsequent years. In a further concession to the urban aesthetic, most cities during the first decade of the twentieth century began placing utility wires underground.

By 1900 southern cities had more to offer their residents in terms of services, attractions, and economic well-being than they did twenty years before. Yet, the fruits of progress were not equally distributed. The primary beneficiaries were the commercial elites who saw to it that the downtowns and the residential areas in which they lived received the lion's share of urban improvements. Members of the working class and especially the poor often suffered from the low priority given to their needs.

Unlike their counterparts in the North, comparatively few of the lower class workers were foreign immigrants. The small number of immigrants has often led historians incorrectly to minimize their impact on southern life. The Irish played a significant role in southern urban politics and as laborers, particularly in Memphis, Richmond, and New Orleans.[91] Jewish merchants, usually of German descent, figured prominently in business affairs and politics; there was a "Jewish seat" on the Atlanta Board of Education, and both the Radical and Redeemer mayors of Montgomery were Jewish. And at the end of the century New Orleans received a large number of Italian immigrants.[92] Nevertheless, despite white attempts to encourage foreign immigration as an alternative to dependence on Negro labor, the percentage of foreign born in southern cities dropped sharply between 1860 and 1900. In Richmond the decline was from 13 percent to 3.4 percent; Charleston, 15.5 percent to 4.6 percent; Savannah,

91. See, for example, Capers, *Biography of a River Town,* and W. D. Miller, *Memphis during the Progressive Era;* Joseph O'Grady, "Immigrants and the Politics of Reconstruction in Richmond, Virginia," *Records of the American Catholic Historical Society of Philadelphia* 83 (June 1972): 87–101; George M. Reynolds, *Machine Politics in New Orleans, 1897–1926* (New York: Columbia University Press, 1936). See also James Joseph Flanagan, "The Irish Element in Nashville, 1810–1890" (Master's thesis, Vanderbilt University, 1951).

92. *Atlanta Constitution,* May 6, 1890; *Montgomery Alabama State Journal,* April 8, 1875. For useful studies of two of the South's most important Jewish communities, see Steven Hertzberg, "The Jewish Community of Atlanta from the End of the Civil War until the Eve of the Frank Case," *American Jewish Historical Quarterly* 62 (March 1973): 250–85, and Mark H. Elovitz, *A Century of Jewish Life in Dixie: The Birmingham Experience* (University: University of Alabama Press, 1974); J. J. Jackson, *New Orleans in the Gilded Age,* 17–19.

21 percent to 6.3 percent; New Orleans, 38 percent to 10 percent. Not on the map in 1860, the new town of Birmingham had only 5 percent foreign born in 1900, when Pittsburgh, its chief rival for iron and steel supremacy, had 26.4 percent.[93]

A larger share of the urban working class was composed of native whites, many of whom had migrated to the cities from the depressed rural areas. Studies of San Antonio, Birmingham, and Atlanta indicate that as a group they enjoyed only limited social mobility during the prosperous closing years of the century; in Atlanta even the foreign element outstripped them.[94] These were the people who worked in the mines or ironworks of Birmingham; the cotton mills of Greensboro, Augusta, and Gastonia; the tobacco factories of Richmond and Durham; and on the docks of New Orleans, Savannah, and Charleston. Their wages low, they inhabited the growing tenement districts of the expanding cities, moving apart physically from the commercial elites and the middle classes, just as they were being left behind economically.[95]

The lower-class whites found comfort in the frequent assurances of their "betters" that they were superior to the Negroes. And not surprisingly, blacks benefitted least from the urban growth of the last two decades of the century. By 1900 only 17.2 percent of the South's blacks lived in cities, but they comprised 30.9 percent of the total urban population. Their percentage of the population in the major cities ranged from lows of 14.1 percent in San Antonio and 27.1 percent in New Orleans to highs of 56.5 percent in Charleston and 51.8 percent in Savannah. Not until after 1900 did the percentage of blacks in the urban population of southern cities decline for the first time since 1860, as significant numbers migrated to the North.[96] Blacks who did leave prior to 1900 enjoyed greater opportunities in the northern cities than those who remained behind. The last twenty years of the century witnessed the improvement of black prospects for economic success in the North, a decline in the extent of legally enforced

93. Bayrd Still, *Urban America: A History with Documents* (Boston: Little, Brown and Company, 1974), 118–19, 264–65.

94. Alwyn Barr, "Occupational and Geographic Mobility in San Antonio, 1870–1900," *Social Science Quarterly* 51 (September 1970): 396–403; Worthman, "Working Class Mobility in Birmingham," passim; Richard J. Hopkins, "Occupational and Geographic Mobility in Atlanta, 1870–1896," *Journal of Southern History* 34 (May 1968): 200–13.

95. See, for example, Kipp, "Urban Growth and Social Change in the South," 272; Russell, "Atlanta," 264–65.

96. Bureau of the Census, *Negro Population, 1790–1915,* 90–91, 93. This definition of the South includes Delaware, Maryland, District of Columbia, Oklahoma, Kentucky, and West Virginia. The percentage of blacks in the urban population of the former Confederate states ranged from 22.9 percent in Texas to 49.3 percent in South Carolina, while a much smaller percentage of the blacks in the eleven states were urban.

segregation, and a greater role for blacks in politics.[97] The economic, social, and political trends for blacks in the South ran in the opposite direction.

For most southern blacks the closing years of the century meant continued economic hardship. The great majority of black workers were disproportionately represented in menial jobs, and black women, unlike their white counterparts, formed a significant part of their race's work force. Out of Nashville's work force of 8,100 black males in 1890, 1,107 were employed as servants and 3,811 as unskilled laborers. Yet of the white male work force of 14,847, there were only 56 servants and 676 laborers. Although there were 991 white carpenters and joiners; only 198 blacks were in those skilled positions. Of the 6,609 employed black women, 2,465 were laundresses and 3,372 were servants; of the 2,989 employed white women, 104 were laundresses and 378 were servants.[98] Outside of the cotton mills, from which they were excluded, blacks made up a large part of the unskilled factory workers and were in great demand as day laborers for such hazardous occupations as well digging or sewer building. The streets, docks, and rail yards throughout the urban South were filled with black workers.

Blacks were hindered by their lack of skills, but many were clearly confined to the low-paying, unskilled jobs because of their race. Much of the opposition to blacks in skilled positions came from white workers, though organized labor sometimes sought to incorporate blacks. Often the Knights of Labor and the local unions that preceded them permitted blacks in their unions, usually in segregated branches. In 1888 the Richmond Knights of Labor had twenty-three white and thirty black assemblies. New Orleans, described by David Bennetts as "most certainly the best organized city in the South," witnessed united action by black and white union members that resulted in increased wages, shorter work days, and improved conditions for most workers. Collapse of the city's general strike, the first in the nation, in 1892, and the depression of the 1890s brought an end to "labor's golden era in New Orleans" and also limited future racial cooperation.[99] By the mid-1890s most white union and nonunion labor in New Orleans, as elsewhere in the urban South, was committed to blocking black access to skilled positions. The replacement of the Knights by the racist American Federation of Labor doomed prospects for a revived biracial alliance.

At the same time that the ranks of the black unskilled were increasing, there

97. See, for example, Gilbert Osofsky, *Harlem, The Making of a Ghetto: Negro New York, 1890–1930* (New York: Harper and Row, 1963); Allan H. Spear, *Black Chicago: The Making of a Negro Ghetto, 1890–1920* (Chicago: University of Chicago Press, 1967).

98. Bureau of the Census, *Eleventh Census of the United States: 1890,* vol. 1, *Population,* pt. 1, 696.

99. *Richmond Dispatch,* January 2, 1888; Bennetts, "Black and White Workers," passim, quotes, 548, 553.

emerged a small business and professional class. Even in the 1870s there had been a class of successful blacks, but many of them, like the Atlanta barber Robert Yancy or the dentist Frederick Badger, had a white clientele.[100] By the end of the century, however, a black elite of undertakers, barbers, lawyers, teachers, grocers, and doctors serving primarily a black clientele had risen to prominence in southern cities. Black business districts along Raleigh's Hargett Street or Nashville's Cedar and Cherry Streets (now Fourth and Charlotte avenues) announced their presence. Yet as an 1899 survey of Negro businessmen in the South suggests, the range of occupations was limited. Better than 40 percent were either grocers, general merchandise dealers, or barbers with $500 or more invested; the next two highest groups were printers and undertakers. Groceries made up more than one-third of Atlanta's sixty-one Negro businesses of sufficient size to be counted.[101] Nevertheless, a group had emerged that was on the other end of the economic scale from the mass of blacks. As of 1891 Richmond blacks owned real estate valued at $968,736; four years later there were six blacks who owned more than $10,000 worth of property in the city's largely black Jackson Ward. By 1886 the combined wealth of Nashville's black population was approximately $1 million, with seventeen individuals worth more than $10,000. More than half of that $1 million was owned by only forty-four families.[102]

The poverty of the black masses plus the racism of whites encouraged the earlier trend toward segregated neighborhoods. Though ward statistics for most cities suggest a high degree of residential integration, a street-by-street survey reveals that in cities such as Richmond, Montgomery, Raleigh, and Atlanta the great majority of whites and blacks lived on totally segregated blocks. Because of racial discrimination, even members of the black elite were confined to black neighborhoods among lower-class dwellings as on Atlanta's Wheat Street. The few whites in black neighborhoods came primarily from three groups with limited mobility: laborers, widows, and grocers. Most blacks in predominantly white areas lived in the rear of fashionable white streets and served whites as laundresses, gardeners, and handymen.[103]

100. Wotton, "New City of the South," 326.

101. W. E. B. Du Bois, ed., *The Negro in Business,* Atlanta University Publications, ed. W. E. B. Du Bois, no. 4 (Atlanta: Atlanta University Press, 1899), 7, 68.

102. Alrutheus Ambush Taylor, *The Negro in the Reconstruction of Virginia* (Washington, D. C.: The Association for the Study of Negro Life and History, 1926), 135; James T. Haley, comp., *Afro-American Encyclopedia; or, The Thoughts, Doings and Sayings of the Race* (Nashville, 1896), 212; *Nashville Banner,* December 18, 1886.

103. Conclusions based on examination of city directories in Raleigh for 1886, Atlanta and Richmond for 1891, and Montgomery for 1895. For Negro sections of other cities, see Greene, *Dallas,* 18; German, "Queen City of the Savannah," 37; Kipp, "Urban Growth and Social Change in the South," 312–13.

The combination of large poor black populations and significant numbers of lower-class whites meant that southern cities generally had a lower percentage of home ownership than their northern counterparts. Of the 420 cities and towns with 8,000 to 100,000 people in 1890, 12 had a rate of home tenancy less than 40 percent; none were in the South; but of the 18 cities with a percentage of home tenency above 80 percent, 11 were in the South. Birmingham ranked highest with 89.84 percent, Norfolk was third with 85.62 percent, and Macon was fourth with 84.6 percent. Overall, the percentage of families who were tenants was greatest in the south central and south Atlantic sections of the country.[104]

The black areas of the cities shared little in the expansion of municipal services during the 1880s and 1890s. Water mains, sewer lines, paved streets, and regular garbage collection rarely reached into black neighborhoods. Neither electricity nor gas illuminated the houses. In Richmond the fire chief unsuccessfully pleaded for a fire station to protect the largely wooden homes of Jackson Ward, while in Atlanta, Spelman Seminary's Union Hall burned down because fire engines had a two-mile run over rough roads to get there. Major black institutions like Atlanta University were not served by streetcars. When streetcar service existed, it was unsatisfactory. Richmond's Jackson Ward had twenty-minute service on a single-track line; nearby white areas had five and ten minute service on double-track lines. In Algiers, a heavily black section of New Orleans, mule cars were still running in 1907, fourteen years after the rest of the city's lines had begun to be electrified.[105]

Other services were available to blacks on a separate but unequal basis. By the 1890s city hospitals and local almshouses in Atlanta and Nashville offered inadequate segregated accommodations to blacks. During the 1880s local black protests finally succeeded in securing the appointment of black teachers in most black schools as the expansion of the white schools provided jobs for the white teachers and scores of teacher exams demonstrated that the blacks were qualified. Only Charleston and New Orleans seem to have lagged behind the other cities. Even this triumph for blacks had its price, since the black teachers received considerably lower salaries than white instructors.[106]

104. U. S. Bureau of the Census, *Eleventh Census of the United States: 1890: Report of Farms and Homes* (Washington, D.C.: Government Printing Office, 1896), 29.

105. Richmond, *Annual Reports of the City Departments of Richmond, Virginia, for the Year Ending January 31, 1886* (Richmond, 1886), 8; *Atlanta Constitution,* June 25, December 23, 1887; Richard Mendales, "Sic Transit Richmond," typescript, Twentieth Century Urban Negro Project, Center for Urban Studies, University of Chicago, July, 1969, 2–3; J. J. Jackson, *New Orleans in the Gilded Age,* 164.

106. See Rabinowitz, "Health and Welfare Services" and "Half a Loaf," reprinted above. As late as 1889 there were only twenty-three Negroes among New Orleans public school teachers. Bennetts, "Black and White Workers," 217. The delay in hiring black

By the 1890s the first Jim Crow statutes were being passed, enforcing segregation in a variety of public accommodations. But even without the passage of laws, de facto segregation or exclusion had become further entrenched during the 1880s in public and private parks, theaters, zoos, and other places of public amusements. The dummy streetcars, for example, that appeared in Nashville, Atlanta, and Montgomery after the mid-1880s were segregated. Jim Crow streetcar legislation passed in Georgia in 1891 and elsewhere after 1900 removed whatever flexibility there had previously been.[107]

Despite widespread de facto and, increasingly, de jure segregation, whites were not satisfied until they had removed the blacks from the political arena. As noted earlier, while Redemption had generally been quickly achieved, blacks remained active in city government in several major southern cities. Though the cases were certainly atypical, blacks were regularly elected to city councils in Nashville and Jackson, Mississippi, until the late 1880s, and in Richmond and Raleigh until the turn of the century. During the 1890s fusion movements returned white and black Republicans to office in a number of North Carolina cities, a development that had taken place in Jacksonville in 1887.[108]

Black councilmen had limited power, as revealed by their assignment to unimportant committees or to none at all, but they were often able to help their constituents. Nashville's leading black politician, J. C. Napier, was instrumental in the opening of new black schools and the hiring of black teachers, while his councilmate from 1883 to 1885, C. C. Gowdey, secured free water for some

teachers in New Orleans may have been due to the failure of the system to expand and thus to provide jobs for white teachers in Negro schools; this was evidently the case in Charleston, where in 1902 there were still only six public schools. Bureau of the Census, *Statistics of Cities . . . 1902 and 1903,* 93–94. For the persistence of white teachers in Charleston's black schools despite Negro protests, see George Brown Tindall, *South Carolina Negroes, 1877–1900* (Columbia: University of South Carolina Press, 1952; reprint ed., Baton Rouge: Louisiana State University Press, 1966), 220–21.

107. *Nashville Banner,* May 1, 1888; Franklin M. Garrett, *Atlanta and Environs: A Chronicle of Its People and Events,* 3 vols. (New York: Lewis Historical Publishing Company, 1954), 2:175; letter of Eliza Bowers to the editor, *Atlanta Constitution,* July 28, 1889. Miss Bowers, an Atlanta white, remembered entering the Negro car in Montgomery by mistake three years earlier; Gilbert Thomas Stephenson, *Race Distinctions in American Law* (London: D. Appleton and Company, 1910), 227–33.

108. For Raleigh, Nashville, and Richmond, see Rabinowitz, "From Reconstruction to Redemption," reprinted above; for Jackson, see Wharton, *Negro in Mississippi,* 167–68; for North Carolina cities, see Helen G. Edmonds, *The Negro and Fusion Politics in North Carolina, 1894–1901* (Chapel Hill: University of North Carolina Press, 1951), 124–35; for Jacksonville, see Edward Akin, "When a Minority Becomes the Majority: Blacks in Jacksonville Politics, 1887–1907," *Florida Historical Quarterly* 53 (October 1974): 123–45 and passim.

Negro neighborhoods and pushed through the organization of a regular black fire company of which he immediately became captain. The four Negro councilmen in Jacksonville in 1887 saw to it that almost half of the police force was black, as were the municipal judge and one of the three police commissioners. Richmond's black councilmen secured improved streets and better lighting in Jackson Ward, the dispensing of coal to the Negro poor, the opening of the first black night school, the appropriation of money for the Negro militia companies, and construction of a separate armory.[109]

Blacks temporarily increased their influence by combining with other groups like the Knights of Labor in Richmond, Mobile, and Jacksonville during the mid-1880s or the Populists in North Carolina cities during the 1890s.[110] But whites came to be more concerned about the role of blacks in the prohibition and local option campaigns, fixtures of local politics in the late 1880s. Liquor was an emotional issue that divided both communities and the Democratic party. Even in Atlanta, where blacks were prevented by the use of the white primary, poll tax, and manipulation of the election procedures from winning public office, the issue of prohibition made them a pivotal force in local politics. From 1885 to 1888 Atlanta witnessed a series of referenda or campaigns in which prohibition was the chief issue. Blacks sought to play off the wets against the drys to win concessions, but the victors never kept their promises, and the net effect was to increase white desires to eliminate totally the black vote. During Richmond's local option campaign of 1885, a local newspaper feared that prohibition would be "forced upon white men by negro votes"; three years later a "race war" in Jackson was attributed to bad feelings generated by a local option election.[111]

Thus, throughout the urban South white Democrats became interested in disfranchisement even before the rise of Populism. The bidding for the Negro

109. See, for example, Nashville City Council Minutes, December 13, 1883, Office of the Metropolitan Clerk, Davidson County Building and Nashville City Hall; *Nashville Banner,* May 26, 1882; November 8, 1884; January 8, 9, 1885; Akin, "When a Minority Becomes the Majority," 136; Luther Porter Jackson, *Negro Office-Holders in Virginia, 1865–1895* (Norfolk, Va.: Guide Quality Press, 1945): 83; Richmond Common Council Minutes, May 7, 1888, Office of the City Clerk, Richmond City Hall. Black councilmen, however, failed to achieve one of their major goals: the purchase of land for a city park in Jackson Ward. See, for example, Richmond City Council Minutes, August 18, October 3, 1887; June 7, August 6, 1888; June 3, 1889; April 7, 1890, Office of the City Clerk, Richmond City Hall, Richmond.

110. Woodward, *Origins of the New South,* 230; Edmonds, *Negro Fusion and Politics.*

111. See my "The Search for Social Control: Race Relations in the Urban South, 1865–1890" (Ph.D. diss., University of Chicago, 1973), 2:774–81; *Richmond Dispatch,* December 1, 1885; Report of the United States Senate Judiciary Committee, reprinted in *Atlanta Constitution,* August 2, 1888.

vote in prohibition campaigns or when independents challenged incumbent Democratic administrations severely upset local elites. The only remedy was to remove the Negro voter, since containment, though successful, was not enough. As they had done during Reconstruction, the urban dwellers turned to the state legislatures for help. And help soon came! Jackson Democrats, who finally ousted their Republican mayor in 1888, secured an amended charter in 1890 which included "changes [in the] wards so as to give perpetual control of the board of aldermen to the white people."[112] The same year the legislature passed the Mississippi Plan, the first clear-cut statewide disfranchisement program in the nation. In 1889 Tennessee passed new voting and registration laws that applied only to Nashville, Memphis, Chattanooga, Knoxville, and their counties in order "to practically exclude the vote of illiterate negroes." The heart of the laws was adoption of the nonpartisan Australian ballot that barred the practice of aiding voters as they selected their candidates from an alphabetically arranged list. This law, plus tighter registration requirements and a two dollar poll tax enacted in 1890, was responsible for the reduction of black voters to less than 250 in the 1890 Nashville municipal election. But even after the passage in Florida in 1889 of an Australian ballot, multiple-ballot-box system, poll tax, and other restrictions, blacks still were being elected to the council in Jacksonville after the turn of the century.[113] By then, however, with the notable exception of Memphis, the passage of disfranchising legislation throughout the South had largely eliminated the black urban voter as a factor in any kind of election. And as a further reminder to blacks of their inferior position in southern cities, there were white-initiated race riots in Wilmington, North Carolina, in 1898, and in New Orleans in 1900.[114]

Postbellum cities failed to fulfill the antebellum hopes of the South's urban boosters. Cotton remained king, northern control of the region was extended, southern urban populations continued to experience a quality of life inferior to that of their northern counterparts, and race was still "the central theme of Southern history." There is no denying the validity of C. Vann Woodward's conclusion, "The Southern people remained throughout the rise of the 'New South' overwhelmingly a country people, by far the most rural section of the

112. *Nashville Banner*, September 18, 1889; *Atlanta Constitution*, January 22, 1890.

113. *Nashville Banner*, April 3, 1889; August 5, 8, 1890; Akin, "When a Minority Becomes the Majority," 140.

114. Paul Lewinson, *Race, Class, and Party: A History of Negro Suffrage and White Politics in the South* (Universal Library Edition; New York: Grosset and Dunlap, 1965); J. Morgan Kousser, *The Shaping of Southern Politics: Suffrage Restriction and the Establishment of the One-Party South, 1880–1910* (New Haven: Yale University Press, 1974); Edmonds, *Negro Fusion and Politics*, 158–77; J. J. Jackson, *New Orleans in the Gilded Age*, 20.

country."[115] Between 1860 and 1900 the proportion of urban dwellers in the South grew from 7.1 percent to 14.8 percent, as compared to a shift from 19.9 percent to 39 percent in the nation at-large, and the region's share of the nation's urban places grew from 13.8 percent to 15.7 percent, but by 1900 the South had none of the country's eleven cities with over 300,000 people and only two of the twenty-seven cities with between 100,000 and 300,000.[116] Nonetheless, only if Woodward is speaking in statistical terms is it true that after the urban boom of the 1880s "the sum total of urbanization in the South was comparatively unimportant."[117] The founding of Birmingham and Miami meant that by 1900 every one of today's major southern cities had been established; their arrival, plus the growth of the young Texas towns, spelled the end of the hierarchy of cities that had existed in 1860.

Furthermore, as in earlier southern history, postbellum cities played a role far greater than their limited share of the total population would suggest. Certainly the expansion of the rail network during the period was tied to the growth of the region's cities, and the South's agriculture depended upon urban marketing. Nor should the impact of urban leaders on the political life of the region be forgotten. Norfolk's Gilbert Walker, Knoxville's William Brownlow, and Raleigh's William Holden were only three of the Reconstruction governors with urban roots. Later, as Woodward himself acknowledges, "Southern progressivism was essentially urban and middle class in nature."[118] Birmingham produced Governor Braxton Bragg Comer; Atlanta, the future governor and secretary of the interior Hoke Smith; Jacksonville, Governor Napoleon B. Broward and Senator Duncan Fletcher; and Houston, future presidential adviser Colonel E. M. House. Meanwhile, the Raleigh editor and future secretary of the navy Josephus Daniels and the Atlanta editor Henry W. Grady exercised great influence as spokesmen of the New South. Despite all the just attention given to the colorful southern agrarian leaders, it should be remembered that the cities were overrepresented among southern political leaders everywhere but in the state legislatures.

Southern cities were also at the core of the momentous decisions that occurred in the area of race relations. As had been the case in the antebellum period, it proved more difficult for whites to control blacks in the cities than in

115. *Origins of the New South*, 139.
116. Number of urban places and percentages computed from U.S. censuses of 1860 and 1900, and tables in Smith, "Emergence of Cities," 28–29, 33. If Kentucky and Oklahoma are included, the percentage of urban dwellers in the South rises from 7.2 percent in 1860 to 15.2 percent in 1900, and the South's share of the nation's urban places grows from 15.8 percent to 18.4 percent. The region's share of places over ten thousand inhabitants increases from 16.1 percent to 19.5 percent.
117. *Origins of the New South*, 139.
118. Ibid., 371.

the rural areas. It is not surprising, therefore, that much of the early stimulus for disfranchisement came from southern cities, and that most of the Jim Crow legislation was aimed at urban blacks.

And if urban services and amenities still left much to be desired, southern cities had at least made noteworthy strides toward the day when the bluster of urban boosters would match the reality of southern urban life. Yet, that time was still far in the future, and the changes in southern urban life between 1860 and 1900 would pale next to those of the twentieth century. Only then, as well, would colonial dependence on northern cities cease and the forces of racial moderation triumph.

The Weight of the Past vs.
The Promise of the Future

Southern Race Relations in
Historical Perspective

The following essay was initially prepared as a lecture for a symposium on "The Future South," which was a featured part of Converse College's centennial celebration in October 1988. Participants were assigned one of several areas of study in southern history from among women, urbanization, race relations, science and technology, and culture and asked to predict developments in the twenty-first-century South based on what happened in the past. The revised (and, in my case, updated) papers were published, with the addition of a chapter on southern literature, three years later. Once again in transforming an oral presentation into written form, I chose to retain a good deal of the original paper's informal and somewhat preachy character.

More has been written about race relations than any other topic in southern history. This is as it should be given the centrality of race in the history of the South. Thus it is no small task to assess the prospects for southern race relations in the future, based on the history of the region's race relations to this point. I have therefore chosen to paint my picture with broad strokes and, to make my task a bit easier, I will basically use only two colors; that is, I will limit myself

Revisions for this essay were completed while I was a Fellow at the Center for Advanced Study in the Behavioral Sciences. I am grateful for financial support provided by the Center, the National Endowment for the Humanities, and the Andrew W. Mellon Foundation. I also want to thank the participants in the Center's seminar series; audiences at the Berkeley, San Diego, and Santa Barbara campuses of the University of California; and Michael Les Benedict, Peter Kolchin, August Meier, and Arthur Mann for their comments about earlier versions of this essay.

primarily to black-white relations, although I think we too often ignore other ethnic groups in our study of southern history and society.[1]

When I told some nonacademic friends that I had been asked to prepare this essay, they immediately wanted to know what I, in fact, thought of black-white relations in the South. My response, of course, was: Compared to what? Any assessment of southern race relations for the future, or for that matter in the present, must place the subject within the proper comparative context.

There are many possibilities for comparison—Mikhail Gorbachev and Ronald Reagan once engaged in such an exercise when they contrasted human rights in Russia and the United States—but I want to simplify things by dealing with the two basic themes in southern history as identified by most southern historians: continuity and distinctiveness viewed within an American context.[2] That is, I want to survey briefly the history of southern black-white relations with an eye on the ways in which such relations have or have not resembled those of the United States in general, and the degree to which southern black-white relations have or have not changed over time.

In doing so, I will divide American race relations a bit arbitrarily into six periods, although allowing for considerable overlap: (1) 1619 to 1787; (2) 1787 to 1865; (3) 1865 to 1900; (4) 1900 to 1954; (5) 1954 to the present; and (6) the future. Despite this volume's emphasis on "the Future South," it is the past that will receive most of my attention, for without an understanding of that past, or what I have termed "the weight of the past," we cannot assess reasonably the prospects for what I have termed "the promise of the future." What is most striking about this comparison between North and South and between different eras of southern race relations is that after decades of troubling continuity in the failure of its race relations, the South now shows signs of breaking new ground and providing the nation's most favorable environment for positive racial change.

The arrival in Virginia in 1619 of twenty blacks purchased from a Dutch sea captain would, of course, seem to mark the beginning of black-white relations in the South, and for that matter in what was to become the United States. As the

1. For the experiences of other groups see, for example, James H. Merrell, "Some Thoughts on Colonial Historians and American Indians," *William and Mary Quarterly*, 3d ser., 46 (January 1989): 94–119; Ira Berlin and Herbert G. Gutman, "Natives and Immigrants, Free Men and Slaves: Urban Workingmen in the Antebellum South," *American Historical Review* 88 (December 1983): 1175–1200; Lucy M. Cohen, *Chinese in the Post–Civil War South: A People without a History* (Baton Rouge: Louisiana State University Press, 1984); Randall M. Miller and George E. Pozzetta, eds., *Shades of the Sunbelt: Essays on Ethnicity, Race, and the Urban South* (Westport, Conn.: Greenwood Press, 1988).

2. For an extended discussion of the limits and possibilities of this approach that focuses on the pre–twentieth century, see Carl N. Degler, *Place over Time: The Continuity of Southern Distinctiveness* (Baton Rouge: Louisiana State University Press, 1977).

historian Winthrop D. Jordan has argued, however, the English colonists brought with them certain ideas about color and religion that predisposed them to consider blacks to be inferior and threatening. Other historians have argued that the badge of slavery tainted blacks rather than blackness itself leading to enslavement, yet all agree that the process of defining blacks as slaves was more complex and drawn out than once assumed.

Nevertheless, for our purposes it is clear that by the end of the seventeenth century slavery was a well-entrenched institution in both the North and the South. First through custom, then through law, most blacks found their terms of service extended to life, and that status passed on to their children. Yet, if present in all of England's mainland colonies, slavery had already begun to give a special character to those in the South. In part this was reflected in the differences in the legal status of slaves in the colonial North and South. Northern colonies, for example, normally recognized slave marriages as binding and the right of slave parents to their children.[3]

There were, however, differences in race relations within the South based on such factors as demography, geography, staple agriculture, and the nature of the slave trade. As the historian Ira Berlin has noted, the character of African-American society and the relationship between blacks and whites emerged differently in the Chesapeake region and in the rural and urban areas of the Low Country. Yet in all parts of the South, after an initial period of greater autonomy or individual opportunity during the pioneering days of settlement, the firmer drawing of racial lines—marked by the legalization of slavery in the 1660s in Virginia and Maryland and the spread of the rice culture in South Carolina and Georgia during the early eighteenth century—restricted the rights of most blacks. This occurred even though such restrictions in the Chesapeake accompanied a decline in the slave trade while the 1770s brought a sharp increase in dependence on importation further south.[4] And as slavery flourished, so too did an ideology of freedom for whites. Indeed, the two were interrelated, for as the

3. Winthrop D. Jordan, *White over Black: American Attitudes Toward the Negro 1550–1812* (Chapel Hill: University of North Carolina Press, 1968), chapters 1 and 2, passim. See also Oscar Handlin and Mary F. Handlin, "Origins of the Southern Labor System," *William and Mary Quarterly*, 3d ser., 7 (April 1950): 199–222; Carl N. Degler, "Slavery and the Genesis of American Race Prejudice," *Comparative Studies in Society and History* 2 (October 1959): 49–66; Edmund S. Morgan, *American Slavery, American Freedom: The Ordeal of Colonial Virginia* (New York: W. W. Norton and Company, 1975); William M. Wiecek, "The Statutory Law of Slavery and Race in the Thirteen Mainland Colonies of British-America," *William and Mary Quarterly*, 3d ser., 34 (April 1977): 258–80.

4. Ira Berlin, "Time, Space, and the Evolution of Afro-American Society in British Mainland North America," *American Historical Review* 85 (February 1980): 44–78. See also Allan Kulikoff, *Tobacco and Slaves: The Development of Southern Cultures in the Chesapeake, 1680–1800* (Chapel Hill: University of North Carolina Press, 1986).

historian Edmund Morgan put it, "by lumping Indians, mulattoes, and Negroes in a single pariah class, Virginians had paved the way for a similar lumping of small and large planters in a single master class. . . . Racism became an essential, if unacknowledged, ingredient of the republican ideology that enabled Virginians to lead the nation."[5]

Thus on the eve of the Revolution slavery had strengthened its grip on the South, and the rights of blacks to their own property or labor had been greatly circumscribed. Yet northern blacks had undergone a similar transformation. Slaves became an increasingly important part of the northern colonial economy, replacing white indentured servants as a prime choice for menial labor. The greater demand for black labor led to the direct importation of slaves and to the emergence of a less acculturated black population. There was already, however, a major difference between the North and the South that was to have significant implications for the future character of race relations in the two regions. Although blacks made up an indispensable part of the urban artisan class in Charles Town, more than 82 percent of southern blacks lived in rural areas, raising wheat or tobacco in the Chesapeake or rice further south. In the North, following an early period in which most blacks worked on small farms, there was a pronounced shift to the urban areas so that by the Revolution approximately 70 percent of northern blacks were urban.[6]

The Revolutionary era helped sharpen the differences between the status of southern blacks and those elsewhere. White southerners were becoming more sensitive about what would soon be their "peculiar institution." This was evident in the striking of Thomas Jefferson's condemnation of the slave trade from the Declaration of Independence, an indictment that Newport, Rhode Island, slave traders admittedly objected to as well. Southerners were further incensed by British efforts to encourage rebellion or desertion by their slaves. And, of course, slavery became a major issue at the constitutional convention as delegates, especially from South Carolina and Georgia, sought to hold onto the foreign slave trade for as long as possible, and debates over the counting of slaves for purposes of representation and taxation helped forge the South's definition of itself as a section.[7]

---

5. *American Slavery,* 386.

6. Berlin, "Time, Space, and Evolution of Afro-American Society," 45–54, passim.

7. Carl L. Becker, *The Declaration of Independence: A Study in the History of Political Ideas* (New York: 1922; repr. Alfred A. Knopf, 1942), 212–21; Paul Finkelman, "Slavery and the Constitutional Convention: Making a Covenant with Death," in *Beyond Confederation: Origins of the Constitution and American National Identity,* ed. Richard Beeman, Stephen Botein, and Edward C. Carter, II (Chapel Hill: University of North Carolina Press, 1987), 188–225; Drew R. McCoy, "James Madison and Visions of American Nationality in

The years between the convention and the end of the Civil War witnessed the continued efforts of white southerners to expand and defend the institution of slavery. In the process, the system lost much of its remaining flexibility, becoming ever more rigid, particularly in response to the prodding of northern abolitionists and perceived or actual threats of black rebellion, such as those associated with Denmark Vesey and Nat Turner.[8] And as southern states passed law after law aimed at tightening their hold over slaves, free Negroes as well began to lose much of their freedom. Just as white southern concern over the need to draw the color line had resulted in the substitution of racial barriers for class barriers in the colonial period, now racial barriers threatened to overwhelm completely the distinction among blacks between free and slave status. Early forms of racial segregation, restrictions on property ownership and marriage rights, and the loss of the vote in the last of the southern states (Tennessee in 1834 and North Carolina in 1835) pushed free Negroes closer to the noncitizen status of the enslaved mass of blacks. Arkansas went so far as to pass legislation in 1858 expelling its free Negroes; only 144, mostly elderly, free Negroes remained in 1860. No other state took such a drastic step, but the variety of measures took its toll. From a peak of 8.5 percent of the South's total black population in 1810, free Negroes were reduced to 6.2 percent in 1860.[9]

On the surface, it would seem that race relations in the South during these years were indeed distinctive. As the southern states moved to buttress slavery, northern states between 1777 and 1817, for a mixture of ideological, religious, and economic reasons, abolished the institution where it had existed. In the new states to be carved out of the Northwest Territory, slavery was prohibited. And in the years between 1790 and 1820, northern blacks, now even more concentrated in the region's cities, often enjoyed the right to vote, formed their own churches and voluntary associations, lived in homes scattered throughout the community, and availed themselves of new economic opportunities that sometimes, as in the case of Philadelphia sail-maker James Forten, made them the employers of whites.

Yet after 1820 and especially 1830, northern blacks lost ground, in part as a result of the influx of European immigrants who competed with them for jobs

---

the Confederation Period: A Regional Perspective," in *Beyond Confederation*, ed. Beeman, Botein, and Carter, 226–58.

8. Richard C. Wade, "The Vesey Plot: A Reconsideration," *Journal of Southern History* 30 (May 1964): 143–61; Stephen B. Oates, *The Fires of Jubilee: Nat Turner's Fierce Rebellion* (New York: Harper and Row, 1975).

9. Ira Berlin, *Slaves without Masters: The Free Negro in the Antebellum South* (New York: Pantheon, 1974); John Hope Franklin, *The Free Negro in North Carolina, 1790–1860* (Chapel Hill: University of North Carolina Press, 1943).

and housing. Either through de facto or, less often, de jure action, segregation was enforced in schools, public accommodations, housing, churches, and most other areas of northern life. Even about Massachusetts, the hotbed of abolition, Frederick Douglass in 1846 could write:

> There was in Boston . . . a menagerie I had long desired to see. . . . I was met and told by the doorkeeper, in a harsh and contemptuous tone, *"We don't allow niggers in here."* . . . Soon after my arrival in New Bedford from the South, I had a strong desire to attend the Lyceum, but was told, *"They don't allow niggers in here!"* On arriving in Boston from an anti-slavery tour, hungry and tired, I went into an eating house near my friend Mr. Campbell's, to get some refreshments. I was met by a lad in a white apron, *"We don't allow niggers in here."* . . . On attempting to take a seat in the Omnibus [Weymouth], I was told by the driver, (and I never shall forget his fiendish hate) *"I don't allow niggers in here!"*

As their Federalist friends lost power, blacks in Rhode Island, New York, and elsewhere either lost the franchise or had access to it sharply restricted at the same time that states implemented universal white manhood suffrage. Many blacks lost even more in the series of race riots aimed at them and their white allies in Philadelphia, Providence, Boston, Cincinnati, and numerous other northern cities during the 1830s and 1840s.[10]

The point is that white northerners could and did oppose slavery on economic, political, social, or constitutional grounds while not embracing racial equality. Indeed, those same states in the Midwest that had slavery barred by the Northwest Ordinance were far more antiblack than their eastern counterparts, some going so far legislatively as to bar Negroes altogether. And although the American Colonization Society drew most of its support from such Upper South whites as James Madison and Henry Clay, its membership also included northerners such as Daniel Webster and William Seward. Advocates of colonization included Abraham Lincoln, who told a political rally in 1858, "I am not, nor ever have been in favor of bringing about in any way the social and political equality of the white and black races— . . . I am not nor ever have been in favor of

10. Leon Litwack, *North of Slavery: The Negro in the Free States, 1790–1860* (Chicago: University of Chicago Press, 1961); Leonard Curry, *The Free Black in Urban America, 1800–1850: The Shadow of the Dream* (Chicago: University of Chicago Press, 1981); Gary B. Nash, *Forging Freedom: The Formation of Philadelphia's Black Community, 1720–1840* (Cambridge: Harvard University Press, 1988); Shane White, "'We Dwell in Safety and Pursue Our Honest Callings': Free Blacks in New York City, 1783–1810," *Journal of American History* 75 (September 1988): 445–70; Douglass quoted in August Meier and Elliott Rudwick, *From Plantation to Ghetto,* 3d ed. (New York: Hill and Wang, 1976), 96.

making voters or jurors of negroes, nor of qualifying them to hold office, nor to intermarry with white people."[11]

By the end of the Civil War then it would seem that the South was distinctive in terms of its support for slavery, but that it shared with much of the rest of the country a belief in Negro inferiority and desire to keep blacks in their place that denied even free blacks the basic rights other Americans enjoyed. And following an initial period of relative openness and flexibility in race relations during the early colonial period, the region had exhibited a remarkable continuity in seeking to fix more firmly the second-class status of its blacks, be they slave or free.

The years between 1865 and 1900 were different. On the one hand, they witnessed the region's sharpest break with its past to that point; on the other, during no period prior to the 1950s were the trends in race relations in the North and South more dissimilar. The primary agents of transformation were northern whites, who either came South or controlled the federal government, and southern blacks themselves.

Following a brief interlude of Presidential Reconstruction between 1865 and 1867—when southern whites were pretty much left to handle their own Reconstruction and responded by seeking to minimize the effects of emancipation through black codes, economic intimidation, and violence—the northern victors imposed a more stringent Congressional Reconstruction on the defeated South. Although never as long or restrictive as white southerners claimed or blacks and most of their white allies had hoped, this Reconstruction forced basic changes in southern race relations. Thanks to the Thirteenth, Fourteenth, and Fifteenth amendments and various civil rights acts, slavery was abolished, blacks were made citizens with equal rights before the law, and racial discrimination in voting was prohibited. And between 1868 and 1877 the national Republican party, with varying degrees of commitment and success, sought to use the power of the federal government to protect the rights of blacks, while at the state level Republican governments, at least in Louisiana, Florida, and South Carolina, held power for as long as nine years.[12]

Yet without the blacks themselves little would have changed in the South. Even before the beginning of political reconstruction southern blacks had begun

11. Litwack, *North of Slavery,* 20–24, 66–74, Lincoln quoted, 276.

12. For the traditional assessment of Reconstruction, see William A. Dunning, *Reconstruction, Political and Economic, 1865–1877* (New York: Harper and Brothers, 1907) and Claude G. Bowers, *The Tragic Era: The Revolution after Lincoln* (Cambridge: Houghton Mifflin Co., 1929); for more recent (and accurate) assessments, see John Hope Franklin, *Reconstruction after the Civil War* (Chicago: University of Chicago Press, 1961) and Eric Foner, *Reconstruction: America's Unfinished Revolution 1863–1877* (New York: Harper and Row, 1988).

the region's social and economic transformation. The former slaves refused to accept their old status. They objected to laboring in gangs, removed their wives and children from the fields, and deserted the old slave quarters. Historians still debate the origins of the sharecropping system, but at the very least it represented a compromise between white expectations and black demands.[13] Other blacks exercised their new freedom of mobility to seek better opportunities further west or in the region's cities. And with enfranchisement after 1867, blacks formed the backbone of the Republican party. They voted, held office, and in general made white southerners wonder what had happened to their world. Blacks, especially those in cities, demanded access to schools, public conveyances, welfare institutions, and public accommodations. They won that right under Congressional Reconstruction, although usually, together with their white allies, accepted the promise of separate but equal treatment. Segregation thus became the rule in most areas of southern racial life, but ironically that was seen as, and indeed was, an improvement for blacks, for what it replaced was not integration but exclusion.[14]

White southerners objected that white northerners were forcing racial changes on them that the North itself would not accept. They had a point. Before the ratification of the Fifteenth Amendment in 1870, blacks could not vote in most northern states, and indeed several states, including New York, Wisconsin, and Connecticut, had voted down Negro suffrage after the war; most states still had antimiscegenation laws and segregated schools and public accommodations; and there was widespread discrimination against blacks in housing and employment.[15] In fact, I would argue that in 1868 prospects generally speaking were better for blacks in the South than in the North.

The situation soon changed. With the return of the former Confederates to power in the South during the 1870s, the triumph of the Democrats in Congress, and the withering of northern determination to protect the rights of blacks in the South, conditions for southern blacks deteriorated.[16] The change was never as

13. Peter Kolchin, *First Freedom: The Responses of Alabama's Blacks to Emancipation and Reconstruction* (Westport, Conn.: Greenwood Press, 1972); Roger L. Ransom and Richard Sutch, *One Kind of Freedom: The Economic Consequences of Emancipation* (New York: Cambridge University Press, 1977); Harold D. Woodman, "Sequel to Slavery: The New History Views the Postbellum South," *Journal of Southern History* 43 (November 1977): 523–54.

14. See my *Race Relations in the Urban South, 1865–1890* (New York: Oxford University Press, 1978) and "More Than the Woodward Thesis: Assessing *The Strange Career of Jim Crow*," reprinted above.

15. Foner, *Reconstruction*, 223–24.

16. William Gillette, *Retreat from Reconstruction, 1869–1879* (Baton Rouge: Louisiana State University Press, 1979).

rapid nor drastic as once believed, but by the 1890s southern states had initiated a successful systematic program of disfranchisement and de jure segregation, blacks had been largely confined to menial jobs in the cities and to sharecropping in the countryside, white politicians spewed forth a vile political rhetoric of racial inferiority and hate, and white mobs increasingly sought to intimidate blacks and entertain themselves through hideous lynchings.[17]

But as things worsened for blacks in the South, they improved in the North, again reinforcing the distinctiveness of southern race relations. With the Republican and Democratic parties evenly matched in many northern states, the black vote became pivotal following ratification of the Fifteenth Amendment, particularly in presidential elections. Whether out of a sense of political necessity or concern for fairness, white politicians responded positively to black demands for better treatment. After the United States Supreme Court declared the Civil Rights Act of 1875 unconstitutional in 1883, northern states passed their own legislation. Segregated schools and public accommodations persisted in many places but were eradicated elsewhere, and in any case were now against the law. Most antimiscegenation statutes were stricken from the books as they were being reinstituted in the South, and the industrializing North provided better economic opportunities for blacks and perhaps less segregated housing.[18]

By the turn of the century, then, Reconstruction had brought southern blacks, in the historian Eric Foner's words, "nothing but freedom."[19] But that was worth much, and in the rush to declare Reconstruction a failure we should not forget that it did confirm the death of slavery as well as lay the constitutional foundation for a more successful attack on southern racial mores in the mid-twentieth

17. Rabinowitz, *Race Relations in the Urban South;* J. Morgan Kousser, *The Shaping of Southern Politics: Suffrage Restriction and the Establishment of the One-Party South, 1880–1910* (New Haven: Yale University Press, 1974); Joel Williamson, *The Crucible of Race: Black-White Relations in the American South since Emancipation* (New York: Oxford University Press, 1984); C. Vann Woodward, *Origins of the New South, 1877–1913,* vol. 9 of *A History of the South,* ed. Wendell Holmes Stephenson and E. Merton Coulter, 10 vols. (Baton Rouge: Louisiana State University Press, 1951).

18. These generalizations about the nature of northern black life are based on a wide variety of studies, including David M. Katzman, *Before the Ghetto: Black Detroit in the Nineteenth Century* (Urbana: University of Illinois Press, 1973); Kenneth L. Kusmer, *A Ghetto Takes Shape: Black Cleveland, 1870–1930* (Urbana: University of Illinois Press, 1976); Elizabeth Hafkin Pleck, *Black Migration and Poverty: Boston, 1865–1900* (New York: Academic Press, 1979); W. E. B. Du Bois, *The Philadelphia Negro: A Social Study* (Philadelphia, 1899); David A. Gerber, *Black Ohio and the Color Line, 1860–1915* (Urbana: University of Illinois Press, 1976); Lawrence Grossman, *The Democratic Party and the Negro: Northern and National Politics, 1868–92* (Urbana: University of Illinois Press, 1976).

19. *Nothing but Freedom: Emancipation and Its Legacy* (Baton Rouge: Louisiana State University Press, 1983).

century. In the short run, however, Reconstruction legislation had a more long-lasting effect in the North. Between 1860 and 1900, most notably after 1880, southern blacks who moved north usually enjoyed greater opportunities than those who remained behind. The last twenty years of the century witnessed in the North a decline in the extent of legally enforced segregation and discrimination, a greater role for blacks in politics, and perhaps an improvement in black prospects for economic success. After a more promising beginning, the social, political, and economic trends for blacks in the South ran in the opposite direction.

Nevertheless, as late as 1900, 90 percent of the nation's blacks remained in the South, more than 80 percent of them trapped in its rural areas,[20] the least dynamic sector of a region that, as a whole, lagged far behind the rest of the country economically and was most hostile to black aspirations. The sharecropping system, which might have been a good temporary solution to postwar agricultural dislocation, had become institutionalized, with the mass of blacks and about one-third of the whites mired in its grip. In other areas as well, despite claims of spokesmen such as Henry Grady and Richard Hathaway Edmonds for the existence of a "New South" (which, with the benefit of hindsight, I've termed the First New South), the detrimental continuity of southern race relations was evident—remaining states, including the new one of Oklahoma (a kind of a southern fellow traveler) disfranchised their blacks, extended segregation laws throughout southern life, permitted the perpetuation of racial violence, made education even more separate and unequal, and elected to office race-baiting politicians like Tom Watson, James Vardaman, and Theodore Bilbo.[21]

World War I seemed to bring encouraging prospects for change. At a time when southern agriculture was threatened by flooding and the boll weevil, northern industry sought workers to replace those lost to the armed services or the suspension of foreign immigration. Despite the often ingenious efforts of southern whites to stop them, southern blacks, especially from the Deep South's rural areas, headed north in the so-called Great Migration. The combination of economic hardship, violence in the South, and opportunities in the North led the black-owned Chicago *Defender* to ask, "Do you wonder at the thousands leaving the land where every foot of ground marks a tragedy, leaving the graves of

20. U.S. Bureau of the Census, *Negro Population, 1790–1915* (Washington, D.C.: Government Printing Office, 1918), 90–91.

21. Woodward, *Origins of the New South;* Kousser, *Shaping of Southern Politics;* Williamson, *Crucible of Race,* part 2; Paul M. Gaston, *The New South Creed: A Study in Southern Mythmaking* (New York: Alfred A. Knopf, 1970); Louis R. Harlan, *Separate and Unequal: Public School Campaigns and Racism in the Southern Seaboard States, 1901–1913* (Chapel Hill: University of North Carolina Press, 1958). See also my *The First New South, 1865–1920* (Arlington Heights, Ill: Harlan Davidson, 1992).

their fathers and all that is dear, to seek their fortunes in the North?" As one migrant to Chicago wrote to her sister-in-law:

> I can get a nice place for you to stop until you can look around and see what you want. I am quite busy. I work in Swifts Packing Co. in the sausage department. My daughter and I work for the same company. We get $1.50 a day and we pack so many sausages we don't have much time to play but it is a matter of a dollar with me and I feel that God made the path and I am walking therein. Tell your husband work is plentiful here and he wont have to loaf if he want to work.

Another person writing from Akron, Ohio, reported simply, "I am making good." Meanwhile, economic conditions improved somewhat for those who remained behind as labor grew scarce, even if little else changed.[22]

It was not long, however, before race relations in the two sections once again renewed their parallel development to the detriment of all blacks. What changed this time was the situation for blacks in the North after 1900, and especially after the Great Migration. If the passage of a state school segregation law in Louisiana in 1877 symbolized the shift in direction in the South, then Kansas's decision in 1903 to reverse thirty years of progress in school relations by enforcing segregation symbolized the North's retreat from social progress.[23] Republican hegemony during the Fourth Party System (1894–1932) eliminated the incentive to woo northern Negro voters, and the growing number of black migrants alarmed whites at the same time that a massive influx of foreigners provided formidable competitors for jobs and housing. Those blacks who went North thus initially found greater economic opportunity, but once the war was over they encountered the wrath of returning white veterans. Whites had already resorted to violence against blacks in the New York City race riot of 1900, but far more frightening and bloody were the Great Migration–induced riots in East St. Louis,

22. *Defender* quoted in Alan H. Spear, *Black Chicago: The Making of a Negro Ghetto, 1890–1920* (Chicago: University of Chicago Press, 1967), 135; migrants quoted in "Additional Letters of Negro Migrants of 1916–1918," collected under the direction of Emmett J. Scott, *Journal of Negro History* 4 (October 1919): 457, 465; see also, Florette Henri, *Black Migration: Movement North, 1900–1920: The Road from Myth to Man* (New York: Anchor Press/Doublday, 1975); Peter Gottlieb, *Making Their Own Way: Southern Blacks' Migration to Pittsburgh, 1916–30* (Urbana: University of Illinois Press, 1987); James R. Grossman, *Land of Hope: Chicago, Black Southerners, and the Great Migration* (Chicago: University of Chicago Press, 1989).

23. J. Morgan Kousser, "Before *Plessy,* Before *Brown:* The Development of the Law of Racial Integration in Louisiana and Kansas," California Institute of Technology Social Science Working Paper 681, October 1988.

Illinois, in 1917, Chicago in 1919, and elsewhere.[24] Although there were occasional riots in the South during these years as in New Orleans (1900), Atlanta (1906), and Houston (1917),[25] the most serious ones were in the North, reflecting the extent to which white southerners had succeeded in keeping blacks "in their place" compared to the continued relative openness of northern society.

The riots were only the most visible manifestation of the assault on black rights. De facto segregation once again became the norm in all areas of northern life, schools became more separate and unequal, blacks lost factory jobs and service positions as waiters, barbers, and caterers to white immigrants, and large-scale black ghettoes emerged not merely in response to the voluntary growth of black community life, but to white-orchestrated discrimination. Whether in New York's Harlem, Philadelphia's Seventh Ward, Chicago's South Side, or Baltimore's Druid Hill Avenue, the reality was depressingly similar. By 1920 in Chicago, for example, 35 percent of the city's blacks lived in census tracts that were more than 75 percent black; only 7.4 percent lived in neighborhoods less than 5 percent black, a sharp reduction from 32.7 percent in 1910.[26]

Black migration slowed in the 1920s, but the persistent decline of the cotton economy, the lure of jobs in the North, and hopes for greater personal dignity kept the movement going until the depression brought it to a halt. Southern blacks continued to leave the rural areas, but the more likely destination was the region's own cities rather than those in the North. Between 1930 and 1940 the percentage of black urban dwellers in the South increased from 31.7 percent to 36.5 percent while the northern black urban population merely went from 88.1 percent to 89.1 percent.[27]

Movement off the farms was often fostered by New Deal agricultural policies

24. See, for example, Gilbert Osofsky, *Harlem, The Making of a Ghetto: Negro New York, 1890–1930* (New York: Harper and Row, 1966), 46–52; Elliott M. Rudwick, *Race Riot at East St. Louis, July 2, 1917* (Carbondale: Southern Illinois University Press, 1964); William M. Tuttle, Jr., *Race Riot: Chicago in the Red Summer of 1919* (New York: Atheneum, 1970).

25. William Ivy Hair, *Carnival of Fury: Robert Charles and the New Orleans Race Riot of 1900* (Baton Rouge: Louisiana State University Press, 1976); Ray Stannard Baker, *Following the Color Line* (New York: Doubleday, Page and Company, 1908); Arthur I. Waskow, *From Race Riot to Sit-In: 1919 and the 1960s* (New York: Doubleday and Company, 1966).

26. Spear, *Black Chicago,* 142. For the causes and effects of growing discrimination on northern blacks see Kusmer, *A Ghetto Takes Shape;* Gerber, *Black Ohio;* Gottlieb, *Making Their Own Way;* Henri, *Black Migration;* Osofsky, *Harlem;* Spear, *Black Chicago;* Thomas Lee Philpott, *The Slum and the Ghetto: Neighborhood Deterioration and Middle-Class Reform, Chicago, 1880–1930* (New York: Oxford University Press, 1978).

27. U. S. Bureau of the Census, *Historical Statistics of the United States: Colonial Times to 1970,* pt. 1 (Washington, D.C.: Government Printing Office, 1970), 22.

that rewarded white landowners rather than black tenants. There were other ways in which the New Deal perpetuated racial discrimination—Civil Conservation Corps camps and public housing were segregated, greenbelt towns excluded blacks altogether, the National Recovery Administration allowed a wage differential for the South, and so on, but through its relatively color-blind relief policies and the publicized activities of enlightened key figures such as Eleanor Roosevelt and Harold Ickes, the New Deal brought northern blacks into the Democratic party and paved the way for the great changes that would follow.[28]

As important as they were in preparing the way for future advances, neither the New Deal nor World War II (which was fought by a segregated armed forces) fundamentally altered the pattern of race relations during the years between 1900 and 1954. A nascent protest movement in the North sought to end segregation, spearheaded in the courts by the NAACP and in the streets by the new Congress of Racial Equality, while those southern blacks and white liberals pushing for change initially sought truly equal separate treatment or an end to the vestiges of exclusion. Although in 1932 a communist-led interracial group defied the law requiring segregated seating at the Norfolk City Auditorium, more typical were demonstrations in the 1930s aimed at more equitable segregated treatment at Raleigh's War Memorial Auditorium and Richmond's Mosque Theater, and a "sit-down strike" at Alexandria, Virginia's, whites-only public library.[29] But despite court suits, marches, sit-ins, bus and school boycotts, "don't-buy-where-you-can't-work" campaigns, and rent strikes that produced occasional victories, prospects for most blacks in the northern urban ghettoes seemed little different from those facing their largely rural southern counterparts. Symptomatic were the race riots in Harlem, Detroit, and Mobile during World War II, although in the South blacks were still more likely to be victims than to share the tendency of northern blacks to initiate their own riots out of frustration over their treatment.[30]

Yet a new era was approaching. Spurred on by black organizations like the NAACP and leaders such as Bayard Rustin, northern blacks effectively chal-

28. See, for example, Harvard Sitkoff, *A New Deal for Blacks: The Emergence of Civil Rights as a National Issue: The Depression Decade* (New York: Oxford University Press, 1978); Nancy J. Weiss, *Farewell to the Party of Lincoln: Black Politics in the Age of FDR* (Princeton: Princeton University Press, 1983).

29. August Meier and Elliott Rudwick, "The Origins of Nonviolent Direct Action in Afro-American Protest: A Note on Historical Discontinuities," in *Along the Color Line: Explorations in the Black Experience,* ed. August Meier and Elliott Rudwick (Urbana: University of Illinois Press, 1976), 307–44, especially 341.

30. Dominic J. Capeci, Jr., *The Harlem Riot of 1943* (Philadelphia: Temple University Press, 1977); Robert Shogan and Tom Craig, *The Detroit Race Riot [1943]: A Study in Violence* (Radnor, Pa.: Chilton Book Company, 1964); James A. Burran, "Urban Racial Violence in the South during World War II," paper presented at the Citadel Conference on the "New South," Charleston, S.C., April 20–22, 1978.

lenged the racial barriers against blacks in politics, education, employment, and public accommodations. Following less visible courtroom triumphs, and benefiting from a cold-war environment in which domestic racial discrimination had become an embarrassment abroad, the *Brown v. The Board of Education* decision in 1954 ushered in our fifth period, the one in which we still live despite the momentous developments in the mid-to-late 1960s. And ironically, this period was to resemble in many ways the years between 1867 and 1877 in that southern race relations came to be distinctive in a positive sense, for, although met with sickening violence, the civil rights struggle seemed to bring greater benefits to southern blacks than to their northern counterparts.

As eighty years before, the central elements of this "New Reconstruction," as C. Vann Woodward once termed it, were the federal government and southern blacks. Yet thanks to the New Deal and the continued migrations north, northern blacks, who formed a critical voting bloc, also played a major role in forcing racial change in the South. In the face of considerable white resistance, the forces of change that combined grass-roots black protest with white liberal (some of it southern) and northern black pressure on the federal government made remarkable gains. In a relatively brief time, they brought an end to legally enforced segregation (despite, as in the case of the Montgomery bus boycott, an initial inclination to settle for the more traditional aim of truly equal separate treatment), abolished the poll tax and removed other barriers against black voting, and opened new economic opportunities for a southern black population that was by 1960 for the first time in history more than 50 percent urban.[31]

In retrospect, the process of change proved easier to accomplish than most people had anticipated. That was because the primary aim was to remove artificial bars to racial equality before the law. And contrary to widespread belief, but

31. For the best introduction to these momentous times, see C. Vann Woodward, *The Strange Career of Jim Crow,* 3d rev. ed. (New York: Oxford University Press, 1974), chapters 4–5, but for the problems involved in substituting "Second" for "New" Reconstruction, see my essay "More than the Woodward Thesis," reprinted above. For an especially good discussion of the conflicting approaches to the civil rights movement, see Charles W. Eagles, ed., *The Civil Rights Movement in America* (Jackson: University of Mississippi Press, 1986). For the slow journey of southern white liberals from a separate but equal to an integrationist orientation, see Morton Sosna, *In Search of the Silent South: Southern Liberals and the Race Issue* (New York: Columbia University Press, 1977) and John T. Kneebone, *Southern Liberal Journalists and the Issue of Race, 1920–1944* (Chapel Hill: University of North Carolina Press, 1985). The nation's black population as a whole had surpassed the 50 percent urban figure in 1950; see Bureau of the Census, *Historical Statistics,* 22, and Reynolds Farley, "The Urbanization of Negroes in the United States," *Journal of Social History* 1 (Spring 1968): 241–58. For the initial aim of truly equal separate treatment in Montgomery, see Martin Luther King, Jr., *Stride Toward Freedom: The Montgomery Story* (New York: Harper and Brothers, 1958), 63–64.

as the psychologist Thomas Pettigrew correctly predicted in 1961, attitudes did not have to be first altered in order to force changed behavior.[32]

The contrast with the North was again instructive; as circumstances improved in the South, they seemed to worsen in the North. One week after Lyndon Johnson signed the Voting Rights Act of 1965, the Watts riot ushered in a period of long hot summers during which it became clear that the solution to racial inequality in this country required more than the eradication of legalized segregation and the protection of the ballot. More troubling were the serious economic imbalances and examples of de facto segregation that could not be altered through legislation or marches—be they in Selma or Cicero.[33] Court challenges to or direct action against unjust southern laws could work because of a growing consensus among whites, even in the South, that such barriers were unfair; there was no such consensus regarding positive steps that included busing, affirmative action, and scattered-site public housing to make up for years of less formal discrimination in the North in the areas of education, jobs, and housing.

The past thirty-five years, then, have brought marked progress in southern race relations to the point where, to many, the South seems to be, as its whites had so long falsely claimed it to be, the best place for blacks. Migration patterns suggest the recency of this development. Although the 1960s was the first decade in a hundred years during which more individuals moved into the South than out of it, it was not until the 1970s that more *blacks* moved from the North to the South than in the traditional reverse direction.[34] And no wonder. Darenda Mason, a black employment agency supervisor who had left Charlotte, North Carolina, for New Jersey in 1968, was amazed "at how much difference fifteen years has made." Explaining her reasons for returning South, she cited "changes in housing and employment opportunities, professional association, and civic and political leadership."[35]

Outside of Charlotte, the story is the same. Thanks to the Voting Rights Act of 1965, increased turnout among black registered voters, and an abatement of the racially charged political atmosphere of the 1950s and 1960s, there are now more elected black officials in the South than in any other region. Although the South contains just over 50 percent of the nation's black population, it had 62

32. "Social Psychology and Desegregation Research," *American Psychologist* 16 (March 1961): 105–12.

33. William Julius Wilson, *The Declining Significance of Race: Blacks and Changing American Institutions,* 2d ed. (Chicago: University of Chicago Press, 1980); Woodward, *Strange Career,* chapter 6.

34. Marcus E. Jones, *Black Migration in the United States with Emphasis on Selected Central Cities* (Saratoga, Calif.: Century Twenty-One Publishing, 1980), 97–98.

35. Quoted in David R. Goldfield, *Promised Land: The South since 1945* (Arlington Heights: Harlan Davidson, 1987), 216.

percent of all elected black officeholders in 1987, well ahead of the North Central states with their 19.2 percent. Led by Mississippi's 548 officials in 1987, four of the five states with the most black officeholders are in the South, as are the next three highest. While concentrated on the local level, these officials include three congressmen, most notably Mike Espy of Mississippi, elected in 1986 and reelected in 1988 following two narrow defeats in the same district by another black, Robert Clark, a veteran state legislator.[36]

Most striking, however, was the election in 1989 of Lieutenant Governor L. Douglas Wilder as governor of Virginia. The fifty-eight-year-old grandson of slaves, who began his political career as a young militant state senator from Richmond, thus became not only the South's, but also the nation's, first elected black governor. To have received the Democratic nomination in the first place was remarkable enough, but to win in a state more than 80 percent white personified the changes at work in this region. As Wilder remarked during the campaign, "This is a far, far different state than it was when I got into politics 20 years ago. After all, I'm now the Lieutenant Governor. A lot of people have moved into the State. There's been a lot of economic and social change, particularly up around Washington and down around Norfolk." Arguing that he was "as Virginian as any Virginian," Wilder maintained, "This race will not be decided on race. Virginia has moved away from that." A less personally involved political scientist, Larry Sabato, agreed: "Any effort by his opponent to make it an outright black-white race will backfire because the state has just grown and changed so much in recent years."[37]

To a certain extent such predictions proved too rosy. Despite preelection polls that showed him well ahead of his Republican opponent, Wilder won by less than ten thousand votes and ran well behind other members of the statewide Democratic ticket. And some polling data suggest that race was more of a factor than anyone chose to admit. Yet several issues (especially abortion) were of greater concern than race to most voters, and, most tellingly, Wilder received an estimated 39 percent of the white vote, roughly the same percentage garnered by the previous two (white) Democratic gubernatorial candidates. By contrast, on the same day, after a campaign involving many of the same issues but in which race was more central, David Dinkins was selected the first black mayor of New York City while attracting less than 30 percent of the white vote.[38]

36. "South Leads in Black Officeholders," *Southern Changes* 9 (December 1987): 25; Bill Minor, "Congressman Espy from Mississippi," *Southern Changes* 8 (December 1986): 1–3; for the changed political environment in the South, see Alexander Lamis, *The Two-Party South,* exp. ed. (New York: Oxford University Press, 1988).

37. *New York Times,* April 16, 1989, sec. 1, 22.

38. *Time,* November 20, 1989, 54–57; *New York Times,* November 8, 1989, sec. 1, 14–

The South seems less resistant to change in other respects as well. Schools in all sections remain heavily segregated but since the early 1970s, southern schools have become more integrated than northern ones, in part because of the artificially forced nature of much of the original segregation and the success of busing and other court-ordered measures.[39] Residential segregation among blacks, although still high even when compared to other minorities, is generally less than in the North. Most recently, two sociologists, Douglas S. Massey and Nancy A. Denton, identified "a significant core of 10 large metropolitan areas within which blacks are very highly segregated on at least four dimensions of residential segregation." Containing 29 percent of all blacks in the United States, the cities were Baltimore (the only one even remotely southern), Chicago, Cleveland, Detroit, Milwaukee, Philadelphia, Gary, Los Angeles, New York, and St. Louis. The concentration and isolation of these black residents is so severe that Massey and Denton had to coin the term *hypersegregation* to describe it.[40]

Economic prospects for southern blacks compared to blacks elsewhere have improved thanks to the decline of northern industry, especially in the cities of the Northeast and Midwest, and the end of the South's separate labor market, which had kept wages low and limited occupational choices. The latter point is especially important, for it reflects the transformation of southern agriculture since the 1940s. On the one hand, agriculture became more mechanized, and on the other, its overall importance to the southern economy, while still great, declined. The effect was to lessen the region's historic dependence on a fixed labor supply for its plantation-style agriculture, a source of continuity that had long clashed with the free-labor ideology, if not always practice, of the rest of the country. With greater options for their labor, southern blacks were more likely to pursue both geographic and economic mobility, and to do so with less opposition from whites.[41]

---

16. For the centrality of race in the New York City mayoral campaign, see Joe Klein, "The Real Thing," *New York Magazine,* November 13, 1989, 16, 19–20.

39. Gary Orfield et al., *School Segregation in the 1980s: Trends in the United States and Metropolitan Areas* (Washington, D.C.: 1987); Sar A. Levitan, William B. Johnston, and Robert Taggart, *Still a Dream: The Changing Status of Blacks since 1960* (Cambridge: Harvard University Press, 1975), 279–83; *New York Times,* January 16, 1972, sec. 1, 60.

40. Douglas S. Massey and Nancy A. Denton, "Hypersegregation in U.S. Metropolitan Areas: Black and Hispanic Segregation Along Five Dimensions," *Demography* 26 (August 1989) 373–91. See also, Douglas S. Massey and Nancy A. Denton, "Trends in the Residential Segregation of Blacks, Hispanics, and Asians: 1970–1980," *American Sociological Review* 52 (December 1987): 802–25; Reynolds Farley and Walter R. Allen, *The Color Line and the Quality of Life in America* (New York: Russell Sage Foundation, 1987), 141, 143, 145.

41. On economic problems in the Northeast and Midwest, see William Julius Wilson,

While many migrants continued to look to the North and West, an increasing number cast their lot with the South's booming cities. For at least some, it must have been a wise choice. One study using 1980 census statistics ranked the nation's forty-eight metropolitan areas with a hundred thousand or more black residents in each of nine categories reflecting opportunities for black advancement in income and homeownership and concluded that many of the most promising communities were in the South. Following Long Island, among the five best economic communities for blacks were Miami, Columbia, Richmond, and Newport News–Hampton. The bottom five were Newark, Milwaukee, Chicago, Cleveland, and Buffalo.[42]

Perhaps most of all in accounting for the growing attractiveness of the South, blacks seem more comfortable there, whether because of the climate, slower pace of life, or because of southern whites themselves, whom most blacks view, at the least, as less hypocritical than northern whites. Too many blacks have encountered or heard about incidents such as that in California, where a department store manager wrote in a memo to her employees, "If any black person returns any sheet sets, refuse a cash voucher or exchange or credit for any reason."[43] As Taylor Wilson, a black electrician from Chicago whose father left Mississippi earlier in the century, said, "I'm moving South for the same reasons my father came here from Mississippi. He was looking for a better way of life."[44]

The South, then, still provides a distinctive environment for blacks, and its race relations are different. Yet now it is distinctive because despite its considerable failures, it seems better; and also, unlike in the past, the region seems to be truly departing from its troubling continuity dedicated to the maintenance of white supremacy. Even those blacks unwilling to place the South ahead of the North recognize the force of change in both sections. As William Cunningham, a Gadsden, Alabama, city councilman and rubber plant worker put it, "I do a lot of traveling, but I think it's just as bad up there [in the North]. I think people have a distorted view of the South."[45]

The Truly Disadvantaged: The Inner City, the Underclass, and Public Policy (Chicago: University of Chicago Press, 1987); on the integration of the South into the national labor market see, Gavin Wright, *Old South, New South: Revolutions in the Southern Economy since the Civil War* (New York: Basic Books, 1986), chapters 6–8; for the emergence of Atlanta's black middle class, perhaps the region's most visible and successful, see Peter Ross Range, "Capital of Black-Is-Bountiful," *New York Times Magazine,* April 7, 1974, 28–29, 68–78.

42. William O'Hare, "The Best Metros for Blacks," *American Demographics* 8 (July 1986): 26–33.

43. "Business Outlook," *Albuquerque Journal,* July 11, 1988, 29.

44. Quoted in Goldfield, *Promised Land,* 216.

45. Quoted in *Wall Street Journal,* February 25, 1988, 15.

At this point I need to make my position explicit, lest it be misunderstood. I am not presenting a brief for the South. Nor do I wish to be thought Pollyannaish. There is still need for much improvement in the region's race relations, as the election of a Klan leader in Louisiana, the sending of letter bombs, or the march of racists in suburban Atlanta reminds us. And one could argue that the present-day South looks good only in relation to its own sorrowful past and the more severe problems in the North. But there is no denying that the break with the past is real and quite remarkable. Referring to what was, let us not forget, very recent systematic racial oppression, a black student at Selma High School told a reporter in 1985: "Try as you can, you can't believe that white people once treated black people that way. It seems like something that happened long, long ago."[46]

But what does the future hold? After all, as the journalist Harry Ashmore pointed out in 1958, the traditional elements of southern race relations seen as defining a distinctive South are in the past—disfranchisement, de jure segregation, the sharecropping system, and one-party rule.[47] Yet departure from the past, while meaning an end to continuity, does not necessarily mean an end to a distinctive pattern of southern race relations. In part this is due to the persistence of one aspect of historical southern continuity and distinctiveness. The South remains the region within the nation in which blacks are most concentrated. Although it is no longer the home for 90 percent of the nation's blacks as it was for most of our history and as late as 1900, it still contains more than 52 percent of the nation's blacks, who make up 20 percent of the region's population.[48]

And thanks to the recent revolution in southern economic, political, and social life and a relatively homogeneous and paternalistically inclined white leadership, together with the new unattractiveness of the Northeast and Midwest, a majority of blacks will continue to remain in the South in the future, although they will be increasingly urban as in the North. If current trends continue, as is likely, their numbers will be augmented by new or returning black migrants from other sections who seek a compatible place to work and raise families.

The presence of large numbers of blacks and the continued acceptance of them, as well as changing racial attitudes by whites, will bring additional blacks into political office, although growing Hispanic influence will present problems in Texas and Florida, the least "southern" of the former Confederate states. (That influence, often in contradictory ways, perhaps accounts for the relative, al-

46. Quoted in Wright, *Old South, New South,* 269.
47. *An Epitaph for Dixie* (New York: Norton, 1958).
48. Bureau of the Census, U.S. Department of Commerce, *Statistical Abstract of the United States, 1988, Negro Population* (Washington, D.C.: Government Printing Office, 1987), 24.

though still limited, success Republicans have had in attracting black voters, evidently largely middle class, in those states.)[49] There will be more councilmembers, state legislators, mayors, and governors to join Douglas Wilder— and U.S. senators as well. In the short run, however, a good deal will depend on the presence of high-visibility issues such as abortion, which, as in Wilder's victory, are likely to undercut the effectiveness of racist appeals. And, of course, even more than is generally the case with southern white politicians, victorious black candidates will, again like Wilder, have to project a nonthreatening, moderate-to-conservative, "let's bring us together" image.

Political power will also contribute to greater economic power as blacks will benefit along with whites as the region continues to move forward economically; perhaps even lowly Mississippi (fiftieth in per capita income) will join the Sunbelt boom. Predictions about income are always risky, especially given the diversified nature of the southern economy and the region's growing ties to a global economy, but if recent trends are any guide, black economic status will continue to improve in absolute and relative terms, both within the region and compared to residents of other parts of the country. In 1939, for example, median income for black men was 67 percent of the white median income in both the Northeast and Midwest, 56 percent in the West, and only 43 percent in the South: the figures for women were 67 percent, 60 percent, 60 percent, and 31 percent. By 1984, southern blacks had sharply closed the income gap in all respects. While the median income for black men in the South was still only 56 percent that of whites, this represented the greatest improvement for any region, left the South ahead of the Midwest, and constituted the only instance in which the gap between whites and blacks had not worsened in the years since 1969. And the black male median income of $8,800 was for the first time greater than that of midwestern counterparts and was much closer to blacks and whites in other sections than it had normally been over the previous forty-five years. Southern black women did even better, so that by 1984, their median income was 84 percent that of southern white women, although this still trailed the other three sections including the West, where the black median income was actually slightly higher than the white one. In short, as the sociologists Reynolds Farley and Walter Allen argue, "Blacks in the South have always had smaller incomes than those in other regions, but the regional disparity has decreased." Equally encouraging for the future are 1979 figures that indicate that southern blacks were less plagued by unemployment than blacks in other sections. And of those who were employed in 1982, 10 percent held higher-status, white-collar em-

49. Lamis, *The Two-Party South,* 296.

ployment (banking, commerce, education, law, and medicine) compared to less than 3 percent as late as 1975.[50]

Increased per capita income will continue the present trend toward decreased forced residential segregation although there will always be blacks who, like members of other successful ethnic groups, prefer to live among "their own kind." Indexes of residential segregation will thus remain high despite years of progress reflected in declines in Atlanta from 94 in 1960, to 92 in 1970, to 86 in 1980; from 92 in 1960 and 1970 to 85 in 1980 in Memphis; and from 95 to 91 to 79 in Richmond. During the same period, Chicago went from 89 to 92, Philadelphia from 87 to 88, and Cleveland remained at 91.[51] And more southern blacks will, like their counterparts elsewhere, move into often heavily, but not exclusively, black suburbs on the fringes of the region's major cities. As southerners increase their commitment to public education, the environment for learning will improve and the less segregated southern metropolitan areas and growing economic parity of the races will widen still further the gap between northern and southern prospects for meaningful desegregation.

Yet the future will also bring some of the problems that have long troubled the North. Some of these will involve changes in the rural ares, but for the first time in the region's history, the nature of southern race relations will depend most on what happens within the region's cities. Open housing legislation, altered attitudes, and economic realities will lead to similar kinds of residential succession struggles, unlike the past, when space for black housing was often found on unwanted, undeveloped land; the influx of northern whites, Asians, Hispanics, and others will create new sources of competition in a more multicultural and less biracial society; economic opportunities that cannot possibly keep pace with rising expectations will probably lead, as they did in the North in the 1960s, to urban race riots such as those most recently in Miami, by those being left behind; the success of some blacks will widen the gap, with the lower or underclass trapped in blighted urban neighborhoods or the decaying countryside; and although forced segregation will be a thing of the past, it will not necessarily be replaced by integration.

The latter point is worth emphasizing because many well-meaning whites are already beginning to despair about the lack of integration now that artificial

50. Farley and Allen, *The Color Line,* 300–303, 238–39, quote, 301; Goldfield, *Promised Land,* 216.
51. Farley and Allen, *The Color Line,* 140–45; Massey and Denton, "Trends in Residential Segregation." Compare the more recent advances in southern residential desegregation with the pessimistic findings based on trends down to 1960 in Karl E. Taeuber and Alma F. Taeuber, *Negroes in Cities: Residential Segregation and Neighborhood Change* (New York: 1965; repr. Atheneum, 1969).

barriers to social interaction have been removed, especially in the schools. For example, David Fleischaker of Louisville, Kentucky, a white liberal who worked hard to bring the races together in local schools, created a highly charged debate by writing a column in a national magazine and appearing on Oprah Winfrey's television show to ask why, despite busing, his youngest children had no black friends and little contact with blacks in schools. "Segregation and integration look like tweedledum and tweedledee," he wrote. "Even the lunchroom looks like a segregated restaurant."

Hazel Lane, who had attended the largely black Duvalle Junior High School in western Louisville in the late 1950s, had a different reaction. She knew that meaningful change had occurred. Having endured secondhand books, old type-writers, and less rigorous classes, she made sure her children would have it better when fifteen years later she became a plaintiff in the lawsuit that led to busing and the merger of the city and county school systems. "What I wanted initially was that the schools would be equal," she said, and she believes that she succeeded. Three of her children were bused to high school and graduated with what she felt was a good education. Her son was one of the first black students from the South to visit the Soviet Union in an exchange program, and, besides, "his very, very best friend was a white boy." She did not understand why Fleischaker was questioning the effectiveness of the city's busing program.[52]

Having white friends, of course, depends as much upon housing patterns, socioeconomic factors, common interests, and family attitudes. Mrs. Lane pointed correctly to the fact that "Social integration begins at home."[53] Yet it should not be forgotten that integration, while a hope for some, was not the primary goal of the civil rights movement; rather it was equal opportunity and freedom of choice. Blacks demanded to have access to the kinds of opportunities open to all other Americans. Such freedom of choice might indeed lead to a continuation of separate Negro churches, voluntary associations, colleges, neighborhoods, or even separate lunchroom tables at school. When truly voluntary, such separa-tion, unlike so much of that in the past, would not represent a failure of Ameri-can democracy, but rather confirmation that America is a pluralistic society in which one should not be prevented by artificial barriers from choosing where or with whom to work, play, and live. Ironically, given the region's tragic history, for the foreseeable future the prospects for such a reality seem most promising in the American South.

52. *Louisville Courier Journal,* August 5, 1988, metropolitan section, 1 and 6.
53. Ibid., 1.

Index

Acton, Lord, 6

African American, as term, xi–xii. *See also* Blacks

African Methodist Episcopal church, 92, 192

Akron, Ohio, 328

Alabama: attitudes toward blacks in, 91; black administrators of welfare services in, 82; black Reconstruction leadership in, 198–203; correctional facilities in, 153; custom versus law in, 162; education of blacks in, 97; gerrymandering used in Montgomery, 129–30; insane asylum in, 74, 84, 86, 139, 147; public school system in, 97; railroads in, 156, 292; scalawags in, 57; separate but equal treatment in, 145; voting requirements in, 130–31. *See also* names of specific cities

Alabama Institution of the Deaf and Dumb and Blind, 74, 82, 88, 147

Alcorn, James, 185, 187

Alden, A. E., 120, 121, 123–24

Alexandria, Va., 269

Alien and Sedition Acts, 259

Allen, E. A., 305

Allen, Walter, 337

Allport, Gordon, 31

Almshouses, 65, 69, 82, 86–87, 121, 139, 141, 212, 284, 312

Alvord, John Watson, 100

AMA. *See* American Missionary Association

American Baptist Home Mission Society, 92

American Colonization Society, 323

American Federation of Labor, 310

American Freedmen's and Union Commission, 92, 93

American Historical Association, 4–5, 8

American Missionary Association (AMA), 64, 92, 93, 98, 99, 100n, 108

Ames, Adelbert, 107, 188

Amusement. *See* Recreation

Andrews, Sidney, 277

Annales School, 10

Annexations: in urban areas, 306–7

Anti-Defamation League, 268

Antimiscegenation statutes, 48, 102, 220, 325

Anti-Semitism: of blacks, 38, 258, 258n; in Civil War, 260, 261–62; before Civil War, 261; groups at forefront of, 260; in the North, 260–61; in the South, 261–70; study of, 257–58; types of, 260–61; in U.S. compared with other countries, 259. *See also* Jews

Apartheid, 33, 54

Arkansas: expulsion of free Negroes from, 209, 322; insane asylum in, 148n; Jews in, 264; public school system in, 139; Woodward thesis applied to, 44. *See also* Little Rock, Ark.

Army. *See* United States Army

Ashmore, Harry, 336

Assimilation: and Anglo-conformity, 229–30, 246; and cultural pluralism, 230–31, 243–46; melting pot model of, 228–30, 246; salad bowl model of, 230

Athens, Ga., 101

Atlanta, Ga.: almshouse in, 312; American Missionary Association teachers in,

341